SO-AHU-217

SACRAMENTUM VERBI

Volume 3

SACRAMENTUM VERBI

An Encyclopedia of Biblical Theology

Edited by
Johannes B. Bauer

Volume 3
Sabbath – Wrath

Supplementary Bibliography
Analytical Index of Articles and Cross-References
Index of Biblical References
Index of Hebrew and Greek Words

KENRICK · SEMINARY · LIBRARY

WITHDRAWN

220.3
S223
V.3

62173

HERDER AND HERDER

1970
HERDER AND HERDER
232 Madison Avenue, New York 10016

Original edition: *Bibeltheologisches Wörterbuch*,
Verlag Styria, Graz–Vienna–Cologne, 1959
This translation is made from the third enlarged and revised edition of 1967

The bible text in this publication is from the Revised Standard
Version Bible, Catholic Edition, copyrighted © 1965 and 1966 by
the Division of Christian Education of the National Council of
the Churches of Christ in the USA, and used by permission

Nihil obstat: Nicholas J. Tranter, S.T.L, Censor
Imprimatur: ✠ Patrick Casey, Vic. Gen.
Westminster, October 23, 1969

The Nihil obstat and Imprimatur are a declaration that a book or
pamphlet is considered to be free from doctrinal or moral error. It is not
implied that those who have granted the Nihil obstat and Imprimatur agree
with the contents, opinions, or statements expressed

Library of Congress Catalog Card Number: 74–114764
© 1970 by Sheed and Ward Ltd.
Printed in Great Britain

Volume 3

Sabbath – Wrath

Catholic Supply

3/23/71

3 vols. $45.40

Sabbath

The word *sabbath* (Hebrew *šabbāth*) is found as a substantive only in the language of religion, and it signifies the seventh day of the week. The longer form *šabbāthôn* is used to designate several feast-days and days of rest, which, however, need not in every instance coincide with a sabbath (Lev 25:4). On grammatical grounds we must exclude the idea that the word is derived from *šebaᶜ* (=seven). As used in the bible the word *sabbath* represents, rather, a noun derived from the Hebrew verb *šābath*. The basic meaning of this verb is independent of the idea of sabbath, for it signifies quite in general 'to cease, keep still' (Gen 8:22; Josh 5:12; Is 24:8), an etymology which is supported by the text of the bible itself (Gen 2:2f).

With regard to the origin of the sabbath, attempts have been made to find this chiefly in Mesopotamia, where the Akkadian word *šapattu* designated a day of the full moon in the middle of the month, or alternatively the seventh, fourteenth, nineteenth (=forty-nine days, ie, 7×7 days, since the beginning of the previous month), twenty-first, and twenty-eighth days were considered to be *ûmu limnû*, ie, 'evil days', on which a series of tabus were in force (eg, the prohibition of eating meat, changing clothes, touching the sick, offering sacrifices, enquiring of oracles, etc.). Since many of the Old Testament passages associate the sabbath with the new moon as a feast day (2 Kings 4:23; Is 1:13; Hos 2:11; Amos 8:5; Ezek 45:18; Neh 10:33), and since, furthermore, the festivals of Passover and Tabernacles were celebrated on days of the full moon, it has been concluded that originally Israel would only have known of this sabbath which falls in the middle of the month as a day of rejoicing. In the exile Ezekiel (see 46:1) would have been the first to introduce the idea of the sabbath as a day of rest after six days of work, and at the same time as a sign of the covenant. Following the pattern of the *ûmu limnû* the sabbath would have had a series of prohibitions attached to it, and in order to avoid any contamination of star worship would have lost its connection with the phases of the moon, and would have been fitted into a calendar of weeks independent of the lunar month. A series of considerations, however, militate against this hypothesis. In contrast to the sabbath the *ûmu limnû* were 'unlucky' days. *šapattu* was used only as a designation of the day of the full moon, and never to signify an *ûmu limnû*. More than this, we have no evidence to justify the supposition that on the *šapattu* work came to a halt. It is true that sabbath and new moon occur in parallelism one to another. But the reason for this is to be found in the festal character which both these days have in common. The obvious relationship between the expressions *šabbāth* and *šapattu* can be explained from the fact that both are derived from the common root *šb/pt* (=cease), for on the *šapattu* the moon ceases to grow larger, and on the sabbath labouring activities come to an end, as also does the week.

Since the sabbath in Israel has come to be recognised more and more as an ancient institution, and since any direct Babylonian influence is improbable, many have supposed that Israel would have taken over the sabbath from the Canaanites after they had appropriated their land, and that these Canaanites would have imported the sabbath at a still earlier date from Babylon. A fact which tells against this view, however, is that this assumption does not explain the difference between sabbath and *šapattu* or *ûmu limnû*, and furthermore neither the sabbath nor the division of time based on weeks were known to the Canaanites.

A theory which is no less ingenious, and also no less unprovable, upholds the view that Israel would have taken over the sabbath from the Kenites. These were related to the Midianites (Num 10:29), and even at a later stage the Israelites continued to have ties with them (Judg 1:16; 4:11, 17; 1 Sam 15:6). The name 'Kenites' would have meant 'smiths', and the working of the mines at Sinai could have accounted for the temporary settlement of a tribe of smiths in the Sinai region. Since one of the earliest sabbath laws prohibits the making of fire (Ex 35:3), this would have implied an interruption in the working of metal. Finally, among certain non-Israelite peoples the seventh day of the week was dedicated to the dark planet, Saturn, which corresponded to the Assyrian Kewân, a god whom Israel may have honoured in her cult during the sojourn in the wilderness (see Amos 5:26). Unfortunately, however, we know almost nothing of the Kenites—neither that they were smiths, nor that they had a time-division based on weeks, nor that they worshipped Saturn. The only fact that remains assured is that the sabbath goes back to the origins of Yahwism, and that the

bible presupposes it as already in force before the promulgation of the law at Sinai (Ex 16:22–30). Indeed one tradition actually assigns it to the beginning of the world (Gen 2:2f).

In the various strata of the Pentateuch the sabbath is recognised as a day of rest after six days of work (Ex 34:21 J; Ex 23:12 [E]; Exod 31:12–17 P). Since the stipulations in Exodus were in force at latest at the beginning of the conquest of the land, and since the sabbath commandment is found in both of the passages of the decalogue (Ex 20:8–10; Deut 5:12–14), there is no room for doubt that the sabbath goes back to the time of Moses, that is to the origins of Yahwism. Whether it is modelled upon a pre-Mosaic institution cannot be established. In any case the seven-day week is irreconcilable with the lunar calendar, and for this reason the sabbath cannot be derived from the phases of the moon. For the rest the seven-day period is often found in Israel and her world (Marriage: Gen 29:27; Judg 14:12; Tob 11:19; Mourning: Gen 50:10; 1 Sam 31:13; Job 2:13; Judith 16:24; Sir 22:12; Sympathetic mourning: Job 2:13; Banquet: Est 1:5; Long period spent in wandering: 2 Kings 3:9; etc). Seven, therefore, was a small round unit used in divisions of time also. But whatever the origin of the sabbath may have been, it does remain a fact that in Israel the sabbath was a specific institution. But it had this significance not by reason of its periodic recurrence, the prescription of resting from work, or the various prohibitions, for all this is found in one form or another elsewhere as well. The distinctive element in the Israelite sabbath consists in the fact that it is held sacred by reason of its connection with the covenant God, and is, therefore, an intrinsic factor in this covenant. Just as the ↗ firstborn of the flock and the fruits of the field constituted a tithe representative of man's work, so the sabbath represented, as it were, a tithe of man's days, the rest of which were spent in toil. Hence the sabbath has its place within the framework of the Sinai covenant (Decalogue) and in the Book of the Covenant, considered as the document of the tribal confederation (Ex 23:12). Since the Deuteronomist writings mention only those festivals at which the Israelites had to come to the central sanctuary, the sabbath is not mentioned in Deut 12–26, but there is certainly a special emphasis on its importance in the Code of Holiness (Lev 19:3, 30; 23:3; 26:2), and the Priestly (P) document (Ex 31:12–17; Num 28:9f). Probably the sabbath commandment as originally formulated in the decalogue exhibited the same short and apodictic form as is apparent in the rest of the decalogue commandments. But when we consider the surviving versions in which it has come down to us, in Deut 5:14f it is associated with the mighty deed of God in freeing Israel from the bondage of Egypt, after which Israel was to find a 'place of ↗ rest' (Deut 12:9) in the land of the promise. During the sabbath rest it was this that she had to recall. Ex 20:11, on the other hand, associates the sabbath commandment with the work of creation, and sees it as following an example provided by God himself (Gen 2:2f). Just as the creation is the first act of salvific history, at the conclusion of which God pauses in

order to conclude a covenant with his creation, and just as it is only at the cessation of the Flood that the covenant with Noah is made possible, its sign being the rainbow (Gen 9:8–17), so in turn the sabbath is a sign of the Sinai covenant (see Ex 20:10, 11). In both of these motivations the sabbath is connected with the covenant. But in this Deuteronomy lays greater emphasis on the covenant people, while the Priestly document lays it on the covenant God. P, therefore, brings out the religious character of the sabbath above all. It is *for* Yahweh (Lev 23:3). It is the day which Yahweh has made holy (Ex 20:11). Therefore the observance of the sabbath carries with it an assurance of salvation (Is 58:13f), and its violation, for which the law requires the death penalty (Ex 31:14f; see also Num 15:32–6), brings down on the individual exclusion from the community of salvation, and on the people as a whole divine punishment (Ezek 20:13; Neh 13:17f).

This theological understanding of the sabbath only developed slowly. In the earlier passages the sabbath is a day of rest and joy (Is 1:13; Hos 2:13), on which no heavy work was done (Ex 20:9f; Deut 5:13f), no trading was engaged in, but probably small journeys were undertaken (2 Kings 4:23) and the relieving of the guard was carried out (2 Kings 11:5, 11). After 586, when the remaining feast days could no longer be celebrated, the importance of the sabbath increased and it came to be the essential sign of the ↗ covenant. Under post-exilic judaism it was laid down that on the sabbath the shewbread should be renewed (Lev 24:5–9) and supplementary sacrifices should be offered (Num 28:9f). The number of sabbath prohibitions were also increased (Is 58:13; Jer 17:21f), though the Jews made little effort to observe these, so that Nehemiah directed that the gates of Jerusalem should be closed on the sabbath (Neh 13:19–22) in order to compel the citizens to observe the sabbath rest. Gradually the sabbath prescriptions were imposed more and more strictly. In the period of the Maccabees the Jews preferred to submit to slaughter rather than to violate the sabbath rest by taking measures to defend themselves (1 Macc 2:32–8). Again, a successful pursuit of the enemy was broken off at the beginning of the sabbath, and only resumed when the sabbath had passed (2 Macc 8:25–8). According to Jub 1:8–12 marital intercourse and the preparation of meals were prohibited on the sabbath. The Essenes refused to move any object on the sabbath (Flavius Josephus, *Bell.* II, 8:9). At the time of Christ the pharisees said that on the sabbath it was unlawful for a man to carry his bed (Jn 5:10), to care for the sick (Lk 13:14), to pluck ears of corn (Mt 12:2) and to walk more than two thousand paces (see Acts 1:12). Jesus respected the sabbath (Mt 24:20; Lk 4:16), but rejected an unduly narrow interpretation of the sabbath commandment, and put man before the sabbath (Mk 2:27; 3:4; see also 2:23–6; 3:1–6; Lk 13:10–17; 14:1–6). In the Mishna the upholders of judaism compiled a list of 39 works which were considered prohibited on the sabbath. In contrast to this Jesus as Lord of the sabbath (Mk 2:28) abrogated these, just as he also brought an end to the Old Covenant by introducing the New. Thus there is no connection either between the Jewish sabbath and the christian Sunday. The former represented the conclusion of the week, the latter its beginning, which, moreover, is for christian minds associated with the resurrection of the Lord (Acts 20:7; 1 Cor 16:2; Rev 1:10). Just as Jesus fulfils the whole of the Old Testament in his own person, so too Sunday, as the ↗ day of the Lord, constitutes a fulfilment of the sabbath which was a type of it.

Bibliography: N. H. Tur-Sinai, 'Sabat und Woche', *Bibliotheca Orientalis* 8 (1951), 14–24; G. K. Botterweck, 'Der Sabbat im AT', *TQ* 134 (1954), 134–47 and 448–57; R. North, 'The Derivation of Sabbath', *Bbl* 36 (1955), 182–201; E. Jenni, *Die theologische Begründung des Sabbatgebotes im AT*, Zurich 1956; W. Kornfeld, *Der Sabbath im AT: Der Tag des Herrn. Die Heiligung des Sonntags im Wandel der Zeit*, Vienna 1958, 11–31; E. Vogt, 'Hat Šabbat im AT den Sinn von Woche?', *Bbl* 40 (1959), 1008–11; E. Kutsch, *RGG* v³, 1258–60; de Vaux 475–83.

Walter Kornfeld

Sacrifice

Although sacrifices were offered in ancient times they were left undefined. Various primitive rites were current, the exact meaning of which was for the most part no longer exactly known, and which furthermore the offerer was able to vary. Thus in a papyrus from Ramesseum we can discern a new interpretation of the coronation rituals pertaining to the myth of Horus and Osiris: the Egyptian priests wished to explain the sacrifice as the victory of Horus over Seth. The popular explanation of sacrificial gifts in Assyria and Babylon is of a similar kind. It is that the gods devour the sacrificial gifts which are brought to them (see Dan 14). It is for the duty of providing these offerings that men are created, as the sixth table of the epic of creation declares (lines 32–9). But both in these regions and among the Hittites of Asia Minor it is even more clear that it was a duty laid upon men to offer sacrifices even though they were ignorant alike of their meaning and of the value of the rites employed in them. One of the pieces of advice which the hero of the Babylonian epic of the Flood gives to his children (see Meissner, *Assyrien und Babylonien* II, 421f) runs as follows: 'You shall honour your god every day with sacrifices, prayers, and the prescribed incense offering'.

The ancients seem to have regarded sacrifice chiefly as a *gift*, the *performance of a duty*, an *act of homage to the protecting deity*, the ruler of mankind. But the texts are not always so clear, and precisely in the case of the Semites and Israelites various theories have been proposed in recent times. The leading theorists interpreted sacrifice as a gift made to the godhead until W. R. Smith published his *Lectures on the Religion of the Semites* in 1889. Here he connected sacrifice not, as formerly, with the idea of a gift, but with that of *communion with the deity*. The believer strove to unite himself physically to the deity so that it would impart its power to him by partaking of a banquet with it consisting of the flesh of the sacrifice. Smith based his theory upon the primitive totemism of the Semites, but he did exaggerate. Lagrange produced a criticism of this work in his *Etudes sur les Religions sémitiques* (1905), and finally arrived at the following conclusion:

'The sacrifice of the Semites is neither a simple compact of participation nor the holding out of a (hungry) mouth to the gods, nor yet the renewal of a blood-bond with the deity by means of a sacrifice divine in character. Rather it is the expression of a ceremonial act with the concomitant idea that everything belongs to God. It is an acknowledgement of this right of his. At the same time, however, it is also an expression of the desire to draw near to God' (p 274). G. B. Gray (*Sacrifice in the Old Testament*, 1925) returns once more to the basic idea of a gift. But according to Gray there would have been a constant deepening of this idea of a gift, and the synthesis of Leviticus provides evidence of what man sought to achieve by it: *a spiritual union with the godhead*.

Great attention has also been paid to the development of sacrifice in Israel's own history. O. Eissfeldt ('Opfer im Alten Testament', *RGG* IV, 711–17) connects the idea of a gift with the entry into Canaan. A. Lods regards Leviticus as an attempt, not altogether successful, at achieving a synthesis of various ideas. Oesterly concentrates particularly on the sacrifices of the nomadic period (*Sacrifices in Ancient Israel*, 1937). He finds that already at this period three ideas of sacrifice had emerged: *gift*, *communion*, and *redemption*. After a syncretistic period during the agricultural stage and the more advanced stage of civilisation in Israel, sacrifices appear in the exilic period as *reconciliation with God*. R. Dussaud (*Origines cananéennes du Sacrifice israélite*, 1941[2]) emphasises that sacrificial rituals in Canaan and Israel were originally identical. Moses chooses Yahweh as his God and in his spirit codifies the Levitical ritual legislation. According to H. H. Rowley ('The Meaning of Sacrifice in the Old Testament', *BJRL* [1950]) Israel already possessed rites of its own when it came into contact with Canaan, but adapted many others to its own purposes. Sacrifice expresses various ideas such as those of gift, of communion, of propitiation, but the single factor which all these have in common is the idea of sacrifice as constituting an effective means in the hand of the offerer of presenting himself before God. L. Moraldi (*Espiazione sacrificale e riti espiatori*, Rome 1956) does not attempt to provide any comprehensive treatment of the problem of sacrifice, but insists on one aspect of it, namely the independent value of sacrifice as a victim substituted for the offerer to undergo his punishment. In an extremely penetrating study of the relevant texts he shows the connections between the Israelite ideas of sacrifice and those current in the world about her, but emphasizes the peculiarly spiritual aspects of the legislation in Leviticus: the clearer idea of sin, of the presence of God in his temple and his holy land, which gives life to his people provided that they do not profane this place by their conduct: the blood sacrifice has a cleansing value inasmuch as↗ blood is life (Lev 17:11, 14).

This presentation enables us to realise how rich in ideas Israelite sacrifice can be shown to be. It would be perilous to attempt to opt for any one of these ideas at the expense of another. As the central idea of all we should probably hold fast to that of *sacrum facere*. The effectiveness of the act of sacrifice consists chiefly in the fact that by means of it the individual or the community transforms a living act into a consecrated act. The community sacrifice is certainly extremely ancient and makes manifest the union of the god with his people above all on festival days. Leviticus, however, does not give first place to these ritual meals, which were very widely practised among the Canaanites, but makes the whole burnt offering, in which everything is destroyed in honour of, or for the sake of the godhead, the chief form of sacrifice. This form of sacrifice, which is likewise extremely ancient, seems at first to have been conceived of as a kind of thanksgiving for an encounter with God (Judg 9, 13), but Leviticus ascribes an atoning value to it, as also to the two other kinds of sacrifice, *ḥaṭāʾâh* and *ʾāšām*, which presuppose transgression and liability to punishment. These sacrifices were well-known in the Semitic world, and had an expiatory value, whether this was achieved through punishment (penance) or through a *kuppuru* rite (in Assyria and Babylon), by which it was sought to heal one smitten with sickness by a deity whose indignation had been aroused by some transgression or fault or uncleanness in him. We believe, although this is still a disputed point, that Leviticus has merely 'canonised' these atonement rituals by attaching them to the Mosaic law, above all the *lex talionis*, but that in the case of the whole burnt offering, the *ḥaṭāʾâh* or the *ʾāšām* the blood of the slaughtered beast was regarded as a substitute for the life of the sinner, who would otherwise have had to die in accordance with the strict letter of this law. Passages exhibiting the same spirit, such as Ezek 30:12-16, connect atonement (*kipper*) with ransom (*kōp̱er*). Thus the lawgiver ruled out all magic practices and all kinds of naturalism. This, however, was not the deepest sense of atonement, which above all represented the healing of an individual sick in body and soul. Christ restores the full value of the communion sacrifice to it. *Kipper* (Greek: *hilaskomai*) becomes in the New Testament the outpouring of the blood of Christ. *hilastērion* (Rom 3:25), which heals man, justifies him in faith by his sharing in the eucharistic meal: 'This Blood will be shed for many' (Mk 14:24). ↗ Eucharist, redemption.

Bibliography: Haag, 1229–35; N. H. Snaith, *VT* 7 (1957), 308–17; R. de Vaux 415–56; L. A. Rutschmann, *Altar and Sacrifice in the OT Nomadic Period, with Relation to Sacred Space and Sacred Time*, 1962 (dissertation, S. California School of Theology); D. Gill, 'Questions to Thysia and šᵉlāmīm', *Bbl* 47 (1966), 255–62; R. Rendtorff, *Studien zur Geschichte des Opfers im Alten Israel*, (*WissMonANT* 24), Neukirchen-Vluyn 1967; N. M. Loss, 'Oblazione quotidiana oppure oblazione stabile', *Rivista Biblica Italiana* 16 (1968), 409–29; H. Muszynski, 'Sacrificium fundationis in Jos 6, 26 et I Reg 16, 34?', *VD* 46 (1968), 259–74.

Henri Cazelles

B. *New Testament*. The many and varied ideas of sacrifice found in the Old Testament do not die out in the New Testament, but are transposed on to a higher plane. In the thinking of the primitive christian community they are concentrated on the death of Christ and given a new interpretation from this standpoint.

Full clarity and maturity are only achieved through separation from the religious community of judaism, theological reflection on Jesus' death on the cross, and the primitive church's deepening understanding of itself as the community of God whose life and duties flow from the sacrificial death of Christ.

1. Relation to the sacrificial ritual of judaism. Jesus' own attitude can no longer be completely reconstructed from the brief and selective accounts of the gospels, which give it a slant reminiscent of that of the great prophets: no total rejection of contemporary sacrificial rites (cf Mk 1:44 and parallels; Mt 5:23f; Lk 13:1), but sharp criticism of external religion (Mk 7:6 and parallels following Is 29:13) and dishonouring the sanctuary (the cleansing of the temple), the placing of the commandment to love above all sacrifices (Mk 12:33f). Jesus probably kept the passover (though hardly in the manner of the Essenes) until he 'reinstituted' it at the last supper (cf Mk 14:12–16 and parallels; Lk 22:15). The 'temple saying' (Mt 26:61; Mk 14:58; Jn 2:19; cf Rev 6:14) is not conclusive evidence of a rejection of the temple and its sacrificial ritual.

The attitude of the primitive church in this respect was at first neither clear nor unified; in spite of their connection with the temple (cf Acts 2:46; 3:1, 11; 5:12), the first christians must from the start have celebrated their own 'Easter' in place of the Jewish passover. In the circle of James the links with the Jewish sacrificial system were presumably maintained (cf Acts 21:23–6), but on the other hand Stephen (and with him the 'hellenisers') completely rejected the temple, Paul distanced himself from the Jewish sacrificial ritual (cf 1 Cor 10:18), and there grew up generally in the primitive (hellenistic) church the consciousness of a new christian system of worship without the Jewish (and pagan) practice of sacrifice.

2. *Theological distancing from the old sacrificial system.* The realisation of the 'new thing' which had taken place in and with Jesus through God's action, together with the destruction of the temple and the end of the sacrificial ritual in AD 70, led to a theologically conscious turning away from the old Jewish sacrificial system, which is surpassed and 'abolished' in the new eschatological order of salvation which came into being with Christ. This is the context in which Matthew uses Hos 6:6 (9:13; 12:7) and inserts in 12:6 the sentence 'Something greater than the temple is here [i.e. in Jesus]. John refers the 'temple saying' to the body of Jesus, the risen one (2:21f), and regards as brought to pass in Jesus the time when true worshippers will no longer pray to God in the temple but 'in spirit and in truth' (4:21–4). For Paul the eucharist surpasses the communion with God which was the aim of the Jewish 'peace offering' (1 Cor 10:14–18), and 'Christ, our paschal lamb, has been sacrificed' (1 Cor 5:7), that is to say, the new ('our'), genuine, eschatological paschal lamb; this idea is echoed in 1 Pet 1:19 and lies behind Jn 19:33f, 36 as a type.

The author of the Letter to the Hebrews, who has no need to take account of any still existing Jewish system of worship, regards the Jewish priesthood and sacrificial ritual as fulfilled and surpassed by Christ, the true high priest 'after the order of Melchizedek', and his once-for-all, complete and permanently valid sacrifice. The old covenant is not merely subordinated to the new covenant sealed in the blood of Jesus, but it is also abolished by it, because perfected (cf 8:13; 10:9b). Since Christ by his sacrifice 'has perfected for all time those who are sanctified' (10:14), and as high priest leads the people of God into the heavenly sanctuary (10:19ff), the meaning of every sacrificial system and the demands of the worshippers are now fulfilled, and the shadow must give way before the reality (10:1).

3. *The atoning death of Christ and ideas of sacrifice.* The earliest community understood the death of Jesus as representative atoning suffering (cf 1 Cor 15:3 'died for our sins in accordance with the scriptures', presumably referring to Is 53), and this idea is also expressed in the saying over the cup at the eucharist (Mk 14:24 'for many'; Mt 26:28 'poured out for many for the forgiveness of sins'; Lk 22:20, applied to the participants in the meal, 'poured out for you') and in Mk 10:45 = Mt 20:28 ('his life as a ransom for many'). This idea of representative atonement, which appears first in Is 53 and then has a continued existence in judaism (esp. 2 Macc 7:38; 4 Macc 1:11; 6:28f; 17:21f; 18:4) should be distinguished from views of sacrifice (cf Lohse), though it can be linked with such views, as perhaps already in the servant song of Is 53 itself (cf v 7, the image of the lamb; v 10 ʾašam). Mk 14:24, with its 'blood of the covenant', recalls the sacrifice which ratified the covenant on Sinai (Ex 24:8), during which the blood was also sprinkled on the people (v 8), and after which a sacrificial meal took place (v 11), and in this way it connects the two ideas. Jesus' death falls under the ideas of

sacrifice in another way when it is treated as the New Testament passover (see above).

In the Gospel of John the 'lamb of God' (Jn 1:29, 36) may be a fusion of the ideas of 'servant of God' (the Aramaic *talja'* can mean both 'servant' and 'lamb') and paschal lamb to describe Jesus. The 'lamb' (Gk *arnion*, strictly 'ram') of Revelation combines royal features with a reminder that it was 'slain' (5:8, 12; 13:8) and washes the garments of the redeemed with its blood (7:14). Wherever the blood of Christ is mentioned, the idea of the covenant founding (Ex 24) and atoning (cf Heb 9:22) effect of the blood of the sacrificial victim should be felt as well.

At the back of Rom 8:32 there certainly lies the typology of the sacrifice of Isaac, and according to Eph 5:2 Jesus gave himself as 'a fragrant offering and sacrifice to God'. The language of sacrifice is also used when, according to Jn 17:19, Jesus 'consecrates' himself for his own. Finally, the view of Christ's death as the once for all and definitive sacrifice which ends and surpasses all the sacrifices of the Old Testament, and of his blood as the totally efficacious, atoning, purifying and sanctifying ransom, is set out in full in Heb 9:11–10:18.

4. Eucharist and sacrifice. The sacrificial character of the eucharist, which many exegetes are unwilling to recognise in the texts of the New Testament, can be seen not only in its close relation to the sacrifice of the cross (the bestowal of the saving power of Christ's blood on the participants in the meal), but is also in the eucharist itself, inasmuch as it is treated as a representation of the sacrifice of the cross and as a sacrificial meal.

But Jesus' institution of the supper means more than a symbolic event which depicts and interprets the death on the cross; it is an action which makes present the sacrifice of the cross, applies and makes effective its atoning power for the time before the parousia (cf 1 Cor 11:26), and thereby shares in the sacrificial character of Christ's death. In 1 Cor 10:14–22 this sacrificial character is made clear by the analogy with Jewish (v 18) and pagan (v 20) sacrificial meals. If Paul is putting the christian celebration of the eucharist—though with a more exalted status—in the place of the previous Jewish sacrifices or sacrificial meals, then 1 Cor 9:13; 10:7; 11:28ff also support this view (S. Aalen).

The idea of the christian eucharist as a sacrificial meal is also present in Heb 13:10–14; its uniqueness, by which it surpasses the Jewish sacrifices, lies in the fact that those who celebrate the atoning sacrifice participate in the atoning event at the altar by sharing the sacrificial gifts. This linking of atonement (the sprinkling with the blood of the sacrificial victim) and sacrificial meal, found in the Old Testament in the sacrifice which ratified the covenant at Sinai, is completely fulfilled in the institution of Jesus (cf Mk 14:24), and gives the eucharistic celebration the character of a new sacrificial meal which makes present and effective the new covenant sealed in the blood of Christ (cf 1 Cor 11:25).

5. Effect of the New Testament idea of sacrifice on christian existence. When Heb 13:15f, after recalling the sacrificial death of Jesus, and the eucharistic community, immediately demands of christians a 'sacrifice' of praise of God and brotherly love, this is a transfer of meaning which can already be observed in judaism but which has developed out of the particular christian understanding of sacrifice and can be seen in other places in the New Testament.

Within hellenistic judaism the cultic ideas of temple, priest and sacrifice came to be 'spiritualised' (Wenschkewitz); in Qumran, where the priestly and sacrificial system of the Jerusalem temple was rejected as illegitimate, great value was placed, in a way formally similar to that of the New Testament, on the 'sacrifice of the praise of the lips' and moral living, as an 'acceptable and voluntary sacrifice' (1 QS 9:5; 10:14; CD 11:21). This did not, however, go with a depreciation in principle of cultic and ritual sacrifices, and there was on the contrary an expectation that these would be legitimately renewed in the last days (cf 1 QM 2:5f).

The renunciation on the part of christians of the old cultic sacrifices and the call to christians to 'offer' spiritual or moral 'sacrifices' arise from the evaluation of Christ's death on the cross as the unique atoning sacrifice, and from the consequences which were derived from this for those who followed him. This can be seen in the primitive christian use and interpretation of the Lord's sayings about taking up one's cross (esp. Lk 9:23 'daily'); there is no mention of 'sacrifice' here, but the idea of sacrifice is contained in those of self-denial and readiness to die. A sacrifice image lies behind the saying about 'being salted with fire' (Mk 9:49; cf the alternative reading of some MSS), and also goes with similar sayings which demand a spirit of sacrifice from the disciples. Paul uses the image of a libation to express his readiness for martyrdom (Phil 2:17; cf 2 Tim 4:6). He requires all christians to present themselves 'as a living sacrifice, holy and acceptable to God' (Rom 12:1), and explains this as being not 'conformed to this world', i.e., renunciation of the world which is hostile to God and leads men astray from him, and inner renewal (v 2). Similarly, in 1 Pet 2:5, christians, as a 'holy priesthood', in the 'spiritual house', are to offer God 'spiritual sacrifices' through Jesus Christ. This refers to actions inspired and made possible by the Holy Spirit, the worship of God, brotherly love, the building up of the church through service, which belong to the 'priestly' vocation of christians. Christ has revealed the way to them through his sacrificial death (cf 1:18f); he himself is the cornerstone of God's holy building, and is to be their model, especially in suffering (2:21–5; 3:17f 4:1f). This is no 'spiritualising' of old cultic ideas, but an application of the central christian idea of sacrifice to the existence of christians in this world.

Bibliography: O. Schmitz, *Die Opferanschauungen des späteren Judentums*, Tübingen 1910; H. Wenschkewitz, 'Die Spiritualisierung der Kultbegriffe Tempel Priester u. Opfer im NT', *Angelos* 4 (1932), 71–230; J. Behm, *TDNT* III, 180–90; J. Blinzler, '*Hierateuma*: Exegese von 1 Pet 2:5 and 9', *Episcopus*, Munich 1949, 49–65; P. Seidensticker, *Lebendiges Opfer*, Münster 1954; E. Ruckstuhl, 'Wesen und Kraft der Eucharistie in der Sicht des Johannesevangeliums', *Das Opfer der Kirche*, Lucerne 1954, 47–90; E. Lohse, *Märtyrer und Gottesknecht*, Göttingen 1955; F. J. Schierse, *Verheissung und Heilsvollendung*, Munich 1955; H. Schürmann, *Der Einsetzungsbericht Lk 22:19–20*, Münster

1955; H. Schürmann, 'Abendmahl', *LTK* I², 26–31; O. Kuss, 'Der theologische Grundgedanke des Hebräerbriefes', *MTZ* 7 (1956), 233–71; J. Sint, 'Schlachten und opfern', *ZKT* 78 (1956), 194–205; J. Carmignac, 'L'utilité ou l'inutilité des sacrifices sanglants dans la *Règle de la Communauté* de Qumran', *RB* 63 (1956), 524–32; R. Schnackenburg, 'Die "Anbetung in Geist und Wahrheit" (Jn 4:23) im Lichte von Qumran-Texten', *BZ* 3 (1959), 88–94; A. Vögtle, 'Blut', *LTK* II², 539–41; H. Zimmermann, 'Mit Feuer gesalzen werden', *TQ* 139 (1959), 28–39; P. Neuenzeit, *Das Herrenmahl*, Munich 1960; J. Betz, *Die Eucharistie in der Zeit der griechischen Väter* I/1: *Aktualpräsenz*, Freiburg 1955; and II/1: *Realpräsenz*, Freiburg 1964²; B. Cooke, 'Synoptic Presentation of the Eucharist as Covenant Sacrifice', *TS* 21 (1960), 1–44; R. Hummel, *Die Auseinandersetzung zwischen Kirche und Judentum im Matthäusevangelium*, Munich 1963, 94–108; J. Bihler, *Die Stephanusgeschichte*, Munich 1963, 134–78; S. Aalen, 'Das Abendmahl als Opfermahl im NT', *NvT* 6 (1963), 128–52; L. Sabourin, 'Sacrificium ut Liturgia in Epistula ad Hebraeos' *VD* 46 (1968), 235–58.

Rudolf Schnackenburg

Salvation

For the extremely wide range of meaning attached to the concept of salvation the Greek bible uses the word-group constituted by *sōzein* (= to save) and its derivatives. In the Old Testament sections this is most frequently used as a rendering of the Hebrew root *yš^c* (266 times in all, of which the verb is used 131 times, the noun *sōtēria* eighty-three times, and *sōtērion* fifty-two times). But roots such as *mlṭ* (forty-eight times: 'to allow to escape', 'to deliver'), *nṣl* (twenty-three times: 'to pull out', 'to rescue'), *plṭ* (verb, twelve times; substantive, seven times: 'to escape', 'to be rescued'), *šrd* (six times: 'to escape', 'to survive'), *ḥyh* (five times: 'to live', 'to let live'), *^czr* (five times: 'to help') are also sometimes translated

by one or other of the forms of the *sōzein* word-group.

First the concept can be used in a completely general sense to signify the setting free from situations of all kinds of need the individual (danger, injustice, sickness) or the community (war, political upheaval, famine). The deliverance thus signified can be effected by the actual person threatened (who 'helps himself', 1 Sam 25:26, 31, 33), or by other men in a purely natural manner (eg, 1 Sam 11:3; 2 Sam 10:11, 19; 2 Kings 16:7), or alternatively by men who are clearly instruments in the hand of God. It can also be effected by interventions in the course of history by means of which God 'works salvation' (on this, see the theology of history of the Book of Judges, eg, Judg 2:16). God is in no way dependent upon the use of these creatures as his instruments, but often in the course of history he so arranges things that no connection whatever exists between the salvation which is effected and the means used by God, men or circumstances which are often quite inadequate to the end achieved. In fact in a certain sense it is precisely the powerless, the poor, who have special grounds for hoping for salvation from God (see many psalms). Thus it becomes ever clearer that in the last analysis it is God alone who 'works salvation' (Ex 14:13), indeed who 'is salvation' (Ex 15:2). In the Old Testament this idea of salvation can be traced from a primitive eudaemonistic optimism (both on the personal and national plane) to the idealised concept (which was regarded as more or less made actual in the age of David) of a salvation achieved on the political and national plane. This was connected with the further idea of a glorified 'remnant' saved in the midst of catastrophes, to which a 'new heart' and a 'new spirit' would be imparted (Jer 24:7; 31:33; Ezek 36:26ff). The idea of salvation was developed further to a point where it was expected to usher in a new creation, and probably also to take a form that was primarily, though not exclusively spiritual in character in the *ᶜōlām habbaᵓ*, the new world which was to come at the end of this present age. It is only after the period of the prophets that the expected salvation becomes clearly connected with the expectation of a messiah (↗ Jesus Christ, ↗ redeemer, ↗ saviour), who is to be the absolute bringer of salvation.

The New Testament takes over in all essentials this wide range of meaning connected with the concept of salvation as this has been developed in the Old Testament, and attaches it to the person of Jesus Christ, the Saviour, who has come to bring salvation to sinners and indeed to all men (1 Tim 1:15; 2:4). The condition for obtaining salvation, whether this signifies the healing of a sick man, the forgiveness of specific sins or the ultimate salvation in the broadest and most spiritual sense of the term, is first and foremost a turning back (↗ conversion) to Jesus Christ in faith, hope and trust. Prayer and the fulfilment of one's duty (Paul instances child-bearing for women 1 Tim 2:15) also belong to the prior conditions necessary for becoming subjectively a sharer in salvation, which objectively Christ has achieved once and for all by his sacrificial death for all mankind.

Bibliography: M. Joseph, *Jüdisches Lexikon* II, 1514–15; E. G. Hirsch, *The Jewish Encyclopaedia* x, 663–4; Löwe, *BTHW* 245; A. Gelin, *Die Botschaft des Heiles im AT*; ↗ hope (bibliography); ↗ redemption (bibliography); W. Wagner, *ZNW* 6 (1905), 205–35; J.-B. Colon, *RSR* 10 (1930), 1–39, 189–217, and 370–415; and 11 (1931), 27–70, 193–223, and 382–412; J. N. Sevenster, *Het verlossingsbegrip bij Philo, vergeleken met de verlossinggedachten van de syn. evangeliën*, 1936; M. Goguel, *RHPR* 17 (1938), 105–44; André Rétif and Paul Lamarche, *Das Heil der Völker*, Düsseldorf 1960; J. Scharbert, *Heilsmittler im AT und im Alten Orient*, Freiburg 1964.

Suitbert H. Siedl

Satan

A. It is consistent with the provisional character of the *Old Testament* that it provides only scanty indications of the nature of Satan and his place in the plan of salvation. The name *Satan* (from the verb *stn* = 'obstruct', 'oppose', 'show hostility to') is used first as the designation of an earthly enemy (1 Kings 11:14, 25). But even here we already find some adumbration of the idea that these 'adversaries' are sent by God to execute his punishment upon Solomon 'because his heart had turned away from the Lord' (1 Kings 11:9). The first mention of Satan as a demonic spirit occurs in 1 Chron 21:1: 'Satan stood up against Israel . . .', while the parallel account in 2 Sam 24:1 runs: 'The anger of the Lord was kindled against Israel . . .'. This correction does indeed attest a certain progress in theological thought, but leaves the actual problem of the part played by Satan still obscure. As *adversary* in the juridical sense, that is, as *accuser*, we encounter Satan in Zechariah (3:1–5), but above all in the Book of Job. Here he plays the part of the 'public prosecutor' of heaven. He is therefore the adversary not of God but of men, and is counted as one of the sons of Elohim. It is his task to go through the earth and to keep watch over men (Job 1:7; 2:2). He is not merely accuser, however, but calumniator and above all *tempter*, who has a double end to pursue: to make men rebel against God and to destroy them. Already here certain essential traits of the biblical portrayal of Satan are to be found, at least implicitly: he is not a partner on an equal footing with God, not an 'anti-God' as in the dualistic religions, but a *creature*, a *servant of God* who constantly needs special permission from God in order to carry out his destructive designs (catastrophes in nature, brigand raids, sickness, etc). The relationship of Satan to the rest of the demonic beings mentioned in the Old Testament, and also the exact reason for his role as adversary remain, however, wholly obscure.

B. It is only in the *New Testament* that we are provided with the definitive answer to this question. Here it is shown how it was possible for a rebellion to be made, an original sin committed in the cosmos created by God, how by Satan's influence this sin was extended from the sphere of the spiritual beings to the world of men, and how it extended its influence still further in this field until Christ 'appeared to destroy the work of Satan' (1 Jn 3:8). It describes the redemption in the form of a mighty struggle between the 'strong man and the stronger' (Mk 3:27 and parallels), which, in spite of the decisive victory of the Cross, will be brought to its conclusion only in the last days of the history of salvation.

As our point of departure we may take the passage in Jn 8:44 which puts the whole 'diabolism' of the bible in a nutshell: 'He [the *diabolos* = 'stirrer-up of tumult', 'calumniator'] was a murderer from the beginning, and has nothing to do with the ↗ truth, because there is no truth in him. When he lies, he speaks according to his own nature, for he is a liar and the father of lies'. *From the beginning*—John does not use any expression such as 'from the first moment of creation onwards', for it is a fundamental doctrine of the bible that 'God created all things as his own' and said that they were 'very good' (Wis 14; Gen 1, 3)—but more probably at the beginning of the *history of salvation*, at the dawn of creation, before man had been made. From that time, therefore, Satan had nothing to do with *the truth*, that is he rejected the truth, the 'word of revelation with which he was confronted' (Kittel), closed his mind to it, rejected the grace that was offered to him and thereby found that he could no longer stand even in *his own truth*, in his creaturely *reality*: 'I will not be that which thou thinkest or as thou hast seen me from eternity . . . I am the creature which escapes thee, which evades thy arm, which turns thy creative word into a lie' (*Satan*, 241).

Corresponding to the johannine expression 'having nothing to do with truth' (lit: 'not standing in the truth') is a passage to which too little attention has been paid in Jude 6–8: 'The [fallen] angels . . . did not keep their own position but left their proper dwelling'. The manner in which they did this can be gathered from the verses which follow, in which the comparison between the gnostics (v 8), the inhabitants of Sodom (v 7), and the fallen angels (v 6) permits an analogy to be drawn between the lower and the higher, the sin of man and the sin of angels. The inhabitants of Sodom rebelled against the order established by God on the sexual plane, and the gnostics on the intellectual and personal plane in that by indulging in unnatural sexual practices or by proudly disdaining the body they denied the need of a creature to be completed, and by this act of autonomous self-glorification they sinned at the same time against their own natures. In just the same way Satan, and with him the rest of the fallen angels, perpetrated on the broadest possible basis what was essentially the same sin: he *willed* to be sufficient to himself, persisted in his blind complacency in his own nature, and thereby lost his true value, his office, his rank (*arkhē*), perverted his nature to lying, and so became the *father of lies* who 'exchanged the truth about God for a lie' (Rom 1:25). So completely did he become the champion and protagonist of lying that between it and him complete identity was achieved: 'Everywhere where lying has become a principle of life, a principle of understanding, of willing, of acting, there Satan is directly at work' (A. Mager, *Satan*, 641).

That this rebellion against God proceeded from a ring-leader who had gathered companions of like disposition about him can be gathered from Rev 12:7-8. Other statements in the New Testament also, among which the 'Beelzebub' pericope (Mk 3:22-7) is particularly clear, permit us to recognize that Satan is the chief of all demons and that his kingdom is single and united. In the light of these statements in the New Testament those of the Old Testament too acquire their full significance. These tell of how a mighty potentate and enemy of God rebelled against him, and how he was punished for this (Is 14:4-20; Ezek 28:12-17; Pharaoh, Nebuchadnezzar, etc).

Thrown down from heaven—the state of proximity to and friendship with God— *to earth* (Rev 12:9), the father of lies becomes a *murderer*, whose first victims are our own forebears. His tactics remain always the same. They consist of deception, of 'laying a smokescreen', of uttering lies which are wellnigh impossible to observe. But here for the first time when the first human couple consented to him (↗ possession by evil spirits) these tactics succeeded, and gained for him a far-reaching influence over the cosmos. He became the *prince, the god of this world* (Jn 12:31; 14:30; 1 Cor 2:8; 2 Cor 4:4; Eph 2:2), the *lord of death* (Heb 2:14), because death is nothing else than the expression in the body of sin in the soul: 'By the envy of the devil sin came into the world, and through sin death' (Wis 2:24; Rom 5:12). The close connection between Satan, ↗ sin, and ↗ death is particularly clearly brought out in the pauline letters. Sin, which entered the world through the disobedience of one man (Rom 5:12)— true to the pauline manner of expressing things, which sums up in a single phrase a whole conceptual range from the original effective cause right down to the ultimate effect which it produces— is nothing else than the sinner *par excellence*, the constant adversary of God who avails himself of the instinctive life of man, the ↗ flesh, and even the law given by God himself in order to bring men under his deathly sway (Rom 7:11, 13–20; 1 Cor 15:26, 54–6). He holds humanity prisoner in the bondage of the fear of death (Heb 2:15) until Christ appears as the bringer of God's dominion (Mk 1:15), binds the strong man and robs him of his booty (Mk 3:27).

The stages in this spiritual combat can be followed exactly in the gospel: it commences in the wilderness and continues in the innumerable accounts of how devils are driven out. In these stories the behaviour of the possessed person clearly reflects the terror, torment and fury of the defeated devil before the irresistible advance of his conqueror. The struggle ends at Calvary, where the prince of this world is *cast out* from the whole sphere of humanity (Jn 12:31) just as formerly he was cast out of the individual whom he had enslaved (see the frequent use of *exebale* = 'he cast out' in the exorcisms of Jesus, eg, Mk 1:34). This victory of Christ over Satan is fully revealed in his resurrection, for in this he 'brought life and immortality to light' (2 Tim 1:10) for all who believe in him, becoming for them a 'life-giving spirit' (1 Cor 15:45), a new principle of life, the author of a rebirth by which they become children of God (Jn 1:12) from being 'children of wrath' (Eph 2:3).

But how can these statements concerning the decisive victory of the cross of Christ (Col 1:13; 2:15; 1 Jn 3:8; etc) be reconciled with those which refer to the work of Satan within the young christian community and in the life of individual christians, generating evil, raising obstacles to christian living and destructive in its effects? This is the real problem with which we have to

deal. The devil steals the good seed from the hearts of the hearers (Mt 13:19), sows weeds among the wheat (Mt 13:25), seduces Ananias and Sapphira into an act of deceit (Acts 5:3), leads the chaste into temptation (1 Cor 7:5), stirs up dissensions in the community (2 Cor 2:11; Rev 2:24), and seeks in every way to inhibit the work of the apostle to the gentiles by crippling infirmity and other adverse conditions (1 Thess 2:18; 3:5; 2 Cor 12:7). But it is in the *secret revelation* above all that the part played by Satan within the church and within the whole course of world history finds its clearest expression. He has his 'synagogue' at Smyrna (Rev 2:9) and his 'throne' (Rev 2:13) at Pergamum, the centre of emperor-worship. The expulsion of the angels is mentioned for the first time here under the figure of the falling star (8:10), and after this in the following section the evil effects of this are described (8:11) and the satellites of Satan are introduced: locusts (9:3–11), hostile cavalry (9:13–19), the image of all that is terrifying, awe-inspiring, destructive, which has taken place or will take place from time to time in the world through the influence of Satan. After the defeat of Satan in heaven (12:8) the extensive description of his activity within human history begins (12:13–20:10). Under the disguise of the 'beast from the sea' (13:1–10) and the 'beast from the dry land' (13:11–17) as the power behind imperialism and pseudo-religion he rules over 'those who dwell on earth' (13:14; Mt 24:11–12; 2 Thess 2:10). But however mighty and terrible this coalition between brute force and glittering lies may be, at basis it is no more than the death-struggle of the 'beast which goes to perdition' (17:8), and is destined to everlasting bondage (Jude 6) and to eternal torment in the lake of fire and brimstone (Rev 20:10).

In the penultimate stage of this struggle, at the time when Satan's power is at its height, we find the saying which leads to the solution of our problem, at least to the extent that it is capable of being solved at all. As in the Book of Job, 'power to make war on the saints and to *conquer them*' (13:7) is *allowed by God* to Satan, only to an immeasurably greater extent. And it is allowed to him—so the seven letters to the churches tell us—in order that the christian may become the victor with Christ (2:26; 3:5, 12, 21; 21:7), his fellow combatant in the struggle against Satan. Those who seem to have been conquered by Satan are in reality those who follow Christ in his victory on 'white horses' (19:11–14). In order to give them an opportunity to prove themselves in battle Satan is allowed this power. In order to enable men to become 'fellow workers with God' (1 Cor 3:9) in full reality the strongholds of the beleaguered enemy remain standing in the territory which Christ has conquered. In the struggle against Satan there is neither neutrality (Lk 11:23) nor secret treaty-making (Mt 6:24; 1 Cor 10:21). Constant watchfulness (1 Pet 5:8), constant preparedness (Eph 6:10) is required, and above all uncompromising sureness of victory! Satan has in fact power only over those who 'give him opportunity' (Eph 4:27), who allow themselves to be led astray by the threefold lust (1 Jn 2:16), and thereby open the doors of their thinking, willing and acting to him.

But he who belongs to the body of Christ is withdrawn from the power of Satan: the Lord, the God of peace, will soon crush Satan under his feet (Rom 16:20) and guard that man from 'the evil one' (2 Thess 3:3; Mt 6:13).

Bibliography: (A): J. B. Bauer, 'Libera nos a malo', *VD* 34 (1956), 12–15; J. Guillet, *Leitgedanken der Bibel*, Lucerne 1954, 156–68; B. Langton, *Essentials of Demonology, a Study of the Jewish and Christian Doctrine, its Origin and Development*, London 1949; E. Lewis, *The Creator and the Adversary*, New York–Nashville 1948; H. B. Kuhn, 'Angelologia VT', *JBL* 67 (1948), 217–32. See also: M. Zerwick, *VD* 27 (1949), 179; B. Noack, *Satanas und Soteria*, Copenhagen 1949; M. Prager, 'Vater der Lüge, Aufriss einer biblischen Diabologie', *Gloria Dei* 7 (1952), 105–18; A. Romeo, 'Satana-Satanismus', *Enciclopedia Cattolica* x, 1948–61; *Satan (Etudes Carmélitaines* 27), Paris 1948 (with numerous articles and a copious bibliography); R. Schärf, 'Die Gestalt des Satans im AT', *Symbolik des Geistes*, ed. Jung, Zurich 1948, 153–319 (see Hempel, *ZAW* 63 [1951], 114f); K. L. Schmidt, 'Luzifer als gefallene Engelmacht', *TZ* 7 (1951), 261–79; F. Zeman, 'De daemoniis in scriptis prophetarum VT in luce daemonologiae Orientis antiqui', *VD* 27 (1949), 270–77 and 321–35; and 28 (1950), 18–28 and 89–97. (B): D. de Rougemont, *Der Anteil des Teufels*, Vienna 1949; C. S. Lewis, *The Screwtape Letters*, London 1942.

Myriam Prager

Saviour

In the Old Testament Yahweh is described, especially in the Psalms and Isaiah, as *Saviour* (Hebrew *yēšaʿ*, *yešûʿâh*, *môšîʿa*). The corresponding word in lxx is *sōtēr*. In Is 19:20 the Messiah is designated as the 'saviour' who is to come. In judaism this title is generally reserved to God. (When Moses is said to 'save' the people or other leaders of the people are given the title 'saviour', as in Judg 3:9, 15, these cases are exceptions which are to be explained precisely by the fact that it is God who works through these, his helpers.)

In hellenistic circles gods, heroes, and rulers are regarded as saviours in cases in which they have supplied some kind of need. The 'saviour' Asklepios brings healing from sickness. The divinised ruler acts as 'saviour' when he creates peace and order. The deity who breaks the power of death and matter in the mystery cults is likewise saluted as 'saviour'. Jesus was probably never called 'saviour' (*sōtēr*) during his lifetime. Nevertheless this honorific title seems to have been employed at a very early stage, as we can gather from Acts 5:31 and 13:23, and also Phil 3:20. In Lk 1:47 this title is used to designate God. But in Lk 2:11 it is Jesus Christ who is the 'saviour'. In the same way, too, in the Pastoral Epistles both God and Christ are designated by the title of *sōtēr*. When this *sōtēr* title is applied to Jesus it is chiefly as the deliverer of the people from sin and death; in other words on the basis of his work of redemption. In addition to this there is an *eschatological element* (absent from the hellenistic concept of *sōtēr*) in the 'epiphany in glory' which is still awaited, and in which the work of redemption will finally be completed (Tit 2:13; Phil 3:20). It may be that John deliberately chooses a mode of designation which closely resembles the formulae employed in the cult of the emperor as *sōtēr* (formulae of this description are applied to Hadrian), or alternatively he may even be reacting against the idea of Asklepios as 'saviour' (his sanctuary at Pergamum is referred to as the 'throne of Satan' in Rev 2:13). But these points cannot be determined with any degree of certainty.

Bibliography: O. Cullmann, *The Christology of the New Testament*, London 1959, 246–52 (with extensive bibliography); K. H. Rengstorff, *Die Anfänger der Auseinandersetzung zwischen Christus-glaube und Asklepiosfrömmigkeit*, Münster 1953; K. Prümm, *Religionsgeschichtliches Handbuch*, Freiburg 1943 (Index); S. Lyonnet, *VD 36* (1958), 3–15; E. Pax, *LTK* v², 80–82; W. Foerster and G. Fohrer, *TWNT* vii, 866–1024; J. Zandee, *Numen* 11 (1964), 52–6 and 62–4.

Johannes B. Bauer

Scandal

The biblical word which we translate 'scandal', and which has entered our language in this form, originally designated the stumbling-block causing a fall, then the fall itself, and finally everything which provides the occasion for stumbling and falling, in other words a 'hostile influence'. The realisation of the image which lies behind this word makes it easier to understand many passages in the bible, and also explains the wider usage and field of significance attached to it.

In the New Testament the word *scandal* is not used primarily of moral danger, but of *influences hostile to faith*, and since faith provides the basis for obtaining salvation, all the words for scandal which bear upon this carry special weight. When it is a question of the agent by whom, or the occasion through which scandals are caused a significant difference is to be discerned: one line of thought leads back to God who in his inscrutable wisdom laid down ways to salvation which are hard for men to understand, and so put their faith to the test, and, indeed, represent a burden upon and a challenge to it. They can take scandal at this. Other statements refer to men who wickedly and culpably set pitfalls for the faithful and lead them to destruction, to falling away from the faith. At the very outset we find the aged Simeon prophesying that the child Messiah is 'set for the fall and the rising of many in Israel' (Lk 2:34), and this prophecy is fulfilled in Jesus' answer to the emissaries of the baptist: 'Blessed is he who takes no offence at me' (Mt 11:6). The significance of this is that the person and actions of Jesus run counter to almost all the contemporary messianic expectations of the Jews: his earthly origin (Mk 6:3; see also Jn 7:27, 41f), his renunciation of external power, and the aim of political liberation (see Jn 6:14f), the works of grace which he performs for sinners and the irreligious without any accompanying condemnation (see the questions addressed to him by the Baptist, Mt 11:2ff), and finally his passion and cross, which are incomprehensible even to his closest disciples (Mk 8:31–3 and parallels). In fact, as Jesus has predicted, the passion shakes their faith for a time, and scatters the little flock of the faithful until the risen Christ assembles them once more (Mk 14:27f). The taking of scandal on the part of the disciples here constitutes a fulfilment of scripture, and, like the betrayal of Judas (Mk 14:21), pertains to the divine plan. For, without absolving the individuals concerned from responsibility (see the presumptuous attitude of Peter (Mk 14:29f), it

was part of this divine plan that the Son of Man should undergo the deepest humiliation and the most total abandonment (see Mk 14:41; Jn 16:32). In the johannine gospel this becomes still clearer, for here Christ simultaneously veils and unveils his divine glory, and so compels men to an inescapable decision between belief and unbelief. The scandal which men take in the person and revealed message of Jesus (6:61) can be endured in faith (6:68f), but unbelief is a sin, indeed is *the* sin (15:22–4; 16:9). Of its nature, then, the divine activity has the effect of challenging faith and putting it to the test, and this effect continues in the subsequent course of salvific history. The hatred and mortal enmity incurred by Jesus are transferred to his disciples, whose faith can be severely shocked by it (Jn 16:1). But only those men whose faith is not deeply rooted enough fall away (cp Mk 4:17). The temptation and scandal to faith to which men will be exposed in the time of eschatological affliction will be especially terrible (Mt 24:10; see also Mk 13:5f, 22f). The faith and constancy of the elect will then indeed be put to the proof (see Mk 13:13, 23).

Scandals are among the inevitable phenomena of this present age. Nevertheless Jesus invokes a terrible woe upon him by whom they come. It would have been better for him that a mill-stone should have been hung about his neck and that he should have been submerged in the sea (Lk 17:1f). This is the other view of the culpable giver of scandal: here too it is certainly the temptation to fall away from faith that is envisaged. For the 'little ones' who must be preserved from scandal are the innocent believers (cf Mk 9:42), the simple members of the community (cf Mt 10:42), whom, nevertheless, no-one may despise (Mt 18:10), since it has pleased God to reveal Jesus' message to those who are childlike in their lack of wisdom (Mt 11:25). A particularly vicious tempter in the last age will be the ↗ antichrist who in the power of Satan will actually perform deceitful signs and wonders (2 Thess 2:9f).

The early church remains conscious of the fact that scandal can be taken at the idea of Jesus as Messiah. It makes an appropriate use of the image of the 'stone of stumbling and rock of scandal' (Is 8:14), which causes unbelievers to fall, but combines with this image that other one which Jesus himself has already employed (Mk 12:10 and parallels), that namely of the stone which the builders rejected and which has become the 'corner-stone', that is, for all those who believe in him (see Rom 9:32f; 1 Pet 2:6–8). Paul regards the event of the cross as the climax of the paradoxical action of God in salvific history, at which men can take scandal. From this he develops his profound ideas on the 'scandal of the cross'. All human wisdom will be confounded at the 'word of the Cross'. It can be received and accepted only by faith. God has deliberately laid down this way of 'folly' because the world with its wisdom has failed to recognise God (1 Cor 1:21). To the Jews, who expect a mighty Messiah and demand signs of his coming, the shamefulness of the cross is a scandal; to the Greeks, proud of their wisdom, it is folly (1:23). But God has chosen those who are weak and foolish in the

eyes of the world in order to confound the exalted and the wise so that no man can boast in his presence (1:29). The scandal of the cross, however, has a profound effect upon christian life, for it demands of christians that they shall take up the cross of their master and with him endure contempt and persecution. In contrast to the judaising teachers of error, who confuse the Galatian communities and in Paul's opinion are merely striving to obtain fame in the eyes of their Jewish compatriots and want to escape persecution (Gal 6:12), Paul himself demands that the scandal of the cross shall not be made void (Gal 5:11). For his part, through the cross of Christ the world has been crucified to him and he to the world (6:14). Thus the scandal of the Cross designates the path that the christian must follow through this world, and it can be overcome only by faith in the resurrection of Christ and its power, which can already be felt in the present (2 Cor 4:16ff; 13:4), and by hope in the christian's own resurrection (Phil 3:10f).

But the New Testament also recognises *moral scandal*. The logion concerning the members of the body which give scandal (Mk 9:43–7 and parallels) has a unique power to unveil all the urgency and radicalism of Jesus in moral matters. When a man's hand, foot, or eye gives him scandal—that is, becomes an occasion of grave sin—he must be ready to pluck it from him and to enter eternal life (or the kingdom of God) without it rather than be thrown into hell with two hands, feet or eyes. In the interpretation of the parable of the tares among the wheat it is said that the angels of God will one day remove 'all causes of sin and all evil-doers' from the kingdom of the Son of Man (Mt 13:41). The similarity of the expressions employed makes it probable that this refers to those men who, being corrupt themselves, give rise to scandal so as to corrupt others. More often we are confronted with exhortations not to give any occasion of sin to our Christian brother by our own behaviour. In the question of whether it is permissible to eat flesh and wine Paul concedes that those who see nothing unlawful in it are right; but at the same time he requires of them that they shall voluntarily go without if by their eating and drinking they lead the 'weak' astray as to act against their conscience and fall into sin. Love prescribes that we should avoid even those actions which, while not in themselves bad, nevertheless by force of circumstances become a cause of sin to others, and can bring about the downfall of a brother 'for whom Christ died' (Rom 14:13–15, 20f; see also 1 Cor 8:13). 1 Jn 2:10 also contains an exhortation to brotherly love. But here, by reason of the figurative language, it is not clear whether he who loves his brother and 'walks in the light' has nothing scandalous in him, or offers no scandal to others, or whether it means that in his walking in the light he does not encounter anything scandalous. To give scandal is always something terrible (see also Rom 16:17; Rev 2:14), because thereby the salvation and redemption of another is threatened, but in the community it is particularly so because 'a little leaven leavens [ie, a little sin corrupts] the whole lump' (1 Cor 5:6), and because 'a "root of bitterness" [can] spring up and cause trouble, and by it the many become defiled' (Heb 12:15).

Bibliography: G. Stählin, *Skandalon*, Gütersloh 1930; G. Stählin, *TWNT* VII, 338–52; A. Humbert, 'Essai d'une théologie du scandale dans les Synoptiques, *Bbl* 35 (1954), 1–28; R. Schnackenburg, 'Vom Ärgernis des Kreuzes', *GL* 30 (1957), 90–95; K. H. Müller, *Der paulinische Skandalon-Begriff*, Würzburg 1965 (dissertation). See also: O. Schmitz, *Vom Wesen des Ärgernisses*, 1925²; W. A. Berruex, *La notion de scandale dans le NT*, Lausanne 1953 (dissertation).

Rudolf Schnackenburg

Scripture

1. *The concept*. Jews and christians have a collection of books which are accounted normative for faith and morals. The collection bears the designation 'scripture', 'holy scripture', or 'bible'. From the aspect of salvific history the compilation is divided into the *Old* and the *New Testaments*, but of these the Jews recognise only the former, while christians recognise both Testaments as normative.

These collective designations have a history which goes back right into the period of pre-christian judaism, or at least into that of early christianity. The New Testament speaks repeatedly of the 'scriptures' (*graphai*) in the sense of books that are normative, and which are already in existence among the Jews (Mt 21:42; 22:29; 26:54, 56 ['scriptures of the prophets']; Mk 12:24; 14:49; Lk 24:27, 32, 45; Jn 5:39; Acts 17:2, 11; 18:24, 28; Rom 15:4; 16:26 ['prophetic writings']; 1 Cor 15:3f; 2 Pet 3:16), but only once of the 'holy scriptures' (Rom 1:2; a similar expression is found in 2 Tim 3:15). Often, too, the New Testament speaks in the singular, but in a collective sense, of 'scripture' (Jn 2:22; 7:38, 42; 10:35; 17:12; 19:28; Acts 8:32; Rom 4:3; 9:17; 10:11; 11:2; Gal 3:8, 22; 4:30; 1 Tim 5:18; 1 Pet 2:6; 2 Pet 1:20; in a non-collective sense 2 Tim 3:16). The word *scripture* here can also be used to designate a particular passage in scripture (Mk 12:10; 15:28; Lk 4:21; Jn 13:18; 19:24, 36f; Acts 1:16; 8:35; Jas 2:8, 23). In a few exceptional cases the term is even applied to a work not elsewhere regarded as authoritative (thus Jas 4:5). In the Old Testament such terms do not yet occur, but the expression 'the holy scriptures' probably is familiar to Philo and the adherents of hellenistic judaism, and that too in a sense corresponding to that in which it is used among the rabbis (instances in *TDNT* I, 750f). Besides this we should mention the Talmudic designation 'writings' for a group of Old Testament books which is additional to the Torah and the Prophets in the narrower sense (Babylonian Talmud, Baraitha, Baba Bathra 14b).

Already in post-exilic judaism we find mention of the 'books' in the sense of normative writings (Dan 9:2), of the 'holy books' (1 Macc 12:9); frequently in Philo and Josephus [*TDNT* I, 615f]). Instances also occur of the singular usage 'the holy book' (2 Macc 8:23). Apart from this the Torah in particular is referred to as the 'Book of Moses' (Ezra 6:18; 7:6, 9), a turn of phrase which is also found in the New Testament (Mk 12:26; see also Gal 3:10: 'The Book of the Law'). Similarly reference is made to the 'book of the psalms' (Lk 20:42; Acts 1:20), the 'book of the words of Isaiah' (Lk 3:4; cp 4:17), and the 'book of the prophets' (Acts 7:42). But the New Testament never speaks of the 'books', the 'holy books', or even of the 'book' without further qualification in the sense of the biblical writings. It is not until the end of the first century AD that the Epistle of Clement (43:1) re-introduces the old Jewish expression 'the holy books'. Such turns of phrase as these were rendered in Greek by the words *biblos* and *biblion*, both terms for 'book', and in Latin this word was retained as a loanword, *Biblia*. In accordance with its Greek origin this word was first treated of as a neuter plural, but later (certainly from the twelfth, and probably from the ninth, century onwards) as a feminine singular. It is this that lies behind the English term *bible* and the corresponding terms in other European languages.

The terms *Old Testament* and *New Testament* represent anglicisations of the Latin designations *Vetus Testamentum* and *Novum Testamentum*, terms which belong initially to salvation history and are primarily intended to refer to the Old Covenant of Moses at Sinai and the New Covenant of Jesus at Golgotha. As early as the prophecies of Jeremiah we find a proclamation of a 'new covenant' (31:31), which Jeremiah contrasts with the earlier covenant made at the time of the exodus from Egypt (31:32). Subsequently the New Testament speaks of a 'new covenant' instituted by Jesus (Lk 22:20; 1 Cor 11:25; Heb 9:15; 12:24), so that Paul can refer to the earlier one as the 'Old Covenant' (2 Cor 3:14). But all these references to covenants do not yet constitute a name for a collection of books. At the same time, however, Paul does speak (2 Cor 3:14) of the 'reading of the old covenant (testament)', and thereby paves the way for the subsequent development in which the expression came to be used as a name for a collection of books. Later, at the turn of the second and third centuries AD, the designation 'New Testament', which had originally been used in the sense of 'New Covenant', likewise comes to stand for a series of writings. It has become general practice in English to speak of the old and new covenants when referring to the institutions in salvation history, but of the Old and New Testaments when it is the collections of books that is in question.

2. *Range and extent.* The books which the Jews or christians hold to be normative for their faith and their lives constitute the 'canon' (a concept which has become native to christian theology at least since the fourth century) of the holy scriptures. 'Canon' here signifies not a list of such writings, but the norm which these books provide for the church. The canon of both the Old and the New Testaments has undergone a prolonged development until it was finally defined as a dogma for the Catholic Church by the Council of Trent (Fourth Session, 8 April 1546: DS 1501-4 [=DB 783ff]). According to this decree, the canon of the Old Testament includes five books of Moses, or the Torah, ie, Genesis, Exodus, Leviticus, Numbers, and Deuteronomy; and further, the books of Joshua, Judges, Ruth, the four Books of Kings, (ie, 1 and 2 Samuel and 1(3) and 2(4) Kings); 1 and 2 Chron-

icles, Ezra and Nehemiah (also called 2 Ezra), Tobit, Judith, Esther, Job, Psalms; the five Books of Wisdom (ie, Proverbs, Qohelet [Ecclesiastes], Song of Solomon, Wisdom, Sirach [Ecclesiasticus]); the so-called four 'major prophets' (ie, Isaiah, Jeremiah [together with Lamentations and Baruch], Ezekiel and Daniel); the so-called twelve 'minor prophets' (ie, Hosea, Joel, Amos, Obadiah, Jonah, Micah, Nahum, Habakkuk, Zephaniah, Haggai, Zechariah, and Malachi); and, finally, 1 and 2 Maccabees— forty-six writings in all, of greater or lesser extent.

The following books are considered to belong to the canon of the New Testament writings: the four gospels (ie, Matthew, Mark, Luke, and John); the Acts of the Apostles; the thirteen letters of Paul (ie, Romans, 1 and 2 Corinthians, Galatians, Ephesians, Philippians, Colossians, 1 and 2 Thessalonians, 1 and 2 Timothy, Titus, Philemon, and also Hebrews); the seven so-called 'catholic epistles' (ie, James, 1 and 2 Peter, 1, 2, and 3 John, and Jude); and finally, Revelation.

References to the normative status of individual books of the Old Testament also occur in the later writings of the Old Testament itself (Sir 46-9, especially 49:10; 2 Macc 2:13), and also in the New Testament (Mt 23:35; Lk 24:44; Jn 5:46, etc). In Flavius Josephus (*Contr. Ap.* 1, 8 §§ 38-42) we also find a reference from about the end of the first century AD to the total number of the books, namely twenty-two. It is evident that various writings which are nowadays enumerated individually have here been taken together. A list of the sacred books dating from the second century AD is also to be found in the Babylonian Talmud (Baraitha Baba Bathra 14b). This Jewish 'canon' includes only books which have been preserved in Hebrew or Aramaic. Those writings which are in Greek or which have been handed down as complete books only in Greek are omitted from it. Such are Tobit, Judith, 1 and 2 Maccabees, Wisdom, Sirach (Ecclesiasticus), Baruch, and the Greek additions to Esther and Daniel, which, since the sixteenth century, have been described as 'deutero-canonical' writings, in contrast to the universally acknowledged 'proto-canonical' writings (the designation *deutero-canonical* was first used by Sixtus of Sienna [1520–1569]). The christian church took over the canon of the Jews, but the 'Deutero-canonical' books, which were prized especially in the circles of hellenistic judaism, only came gradually to have equal value with the proto-canonical writings. As early as the fourth century there is evidence that they had this value here and there in the Western church (Synod of Rome, AD 382; Augustine, *De Doctrina Christiana* II, 8, 13). But against this they were not so valued by Jerome, who on this question allowed himself to be guided by the views of the synagogue, whereas in the East it is only from the seventh century onwards that they can be shown to have been accorded canonical status (Trullanum 692).

The canon of the New Testament has been developed within the christian church. Apart from the heretical list of the scriptures composed by Marcion, it is first attested in the so-called Canon of Muratori (called after the Italian historian Ludovico Antonia Muratori [1672–1750], who discovered it in the Ambrosiana at Milan), which belongs to the second half of the second century. Admittedly it is not yet as extensive as subsequent versions, which appear in the West at the end of the fourth century (Synod of Rome, AD 382), and in the East perhaps already in the third century in Origen (*In Jos. Hom.* VII 1), and certainly in the fourth century in Athanasius (*Festal Epistle* 39 from the year 367; *Ench. bib.* n 15). The canonicity of certain of the writings of the New Testament was disputed in the first centuries: that of Hebrews in the West, and that of Revelation in the East. Furthermore the canonicity of the catholic epistles was everywhere disputed, even though 1 Peter and 1 John were recognised as canonical in most cases.

In the Middle Ages the limits of the canon were not seriously called in question either in the case of the Old Testament or in that of the New, and the Council of Florence confirmed the canon as it had come down to it in its Bull *Cantate Domino* of 4 February 1441 (*Decretum pro Jacobitis*: DS 1334 [=DB 706]). In the sixteenth century, however, questions arose in catholic and reformation circles alike concerning the full authority of several books for questions of the faith, and doubts were raised as to whether entire writings or particular parts which had not been included in all the earlier manuscripts did in fact belong to the canon. Against such ideas the Council of Trent issued its decree mentioned above, and in the nineteenth century this was invoked by the First Vatican Council (c.4, *De Revelatione*: DS 3029 [=DB

1809]). In Luther's time, although the canon had been established by tradition, it had not yet been formally defined. He and the protestants who followed him admitted only those Old Testament books which were recognised by the Jews as canonical. The rest, the Deutero-canonical writings, were called 'apocrypha'. Luther also excluded from the New Testament Hebrews, James, Jude, and Revelation. Since the seventeenth century, however, the lutherans have reverted to the traditional canon of the New Testament, to which the calvinists have consistently adhered.

3. *The nature of scripture.* The declaration that a document belongs to the canon *ipso facto* implies that it is inspired by God. Logically speaking, the difference between being inspired and being canonical corresponds to the difference between being something and being recognised as such.

Inspiration (as a technical term for the biblical authors and books the word is current from the seventeenth century onwards) in the passive sense implies that sacred scripture is of divine origin, while in the active sense it signifies the charisma of the biblical author, which enables him to compose an inspired work.

The New Testament does indeed notice in passing that every scripture (by this it means the normative books of the Old Covenant) is inspired by God (2 Tim 3:16: *theopneustos*; Vulgate: *divinitus inspirata*), and further that God, the Holy Spirit, or even Christ himself has spoken in the books of the Old Testament (God: Rom 1:2; 3:2; Heb 1:7–13; 2:6, 11:11–13; 5:5f; the Holy Spirit: Acts 1:16; Heb 3:7;

Christ: Heb 10:5–9); but the compelling proof for the inspiration of the biblical writings as a whole is found in the tradition which already manifested itself in the Epistle of Clement (45:2; 63:2). The church has defined her views on this conviction that the holy scriptures are inspired in the Bull of the Council of Florence already mentioned (*Decretum pro Jacobitis*: DS 1334 [=DB 706]), and has proclaimed it as a dogma at the Council of Trent (Fourth Session: DS 1501 [=DB 783]). The Tridentine decision was renewed by the First Vatican Council (Third Session, 24 April 1870, *Constitutio dogmatica de fide catholica*, c. 2: DS 3006 [=DB 1787]; also c. 4: DS 3029 [=DB 1809]). According to the doctrine of the church, inspiration is a grace exercising a supernatural influence by which God moves the intellectual faculties of the author in such a way that he conceives of within his own spirit, intends to write down, and faithfully does write down that which according to the will of God must be written and must be imparted to the Church (see Leo xiii, *Providentissimus Deus*, 18 November 1893; DS 3293 [=DB 1952]).

This inspiration of holy scripture must be distinguished from prophetic inspiration, which does admittedly also represent a supernatural and divine influence upon an individual man. The purpose of prophetic inspiration, however, is not the composition of a book but rather that the man endowed with the grace of it may impart some message to others in accordance with God's will. Moreover as a rule the message is an oral one. Certainly prophetic inspiration and scriptural inspiration can be bestowed upon the same man if he is both prophet and biblical author at the same time, but there is no necessity in such a combination. Either kind of inspiration can be bestowed without the other. This important distinction is numbered among the achievements of the more recent theology. In taking over Jewish views on prophetic and scriptural inspiration, all earlier christian authorities combined the two (hence, too, they spoke of 'prophecy' and 'prophetic' where we today speak of 'inspiration'). The effects of this conception have survived to the present day, and have raised unnecessary difficulties in the solving of many questions relating to the bible. The consequence of this earlier opinion was that scholars were compelled to seek among prophets or apostles (to whom a similar endowment of the Spirit was ascribed) for the authors of the biblical books, for on this view there was no other way of explaining the inspiration of a given document than through the prophetic or apostolic charisms with which its author was endowed. It is not until recent times, and as a result of the progress in historical and critical knowledge of the New Testament now summed up in modern works of introduction to it, that a change has gradually come about, and that the fresh knowledge which scholars have acquired concerning the manner in which the biblical writings were composed has compelled them to draw the necessary distinction between prophetic or apostolic inspiration on the one hand, and scriptural inspiration on the other.

The fact that a biblical writing is divinely inspired does not diminish the human freedom of its author. In the writing of it God is at work in a mysterious and, for us, an inscrutable manner, and simultaneously the human author works with complete freedom. Thus a biblical document is wholly a product of God and no less wholly a product of its human author. This explains why the books of the bible should differ one from another in presentation and style. Such differences, and many shortcomings as well, derive from the work of the human author whose personal qualities are no less actively present for the fact that he is inspired. Thus a certain tension prevails between the divine and the human elements in the bible, a duality of effect which is remarkable.

Certainly inspiration extends to the actual truths which are taught in sacred scripture, and even to the individual words to the extent that these are necessary for rightly expressing such truths. We must at least, therefore, recognize the presence of a so-called 'real' inspiration. But as soon as one reflects more deeply upon the nature of inspiration one feels inclined to postulate an influence which extends still further, one namely which bears even upon the individual choice of words. This is the so-called verbal inspiration, admittedly not in the antiquated sense of a mechanical influence exercised upon the human author by God, but in the sense of an inspiration that is verbal in the psychological sense. On this hypothesis not only the content of the bible, but the actual biblical text itself would be wholly the work of God and wholly the work of man. This view has the advantage of consistency, but various observations with regard to the biblical books themselves seem to exclude it and to indicate simply a 'real' inspiration (thus the possibility that an uninspired collaborator imposed his own style on the ideas of the inspired author, and committed them to writing (see DS 3395 [=DB 1998]; and DS 3593 [=DB 2178]), or errors of memory such as are found in Mk 2:26; 6:17; Mt 23:35; 27:9; 1 Cor 1:14, 16. Again the loss of the original text of several of the writings of the bible, and the high estimation in which a translation, namely the Vulgate, has been held rather than the original text throughout many centuries of the church's life might be adduced in favour of this view).

The principal effect of inspiration is the so-called inerrancy of sacred scripture. This fact follows necessarily from the concept of inspiration, but it is important to obtain a correct understanding of what this inerrancy really means. It is not an absolute inerrancy, though the not altogether happy expression 'inerrancy' might be taken to suggest this. On the contrary the term 'inerrancy' requires to be qualified in certain particular respects. It is not possible to enter more deeply into these extremely difficult questions at this point. Here we must confine ourselves to a brief mention of certain aspects which are important for a correct understanding of what inerrancy means.

Inerrancy applies only to the assertions, the judgements of the inspired author, not simply to everything which is included in the bible. Admittedly it is not always easy to say what the author intends to assert or to teach. In every case a distinction must be drawn between the actual content of the saying and the form in which it is presented. The literary genre of a passage, or indeed of whole books, must be taken into account before one is able to recognize the true significance of a saying or the presentation of an idea. If it is apparent that earlier traditions have been edited, as is very frequently the case, the biblical author must not be held responsible for them, at least not in all details, without further qualification. The question arises, therefore, of what he himself intends to assert or to teach. Because inspiration is not revelation, not the unveiling of things otherwise unknown, it follows that the biblical recorder of history, just like any other, had first to look for sources on which to base his work, and had to edit them. In this there was much that he was no longer in a position to verify in all its details, a fact which subsequently appears in his own presentation. Finally the inspired author writes history as a child of his age in the manner appropriate to his age, with a freedom which was common in antiquity, but which may seem strange to us, accustomed as we are to modern methods of historical research.

Divine truth is made present in the bible through men who, even though inspired, did not cease to be men, and it is only through the medium of their human modes of expression, conditioned as they are by circumstances of epoch and environment, that we are allowed to have access to the truth of God.

4. *Interpretation.* The interpretation of holy scripture, or 'hermeneutics' (*hermeneutikē* [*tekhnē*] = [the art of] interpretation) was concerned with the

question of the multiplicity of senses in the bible. After a prolonged development originating far back in antiquity the following presentation of the matter was arrived at by Aquinas (*Summa Theologiae* I, q. 1, a. 10): he drew an initial distinction between the literal and the spiritual sense. Then he subdivided this spiritual sense first into the *allegorical* sense, as he called it—the sense which today we call the typical, or typological, sense—in which episodes which took place under the old covenant foreshadow those of the new. Aquinas' second subdivision of the spiritual sense was the *moral* sense, in which that which befell Christ or those who went before him and foreshadowed him is presented as an example for us to imitate in our conduct. Aquinas' third subdivision of the spiritual sense was the *anagogical* sense. In this the events in the life of Christ or those who foreshadowed him are once more taken as types and patterns, but now patterns of what is to come in the future age of eternal glory.

All sound interpretations of scripture invariably take as their starting-point the literal sense, the sense which arises directly from the actual words and the context in which they appear, except in cases in which the words are intended to signify something different from what is immediately expressed (as, for instance, in an allegory). But this is to be determined from the context. Again, according to Aquinas (*Summa Theologiae* I q. 1, a. 10, ad 1), who adduces Augustine in his support (*Epistola* 93 [*Contra Vincentium Donatistam*] 24), theological truths can only be adduced by means of the literal sense. Nevertheless the question of the existence of a spiritual sense over and above the literal one, which in recent times has been thrust into the background with the development of an exegesis based on historical criticism, still has its importance in certain spheres even to this day. Thus it enables us to understand the use of the Old Testament in the New or the importance of the bible in the liturgy and in other departments of the church's life.

But in contemporary thought hermeneutics has acquired a new meaning, now that the question has arisen: How is scripture to be understood as a whole? This problem initially arose from the modern conception of the world, which in recent times has ousted the ancient and mediaeval ideas on the subject. As a work deriving from antiquity the bible shares these latter views concerning the cosmic order, which are today so outmoded. In addition to this the history of religion and culture has contributed further new insights and also not infrequently ideological prejudices, so that all this, whether justifiably or not, has contributed to a transformation in our understanding of scripture. The case of Galileo in the seventeenth century constitutes an outstanding landmark in this development, and in our own times the call for a demythologising of the New Testament raised by Rudolph Bultmann has drawn attention to the problem of understanding scripture in a manner which cannot be ignored.

Under the influence of the modern natural sciences it has long been customary to take the work of the six days in Gen 1 no longer in a literal sense. A different interpretation of it is necessary than that which earlier generations made. But should we not come to a similar conclusion with regard to ↗ angels and ↗ demons, and with regard to concepts such as those of the Holy Spirit and ↗ grace, and doctrines such as the virginal conception of Jesus (↗ virgin birth) and his ↗ resurrection? It is indeed possible to decide in general terms how the biblical authors would have understood their own statements. But in particular cases are not we of the present day, with our new knowledge and new insights, justified and perhaps indeed compelled either to interpret the data afresh or simply to disregard it altogether? Often enough, it is true, we cannot arrive at any short conclusion on the basis of scripture alone. Illustrations of this are, for instance, the discussions carried on in protestant circles concerning the significance of the virginal conception of Jesus or the message of his resurrection.

In the sphere of catholicism the case is different. Here, in addition to scripture itself, we have tradition as a further aid for the interpretation of scripture, and finally we have the teaching of the church in her official function as interpreter of the bible. Certainly even with this assistance many questions do still remain open as to how such and such a passage in scripture should be understood. But in those points which are basic to Christian faith sureness is the predominant note. Not only doctrines such as that of the virginal conception of Jesus and his resurrection, but also those of his messianism and his sonship of God, and many other points, which have long since been proclaimed and estab-

lished by the church as dogmas, can never be revoked or reinterpreted in a different sense. In this way biblical research, while remaining constantly aware of the problems entailed by bringing contemporary knowledge and thought to bear on sacred scripture, does have a firm guiding line by which its course can be directed.

Bibliography: Apart from works of introduction to the Old and New Testaments and the appropriate sections in general treatises of dogmatic theology, *In general and on 1*: G. Schrenk, *TDNT* I, 615–20 and 742–69; B. Hessler, *LTK* II², 335f. *On 2*: *SB* IV, 1, 413–34; P. Katz, 'The Old Testament Canon in Palestine and Alexandria', *ZNW* 47 (1956), 191–217; F. V. Filson, *Which Books Belong in the Bible? A Study of Canon*, Philadelphia 1957; H. Bacht, 'Die Rolle der Tradition in der Kanonbildung', *Catholica (Jahrbuch für Kontroverstheologie* 12), Münster, 1958, 16–37; A. Jepsen, 'Zur Kanongeschichte des AT', *ZAW* 71 (1959), 114–36; J. Schildenberger, J. Michl, and K. Rahner, *LTK* v², 1277–84; F. Hesse, 'Das AT als Kanon', *ZST* 3 (1961), 315–27; P. Neuenzeit, *HTG* I, 777–90; K. Aland, 'Das Problem des Ntl. Kanons', *ZST* 4 (1962), 220–42. *On 3*: *SB* IV 1, 435–51; A. Bea, *De inspiratione et inerrantia Sacrae Scripturae*, Rome 1947; A. Bea, *LTK* v², 703–11; E. Florit, *Ispirazione biblica*, Rome 1951²; N. H. Snaith, *The Inspiration and Authority of the Bible*, London 1956; J. Schildenberger, 'Inspiration und Irrtumslosigkeit der Heiligen Schrift', *Fragen der Theologie Heute*, ed. J. Feine and others, Einsiedeln 1957, 109–21; L. Vagaggini, 'Ispirazione biblica e questioni connesse', *Problemi e orientamenti di teologia dommatica*, Milan 1957, 171–229; B. Brinkmann, 'Inspiration und Kanonizität der Heiligen Schrift in ihrem Verhältnis zur Kirche', *Scholastik* 33 (1958), 208–33; K. Rahner, *Inspiration in the Bible*, London and New York 1961; K. Rahner, 'On the Inspiration of the Bible', *The Bible in a New Age*, London 1965, 1–15; S. Tromp, *De S. Scripturae inspiratione*, Rome 1962⁶; D. M. Beegle, *The Inspiration of Scripture*, Philadelphia 1962; W. Harrington, 'The Inspiration of Scripture', *ITQ* 29 (1962), 3–24; A. V. Bauer, 'Inspiration als sakramentales Ereignis, zum Verhältnis von Wort, Sakrament und Menschheit Christi nach der Theologie Karl Barths', *TTZ* 72 (1963), 84–104; P. Grelot, 'L'inspiration scripturaire', *RSR* 51 (1963), 337–82;

P. Benoit, *Inspiration and the Bible*, London 1965. *On 4*: J. Coppens, *Les Harmonies des deux Testaments, Essai sur les divers sens des Écritures et sur l'Unité de la Révélation*, Paris 1949; J. Coppens, *Vom christlichen Verständnis des AT*, Louvain 1952; J. Schildenberger, *Vom Geheimnis des Gotteswortes, Einführung in das Verständnis der Heiligen Schrift*, Heidelberg 1950; W. Schweitzer, 'Das Problem der biblischen Hermeneutik in der gegenwärtigen Theologie', *TLZ* 75 (1950), 467–78; R. Bultmann, 'Das Problem der Hermeneutik', *ZTK* 47 (1950), 47–69; J. Daniélou, *Sacramentum Futuri, Études sur les origines de la typologie biblique*, Paris 1950; O. Schilling, 'Der geistige Sinn der Heiligen Schrift', *TG* 44 (1954), 241–54; A. Bea, 'Biblische Hermeneutik', *LTK* II², 435–9; A. Bea, '"Religionswissenschaftliche" oder "theologische" Exegese? Zur Geschichte der neueren biblischen Hermeneutik', *Bbl* 40 (1959), 322–41; E. Fuchs, *Hermeneutik*, Bad Cannstatt 1954; E. Fuchs, *Zum hermeneutischen Problem in der Theologie: Die existentiale Interpretation*, Tübingen 1959; E. Fuchs, 'Das NT und das hermeneutische Problem', *ZTK* 58 (1961), 198–226; R. Hermann, *Gotteswort und Menschenwort in der Bibel, Eine Untersuchung zu theologischen Grundfragen der Hermeneutik*, Berlin 1956; R. Hermann, 'Zur Theologie der Schriftauslegung: Bild und Verkündigung', *Festschrift H. Jursch*, Berlin 1962, 71–83; K. H. Schelkle, 'Heilige Schrift und Wort Gottes, Erwägungen zur biblischen Hermeneutik', *TQ* 138 (1958), 257–74; K. H. Schelkle, 'Hermeneutische Zeugnisse im NT', *BZ* 6 (1962), 161–77; K. H. Miskotte, *Zur biblischen Hermeneutik*, Zollikon 1959; H. Wildberger, 'Auf dem Wege zu einer biblischen Theologie, Erwägungen zur Hermeneutik des AT', *ET* 19 (1959), 70–90; H. de Lubac, *Exégèse médiévale, Les quatre sens de L'écriture* (2 vols), Paris 1959/61; C. Westermann (ed.), *Probleme atl. Hermeneutik: Aufsätze zum Verstehen des AT*, Munich 1960; R. Rendtorff, 'Hermeneutik des AT als Frage nach der Geschichte', *ZTK* 57 (1960), 27–40; S. Amsler, *L'Ancien Testament dans l'Église, Essai d'herméneutique chrétienne*, Neuchâtel 1960; L. Steiger, *Die Hermeneutik als dogmatisches Problem, Eine Auseinandersetzung mit dem transzendentalen Ansatz des theologischen Verstehens*, Gütersloh 1961; J. D. Smart, *The Interpretation of Scripture*, New York 1961; E. Käsemann, 'Zum gegenwärtigen Streit um die Schriftauslegung', *Das Wort Gottes und die Kirchen*, Göttingen 1962, 7–32; P. Grelot, *Sens chrétien de l'Ancien Testament*, Tournai 1962; A. N. Wilder, 'New Testament Hermeneutics Today: Current Issues in New Testament Interpretation', *Festschrift Otto A. Piper*, New York 1962, 38–52; O. Rodenberg, *Um die Wahrheit der Heiligen Schrift, Aufsätze und Briefwechsel zur existentialen Interpretation*, Wuppertal 1963²; R. Marlé, *Le problème théologique de l'herméneutique, Les grands axes de la recherche contemporaine*, Paris 1963; L. A. Schökel, 'Hermeneutics in the Light of Language and Literature', *CBQ* 25 (1963), 371–86; W. Vischer, 'Zum Problem der Hermeneutik', *ET* 24 (1964), 98–112; S. Neill, *The Interpretation of the New Testament 1861–1961*, London 1964; *A. Deissler, R. Schnackenburg, A. Vögtle, H. Schlier, and K. H. Schelkle, *The Bible in a New Age*, London 1965, 16–152.

Johann Michl

Sea

In ancient cultures we usually encounter the idea of a deity of the sea, as a rule conceived of as masculine, who rules over all the waters. We also meet with a belief in various spirits and demons which inhabit streams, springs, etc. Certain Old Testament passages contain geographical references (eg, 'spring of the goats', Josh 15:62; 'spring of the serpents', Neh 2:13; 'mistress of the well', Josh 19:8; 'god of the river', Num 21:19) which perhaps represent an echo of ancient local traditions and remnants of what were once popular beliefs. At all events Yahwistic monotheism recognises Yahweh alone as creator and ruler (see Ps 93:4; 135:6) of the three divisions of the cosmos, heaven, earth, and sea (Gen 1; Ex 20:4; 1 Chron 16:31f; Hos 4:3). In accordance with the idea of the cosmos which was general throughout the ancient Near East, the Israelites distinguished between the 'upper sea' above the firmament, in which Yahweh dwells (Ps 104:3; see also Amos 9:6; Ezek 28:2) and the 'lower sea' (see Gen 1:2–9), which is referred to either as *tᵉhôm* (= 'primordial waters', Gen 1:2; 'cosmic sea on which the earth rests', Ezek 26:19; 'flood', Ps 42:7; 'depths of the sea', Ps 107:26) or as *yām* (='open sea', Ps 104:25, a term for the various oceans of the earth).

In the cosmogonies of the peoples of the ancient Near East it is emphasized that the character of the divinised sea is a hostile one, and that it must be conquered in a struggle between the gods. In Chapter 175 of the Egyptian Book of the Dead the sea is considered as a remnant of primeval chaos which constantly threatens the world. In Ugaritic mythology Yam, the god of the wide and dangerous sea, tries to subjugate the earth and the gods, and is ultimately conquered by Baal, the god of the wind. In the Mesopotamian epic *Enuma eliš* two primeval oceans are mentioned: Apsu, the soft sweet water on which the earth is constructed, and Tiamat, the salt water, peopled by monsters. Tiamat is killed by Marduk, the city god of Babylon, by means of the hot wind, and then dismembered. Many of the turns of phrase in Gen 1 (P) are reminiscent of the extra-biblical cosmogonies, but there are essential differences in the way in which the content of the creation narrative is arranged, for it contains above all a revelation of the power, person and absolute authority of Yahweh. *Tᵉhôm* (parallel to the Babylonian Tiamat) is here wholly demythologised and is presided over by the *rûaḥ* of Yahweh (= ↗ 'spirit of God', not wind as in the *Enuma eliš*). The work of dividing light from darkness (= the chief allies of Tiamat in the Babylonian epic), and the division of the upper and lower

waters (death and dismemberment of Tiamat) may to some degree be reminiscent of the Mesopotamian cosmogony (see *ANET* pp 60–61). At any rate in its theological and psychological presentation the Old Testament commits itself to the idea of *creatio ex nihilo* (↗ creation) even though it does not refer to the making of the *tᵉhôm expressis verbis* (according to Prov 8:24 wisdom existed before the *tᵉhōmôth*), and even though it only mentions God's 'power over the *yām*' (Ps 95:5; Jon 1:9).

Again, in the narrative of the flood Yahweh appears as absolute Lord (Gen 7:4; 8:1f), whereas in the Babylonian epic of Gilgamesh the gods flee from the floods to the highest heaven of Anu. The poetic and prophetic passages of the Old Testament employ images of a contest (Ps 104:6ff; Hab 3:15), victory (Ps 65:7; 89:10; Job 38:8ff) and destruction (Job 9:8), to express Yahweh's position of sovereignty over the sea. In particular mention is often made of Yahweh's contest with the sea monsters Tannin and Rahab (Job 7:12; 26:12; Ps 74:13), as well as with Leviathan (Job 3:8; 41:1; Ps 74:14; 104:26; Is 27:1), which are stabbed and dismembered or caught like a great fish (Ezek 29:4f; 32:3ff). Whether these presentations are influenced to any extent by the divine struggle as set forth in the *Enuma eliš* or in the Ugaritic myth of the contest of Baal with Yam cannot be established with any certainty. But in no case is it a cosmogonic theme that is being treated of in the passages in question. However it is plausible to regard the sea monsters as images of political sea powers which were hostile to Israel, for Tannin and Rahab are used as symbols of Egypt (see Ps 87:4; 89:1of; Is 30:7; Ezek 29:1–16). At any rate the monsters are not on an equal plane with Yahweh but are his creatures (eg, Leviathan in Job 41:25), for which he alone is a match.

In spite of Yahweh's sovereignty over it the sea constitutes a continual danger for sailors (Ps 107:23ff), and is associated with the abode of the dead. The dead fall into the sea, into its currents (Ex 15:5; Ps 69:2, 15), into its streams (2 Sam 22:5), into its innumerable waters (2 Sam 22:17), into its depths (Ps 88:7). It is in the sea that the gates to the world of the dead are to be found (Job 38:16f), ie the sea is connected with the underworld, although how it is connected is nowhere systematically set forth. The *t^ehôm* instills fear into men. It is the 'land without return' (Jon 2) where man is no longer united to God (Ps 88:11f). God alone can draw his faithful ones out of these depths (Ps 32).

This brings us to the part played by the sea in apocalyptic and eschatological literature. The sea contains the enemies of God (Ps 68:23; Amos 9:3), as also darkness and unclean spirits (Mk 5:13). The waters of the *t^ehôm* foster and nourish the tree which is a symbol of Egypt in her hostility to God (Ezek 31:4ff). From the sea the monstrous enemies of God arise (Dan 7:2f; Rev 13:1–8). The roaring of the sea is a sign of the return of Christ (Lk 21:25), and it is only at the end of the aeons that the sea will disappear together with the danger of destruction and death which it represents (Rev 21:1).

But for all its diverse aspects, the sea remains a creature of God and manifests the glory of Yahweh (Ps 69:34; 96:11), and by reason of the springs that issue from the lower ocean and the rains coming down from the upper it can be referred to as a medium of blessing (Gen 49:25).

Bibliography: O. Kaiser, *Die mythische Bedeutung des Meeres in Ägypten, Ugarit und Israel* (*BZAW* 78), Berlin 1959; bibliography ↗ water.

Walter Kornfeld

Seal

Seal (Hebrew: *hôthām*, many times; LXX [usually] and New Testament: *sphragis*): means first the instrument with which one seals, that is the stamp or signet, and then the actual imprint made by the seal.

A. *In the history of culture.* Nowadays when we want to give legal validity to a document we sign it. But not infrequently we also affix a seal, or at least a stamp as well. This usage represents the survival of an ancient custom. The use of a seal impress instead of a signature was familiar throughout the entire ancient Near East (1 Kings 21:8; Is 29:11; Jer 32:10). Lengthier documents were closed by being rolled up into a scroll and then sealed (Is 8:16; Dan 12:4–9; Rev 5:1f; 22:10). Stones used for closing the mouths of tombs, vaults, pits, etc were also sealed in order to guard against unauthorised opening of the place concerned (Dan 6:17; Mt 27:66; Rev 20:3). Every free citizen could carry his seal. Many seals still survive, and provide some detailed information of the various forms which were used. From the aspect of the particular techniques employed we must distinguish between two kinds of seal, the roller or cylinder seal and the seal stamp. The special technique employed for the first of these consisted of rolling it on clay tablets so that the device affixed to the cylinder was impressed upon the tablet. The imprint of the seal stamp, on the other hand, was obtained merely by pressing it down on the tablet. Seals bore the names of their owners and often, a picture (symbol, distinguishing mark) in addition. They were made of stone (semi-precious stones, chiefly quartz: see Ex 28:9–11; Sir 32:6), and were carried on a neck band (Song 8:6; see also Gen 38:18, 25) or a ring on the finger (Gen 41:42; Esther 3:10; 8:2; Jer 22:24; Hag 2:23).

B. *As used in figurative language.* Even in the Old Testament seals are referred to in a symbolic sense, although there are only a few instances of this. Thus the earth is said to be changed under the light of morning 'as clay under the seal' (Job 38:14), ie, as a lump of clay receives the picture affixed to the seal when this is pressed down upon it, so the light of morning makes the forms and outlines of the earth appear under it, all of them having previously been unrecognisable in the darkness of night. Another passage, of which the precise interpretation is uncertain, is Ezek 28:12. Here the king of Tyre is called a 'fairly fashioned seal full of wisdom and perfect in beauty'. 'Seal' here may be an expression of the underlying meaning of the qualities which are being praised.

The New Testament speaks especially frequently of 'seals' and 'sealing' in a figurative sense. God has 'sealed' Jesus (Jn 6:27), ie, authorised him as the bringer of his salvation, made manifest in the works of divine power which Jesus performs. When a man by receiving Jesus' words with faith 'sets his seal to the fact that God is true', (Jn 3:33) this means that he confesses, recognises by his faith, the revelation of God which has taken place in Jesus as truth, and thereby confesses also that God himself is true. When Revelation tells us that the book of God is closed with seven seals (5:1f etc) this idea is based upon an ancient usage. What it means is that the decrees of God for the world are hidden, and are disclosed and executed only by Christ. Thus Abraham receives circumcision 'as a seal of the righteousness which he had by faith' (Rom 4:11), so that in his case circumcision was equivalent to the confession mentioned above in bringing about his justification from faith alone. When we read that the community at Corinth is 'the seal of his apostleship' for Paul (1 Cor 9:2), it means that the existence of this community is the guarantee of the fact that Paul really has an apostolic task, the 'seal' which Christ has, so to say, imprinted upon this apostolate. In another passage (2 Tim 2:19) the church is said to bear as a 'seal' the words: 'The Lord knows those who are his own' and 'Let everyone who names the name of the Lord depart from iniquity'. This means that the sayings quoted are, so to speak, affixed to the edifice of the church as seal inscriptions, signifying that they apply to the church. Paul wishes to 'seal' his collection conveyed to the christians in Jerusalem from the communities in the hellenistic sphere (Rom 15:28). One meaning of this is certainly that the undertaking is now definitively discharged. Whether the phrase is intended to express still more than this we cannot discern—at any rate not with any degree of certainty.

In particular the seal which is metaphorically said to be imprinted on a man is a sign that he belongs to the possessor of the seal, whether God or Christ, and can rejoice in the protection of his owner (Rev 7:2–8; 9:4; see also Ezek 9:4, 6; Rev 14:1; 22:4). Thus God has 'sealed' the christians (2 Cor 1:22) in that he has made them his own in the act of ⟋ baptism, and has, indeed, sealed them with the Holy ⟋ Spirit (Eph 1:13; 4:30). It is in line with this manner of speaking that from the second century onwards (Hermas, *Sim.* VIII 6:3; IX 16:3–5, 7; 17:4; 31:1, 4; 2 Clem 7:6; 8:6; Acta Pauli et Theclae 25; etc) 'seal', *sphragis*, becomes a name for baptism.

Bibliography: F. J. Dölger, *Sphragis, Eine altchristliche Taufbezeichnung in ihren Beziehungen zur profanen und religiösen Kultur des Altertums*, Paderborn 1911; F. Nötscher, *Biblische Altertumskunde*, Bonn 1940, 67 and 233–5; K. Galling, 'Beschriftete Bildsiegel des ersten Jahrtausends v. Chr. vornehmlich aus Syrien und Palästina', *ZDPV* 64 (1941), 121–202; S. Moscati, 'I Sigilli nell' Antico Testamento', *Bibl* 30 (1949), 314–38; A. Reifenberg, *Ancient Hebrew Seals*, London 1950 (with illustrations); Haag 1512–14; W. Michaelis, 'Zeichen, Siegel, Kreuz, Ein Ausschnitt aus der Bedeutungsgeschichte biblischer Begriffe', *TZ* 12 (1956), 505–25; N. Avigad, '*ḥotām*', *Encyclopaedia Biblica* III, Jerusalem 1958, 68–86 (with illustrations); J. G. Février, 'Les sceaux et cachets', *DB(S)* XXXIII, 955–64; G. Fitzer, *TWNT* VII, 939–54.

Johann Michl

Seeking God

A. *In the Old Testament.* The expression 'to seek God' (*darāš* or *biqqēš ʾet YHWH*; from *daraš* the word *midrāš* is derived: it stands for a literary category characterized chiefly by the activity of *seeking* for that meaning in an Old Testament passage which is relevant and appropriate to a given age) signifies a basic religious attitude of the man of the old covenant which is closely related to ⟋ fear of God and ⟋ faith. The occurrence of this term, so pregnant in meaning as it is, in relatively early passages enables us to recognise that even in the earliest times the relationship between God and Israel, far from being maintained on a mere collective basis, was in the highest degree personal and individual.

In the J and E passages of the *Pentateuch*, as also in the books of Samuel and Kings, the primary meaning of the phrase 'seeking God' is to ask the Lord for counsel in some specific matter, to request an oracle from God. Thus Rebekah sought the Lord when she felt twins moving in her womb—that is, she went on pilgrimage to a sanctuary in order to ask the Lord the meaning of this preliminary sign, perhaps through the mediation of a non-Israelite 'man of God' (Gen 25:22 J). Later Israel was able to seek judgement from Yahweh through Moses, the accredited spokesman of God (Ex 18:15[E]) or to seek the Lord directly in the Tent of Meeting (Ex 33:7[EJ]). The fact that even after the death of Moses there was no lack of God-given mediators for the people is attested in 1 Sam 9:9: 'Formerly in Israel when a man went to enquire of

God he said "Come let us go to the seer"'. Again it is related of Jehoshaphat (1 Kings 22:5; 2 Kings 3:11) and Josiah (2 Kings 22:13, 18), as also of the wife of Jeroboam 1 (1 Kings 14:5), that in difficult situations they sought Yahweh or alternatively Yahweh's decision, in other words, that they obtained through the prophets a revelation of his will. But it is especially often stated of David that he made no decision on his own, and undertook no military operation without having first sought Yahweh (1 Sam 23:2, 4; 30:8; 2 Sam 2:1; 5:19, 23; 21:1; etc). The fact that this enquiry of God took place through the high priest and by means of the sacred lots which were kept in the ephod is illustrated in 1 Sam 23:9–12 etc.

The all-pervasive change in Israel's religion to personal and interior piety, which was achieved under the influence of the *prophets*, also left discernible effects upon the use of the expression 'to seek God', which henceforward exhibits fresh shades of meaning: voluntarily to turn to God, to turn away from evil, to fulfil the will of God, to turn to him with entreaty. Thus Amos contrasts the worthless externalism of the cult at Bethel, Gilgal and Beersheba, the homes of idolatrous cults, with that genuine seeking for God which alone can avail to ward off the catastrophe: 'Seek me that you may live . . . Seek the good and not the evil' (Amos 5:4, 14; see also Hos 5:6). Zephaniah, too, establishes the closest connection between seeking for God and morally good behaviour. Moreover in the message of this prophet of the ↗ 'poor of Yahweh', this attitude appears simultaneously as

the 'virtue appropriate to the class' of the poor and humble (Zeph 2:3). But those who do not seek God and do not concern themselves with him (Zeph 1:6; Is 9:13), or else do this only with a penitence that is superficial and ungenuine (Hos 6:6; Ps 78:34, 36) prefer to rely upon earthly covenants and alliances as their defensive equipment instead of 'looking to the Holy One of Israel and seeking the Lord of Hosts' (Is 31:1). Such as these shall not escape the condemnation and punishment which is threatened.

Since the inevitable national downfall is ultimately intended simply to bring back the people to a true seeking for God, the pre-exilic prophets already proclaimed: 'I will return again to my place, until they acknowledge their guilt and seek my face, and in their distress they seek me' (Hos 5:15). It is not until the exile and the post-exilic period, however, that we are brought to recognise that it was indeed their apostasy from the true God that brought about the downfall of the two kingdoms (2 Kings 17:7–23; 24:1–4), but that a radical conversion, a true seeking of God, will discover a God who is forgiving and compassionate. 'From there [the exile] you will seek the Lord your God and you will find him if you search after him with all your heart and with all your soul . . .' (Deut 4:29; see also Jer 29:12–14; etc). This sure hope is taken up by Deutero–Isaiah and combined with an urgent exhortation to prayer and penance: 'Seek Yahweh *for* he can be found, call him *for* he is near. Let the wicked forsake his way . . . Let him return to the Lord' (Is 55:6; see also 45:19. P. Troadec has established convincingly, in his article cited below, that the particle *b^e* here, which is generally translated 'so long as', 'while', has here, as elsewhere in Deutero–Isaiah,—eg Is 60:1; 53:5; 57:17—a causal sense). God is near, and, for those who genuinely seek him, easy to find, for in a short time he will reveal himself by a mighty intervention in Israel's fate as her rescuer and redeemer. The point at which he leads her home from the exile is close at hand. The same promise, now on a universal scale, which prepares the way for the New Testament message of God's will to save all mankind, occurs in the final section of the Book of Isaiah: 'I was ready to be found by those who *did not seek* me (Is 65:1; see also Rom 10:20; a similar universalist expansion in Zech 8:22; Bar 4:28–9).

The expression 'to seek God' has a privileged position in the Books of Chronicles, in which it virtually constitutes a principal motif and recurs again and again with new applications. A comparison with the parallel passages in the Books of Kings reveals that by inserting the term 'to seek God' the author of the Books of Chronicles intended to give expression to his conception of the ideal king and of true devotion to Yahweh (compare eg, 2 Chron 14:3, 6 with 1 Kings 15:11–12; 2 Chron 16:12 with 1 Kings 15:23; 2 Chron 19:3 with 1 Kings 22:46; 2 Chron 22:9 with 2 Kings 9:28; 2 Chron 26:5 with 2 Kings 15:3). In all these passages, each according to the particular context, seeking for God would have to be rendered as 'pure faith, covenant loyalty, whole-hearted acknowledgement of Yahweh, conversion from idolatry, abolition of false cults', etc. When, for instance, it is said of Josiah that 'while he was yet a boy he began to seek the God of David, his father' (2 Chron 34:3), what is hinted at in this laconic statement is the religious reform just then commencing, and the final flowering of the Davidic kingdom (see 2 Chron 15:13, 15; Ezra 6:21; etc).

According to this, then, seeking for God is the attitude of one who turns wholly to God, an attitude which, in conformity with the stage reached by ↗ 'reward' theology at that time, brings ↗ peace and ↗ life, the very essence of all blessings. Correspondingly the opposite attitude, 'to pay no heed to God, to abandon him, to forget him, to turn aside from him', condemns those guilty of these sins to misfortune and ↗ death as already foretold by the prophets: 'Saul did not seek guidance from Yahweh [but rather from the spirits of the dead]. Therefore Yahweh slew him' (1 Chron 10:14; see also 2 Chron 12:14; 16:12).

A concept so rich in religious overtones was naturally used copiously in the *Psalms*. Here the chief applications of it are 'seeking the face of God', and 'rejoicing in being near to him in the temple' (Ps 24:6; 27:8; 34:10; 40:16; 69:32; 70:4). The exhortation 'always to seek' God's face (Ps 105:4 = 1 Chron 16:11) found an echo in the liturgy and in the christian life of prayer. In fact according to Augustine, 'the soul is never satisfied with what it has found, but continues seeking all the more eagerly the more it loves' (*PL* 37, 1392; see the postcommunion prayer of Septuagesima Sunday: 'Et percipiendo requirant, et requirendo sine fine percipiant').

In the *Wisdom books* we find echoes of the motifs in the Psalms (Prov 11:27; 15:14; Sir 14:22; 32:14; Wis 1:1). Special mention should be made of those passages in which Wisdom appears as a person in its own right, one emanating from God and one whom the wise man seeks to bring home 'as a bride' (Wis 8:2). She lets herself be found by those who love her easily and willingly (Wis 8:21). The same theme of 'seeking and finding' occupies a central place in the Song of Solomon. However much the question of the literary category to which this book should be assigned may be disputed, there can be no doubt that the bride who tirelessly seeks her beloved among the↗ shepherds (1:7), upon her bed (3:1), in the streets and squares of Jerusalem (3:2; 5:6), is a figure of the covenant people of the post-exilic age which has finally taken to heart the prophetic exhortation to seek God in truth by interior conversion and renunciation of idols. The difference between the biblical and the Greek ideas of seeking appears very clearly precisely in the Song of Solomon. When the biblical man seeks God he does so like the bride in the Song of Solomon by engaging his whole person in the search, seeking genuinely with his whole heart (2 Chron 11:16), with the true resolve of his will (2 Chron 15:19), with his whole soul (2 Chron 15:13), with contrition of↗ heart and abasement of soul (Dan 3:39[LXX]). By contrast for the Greeks seeking is first and foremost an intellectual activity. This is shown by the use of the expression *zēteō* (=examine), *zētēsis* (=investigation), and *to zētoumenon* (=subject under examina-

tion) as *termini technici* of philosophical speculation.

B. *In the New Testament*. The idea that God will allow himself to be found even by those who *do not seek him* (Is 65:1) represented the highest point to which the Old Testament could attain in the knowledge of God. But that God himself was to come in Christ in order to '*seek* and to save the lost' (Lk 19:10), and that having found them he would rejoice over them as a shepherd over a lost sheep that he has found, and as a woman over the recovery of a lost drachma (Lk 15:2–8), was reserved to the christian revelation. The christian himself must now respond to this experience of having been sought by himself seeking—and at this point the New Testament takes over all the depths of meaning inherent in the idea of seeking God in the Old Testament and brings it to its consummation. Whatever the Christian is directed to seek, whether it be 'the kingdom of God and his justice' (Mt 6:33; see also Gal 2:17) or 'that which is above' (Col 3:1) or the 'true fatherland' (Heb 11:14; 13:14), or 'glory, honour and immortality' (Rom 2:7)—at basis he is always seeking God in Christ Jesus, in the person of whom the kingdom of God has entered into the world, and who, as the bringer of salvation, is present and future both at once (*TDNT* 1, 589). Therefore, when he engages in this seeking he must commit himself to it far more unreservedly, and be far more constant in his practice of it, than his forebears were under the Old Covenant. Like the pearl-trader who, in order to obtain the precious pearl which he seeks, joyfully surrenders everything else (Mt 13:45), so too the christian's *first* preoccupation, prior to all earthly cares or concern about food and clothing (Mt 6:31–2), must be to be a follower of Christ and to devote himself to his cause.

The promise which Jeremiah gave to those who truly seek God (29:12–14) is taken up by Jesus and confirmed: 'He who seeks finds' (Mt 7:7–11 and parallels). The context of this passage enables us to recognise clearly that seeking here is equated with praying: 'For prayer is seeking God if it is to be successful prayer, to open the door and to give access to God.' (Greeven, *TDNT* II, 893.)

Since the redemptive death of Christ all men are called and equipped for this task of seeking God. James gives expression to this truth at the first Council of the Apostles when (quoting freely from Amos 9:11–12 and Jer 12:15–16) he proclaims that the 're-building of the fallen hut of David' by Christ, the Son of David, is intended to make it possible for 'all the gentiles who are called by name to seek the Lord' (Acts 15:17). The expression has the same world-wide sense as it occurs on the lips of the apostle to the gentiles, when in his Areopagus speech to those who were groping to seek God he promises that fulfilment and the attainment of that goal will be found in Christ for *all* men who inhabit the face of the earth' (Acts 17:26–7).

Finally the Letter to the Hebrews records the conviction that God 'rewards those who genuinely seek him' (11:6), and who show that 'minimum of faith' which, as it is promised, will be rewarded by eternal salvation.

Bibliography: Eichrodt II, 157–207; M. Prager, 'Gottsuchen in der Heiligen Schrift', *Erbe und Auftrag* 6 (1959), 444–52; P. Troadec, 'La Parole vivante et efficace', *Bible et Vie chrétienne*, XI, 57–67.

Myriam Prager

Self-denial

When we speak of 'self-denial' we are, for the most part, thinking of that *agere contra*, that *abstine et sustine* by which we distinguish between the conquest of our evil inclinations and our endurance of suffering and trials. The first of these is conceived of as self-mastery and mortification, the second as sacrifice or love of the cross. While these requirements actually belong to the basic stock of christian 'asceticism' and religious training, they do not cover what is essential to the biblical concept of self-denial. This concept of self-denial in the traditional sense provides a graphic example of how, in the process by which theology, moral teaching and ↗ asceticism are progressively emancipated from holy scripture, a saying of Jesus that is genuine has become obscured and changed from its original meaning so as to have a purely moralising application. The good tidings of the biblical message have been replaced by a gloomy 'ascetic' imperative, and this represents an impoverishment of one of Jesus' demands which is genuine and important.

A. Self-denial is a New Testament concept, and in the strict sense appears only in the synoptic gospels (Mk 8:34 and parallels) and in one passage in Paul (2 Tim 2:13). The New Testament knows only of the *verb* 'to deny one'self': *arneomai* or *aparneomai*.

In order to gain a deeper understanding of the concept all those passages must be adduced in which this verb appears either in its simple or its composite form. *arneomai* is used thirty-three times (Mt 10:33 ab = Lk 12:9a—Mt 26:70, 72 = Mk 14:68, 70; Lk 22:57; Jn 13:38; 18:25, 27—Lk 8:45—Lk 9:23—Jn 1:20—Acts 3:13, 14; 4:16; 7:35—1 Tim 5:8; 2 Tim 2:12ab, 13; 3:5—Tit 1:16; 2:12—Heb 11:24—2 Pet 2:1—1 Jn 2:22ab, 23—Jude 4—Rev 2:13; 3:8). *aparneomai* is used eleven times and, moreover, only in the synoptic gospels (Mt 16:24 = Mk 8:34—Mt 26:34, 35, 75 = Mk 14:30, 31, 72; Lk 22:34, 61—Lk 12:9b). The composite form of the verb, however, does not express any intensification of the concept, for both verbs are used interchangeably, both in the parallel passages (eg, Lk 9:23 = Mk 8:34—Mk 14:30, 31, 72; Lk 22:34, 61 = Jn 13:38—Mt 10:33ab; Lk 12:9a = Lk 12:9b) and within one and the same sentence as well (eg, Lk 12:9).

B. As in classical Greek so also in the New Testament, *arneomai* is used in its original meaning of 'to say no': 'to refuse, renounce' either an admonition or acclaim, eg, 'to renounce irreligion and worldly passions' (Tit 2:12; see Acts 3:13, 14; Heb 11:24), or 'to give a negative answer' to a question, 'contest' it, eg, to Jesus' question, 'Who has touched me?' all *reply in the negative* (Lk 8:45). Peter gives a *negative answer* to the question of the maidservant as to whether he belongs to the group of Jesus' disciples (Mk 14:68, 70 and parallels; Jn 18:25, 27; see also Acts 4:16; Jn 1:20; 1 Jn 2:22).

Since the gospel lays the principal emphasis not on the truth of salvation but on the bringer of salvation, the Saviour, the New Testament authors have perforce had to give a fresh meaning to the verb under consideration, that namely of 'to *deny a person*'. One can 'give a negative answer' to a truth, but one 'denies' the *proclaimer* of that truth. In contexts concerned with the person of Christ there may already be some underlying connotation of this latter meaning in the use of the word as signifying 'to give a negative answer to' (compare Mk 14:68, 70 with 5:30; Mt 26:70, 72; Acts 3:13, 14; Jn 1:20).

This fresh meaning appears in all those passages which primarily refer to the *person of Christ*, and it is palpably evident that it is only the *disciples* who can be said to deny Christ, and not Jews or gentiles. For only he who has once professed loyalty to Christ can deny him.

The disciple denies Christ when he fails voluntarily and solemnly to confess the *person of Jesus Christ* in his whole conduct. In this sense Peter *denies* his Lord and Master (see Mk 14:30, 31, 72; Mt 26:34, 35, 75; Lk 22:34, 61; Jn 13:38). About disciples who are disloyal Christ says: 'Whoever denies me before men, I also will deny before my Father who is in heaven' (Mt 10:33; Lk 12:9; see also 2 Tim 2:12; Jude 4). It comes to the same thing when the New Testament authors speak of 'denying faith in Christ', or 'denying the word and the name of Christ', rather than of 'denying Christ himself' (Rev 2:13; 3:8; see also Tit 1:16); this means failing to acknowledge the truth of his teaching (1 Jn 2:22, 23; 2 Pet 2:1), or refusing the just claims of one's brother (1 Tim 5:8; 2 Tim 3:5).

'To deny' Christ, therefore, means nothing else than 'to say no' to Christ, to refuse Christ, to fail to acknowledge him before men, 'to be ashamed of him and of his word' (Mk 8:35; Lk 9:26). The opposite of this is 'to say yes' to Christ, 'to acknowledge, bear witness to' Christ before all the world, to remain constant to Christ in life and death, to give up all things for Christ, to be prepared to lose one's possessions and shed one's blood, and even to lay down one's life itself. This requirement arises from Christ's claim to absolute dominion.

C. Self-denial must be regarded from this christological aspect. The classic passage is found in the following major section of Mark: 'And he called to him the multitude with his disciples, and said to them: (1) "If any man would come after me let him deny himself (*aparnēsasthō*) and take up his cross and follow me. (2) For whoever would save his life will lose it; and whoever loses his life for my sake and the gospel's will save it. (3) For what does it profit a man to gain the whole world and forfeit his [future] life? (4) For what can a man give in return for [to obtain once more] his life? (5) For whoever is ashamed of me and of my words in this adulterous and sinful generation, of him will the Son of Man also be ashamed when he comes in the glory of his Father with the holy angels". (6) And he said to them "Truly I say to you, there are some standing here who will not taste death before they see the kingdom of God come with power"' (Mk 8:34–9:1; see also Mt 16:24–8; Lk 9:23–7).

I. Taken as a whole the six sayings contained in this section were spoken by Jesus himself, even if not all on the same occasion (see V. Taylor, 380). The first, second, and fifth are found in different contexts in Matthew and Luke. From this it can be concluded that the word *for* (*gar*) which joins the individual sayings one to another is merely a particle of transition. The evangelist probably derived these sayings from an original collection of sayings, and all of them, or at least the first four (vv 34–7), teach us in what true 'following of Christ' consists. Mark has skilfully inserted them between on the one hand Peter's acknowledgement of the Messiah and the first passion prediction, and on the other the account of the transfiguration. Christ requires an acknowledgement not merely of his message, but of his person also as Son of Man, as suffering and glorified Lord, whose fate in life and death the disciple is called upon to share in obedience.

In the first saying it is striking that *twice* in the first sentence (Mk 8:34; Mt 16:24; Lk 9:23) Christ demands discipleship together with self-denial and bearing one's cross, even though in other contexts in Matthew and Luke (Mt 10:38 = Lk 14:27) he requires only the bearing of the cross and discipleship. This provides a basis for suggesting that in Mk 8:34 and parallels two originally independent sayings have been blended together: 1. 'He who will *follow me*, let him *deny* himself'; and 2. 'He who *does not take up his cross* and *follow* me is not worthy of me' (Mt 10:38), or: 'He who *does not bear his cross* and *follow* me cannot be my disciple' (Lk 14:27).

II. However this may be, self-denial and bearing one's cross ($\nearrow$ cross) are constitutive elements in the discipleship of Christ. The section as a whole (Mk 8:34–9:1) is preceded by the account of the confession of Peter at Caesarea Philippi, and of Christ's prediction of his passion (8:27–33); and followed by the narrative of the transfiguration of the Lord (9:2–8), which is led up to by the reference to the coming of the kingdom of God with power (9:1). Everything focuses upon the following of Christ, and on bearing witness to the suffering and glorified Lord by self-denial and carrying one's cross.

1. Viewed in this christological perspective the expression 'to deny oneself' is equivalent to 'to say no' to oneself as person, 'to yield oneself up', 'surrender oneself', that is to give up the individual 'I' with all its ideas, aims and desires, or as it is expressed in Luke: 'To hate one's life' (Lk 14:26).

The same demand that one should ruthlessly divest oneself of one's own selfish interests also finds expression in the verse which follows: 'Whoever *loses his life* for my sake and the gospel's will save it' (Mk 8:35; see also Mt 16:25; Lk 9:24; Mt 10:39; Lk 17:33; Jn 12:25). He who boldly exposes himself and his earthly life to a martyr's death will gain possession of his true self, and together with this, the true and the eternal life, and will enter into the kingdom of God. *psukhē* (lit. = soul) here means not the immortal soul as contrasted with the mortal body—this is a Greek idea—but that form of life which corresponds to the Hebrew *nepeš*, which embraces both body and soul, the man as a whole. If the disciple courageously surrenders himself in life and death he will win possession of himself and

eternal life at the resurrection. The anthropology of the Old Testament recognises no blessing which applies to the soul exclusively, only blessings which apply to man as a whole. The well-known missionary apostrophe, 'Save your souls!' is derived from Aristotelian thought. The question arises of whether the hypothesis which has recently been forwarded, to the effect that the 'resurrection of the flesh' begins to take place immediately after death, does not come closest to representing the true view of the bible, even though holy scripture itself does not pronounce explicitly upon this point.

Christ requires us to say 'no' to ourselves in a manner that is truly radical: 'He who will be my disciple, *let him take up his cross*' (Mk 8:34 and parallels). Was this demand in any sense comprehensible *before* Jesus' crucifixion? Would it not have been laid retrospectively upon Jesus' lips by the apostles or evangelists? Or may we even suppose that the saying of Jesus originally ran, 'Let him take up his yoke' (Mt 11:29), and that this would subsequently have been changed by the early church into 'Let him take up his cross'. Certainly the rabbinical literature knows nothing of any proverbial saying of this kind (see SB 1, 587), yet death by crucifixion was not unknown in Palestine under Roman domination (see Josephus, *BJ* II, 12:6; II, 14:9; *Ant* XVII, 10:4–10). Probably, therefore, what we have here is a genuinely dominical saying. In it Jesus is thinking of the moment at which one condemned to death by crucifixion takes the crosspiece (*patibulum*) on his shoulders and, amid mockery and insults, crawls as a defenceless and ignominious criminal to the place of execution. 'Everyone who decides to follow me must be ready to endure the pillory like a criminal on the way to execution'. Another question is whether Jesus was thinking of his own death on the cross, for he does not say, '. . . take up *my* cross', but '. . . take up *his* cross'. Jesus does not speak *expressis verbis* of his own death on the cross. The solitary mention of the crucifixion in the passion predictions (Mt 20:19) cannot be adduced against this. In the parallel passages in Mark and Luke (Mk 10:34; Lk 18:33) it is absent, which shows that it represents a subsequent insertion on Matthew's part. But the whole tenor of these sayings suggests that in view of the murderous hatred of his enemies our Lord did indeed have in mind a violent death, precisely the ignominious death of crucifixion.

The witness which the disciple must bear to Christ is pressed to its utmost possible limits, that is to martyrdom in the true sense of the word, the witness in blood which Stephen, the initiator of the endless procession of 'martyrs', was the first to bear. Certainly God requires martyrdom neither every day nor from all of his children. But this should not be taken as showing that martyrdom is a mistaken way of bearing witness, only that it represents an 'extreme situation'.

In view of the altered circumstances of the early christian communities, Luke (or the early church) speaks of a 'daily' bearing of one's cross. This does not represent any weakening of the sense; the accent is simply laid more upon one's interior readiness for mar-

tyrdom. The disciple must always be ready, if God wills it, to follow his Master on the way of the passion to the place of execution, and to undergo violent death in order to bear the witness of blood to his Lord. Everything bears upon the necessity of readiness. The underlying intention of Luke's retrospective interpolation is precisely to bring out the meaning of this readiness. It entails a radical renunciation of self as an essential and abiding attitude of spirit. In this sense those christians who are forced to renounce much in order to live chaste married lives, and perhaps to endure mockery on that account, are true witnesses to Christ. Again the Carmelite nun who in her quiet and hidden life follows the hard way of total self-renunciation practices self-denial in the truest sense. 'Martyrdom was the dream of my youth, and this dream returned in an intensified form in my convent cell' (Therèse of Lisieux).

In Mk 8:36–7 Jesus goes on to speak of a concrete instance of self-denial. He sets side by side for comparison the two possibilities of gaining the world and losing one's life. This verse is connected with v 35 not merely in terms of externals, by the recurrence of the stich-word 'life', but also in terms of its actual interior meaning. He who decides to follow Jesus must be ready to surrender all worldly riches not merely because he will have to lose them all at his death, but primarily because he stands to lose eternal life. With the greatest possible emphasis Jesus warns us of the great dangers to the attainment of eternal life which earthly possessions entail. The *Sitz-im-Leben* of the saying here under consideration is to be sought in the circumstances of the land-owning classes in Palestine. According to Jesus' teaching in the synoptic gospels, what represents the greatest danger to eternal life for these is not the temptations of sex but the thirst for money. In the gospel of John the question of money does not enter in. For Paul the immorality and idolatry of the hellenistic cities conjure up dangers which are at least as great as those entailed by avarice, even if he does also stigmatise this latter vice with extreme severity: 'The love of money is the root of all evils' (1 Tim 6:10; see also Col 3:5). In this the teaching of the apostle to the gentiles is in harmony with that of Jesus, who incessantly renews his warnings of the immense danger of riches. Almost infallibly they lead to eternal perdition: 'How hard it will be for those who have riches to enter the kingdom of God . . . It is easier for a camel to go through the eye of a needle than for a rich man to enter the kingdom of God' (Mk 10:23, 25; Mk 10:24, which interrupts the sequence of thought, is omitted in Mt 19:23 and Lk 18:24). The disciples rightly understood the words of Jesus as signifying that the difficulty spoken of here amounts to almost total impossibility. Hence the fear with which they ask, 'Then who can be saved?' (Mk 10:26 and parallels). Christ reminds them of the omnipotence of God: 'With men it is impossible, but not with God. For all things are possible with God' (Mk 10:27 and parallels). It is precisely when man is reduced to utter impotence that the power of God really comes into its own (see Gen 18:14; Job 10:13; Mk 14:36). God alone can

show himself supreme over the idol Mammon, which, like some sinister demonic power (see Gen 4:7), threatens to draw down the avaricious man into the eternal abyss (see Lk 16:13). And this means eternally and for ever; for at the last judgement man will have no redeeming price to offer in order to buy back or redeem the life he has lost (Mk 8:37).

2. Christ himself points out the supremely salient factor in the biblical idea of self-denial: 'For my sake and the gospel's' (Mk 8:35). This dominical saying tells us what is the definitive mark of self-denial, for it embodies the fundamental motivation which underlies all true self-denial.

The words 'and the gospel's' do not belong to the dominical saying in its original form. They bear the impress of the early church. For according to the evidence of the synoptics Christ himself constitutes the heart and centre of the 'euangelion'. For this reason the expression has actually been omitted in the parallel passages in Matthew and Luke, and rightly so (Mt 16:25; Lk 9:24; see also Mt 10:39). According to Mk 10:29 the disciple of Jesus leaves relations and possessions alike 'for my sake and the gospel's', whereas according to Mt 19:29 it is only 'for my name's sake', and according to Lk 18:29 'for the sake of the kingdom of God'.

One can only speak of self-denial in the biblical sense if it is exercised for Christ's sake. The person of Christ lies at the very roots of self-denial. Thus it is not primarily self-control or character-building or the purifying and perfecting of one's own personality that is in question, though certainly all this is not excluded. It will 'be added to you' (Mt 6:33).

The decisive factors, however, are bearing witness to Christ, giving up what is one's own, and unreserved consent to the divine will. Without Christ self-denial would be distorted into a rigid self-discipline. By the practice of self-denial in the biblical sense man grows beyond himself and shares in the glorious destiny of the life and death of his Lord. His individual personality, with the special talents belonging to it, is not thereby suppressed. It simply becomes free from the perverse inclinations of fallen humanity, free for the love of God, and free for the loving service of his neighbour (see Mk 12:28–34 and parallels; Lk 10:25–8 and parallels). In this way, therefore, the human personality can be developed and perfected. This imparts to self-denial as understood by the bible a dynamic quality, a true moral greatness, and an immense power to affect others.

Bibliography: Apart from the commentaries on the gospel of Mark by M. J. Lagrange (1947), J. Schmidt (1958), V. Taylor (1959), W. Grundmann (1962), and *D. Nineham (1963), see above all A. Friedrichsen, '"Sich selbst verleugnen"', *Coniectanea Neotest* 2 (Uppsala 1936), 1–8; R. Raitz von Frentz, *Selbstverleugnung*, Einsiedeln 1936; R. Raitz von Frentz, 'Selbstverleugnung oder Selbstveredelung', *Zeitschrift für Askese und Mystik* 15 (1940), 45–55; J. Lebreton, 'La doctrine du renoncement dans le Nouveau Testament', *NRT* 65 (1938), 385–412; J. Lebreton, '"Le Renoncement"', *Lumen Christi* (Paris 1947), 171–96; H. Riesenfeld, 'The Meaning of the Verb *arneisthai*', *Coniectanea Neotest.* 11 (Lund–Copenhagen 1947), 207–9; K. H. Schelkle, *Die Passion Christi in der Verkündigung des NT*, Heidelberg 1949, 217–38; A. Decourtray, 'Renoncement et amour de soi selon saint Paul', *NRT* 74 (1952), 21–9; F. Wulf, 'Selbstverleugnung und Abtötung als Übung der Nachfolge Christi und als Kennzeichen des neuen Lebens in Christus', *GL* 25 (1952), 4–42; R. Koolmeister, 'Selbstverleugnung, Kreuzaufnahme und Nachfolge. Eine historische Studie über Mt 16:24', *Charisteria Johanni Kopp octogenario oblata*, Stockholm 1954, 64–94; E. Dinkler, 'Jesu Wort vom Kreuztragen', *Neutestamentliche Studien für Rudolph Bultmann*, Berlin 1954, 110–29; W. K. Grossouw, *Bijbelse Vroomheid*, Utrecht–Antwerp 1964⁶; K. Rahner, 'Passion und Aszese. Zur philosophisch-theologischen Grundlegung der christlichen Aszese', *Schriften zur Theologie* III, Zurich 1955, 73–104; H. Schlier, *TDNT* I, 469–71; J. Jeremias, *Die Gleichnisse Jesu*, Göttingen 1958³, 183–4; H. van Oyen, *RGG* v, 1961³, 1679–82; J. Kahmann, 'Het volgen van Christus door zelfverloochening en kruisdragen', *TT* 1–2 (1961/2), 205–26; A. Schulz, 'Nachfolge und Nachahmen', Munich 1962, 79–92; W. Pesch, *LTK* IX², 629–30; *BTHW* 537.

Robert Koch

Servant of the Lord

A. *In the Old Testament.* 1. In the bible we find repeated references to men of virtue who are called the 'servants' (ᶜ*eebd*) of God. This is the designation which Jacob applies to himself in his prayer to be rescued from the threat of Esau's anger (Gen 32:10). Solomon does the same in his prayer at Gabaon (1 Kings 3:7f). In various passages of the bible the expression is applied to Abraham (Ps 105:6, 42), Joshua (Josh 24:29), David (Ps 18:1), and Job (Job 1:8). Its original meaning, prior to subsequent modifications, is known to us both from the bible and from other texts of the ancient Near East. When the kings of Assyria, such as Assurbanipal, are addressing their gods they describe themselves as their servants. We find the Phoenician king Azitawadda calling himself the servant (ᶜ*bd*) of Baal in only the second line of his inscription. This role of servant includes the service of the cult, a fact which is reflected in the Babylonian epic of creation. According to this man was created after the rebellion of Tiamat so that he could be made responsible for the service of the gods. But this service has a much wider ambience than this. It comprises obedience in all areas of life. The kings are the servants of the nation's god, whose interests they uphold, and we even find King Sargon after his eighth campaign addressing a letter to the god Assur in which he submits a reckoning to him of the campaign he has conducted. For similar reasons the Canaanite princelings in the Tell-el-Amarna letters are called Abdi-Addi, ie, 'servant of the god Adad', Abdi-Aširta ('servant of Asherah), Abdi Ninurta etc. They also refer to themselves in quite general terms in their letters as 'servants' of Pharaoh, who, according to Egyptian ideology, is god and lord. But in the Letters of Lakish and on Israelite seal cylinders this expression is used in so general a manner that it cannot of itself be taken as implying the divinisation of the king.

2. The community of Israel was organised as a direct theocracy, and it is not primarily the prophets who are the 'servants of Yahweh' the true god, but even in the earlier passages (Ex 4:23; 7:16, 26; etc) it is said that Israel must 'serve' Yahweh. However it is only in later passages that we find mention of Israel as the 'servant of God'. Even the plural form 'servants of Yahweh' (2 Kings 9:7; 10:23) designates not the Israelites as a whole but the faithful who share the beliefs of the prophets.

3. It is not until we come to Is 40–55,

chapters which are now generally assigned to the final years of the exile, that the people of Israel in bondage appears as 'the servant of Yahweh'. As Babylon has the status of servant in relation to her gods Bel and Nebo (Is 46:1), so too Israel serves Yahweh, or, more accurately, should serve him; for God reproaches Israel for having neglected to bring him either sheep or sacrifices (43:22–4). Israel is a blind and deaf servant (42:19)—indeed a sinful servant (42:24; see also 43:24), yet God insists that he has chosen her from all the ends of the earth: 'You are my servant, I have chosen you and not cast you off' (41:9 see also v 8: 'Israel my servant, Jacob whom I have chosen, the offspring of Abraham, my friend'). This servant whom he has chosen is his witness (43:10); through him God will reveal himself. His descendants will receive the spirit and blessing of Yahweh, and will have nothing more to fear (44:2); he has a prophetic mission like that of Jeremiah, who was chosen and prepared for his mission from his mother's womb (44:2). This servant will never be forgotten by God, and his sins will be blotted out (44:22f). For his sake, and in order to keep his word, God raises up Cyrus (44:28; 45:4). Yahweh leads this servant, whom he has delivered, through the wilderness (48:21). In order that all may hear the voice, the word of this servant (50:10; see also 44:26), the command of God will become a light to the peoples (51:4), and the new Jerusalem will be far greater and more glorious than the former one, and all who hearken to God, seek Yahweh and abandon their sinful ideas will be able to be healed there (54f).

4. Understandably many authors, seeing the theme of Israel and its prophetic mission to the Gentile peoples, are inclined to regard the four songs inserted into these chapters, which treat in a quite special manner of the mission of the servant of Yahweh, as instances of the same theme. In language, in imagery, and in their general tendency these verses approximate very closely to the remainder of the chapters, but have noticeably abrupt beginnings (42:1; 49:1; 50:4; 52:13). Moreover, if this point too is contested, it can be shown that they interrupt the development of ideas in Is 40–55. The limits of the individual songs can best be determined by the following considerations: (a) the disquisition on idols, which is broken off in 41:29, is resumed in 42:8; (b) the description of the new exodus, which is interrupted by the gloss in 48:22 (from 57:21) and by the second 'Servant' song, is continued in 49:9b; (c) the divine judgement and condemnation outlined in 50:3 is completed in 50:9b—the images find their explanation in 51:6f; (d) finally, the return of the exiles to Jerusalem in 52:9f is completed by a renewed appeal to the repopulated Jerusalem in 54:1ff.

The four songs, the limits of which have been determined in this way (42:1–7; 49:1–9a; 50:4–9a; 52:13–53:12) 'individualise' the servant of Yahweh much more strongly, and distinguish him from sinful Israel. Each of these songs takes up, at least in its opening section, the theme of the mission to the Gentiles, which has already been adumbrated in 41:4f. The servant has the mission of imparting the law entrusted to him to the Gentiles (42:4). He is therefore a light to the gentiles, the glory of the peoples. He ensures that the gentile peoples and their kings shall receive not only knowledge of the Torah, but ↗ salvation and ↗ peace (*šālôm*: 53:5) as well. But he has also a further mission, that namely of setting free the blind and imprisoned Israel (42:7), of restoring the tribes of Israel and leading the remnant of Israel home (49:6), of justifying many and interceding for sinners (52:11f ↗ justification, mediator).

Whereas in chapters 40–55 the mission to the gentiles is only mentioned in passing, in these songs it constitutes the main theme. They even ascribe to the servant that mission of liberation which in the rest of these chapters appears to be ascribed to Cyrus. For this reason many have wished to regard Cyrus as the servant of God. Others again have seen in this figure a king or prophet of the past, present or future. The interpretation which is preferred at the moment would seem to be the collective one, according to which the servant of God is interpreted if not as Israel in general, then at least as the Israel that has been converted—all the more so since most of the manuscript traditions contain the reading in 49:3, 'Israel my servant'. Many speak of a *corporate personality*, and in terms of this suggest that the servant would have been *individual and collective simultaneously*. But traditional exegesis, which is derived from the New Testament, regards the servant as the Messiah, the heir of David, and this view still retains its force: in terms of the first view it is difficult to see how the converted Israel could conduct its liberating mission towards Israel as a whole, especially in view of the fact that this mission is directed precisely to the remnant, the 'redeemed' or 'preserved' of Israel (49:6). The servant does still retain in his own person certain traits which in the rest of Is 40–55 are ascribed to Israel. These are the sufferings which she underwent during the exile, her debasement, her humiliations, her condemnation and punishment, in other words her death, although it is surely far more difficult to assert this of Israel in spite of Ezekiel's vision of the dry bones (Ezek 37). The servant can be called 'Israel', for he takes upon himself all the sufferings of an Israel that has been contaminated with the sins of the Gentiles, and has incurred the same punishment on their account (53:4). Essentially he is the priest-redeemer who 'intercedes for sinners' (Is 53:12).

Against this view it does not appear difficult to see the victorious Emmanuel of Is 9 in this figure who liberates Israel—the more so since the same figures of light and victory recur in this final chapter. The David of Is 55:3–5 is prince and ruler of peoples whom he has never known hitherto. The author of the servant songs seems to have combined the liberating mission of First Isaiah with the universalist vision of Second Isaiah, and to have systematically inserted his oracles in such a way that the conclusion of the songs is connected with those passages in Is 40–55 which follow it. In this way he has imparted the depths of meaning in his songs to the earlier oracles also, and has given them the definitive traits of that universalist messianism which the New Testament constantly regards as fulfilled in the person of Jesus of

Nazareth (Mt 27:29–31; Jn 12:38; 19:5; Acts 8:32f; etc).

Bibliography: *DB(S)* III, 90–100; A. Feuillet, *DB(S)* IV, 709–14; J. Jeremias, *TDNT* v, 654–700; J. Fischer, Haag 609–19 (all with copious bibliographical references); J. Scharbert, *BZ* 2 (1958), 190–213; H. Haag, 'Ebed Jahwe Forschung', *BZ* 3 (1959), 174–204; V. de Leeuw, *De Ebed Jahweh Profetieën*, Assen 1956.

Henri Cazelles

B. In the *New Testament* Israel (Lk 1:54), *David* (Lk 1:69; Acts 4:25), and five times Jesus (Mt 12:18; Acts 3:13, 26; 4:27, 30) are described as the *pais* (servant) of God. In the connected literature the title *pais theou* is found four times applied to Jesus in ancient prayers in the Didache (9:2f; 10:2f; 10:7: copt. fragm.), three times in 1 Clem (59:2ff), three times in MartPol (14:1–3; 20:2); always in liturgical and doxological formulae in which ancient phraseology has been preserved. Since in the New Testament Israel, too, and especially David are described as the servant of God, it is in no sense certain that in the 'christological' use of the title 'Servant of God' Jesus is always being interpreted as the *Isaian* servant of God—the more so as, in the passages quoted in Acts with the exception of 3:13, the idea of the (substitutional) suffering of the servant of God does not appear. It is probable, rather, that Jesus is thought of as the servant of God first and foremost simply in the sense of being the just one who obeys, who fulfils the will of God without reserve (see Mt 3:15). In particular in Acts 3:26 ('God raised up his *servant* for you first') it is not the Isaian servant of God that is being thought of but rather Jesus as *Moses redivivus* (see also 3:22; 7:37; and, on this, Deut 18:15, 18), especially as Moses is described as 'the Servant of God' in the Old Testament (Josh 14:7 [LXX]: *Mōusēs ho pais tou theou*; see also Josephus, *Ant.* v, 39). Jesus himself, as also the apostolic preachers, have viewed his messianic service in the light of the Isaian prediction of the servant of God, as a whole series of passages containing direct or indirect references attest. More important examples: 1. *In the preaching of Jesus*: the logion on ransom, Mk 10:45 and parallels (see also Is 53:12; but probably the formulation of this logion is secondary; see Lk 22:27); the words of Jesus expressing the significance of the distribution of the chalice in the eucharist: *ekkhunomenon huper pollōn* (see Is 53:12; this *huper* [*anti*, *peri*], which precisely gives expression to the 'substitution' idea, plays an important part in the apostolic preaching of salvation; Schelkle, *Die Passion*, 131–5); Lk 22:37 (see Is 53:12); the silence of Jesus at his trial (see Is 53:7); Jn 10:11, 15, 17 (see Is 53:10); behind the 'must' (*dei*) of his passion (see Mk 8:31 and parallels; Jn 3:14) Jesus certainly saw the will of God as revealed in the *scriptures* (see especially the psalms of lamentation and Is 53). 2. *In the apostolic preaching of the gospel*: (a) *direct*: Mt 8:17 (Is 53:4); 12:18–21 (Is 42:1–4); Lk 22:37 (Is 53:12); Jn 12:38 (Is 53:1); Acts 8:32f (Is 53:7f); Rom 15:21 (Is 52:15); (b) *indirect*: 1 Cor 15:3–5 (a very ancient tradition containing a reference to the fact that the atoning death of Jesus on behalf of others was *in accordance with scripture*); Rom 4:25 (Is 53:4, 5, 12

[LXX]); 8:32; Phil 2:6–12 (*doulos* = slave); humiliation—exaltation); Acts 2:23 (see Is 53:10); 1 Pet 2:21–5; Mk 1:11 and parallels (see Is 42:1); Jn 1:29, 36 ('Lamb of God'); 1 Jn 2:2; 4:10 (*hilasmos* = expiation); Heb 9:28 (see Is 53:12). Jesus also seems to have imparted a new dimension to the idea of the Son of Man by introducing aspects of the Isaian servant of God (see especially the predictions of the passion): the Son of Man must pass through his earthly life as the (anonymous) servant of God. Probably, too, the so-called messianic secret of the synoptic gospels is connected with this: precisely because Jesus is the unknown and unrecognised Servant of God his messianic secret must at first remain unspoken and hidden in public. This tension between the glorious and the suffering Messiah also determines the structure and way of life of the church and its members, and it is for this reason that Is 53 has a part to play in early christian parenesis (eg, Mk 10:45 and parallel; Phil 2:5–11; 1 Pet 2:21–5; Schelkle, 217–38). The description of Jesus as the servant of God belongs to the earliest tradition. Yet it soon died out because it was open to the danger of being misinterpreted in a subordinationist sense, and with the christological kerygma of↗ exaltation greater and greater emphasis came to be laid upon the↗ glory of Jesus *as God in heaven*. Since *pais* has also the meaning of 'child', the transition from the *pais* (= servant, child) to the *huios* (son) christology could be made without any difficulty.

Bibliography (a selection): A. von Harnack, *Die Bezeichnung Jesu als Knecht Gottes und ihre Geschichte*, 1926; K. F. Euler, *Die Verkündigung vom leidenden Gottesknecht*, 1934; J. Gewiess, *Die urapost. Heilsverkündigung nach der Apg.*, 1939, 38–56; K. H. Schelkle, *Die Passion Jesu in der Verkündigung des NT*, 1949; H. W. Wolff, *Jesaja 53 im Urchristentum*, 1949³; T. W. Manson, *The Servant-Messiah*, London 1953; C. Maurer, 'Knecht Gottes und Sohn Gottes im Passionsbericht des Mk-Ev', *ZTK* 50 (1953), 1–38; E. Lohmeyer, *Gottesknecht und Davidssohn*, 1953²; H. Hegermann, *Jesaja 53 in Hexapla, Targum u. Peschitta*, 1954; J. Jeremias, *TDNT* v, 700–717 (with bibliography); E. Schweizer, *Erniedrigung u. Erhöhung bei Jesus und seinen Nachfolgern*, 1955, 81–6; E. Sjöberg, *Der verborgene Menschensohn in den Evv.*, Lund 1955; E. Lohse, *Märtyrer und Gottesknecht*, 1955; G. Bertram, 'Praeparatio evangelica in der LXX', *VT* 7 (1957), 235–9; J. E. Menard, *Pais Theou, a Messianic Title in Acts*', *CBQ* 19 '(1957), 83–92; O. Cullmann, *The Christology of the New Testament*, London 1959; J. N. Sevenster, 'Jezus in de EJ', *TT* 13 (1958), 27–46; E. Fascher, *Jesaja 53 in christl. und jüdischer Sicht*, Berlin 1958; J. L. Price, 'The Servant Motive in the Synoptic Gospels', *Interpretation* (1958), 28–38; L. Krinetzki, 'Die Gottesknechtstheologie des hl. Paulus (Phil 2:6–11)', *BM* 34 (1958), 180–91; L. Krinetzki, *Der Einfluss von Is 52:13–53:12 Par auf Phil 2:6–11*, Rome 1959; M. Hooker, *Jesus and the Servant*, 1959; U. Wilckens, *Die Missionsreden der Apg*, Neukirchen 1961, 163–7; F. Hahn, *Christolog. Hoheitstitel (FRLANT 83)*, Göttingen 1963, 54–66; M. Rese, 'Überprüfung einiger Thesen von J. Jeremias zum Thema des Gottesknechtes im Judentum', *ZTK* 60 (1963), 21–41; W. M. W. Roth, 'The Anonymity of the Suffering Servant', *JBL* 83 (1964), 171–9; J. Jeremias, *Abba*, 1966, 191–216.

Franz Mussner

Shepherd

The work of a shepherd was familiar to the ancients as a matter of living experience. It is this that provides the basis for the figurative use of the term. In Sumer, Babylon, and Assyria 'shepherd' is already found as a soubriquet of the ruler who 'pastures' his subjects, gathers them when they are scattered, carries and cares for the weak. In Egypt it is the God of the other world who is the shepherd and tends his flock. The term is applied to the gods generally. Men are the 'flock of God, which he has made'. The idea of 'shepherd of the peoples' is familiar to Homer, and the image is current throughout antiquity.

The *Old Testament* is unfamiliar with the formalised use of the term (*rō'eh*) for gods and rulers, a usage which is customary elsewhere in the ancient Near East. Instead the manner in which individual traits of the shepherd function are applied to Yahweh shows that here the image is wholly subordinate to the context of a living faith. Yahweh leads his people, his flock (Ps 68:7; 23:3; etc), searches out pastures for them (Ps 23:2; Jer 50:19), calls them together when they are scattered (Zech 10:8), collects them (Is 56:8), bears them (Is 40:11; Ps 28:9). In the accounts of the exodus in Exodus and Deuteronomy terms drawn from the work of shepherds are used. Perhaps too Ps 23 has been influenced by these if we may take 'waters of rest' as referring to the promised land, and the 'restoration of my soul' (v 3) as referring to the miracle of the manna (Guillet, *Leitgedanken der Bibel*, 22f). The psalms and prophecies of consolation composed during the exile make manifold use of the 'shepherd' image, but Yahweh can also assume the other aspect of a shepherd. He can hand his people over as a flock to the slaughter and (instead of gathering them) can scatter them among the peoples (Ps 44:11; see also the image in Ps 44:22; Jer 12:3; Zech 11:4, 7).

The term *shepherd* does not occur in the Old Testament as a title for the king. The Messiah who is to come from the house of David is the first to whom it is applied. He will exercise the function of a shepherd, and he alone as the only shepherd will pasture his people (Ezek 34:23f; Israel and Judah will become one people under one shepherd: Ezek 37:22, 24). In this way the more ethical and social aspect of the task of the messianic ruler who is to come is set in contrast to a purely political understanding of the Messiah (significantly the 'shepherd' does not appear in the Qumran literature!).

In the *New Testament* the figurative use of the 'shepherd' (*poimēn*) idea continues. The image is applied to God only in Lk 15:4–7 in the parable of the lost sheep—if, indeed, it is not intended even there to apply to Christ 'who, by God's commission, brings back the sheep that has strayed' (W. Michaelis, *Die Gleichnisse Jesu*, Hamburg 1955², 133). It may be this latter interpretation that finds expression in the Gospel of Thomas (logion 107) when it declares: 'He left the ninety-nine and sought the one until he found it. After he had toiled [a reference to the Passion?] he said to the sheep, "I love you more than the ninety-nine"'.

Jesus does indeed apply to himself the saying in Zech 13:7 when he says that he goes to his death as a shepherd on behalf of his own (Mk 14:27 and parallel; see also Jn 10:11). He repeatedly insists that he has been sent to the lost sheep (Mt 15:24, etc), in order to seek out the lost, to gather them, to rescue them (Lk 19:10). Jesus is the true shepherd of those who believe in him, hearken to him, those whom he knows and who know him

(Jn 10:4, 14f). But he insists that it has been laid upon him as a shepherd to care for the 'other sheep who are not of this fold' (Jn 10:16). The early church describes Jesus with special emphasis as the 'great shepherd' (Heb 13:20), the 'shepherd and guardian' of our 'souls' (1 Pet 2:25), he who is the 'chief shepherd' (1 Pet 5:4) over the bishops and priests (Jn 21:15ff; Acts 20:28) who pasture the flock of God. In Rev 7:17 the image of the ⁊ lamb is combined with that of the shepherd: he will be the shepherd and will lead the perfect to the springs of life (see Jn 10:28). Again in Rev 12:5; 19:15 (see also 2:27) the power of the victorious Christ as judge is expressed as a power 'to lead to the pastures' (*poimainein*: see Ps 2:9 [LXX]) 'with a rod of brass'. In the same way in Mt 25:32ff Jesus himself had already described the carrying out of the last judgement by means of the image of the shepherd who gathers the whole flock in the evening and divides the (white) sheep from the (black) goats.

Bibliography: L. Dürr, *Ursprung und Ausbau der israel.-jüd. Heilandserwartung*, Berlin 1925, 116-24 F. Hintze, 'Noch einmal die Menschen als "Kleinvieh Gottes"', *Zeitschrift für ägypt. Sprache* 78 (1943), 55ff; J. M. A. Janssen, 'De Farao als goede Herder, Mens en Dier', *Festschrift F. L. R. Sassen*, 1954, 71–9; V. Hamp, 'Das Hirtenmotiv im AT', *Episcopus (Festschrift Faulhaber)*, Munich 1949, 7–20; E. Vogt, 'The "Place in Life" of Psalm 23', *Bbl* 34 (1953), 195–211; R. Criado, 'Los símbolos del amor divino en el AT', *Cor Jesu*, Rome 1959, 411–60 (esp. 427ff); M. Rehm, 'Die Hirtenallegorie Zach 11:4-14', *BZ* 4 (1960), 186–208; J. Jeremias, *TWNT* VI, 485–502; W. Jost, *Poimen, Das Bild vom Hirten in der bibl. Überlieferung und seine christologische Bedeutung*, Giessen 1939; T. K. Kempf, *Christus der Hirt*, Rome 1942; R. Schnackenburg, 'Episkopos und Hirtenamt', *Episcopus (Festschrift Faulhaber)*, 1949, 66–88; P. Samain, 'Le pasteur dans le

Bible', *Rev. Dioc. de Tournai* 5 (1950), 15–25; J. G. S. S. Thompson, 'The Shepherd-Ruler Concept in the Old Testament and its Application to the New Testament', *SJT* 8 (1955), 406–18; N. Catavassi, 'De munere "pastoris" in NT', *VD* 29 (1951), 215–27 and 275–85; J. B. Bauer, '"Oves meae" quaenam sunt?', *VD* 32 (1954), 321–4; V. Hamp and J. Gewiess, *LTK* v², 384–6; J. Botterweck, 'Hirt und Herde im AT und im Alten Orient', *Festschrift J. Frings*, Cologne 1960, 339–52. On the representation of the bearer of the sheep, see: T. Klauser, *Jahrbuch für Antike und Christentum* 1, 1958, 20–51; D. Müller, 'Der gute Hirte', *Zeitschrift für ägypt. Sprache* 86 (1961), 127–44; H. Thomann, *Jahwe, Hirte der Seinen*, Rome 1963 (dissertation); W. Tooley, 'The Shepherd and Sheep Image in the Teaching of Jesus', *NT* 7 (1964), 15–25; A. Stöger, 'Jesus der Hirte', *Oberrhein. Pastoralbl.* 66 (1965), 97–106.

Johannes B. Bauer

Sickness

A. *The Old Testament*. 1. *Sickness as a harsh Experience.* Old Testament man is conscious of the bitterness of being sick, and complains of it to God (see eg, Ps 31:11; etc). He knows how to prize the great benefit of good health (Sir 30:14–20: 'It is better to be poor and healthy of body than rich but physically sick').

2. *Sickness as a punishment for sin and a sign of sinfulness.* See, eg, Ps 32:3–5; 38:3 ('There is no soundness in my flesh because of thy indignation'); 41:4 ('Heal me for I have sinned against thee'), 8f; Job 8:13; 22:5–14; Sir 38:15 ('He that sinneth in the sight of his Maker shall fall into the hands of the physician'); 1 Sam 16:14; 2 Kings 5:27; 2 Chron 21:12–15, 18f; 1 Macc 9:54–6; 2 Macc 9:11f.

3. *The image of the 'sick' people as an expression of its sinful state.* See Is 1:5f; Jer 8:21–3; 30:12–15; 51:8f. (There is no healing for Babylon).

4. *Sickness as the threatened penalty for falling away from Yahweh and his commandments, health as a reward for faithfulness.* See Ex 15:26; 23:25; Lev 26:15f; Deut 7:12, 15; 28:20–22, 27, 59–61.

5. *Prayer in sickness.* See, eg, Ps 6:2–8; 13:4; 30; 88; 102:24f; 118:17f; 119:149; Sir 38:9 ('Pray to the Lord and he shall heal thee').

6. *Help from Yahweh.* Ex 15:26 ('I am Yahweh your healer'); Ps 34:3f; 41:2–4; 103:3; 107:20; Jer 30:17; 33:6–8. But the human physician too is highly prized by reason of his skill in healing (Sir 38:1–15).

7. *The healing of sickness in the messianic age.* See especially Is 35:5f.

8. *The servant of God as the bearer of our infirmities.* See Is 53:3–5 (v 4: 'Surely he has borne our griefs and carried our sorrows'), and compare this with the promise in v 10 that Yahweh will heal him when he has been wounded. 'Infirmities' are already being used as an image of sins.

B. *The New Testament.* 1. *Jesus and sickness.* According to the witness of the gospels Jesus healed numerous sicknesses of the most diverse kinds. (Apart from the numerous individual narratives concerning healings of the sick, see the summaries in Mk 1:32–4 and parallels; 3:10 and parallels; 6:55 and parallels; Lk 5:15; 8:2. The apostles too receive the commission to heal the sick and the power to execute it from Jesus: Mt 10:8; Lk 10:9). In this the inauguration of the promised messianic age of salvation manifests itself irrefutably (see Mt 11:5 and parallels; 12:28 and parallels), and according to Mt 8:17 it represents a fulfilment of the prophetic saying concerning the servant of God: 'He has taken away our infirmities and borne our sicknesses' (Is 53:4). 'In his name' the apostles too heal the sick (see Lk 10:17; Acts 3:6, 16; 4:10; 9:34: 'Aeneas, Jesus Christ heals you'; Jas 5:14). In the saying which Jesus applies to himself, 'Those who are well have no need of a physician, but those who are sick' (Mk 2:17 and parallels). The passage which follows ('I came not to call the righteous but sinners'), and the context as a whole, together show that Jesus also considers his salvific work for the 'publicans and sinners' as a work of his office as messianic 'physician', who sees in sin a sickness from which man suffers and from which he must be healed.

2. *Sickness and sin.* In the New Testament it is recognised throughout that there is a connection between sin (the dominion of Satan) and sickness (see Mt 12:28f; Lk 13:16; Jn 5:14; Acts 12:22f; Rom 8:20, 22; 1 Cor 11:30; Rev). But Jesus breaks through 'the mechanical dogma of retribution' (Oepke), which was widespread in the Old Testament (see A 2) and later judaism (see Test xii Gad 5:11: 'That in which a man sins, in that will he be punished also'; Jn 9:2, 24). As illustrations of this, see Jn 9:3: 'Neither he nor his parents have sinned'; 11:4: 'This sickness . . . is for the glory of God, so that the Son of God may be glorified by means of it'; Lk 13:1–5). Admittedly God can also permit a sickness to fall on a man as a means of healing chastisement (see 1 Cor 11:32; 2 Cor 4:17; 12:7ff).

3. *Sickness as vicarious suffering entailed in the vocation of the apostle.* Paul speaks of this in 2 Cor 12:7f; see 2 Tim 2:10f. He boasts of his infirmity, which is manifested in his illness 'that the power of Christ may rest upon me' and 'that the life of Jesus may be revealed in our mortal flesh'. In this he sees a sharing in the 'sufferings of Christ' (2 Cor 1:5; Col 1:24), which vicariously benefit his 'body', the church (see the adumbration of this in Ezek 3:22–7; 4:4–8). This must apply to every christian who accepts his sickness as coming from the hand of God.

Bibliography: A. Lods, 'Les Idées des Israelite, sur la maladie, ses causes et ses remèdes', *BZAW* 41 (1925), 181–3; F. Fenner, *Die Krankheit im NT*, Leipzig 1930 (with bibliography); C. J. Brim, *Medicine in the Bible*, New York 1936; H. Greeven, *Krankheit und Heilung nach dem NT*, Stuttgart 1948; J. Scharbert, *Der Schmerz im AT*, Bonn 1955; J. Hempel, '"Ich bin der Herr dein Arzt" (Exod 15:26)', *TLZ* 82 (1957), 809–826; J. Hempel, *Heilung als Symbol und Wirklichkeit im biblischen Schrifttum*, 237–314; F. J. Schierse, 'Hat Krankheit einen Sinn?', *SZ* 84 (1959), 241–55; *DB(S)* v, 957–68; Haag 963f; G. Stählin, *TDNT* i, 490–93; A. Oepke, *TDNT* iii, 200–15; iv, 1091–8; L. M. Weber, *LTK* vi², 591–5.

Franz Mussner

Simplicity

The concept of simplicity is closely related to that of ↗ perfection.

It connotes not simplicity in the derogatory sense of silliness, but rather the virtue of a straightforward, upright and wholehearted disposition, which is immune to any kind of duplicity or deceit. This attitude, which bears the stamp of the union of God with men, is called *haplotēs* by the Greek translators of the bible and by the New Testament, and for this the most favoured translation in Latin is *simplicitas*.

For Plato and Aristotle this concept coincides with those of truthfulness and uprightness. For adherents of the Stoa it is the idea of being faithful to what is natural and unfalsified that is most emphasised. The simplicity of the cynics and the naturalness of their way of life are recommended. A philosopher who comes closer to the biblical concept of simplicity is Marcus Aurelius: in the virtuous man all must be honest and simple and full of good will (3, 4, 3). He decides for the good from a disposition that is simple and free (3, 6, 6). But Marcus Aurelius' 'simplicity' is strongly and decisively conditioned by the Stoic concept of impassivity as an ideal. One must be simple in the sense of refusing to allow oneself to be perturbed by anything (4, 26, 2). 'Simple' is related to 'immune to suffering', 'free from illusion' (4, 37). In 1 Macc 2:37 the doomed Jews encourage themselves by saying: 'Let us all die in the innocence of our hearts!' The ancient translations of 1 Kings 9:4 and Josh 24:14 may be compared with this. 'Simple' comes to express the inner meaning of all virtues, as is seen in the case of the *vir simplex et rectus*, Job (Job 1:1). Such is the simplicity of heart with which one must seek the Lord (Wis 1:1).

The derogatory sense of 'simple', which appears in non-biblical Greek, is unknown in the Old Testament. It is precisely the Proverbs of Solomon which praise the virtue of walking with an upright heart before God (↗ way). In the Testaments of the Patriarchs 'simplicity' is particularly emphasised,

and here the concept seems to have been developed still further, for it embraces all virtues and is equivalent to integrity (TestIss v 4) and innocence.

In the New Testament the word does not occur so often (see Rom 12:8; 2 Cor 8:2; 9:11, 13; 11:3; Eph 6:5; Col 3:22 for the noun; and, for the adjective, Mt 6:22; Lk 11:34), but the reality signified by the word simplicity is to be found in children and those of tender age (Mt 18:3), who are the example used to illustrate this attitude. Christians must be 'as simple (ie, as immune to falsehood) as doves' (Mt 10:16). In the logion concerning simplicity (soundness) of the eye (Mt 6:22; Lk 11:34) Jesus requires entire and undivided self-giving to God's will as opposed to the divided and ambiguous piety of the pharisees. To be 'simple' means to be free from ulterior motives of self-interest, and carries the further implication of honesty and ↗ humility. Thus after the breaking of bread the community partake of food with joy and simplicity of heart, praising God (Acts 2:46f), and he who has anything to give gives it with simplicity (Rom 12:8).

Bibliography: C. Spicq, 'La vertu de simplicité dans l'Ancien et le Nouveau Testament', *RSPT* 22 (1933), 5–26; O. Bauernfeind, *TDNT* 1, 386f; G. Bertram, *TDNT* IV, 912–23; C. Edlund, 'Das Auge der Einfalt', *Acta Sem. neotest. Upsaliensis* 19 (1952); H. Bacht, 'Einfalt des Herzens', *GL* 29 (1956), 416–26; H. Bacht, *RAC* 4, 821–40; O. Hiltbrunner, *Latina Graeca: Semasiologische Studien über lateinische Wörter im Hinblick auf ihr Verhältnis zu griechischen Vorbildern*, Bern 1958, 15–105; J. Kürzinger, *LTK* III², 746; G. W. H. Lampe, *A Patristic Greek Lexikon* I, 1961, 186f.

Johannes B. Bauer

Sin

A. *Sin in the Old Testament.* It is difficult to define what sin is, but by means of the particular expressions which are employed for it we can deduce from the history of revelation in what it essentially consists.

1. 'Your iniquities have made a separation between you and your God!' (Is 59:2). This is, perhaps, the clearest saying concerning the essence of sin in the Old Testament (Köhler, 164). Something sundering comes between man and God. The first sin that is committed is recorded in the narrative of the fall in paradise. It is a sin of disobedience both interior and exterior. The ancestors of the race wish to be sicut dii, like gods, knowing good and evil! This is not equivalent to saying that they 'wish to know everything', or 'to distinguish between good and evil', but that they wish 'to decide for themselves what was good and what was evil, and to live according to this decision' (thus Coppens, de Vaux, etc). It is a question, therefore, of nothing less than outright moral autonomy which finds expression in pride and rebellion against the dominion which God claims for himself!

At the suggestion of the serpent, Eve believes that the word of God may not be absolute; she doubts the word of God and thinks that the command that comes from God has been given not for man's benefit but for the benefit of God himself (1. 'You will by no means die', 2. 'For God knows that you will be as gods'). Thereby man becomes a rival to God. The whole conception of the relationship between God and man is radically inverted. The evil of sin consists, therefore, not so much in the external act of disobedience as in the interior inversion of the right order.

The indirect effect of sin is an alteration in man by reason of which he flees from God (Gen 3:8: 'And they hid themselves', whereas formerly, on the contrary, 2:25: 'They were not ashamed'). At the same time punishment ensues also: ↗ death and expulsion from paradise. Man no longer had access to the tree of life (3:22–4). ↗ Life has the value of a supreme gift, one which God alone can give. Death, on the other hand, is nothing else than the deprivation of life. So long as no revelation has yet been given of survival after death, death means the absolute deprivation of all benefits without exception, and so the loss of salvation too. Wis 2:23 has also interpreted our passage in the same sense: 'God created man for immortality, and made him to the image of his own eternity. But by the envy of the devil death came into the world, and they experience death who are on the side of the devil'. In Rom 5:12 Paul adduces the revelation of Genesis in the literary form which it has acquired in Wisdom. With the transgression of Adam sin has entered the world of men, sin, here formally personified as a power which sets itself against God, and which so long as it remains in mankind separates it from God. This is the condition of separation which is of itself final and irremediable, and which Paul—in agreement here with the whole of tradition—calls 'death'—death, which is in consequence of the spirit and everlasting, the sign of which is physical death, which will not be followed by any glorious resurrection.

The chapters which follow in the primitive history of the bible relate how sin makes ever deeper incursions into the world of men, and how at the same time it takes away 'life' (see the genealogies in chapter 5, and 6:3). Indeed life would have been completely wiped out by the flood had not God relented and 'saved' Noah together with his family in the ark. (Hence it is that the ark becomes a type of salvation in the New Testament: 1 Pet 3:20ff). They are saved by God who makes his↗ covenant with them. Men would not have been able to achieve salvation of themselves.

In the minds of the Hebrews the land of Egypt (see Ezek 20:5–9) was the land in which man lived *far* from God, the land of *sin*. And it is precisely there that it is revealed with unsurpassable clarity (the miracles of Moses!) that without the miraculous intervention of God all thought of deliverance would have been senseless from the very outset. Hence the constantly recurring motivation: 'For I am the God who brought you out of the house of bondage, out of Egypt'—thus especially in the prelude to the decalogue, Ex 20:2 and Deut 5:6 (see also Lev 22:33 and Ps 81:10), for the commandments of God are meant precisely to be a help to salvation and to life. They are given for man's well-being, so that he shall not fall into sin and finding himself far from God, encounter death.

What does sin mean for God? Does the Old Testament teach only that sin is committed against God, or does it go still further and say that it constitutes an actual injury to God? In itself the word *offence* does express this. In our terms it means 'damage' (as for instance it might be said that the malignant talk of someone else has 'damaged' me), 'scandal', 'injury'. Admittedly the actual term is not exemplified in the Old Testament. Nevertheless the idea is there.

2. *The words for sin* in the Old Testament seem at first not very enlightening: *ḥāṭāʾ*, properly 'to miss a goal, blunder, commit a moral error', applies to the sin which is committed externally and which is apprehensible and visible to others; *pešaᶜ* as a designation for sin usually emphasises the aspect of rebellion, opposition to God; the word *ᶜāwôn* lays the chief emphasis on bad conscience, the evil intention involved in sin, and then (as can readily be understood) the fault.

3. Rather more can be deduced from the consequences arising from sin according to the teaching of the Old Testament. It provokes God's↗ wrath (Deut 32:21); see especially Jer 7:18f; 'The children gather wood, the fathers kindle fire, and the women knead dough, to make cakes for the queen of heaven. And they pour out drink offerings to other gods to injure (insult) me. Is it I whom they injure? says Yahweh'. Is it not themselves, to their own confusion?' From these two verses one receives not merely their own particular message but also a striking insight into the theology of Jeremiah. Properly speaking it is not God who is injured but man! Again the word *nāʾats* means to 'treat irreverently'. The Greek bible (and, following it, RSV) translates 'to provoke to anger'. In any case it is precisely by this word that the idea of injury and offence is expressed, although in practice it is confined to the rejection of the counsel, law, or com-

mandment of God. The Old Testament strives as far as possible to uphold the transcendence of God. However certain it may be that sins are directed against God, it is no less certain that man cannot really affect him by them (Job 35:6: 'If you have sinned, what do you accomplish against him? And if your transgressions are multiplied, what do you do to him?').

Nevertheless the Old Testament does contain many contexts and many individual narratives from which it can clearly be shown that there is a true sense in which the sin of man does affect God also, without impugning his transcendence. In pagan sources we already have abundant evidence for the idea that by sin God is robbed of something, that he does not obtain something that is his by right. Traces of some such idea may well be found from time to time in the earlier passages of the bible, as for instance in the narrative of the sacrifice of the sons of Eli (1 Sam 2:12ff, especially v 17), and similarly in the story of the ark of the covenant among the Philistines (1 Sam 5:7ff). As a whole, however, the Old Testament adopts a hostile attitude to ideas of this kind. The prophets, for example, struggle to eradicate that attitude of mind among the Israelites in which they strive to appease God and offer him compensation in the manner of pagans: see Is 1:11; Ps 50:9ff, similarly in the section on the right kind of fasting, Is 58:5ff.

Sin is an 'injury', an 'insult' to God to the extent that it injures or damages a man whom God has under his protection. In 2 Sam 12 Nathan reproaches David with his sins against Uriah and his wife (vv 7f)—what ingratitude to God who has made David so great and rich, and has bestowed wives in plenty upon him! v 9: David has despised the commandment of God, therefore punishment will fall upon him; v 10: 'because you have despised *me*, and have taken the wife of Uriah the Hittite to be your wife'. But when the sinner acknowledges his sin and repents God removes his guilt from him (v 13). Only part of the punishment still stands in order that others may not be scandalised and imagine that David's guilt might go unpunished. In one way, therefore, sin does indeed affect God, namely by doing injury to men whom God protects and loves. The same idea is expressed in Ps 83 when it is said that the fury of the ↗ enemy is directed against God, and yet it is made clear in the same breath that it is only the Israelites who will experience it. They are, after all, *his* people! Whoever sins against them sins against God.

It is even more true that sin constitutes 'injury' and 'insult' against God in that it is a breach of the ↗ covenant between God and men, the covenant which came increasingly to be deemed as close as the marriage bond. Adam and Eve forfeit not only life as such, but life in friendship with God. God who, of his own free will, had bestowed every kind of love and every possible benefit upon them, is regarded by them as a tyrant and a rival. Then we have to take into consideration all the covenants (see Rom 9:4) which he made with Noah, Abraham and Moses. For this reason it is precisely idolatry (see Rom 1:21ff) which can be described as the sin of sins from which all other sins derive.

For in Israel's choice of other gods besides Yahweh, Yahweh himself is precisely supplanted as inadequate for the role of protector and friend. From early times onwards we find sin regarded as *adultery*. The marriage between people and God is broken. The marriage of Hosea perforce bears moving witness to this, the actual circumstances of it taking on this prophetic meaning (see also Ps 45, the Song of Solomon, Ezek 16, Is 5, and 54:5ff; etc). God loves his people as a wife, with a perfect and boundless love. Every time she is unfaithful and separates herself from him he follows her to induce her to ↗ convert her ways and return home. He does this with all the urgency of a husband who cannot go on living without her. It is against this background that the expressions of divine jealousy are to be understood (the classic passages: Ex 20:5 = Deut 5:9; Ex 34:14; Deut 4:24; 6:15; Josh 24:19). This jealousy is turned into anger when confronted with the enemies of his people, but can also be turned against the Israelites themselves when they are unfaithful, in order to bring about their conversion (see Ezek 23:25 and 14:11). Thus the very punishment inflicted upon sinners by God can be regarded as an expression of his love for them. For if he did not love them, then he would not chastise them in order to induce them to convert their ways. Nowhere in pagan tradition is there any mention of such a love of God for his creatures, his men.

To summarise the doctrine of the Old Testament on sin: Sin is directed against, and in a true sense affects, God in that it 'strikes his love in the face'. For this reason it can be forgiven only by him. Equally sin is an *evil*, the evil that falls upon man himself because it deprives him of true life, and subjects him to the rule of Satan. The effect of sin upon the interior man is to produce in him a profound change for the worse, a change which the man himself cannot be the sole, or even the primary agent in removing and repairing. For this God himself must intervene—must 'wash him clean', 'renew his life', 'create him anew', to invoke the words of the unknown suppliant in Ps 51. It is precisely this sublime psalm of repentance which can be pointed to as the compendium of the Old Testament teaching on sin.

B. *Sin in the New Testament.* 1. *The synoptics.* The vocabulary does not throw much light on the nature of sin. On the contrary, one could be led astray by it if one decided to take as one's starting-point the word most frequently used in the synoptics and Acts, namely *aphienai* (lit. = 'to let go'), and assumed from this that sin in the New Testament is conceived of in purely juridical terms. Instead of such an examination of individual words it will be far more suitable to our purpose to take the New Testament as a whole, the sequence and context of the accounts it contains as the basis for our investigation of the nature of sin.

'Forgive us our debts as we also have forgiven our debtors' (Mt 6:12). Here Jesus is using an expression which was familiar to the Jews: *debt*. See Sir 11:15, where it appears as equivalent to *ḥaṭāʾ*. Thus also, in Ps 25:18, in place of the Hebrew word *ḥaṭat* (=sin), the Targum (Aramaic paraphrase) puts *ḥôbāʾ* (=debt). In exactly the same way Lk 11:4, the parallel text to Mt 6:12, reads 'sin' in place of 'debt'. Naturally the use of this word does not open the way to a purely legalistic view of sin. It is rather that all must lay to heart the commandment of mutual forgiveness (see Sir 28:2ff; Mk 11:25; Mt 18:23–34). More can be learnt of the New Testament idea of sin from the concept of↗ 'conversion', which is extremely closely connected with it. Like John the Baptist, Jesus commences his preaching with a summons to repentance (see Mk 1:4, 15; Mt 3:7–10 and parallels; Lk 3:7ff). This presupposes that the men to whom it is addressed have already *turned away* from God. It is precisely in this turning away that sin consists. It is disobedience to God (Lk 15:21) and lawlessness (Mt 7:23; 13:41). In the ethics of christianity, God is the Lord and man is bound to obey him, whereas in the Stoa sin is regarded simply as a deviation from the ideal, from that which is in conformity with nature. Hence every sin carries with it the awareness of guilt, the awareness of having deserved punishment from God.

A still more perfect and more exact idea of sin is to be obtained from the parables concerning God's kindness, above all that of the prodigal son (Lk 15). In his case sin begins in the moment when he demands his share of the estate with the intention of spending it all on his own pleasure, to which end he takes himself abroad in order to withdraw himself from the surveillance of his father. These two elements, departure from the father's house and living for pleasure, together constitute a sin.

The three parables in Lk 15 carry us further, for they all exhibit one trait in common, namely that the Father, God,

of his kindness brings his lost children (sinners) home from afar. It makes no difference here whether the evangelist was in fact the first to put these parables together. The point is precisely that man, left solely to his own resources, cannot live for long without grave sin. Not only the psalmists but also the devotees of the Qumran sect were utterly convinced of this, and gave expression to their conviction again and again: it is God who guides man's steps into the right way (that is, the moral life). Without his help man cannot live a good life. When↗ temptation comes he is powerless before it without the divine help, like the prodigal son in the far country when a famine broke out. His position is brought home to him even more by this, and he is forced to notice how isolated and desolate man is far from his home. No-one is willing to help. This motif appears in all three parables, if indeed the leading figure is taken to be the Father in his kindness. It is manifest that sin is represented by the element of total deprivation, deprivation of the very meaning of existence by separation from God. The lost sheep is perishing in isolation, and, more than this, has thwarted the very meaning of its own life, namely to be of service to man. The same applies to the lost drachma. The sole purpose of its being there, the very meaning of its existence is that men shall avail themselves of it. When it is lost people can no longer avail themselves of it, and it is like a coin which has been withdrawn from currency, common metal, or— still worse—like forgotten matter. In a word, its 'drachma-being' is meaningless precisely because it has been cut off from its proper sphere of life. So it is with man. The meaning and goal of his life is God, the luminous will of God, his overflowing love. He who wilfully separates himself from this is not only lost but makes his very 'being a man' meaningless in itself. The necessary condition for the sinner receiving grace always remains his conversion (see Lk 15:7, 10). Admittedly this conversion does not of itself bring about the forgiveness of the Father, but rather the Father has been waiting for it from the first. As Augustine trenchantly puts it: 'Iam diligenti nos reconciliati sumus', 'He loves us already before we have been reconciled to him'. If Christ appears as ↗ mediator between God and ourselves, then this is not to alter God's attitude towards us, but to demonstrate to us the love of God, who offers his only begotten Son on our behalf, who only waits for our conversion. This conversion, therefore, is necessary because man is free and a person, possessing free will and taking his own decisions (↗ freedom). Jesus therefore has to alter our attitude, our state of lostness far from God, by his preaching of penance and conversion. By these means he prepares men to receive the forgiveness of their sins, for as the suffering ↗ servant of God he lays down his life in expiation for many who come before and after him. It is only thus that the promise of the angel is fulfilled in its deepest sense. The name 'Jesus' means salvation, that is, that he will save men 'from their sins' (Mt 1:21; ↗ redeemer, ↗ Saviour). This significant feature in the messianism of Jesus was unknown to judaism (in spite of Is 53, etc: see H. Hegermann, *Jesaja 53*, Gütersloh 1954, 131f), and *a fortiori* has no counterpart in any

of the saviour-figures in hellenistic religions.

A further point of fundamental importance (see Schmid) is the 'polarity' of the christian idea of God. God is at once absolute ↗ holiness, and therefore the strict and immovable Lord and judge, and at the same time absolute ↗ love, the kind Father who recognises even the most abandoned of sinners as his child and takes him into his grace when he turns back to him. Both aspects of the christian idea of God are accorded their full force in the teaching of Jesus on sin. Hence the radicalism of Jesus' moral demands, his sayings on judgement and 'woes'. On the other hand Jesus teaches no less decisively that the Father's love knows no limits, that he does not will the death of the sinner, but rather his life, and that he only waits for the conversion of that sinner with open arms—indeed that he actually comes to meet him when he repents. This polarity in the idea of God is again underlined by the circumstances of Jesus' own life. Certainly, the Father loves him in an infinitely higher manner than in his love for his human creatures, but on the other hand in a certain sense he owes it as an act of atonement to his affronted holiness (at least in the order of atonement once he has chosen this) that he both wills and accepts the sacrifice of the life of his beloved Son in expiation for the guilt of humanity.

↗ *Satan*. In the preaching of Jesus and the apostles a further element of decisive importance can be discerned. Jesus comes to establish the kingdom of God in place of the kingdom of Satan (Jn 12:31; Col 1:13; Acts 26:18). This appears quite clearly from the narrative of the ↗ temptations of Jesus. In any case the Lord intended to lay it before his apostles as a fact of special importance for the understanding of his mission. As soon as he had received his solemn messianic investiture at baptism—anointing as messianic king by the Holy Spirit (see Acts 10:38)—he was impelled by the Spirit to go into the wilderness 'in order to be tempted by Satan'. However we choose to explain the individual elements in the temptation, one point is clear. We have here the prologue to the entire life of Jesus. His whole mission consists in the victory over Satan, and a victory won not with any kind of weapons but with those provided by the Father, which alone were effective. Satan suggests various apparently good means, and above all opportune means. Certainly in order to assuage his hunger he could legitimately make use of his power of working miracles. In order to convince the Jewish people he could hardly have thought of a more appropriate miracle than to cast himself down from the pinnacle of the temple, for then they would truly have been able to recognise him as the Son of Man in the guise foretold in Daniel's promise as 'he who comes upon the clouds of heaven'. The Jews themselves demanded a miracle of this kind from Jesus (Mt 12:38; 16:1; Jn 6:30). Josephus has a similar story to tell about the Jews of his time (see *Antiq.* 20:5, 1; 8:6). Jesus would indeed perform miracles, but of a different kind: the sign of Jonah, death as a proof of his love, and resurrection as a proof of his power, but all without eye-witnesses! And when (Jn 6:30) the Jews wanted a

miracle like the miracle of manna Jesus promised them a still greater, more sublime and more effective sign: the true bread from heaven. But they said 'this saying is hard' (v 60).

Christ rejects Satan's suggestions in the clearest possible manner. For him there can be no question of using any other means to establish the kingdom of God except those willed by God himself. Then Satan sees that he has been defeated by the steadfastness of Jesus and reveals his real intentions: I will give you all the kingdoms of the earth if you will adore me . . . the Son of God could no longer be in doubt. Satan, the conqueror of the old Adam, is now himself conquered by the new. But this conquest is only preliminary, only on the occasion of these temptations. Luke adds the significant statement: 'Satan departed from him until an opportune time' (4:13). This victory is only a preliminary one, an anticipated one (as in the transfiguration)—only now will the struggle with Satan run its full course through the entire life of Jesus.

Jesus and Satan during Jesus' public mission. The Jews held the conviction that sickness was a sign of bondage to sin and Satan. The 'woman who was bent over' (Lk 13:11ff) had a 'spirit of infirmity' (v 11). She was 'bound by Satan' (v 16), although it is not stated in so many words that there was a devil to be cast out of her. Certainly Christ does correct the opinion of the Jews and of his own disciples, but he also confirms what is true in this opinion: see Lk 13:1ff: Jesus receives news of the massacre of certain Galilaeans as they were in the act of offering sacrifice at the temple: 'And he answered them, "Do you think that these Galilaeans were worse sinners than all the other Galilaeans because they suffered thus? I tell you, No; but unless you repent you will all likewise perish". There is, therefore, a real connection between men's unhappy fate and sin. In a not dissimilar manner in the case of the man born blind (Jn 9:2f) Jesus explicitly denies that this man or his parents have sinned, but he sharply admonishes the man who has been healed at the pool of Bethzatha (Jn 5:14): 'See, you are well. Sin no more, that nothing worse befall you'. The healing miracles, therefore, are meant to prove more than that Jesus is the awaited Messiah (Mt 11:4), more too than that Jesus has power to forgive sins (Mk 2:10ff), or that he is the sole redeemer (Acts 4:12). These miracles prove more than this in that they constitute in themselves the beginning of redemption to the extent that they free men from the tyranny of the devil. It is no accident that the exorcism stories above all are told at great length. The casting out of devils bears witness to the fact that the kingdom of God has come (Mt 12:28; Lk 11:20). For the same reason the disciples too receive power to heal the sick and to cast out devils (Mk 3:15; 6:7; Lk 10:19). This downfall of Satan is to be understood figuratively as a spiritual demonstration by Jesus (see Is 14:12), and it signifies that the devil has lost the position of power which he has hitherto enjoyed (see Jn 12:31; 16:11). The struggle is at its keenest during the passion of Jesus. Luke has clearly brought↗ temptation and↗ passion into connection with one another (4:13): 'Then Satan departed from

him until an opportune time'; and (22:53): 'This is your hour and the power of darkness'; compare Acts 26:18, in which the phrase 'out of darkness' is used as a synonym for 'from the power of Satan'. Satan is quite exceptionally active at this time. He enters into Judas (Lk 22:3; see also Jn 13:2, 27). He wants to sift the apostles like wheat (Lk 22:31). Paul asserts the same thing in 1 Cor 2:8 when he holds the devils responsible for the death of Christ (the *arkhontes* have crucified the Lord). But as at the temptation Jesus triumphs over Satan in that he subjects his own will to that of the Father: 'Having become obedient to the death of the cross'. And while the others believe that he has succumbed to Satan and to the power of evil, in reality he conquers the devil by his most perfect act of love and obedience. Thus that dominion over all the kingdoms of the earth which Satan had promised to give to him (Lk 4:6) is indeed transferred to Christ: 'All power is given to me . . .' (Mt 28:18; see also Phil 2:9: 'He bestowed upon him the name which is above every name [ie, *Kurios*], that at the name of Jesus every knee should bow in heaven and on earth and under the earth').

Now every christian must obtain a share in this victory of Christ. As the whole life of Jesus was a struggle with Satan, so too the whole life of Christ's disciple must be the same (Eph 6:11). Compare the synoptics: the enemy sows weeds in the field of the farmer (God). This enemy is the devil (Mt 13:39), who avails himself of the night hours because he shrinks from the light of day. The 'evil one' snatches away what has been sown in the hearts of men (Mt 13:19), and Luke, who calls him by his name ('the devil') adds: 'Then the devil comes and takes away the word from their hearts that they may not come to ⁊ faith and be saved' (8:12).

As long as the christian remains united to Christ his struggle with Satan can only have a successful issue. In the light of this the duty of ⁊ prayer becomes manifest (⁊ temptation).

To summarise then: the message of the synoptics goes even further than that of the Old Testament. Here sin is regarded as something even stronger than 'bondage under the devil', not in external terms, as simply a 'debt', but as a state of being sundered from God and enslaved to Satan.

2. In the case of *John* it is striking that, unlike the synoptics, who constantly speak of 'sins' in the plural, he employs the singular form: Christ has come to take away the *sin* of the world (Jn 1:29; see also 1 Jn 3:5). Jesus takes all the sins—that is, the debt of sin— upon himself in order to lead the world home from its state of separation from God. In John the nature of sin as a state of being sundered from God finds its clearest expression. Jesus, who is one with God, is *without* sin (Jn 8:46). He is the light and the sinners are darkness (3:19). He is always heard by God, whereas God does not hearken to the sinners (9:31). For this reason John refers to sin simply as *anomia* (= lawlessness, godlessness) (1 Jn 3:4), that which places men in constant opposition to the will of God.

By sin, then, the sinner becomes precisely a child of Satan (1 Jn 3:8): 'He who commits sin is of the devil; for the devil has sinned from the beginning. The reason the Son of God appeared was to destroy the works of the devil'. In 1 Jn 3:9, on the other hand, we are told; 'No-one born of God commits sin'. The opposition between righteousness (= virtuous life 1 Jn 3:7) and sin is every bit as real and as insuperably great as the opposition between God and Satan.

The gospel has the same message to convey (8:34): The sinner is a son of Satan: 'You are of your father, the devil' (8:44); and this is intended in the full sense, as the context shows. The Jews practise lying and murder inasmuch as they set themselves against Jesus, who is truth itself, and inasmuch as they intend to kill him. This applies to every sin. In every sin the sinner does the works of the devil (1 Jn 3:8–11), that is he sets himself against the truth and becomes a murderer like Cain who, inspired by Satan, slew his brother because the works of that brother were good, whereas his own were evil. Why is the sinner a murderer? Because he who hates his brother is a murderer (v 15). The sign that men possess this ⁊ 'life' (the germ of eternal life which is what John means by 'life') is their love for their fellow men (1 Jn 3:10; Jn 13:35). Hatred of one's brother destroys this (eternal) life. Sin now means not merely a state of being sundered from God but hatred against God. The sinners are indeed impelled by the devil (as, according to John, Judas and Cain were), and do the works of the devil (Jn 3:19ff: 'This is the judgement, that the light has come into the world and men loved darkness rather than light, because their deeds were evil. For everyone who does evil hates the light'. This hatred against Christ, and thereby against God also, has led men to a point at which they will kill him. 'Now they have no excuse for their sin. He who hates me hates my Father also' (15:22f).

This is the drama of human existence: either love of God or hatred of God. Thus Christ becomes a sign of contradiction in that he reveals what sin really is, how penetratingly it takes possession of us, piercing into our innermost depths. In this situation only love could avail to help. There was no other way in which sin could be blotted out except by love. Only in this way could man attain a share in the divine love, in the love of him who is love itself and whose love is the ultimate and absolute love. As Ralph Luther says (*Ntl. Wörterbuch*, Hamburg 1951, 32f), Christ has in our name given to the Father that love which humanity should have given to God but did not give. A debt which we owed he has paid.

Satan is referred to by John no less than by the synoptics. It is the devil that impels the Jews, so that the passion of Jesus is described as the work of the devil and of the ↗ 'world', which for its part is the instrument of Satan. Thereby the death and resurrection of Christ (both referred to by John by the single term 'glorification'), his victory over Satan, is the 'hour in which the prince of this world shall be cast out' (or better, 'cast away': Jn 12:31; see also Lk 10:18; the same image in Rev 12:9: 'And the great dragon was thrown down, that ancient serpent who is called the devil and Satan, the deceiver of the whole world . . . conquered by the Blood of the Lamb . . .'). These last words signify that the fall of Satan is brought about by Christ's death on the cross. This brings us to the Book of Revelation. Here this idea is developed further, especially in chapter 12. Before the seer depicts the hard struggle of the church in chapters 13ff he places at the beginning that vision which can actually be regarded as a synthesis of this struggle as a whole and of its successful outcome, namely the victory of Christ. In a similar manner in the gospel John records the words expressing the triumph, the final victory, spoken by Jesus before his passion: 'Fear not, I have conquered the world' (16:33).

3. In *Paul* the Jewish mode of expressing sin and forgiveness, namely, 'debt' and 'remission of debt', only occurs incidentally, and where it does occur the word *remission* (Col 1:14: *aphesis tōn hamartiōn* = 'remission of sins'; Eph 1:7: *aphesis tōn paraptōmatōn* = 'remission of trespasses') is sometimes explained by other words such as *apolutrōsis* (= redemption) or *hilastērion* (= propitiation). The nearest Paul comes to this idea of sin is to be found in his reference to the cancellation of the bond (Col 2:14); see on this the Jewish prayer for the New Year, Abînu Malkênu: 'Of thy great mercy cancel all our bonds'. But in both these passages it is to be noticed that it is not a question of a debt being paid by a debtor, but of the total cancellation of the bond of debt. Moreover in the passage in Col 2:14 God the Father is the subject.

What therefore can be deduced from the actual words which Paul uses for sin? We have already referred to the fact that the synoptics always use *hamartia* in the plural, whereas John employs the singular form far more frequently. He speaks of the Lamb who takes away *the* sin of the world. Paul goes still further. He reserves this word for cases in which he has a special meaning to express, elsewhere employing other terms. For him *hamartia* is a power, an active force in men which entered the world with the fall of the first parents and brings its lethal effects to bear through the law. In Rom 5:1–11 Paul refers to the christian's experience of peace with God and harmony of soul, which is based upon the unshakeable firmness of christian ↗ hope. And this in turn is based upon the ↗ love which God has for us as the ↗ Spirit attests to us. Christ actually underwent death for us while we were still sinners. Now a prior condition for this experience is that Christ has redeemed Christians from sin, ↗ death, ↗ law and ↗ flesh. In other words the entire redemptive work of Christ is aimed at removing this 'sin', *hamartia*.

From Rom 6 it can be deduced that man can be freed from this sin only by the death and resurrection of another, that is inasmuch as he becomes like the dead and risen Christ. This gives expression to the fact that man before and man after ↗ baptism differ basically from one another alike in their state of being and their mode of action. 6:4: we must walk in newness of life. To the extent that the sacrament of baptism makes the christian one with the being of Christ, it has reformed and fashioned anew our entire being. If we are one with him in death then we are one with him also in resurrection. In v 6 the old man is called the man with *hamartia*

(man before baptism). Our body was a body of sin, but when this was deprived of its effectiveness by baptism it ceased to be an instrument of sin. He who (according to v 7) has died has abandoned this body of sin, this instrument of sin, and is justified. The fact that man can fall back into sin once more appears from the whole tenor of the exhortation of the apostle of the Gentiles (vv 12ff). Sin, therefore, as we have already seen in Gen 3, is something which alters the whole man to his very depths. In Rom 7 Paul develops his doctrine of sin still further. Christ has redeemed man from sin, death, and flesh, but also from the law—in spite of the good effects which the law has had as leading up to Christ. As a wife is no longer bound to her husband by the law after he has died, and no longer becomes an adulteress if she takes another husband, so christians are free from the external law, the Mosaic law, for they are no longer in the flesh but in the Spirit. This death to sin and the flesh takes effect in them through the Body of Christ. In other words they have already begun to share in the life of Christ who, by his death and resurrection, has rid himself of his fleshly body in order to assume a spiritual body.

How is law now related to sin? Is it a cause of it? Is it identical with it? Law is indeed a cause of sin (Gal 3:19), but only as providing the occasion (*causa occasionalis*) for it, that is not a cause of sin in the strict sense, but of transgression of the law itself. This was in fact the case with the first sin. Two elements are present in it, the factor of evil cupidity, concupiscence, and the factor of the commandment. In fact the

LIBRARY
KENRICK SEMINARY
7800 KENRICK ROAD
ST. LOUIS 19, MISSOURI

devil, as always, avails himself of this divine commandment, a commandment which, holy and God-given as it was in itself, was bestowed for the benefit of the first human pair and not for them to transgress. Without this law the devil would have remained powerless for ever. It was not without reason that God permitted this state of affairs. Man's first experience of the power of sin is of its death-dealing effects. By sin man is brought to an awareness that it sets him in opposition to God, sunders him from God, deprives him of his life. For life is a privilege granted by God. Thus the true sense of what Paul says can be recognized: 'It is only through the law that I have knowledge of sin'. Law is the *epignōsis hamartias*.

In vv 14ff Paul describes the consequences of sin for sinful man (not, as Augustine assumed after his Pelagian conversion, for the just). It is not man's nature that is totally corrupt; this remains sound, 7:22: 'I delight in the law of God, in my inmost self'.

The question therefore arises whether what Paul understands as *hamartia* is what we call original sin, the effects and the power of which are blotted out by baptism. Paul at least intends *hamartia* as *including* personal sin, for he speaks of sin having grown (see Rom 5:12).

A further question is whether he understands *hamartia* as meaning concupiscence, as the Council of Trent presumes. This can be maintained provided that the term *concupiscence* is taken to mean something more than merely fleshly concupiscence—in other words, if it is taken in a broader sense, in which its meaning might be paraphrased somewhat as follows: we are all led by a certain egoism with regard to ourselves, our neighbour, and God— ie, concupiscence here would mean what Augustine calls *amor sui ipsius*, self-love.

For our understanding of Paul's idea of the nature of sin it is also particularly illuminating to compare Rom 7 and 8. Here the state of grace is expressed in other terms, namely as the presence of the Spirit, while the state of sin is made equivalent to the absence of the Spirit (see the adumbration of this in Ezek 36). The restoration of man now consists in the fact that he passes from the state of being in the flesh to the state of being in the Spirit, from egoism to love (in the sense of *caritas*). Rom 8 shows us further that in the man whom Christ has redeemed there is no longer anything worthy of condemnation (8:1). He can now live the life that is divine, the life of the Spirit, and therefore too fulfil that which the law prescribes, or rather, what the law prescribes is fulfilled in him (v 4 in the passive); for it is rather that an effect is produced in the redeemed man than that he himself brings it about. Paul adds a further point of special importance: 'Insofar as he walks not according to the flesh but according to the Spirit'. For even when christians have been redeemed from sin and no longer live in the flesh (vv 8, 9), still they can once more hearken to that which is fleshly, and so fall victim once more to the dominion of sin. Thus right through their lives they remain under the law, but only as a matter of duty, not as a matter of compulsion.

The redeemed christians are not subject to the compulsion of the law because he who loves acts not because of the law but out of his love. They are indeed, however, under the obligation of the law because when they are lacking in love they see in it what they have to do.

From all this the position of law and sin in relation to each other is again made clear. If man lived wholly in the Spirit, and could no longer fall victim to the impulse of the flesh, then law would indeed be superfluous. Hence the assertion of the apostle of the gentiles in 1 Tim 1:9: 'The law is not laid down for the just but . . . for sinners' (see Gal 5:23).

Still further light is thrown upon the opposition between Spirit and flesh in the christian in Rom 8:5ff and Gal 5:16ff: 'The mind that is set on the flesh is hostile to God'. Actual transgression of the law is only the expression of this hatred against God. The essence of sin consists in the fact that he who hates God does not and cannot hearken to him. Paul's idea of sin as set forth here also appears in passages in which he is not speaking of sin in general, as in Rom 5–8, but in which he has specific transgressions in mind, as in Rom 1:21ff and 1 Cor 6:12ff. In Rom 1:21ff the sins of the pagans are described in the selfsame terms that are used of Israel (see Ps 106:20), who, even as God was speaking with Moses concerning the covenant, made idols for herself. Israel did not wish to have a distant transcendent God, but one to whom she could constantly have recourse, whom she could influence according to her own wishes, a God who would be 'at hand' for man. Like Adam and Eve the Israelites wanted to decide for themselves what was good and what was evil, what they

should do and what they should omit. This is precisely the reproach that is levelled against the pagans. They have not given due honour to God as God, and have not shown gratitude to him; both expressions have the same essential meaning.

Sin, therefore, is to be regarded as consisting essentially in the fact that man is no longer content to be dependent upon God but decides to be the principle of his own life, no longer acknowledging that it is God and not himself who has made him what he is. In sin man turns away from God and towards himself (see the statements in Col 1:21 and Eph 4:14f).

In 1 Cor 6:18 Paul says that the unchaste man likewise sins against his own body. But the gravity of the transgression consists in the fact that the body exists for the Lord, is the property of the Lord. Thus unrighteousness is directed against Christ. It has the effect of tearing his members from him (the christian is still a member of the body of Christ). Unrighteousness is directed against the Spirit and against the Father in heaven, whose temple the christian is. Even one who sins only against his own body is acting against God, and commits a crime of robbery against God, a sacrilege. When man offends against God it is not as though he could deprive him of something, but rather that he withdraws from him the man whom he loves. Thus Christ's entire work of ↗ redemption and ↗ atonement is aimed at giving back to the Father the man who has once more become Christ and is in Christ.

In the *Letter to the Hebrews* sin is conceived of in a manner wholly in conformity with the underlying meaning of the Hebrew *ḥāṭāᵓ* ('to miss the goal'). It is the sin of one who is *en route*. As the leader of the caravan God requires obedience (3:7, 12:25). But the people murmur and doubt (3:8). Sin, therefore, is disobedience (2:2) and mistrust (4:6, 11). The result is that the sinner loses his orientation (3:13). He is a wanderer who has lost the caravan. He advances without any plan (2:1; 5:2; 13:9). His knees become weak (12:12). He becomes ever more feeble (4:15; 5:2; 7:28) and gives up (10:39; 4:1). He falls (3:17; 4:11; 6:6) and has no further hope of being rescued. Because he has given in to the temptations of fatigue he is condemned (6:8) and draws down upon himself the ↗ Wrath of God (3:11, 17; 10:31). Sin is directly opposed to perseverance (10:36; 12:1f, 7; ↗ hope): man must hold out 'to the point of shedding your blood' (12:4). The gravity of sin consists in the fact that it constitutes mistrust and unbelief in God (3:12, 19; 12:25). This giving up along the way (to God in obedience and trust) is the worst evil of all (6:4) because it sets us at a distance from God for ever (12:14). The meaning, goal and purpose of all human existence is thereby frustrated (see Prov 8:35f: *ḥāṭāᵓ* = 'to miss the goal' on the one hand, and *mātsāᵓ* = 'to find' on the other). For this meaning, goal and purpose of life is draw near to God and finally to find him.

Bibliography: Above all, see S. Lyonnet, *De Peccato et Redemptione* i, Rome 1958; S. Lyonnet, series of articles in *VD* 35 (1957)f. See also: G. Quell, G. Bertram, G. Stählin, W. Grundmann, and K. H. Rengstorf, *TDNT* i, 267–335 (= *BKW* iii); F. Hauck, *TDNT* v, 559–66; Eichrodt iii, 81–141; Procksch 632–53; Köhler 155–71; Jacob 226–39; Imschoot ii, 278–314; J. Guillet, *Leitgedanken der Bibel*, Lucerne 1954, 112–55; A. George, *RB* 53 (1946), 161–84; J. Scharbert, *BZ* 2 (1958), 14–26; A. Kirchgässner, *Erlösung und Sünde im NT*, Freiburg 1950; J. Haas, *Die Stellung Jesu zu Sünde und Sünder nach den vier Ev.*, Fribourg 1953; J. Schmid, *Das Ev. nach Lukas* (*RNT* 3), 1955³, 150–55; E. Lohmeyer, *Probleme paulinischer Theologie*, Stuttgart n.d., 77–156; C. Spicq, *L'Epître aux Hébreux* i, Paris 1952, 284–7; K. G. Kuhn, *ZTK* 49 (1952), 200–22; O. Kuss, *Der Römerbrief*, Regensburg 1957, 241–75; P. Palazzini (ed.), *Il peccato*, Rome 1959; H. Vogel, 'Die Sünde im bibl. Verständnis', *ET* 19 (1959), 439–52; D. Daube, *Sin, Ignorance and Forgiveness in the Bible*, London 1961; E. Beaucamp, E. des Places, and S. Lyonnet, *DB(S)* 7 (1962), 407–568; E. Beaucamp, *Données bibliques pour une réflexion théologique sur le péché*, Paris 1963; S. Porubčan, *Sin in the Old Testament*, Rome 1963; J. Becker, *Das Heil Gottes. Heils- und Sündenbegriff in Qumrantexten und im NT*, Göttingen 1964.

Johannes B. Bauer

Sonship

1. *Pagan sources.* The fact that in his prayers man thinks of and describes his relationship to God as the relationship of a son to his ↗ father is one of the earliest of religious phenomena (see N. Söderblom, *Das Werden des Gottesglaubens*, Leipzig 1916, 176f). Among primitive peoples, who are close to nature, the earliest and most frequent name applied to the deity is that which designates him as father. The highest being recognised by the early Indo-Germanic peoples is called 'Father Heaven' (Dyāuš pitā, hence *Zeus patēr*, Jupiter). For Homer, Zeus is 'the father of men and gods' (Odyssey 1:28, etc). In general when he appeals to his relationship with God as son, all that man intends to express thereby is that he owes to the deity his life and existence, that he recognises his absolute

dependence upon that deity, and yet that in spite of this he can have confident recourse to him as of right. The 'father/son' relationship, however, was in various ways also understood in a natural sense in ancient pagan belief, and specifically among the Greeks. It was assumed not only of heroes but of whole tribes and families as well that they were descended from a divine ancestor. Like the kings of ancient Egypt, so later the hellenistic rulers and outstanding heroes such as Apollonius of Tyana liked to have themselves described as sons of god. The idea that every man is a son of god by nature found strong expression among the Stoics. We are all sons of god 'because we have all come to being through god' (Epictetus 1, 3, 1), 'have all sprung from him' (Cleanthes, *Hymn to Zeus*), and hence are 'of his race' (Aratos, Prologue to the *Phainomena*; see Acts 17:28). In the mysteries and the hermetic writings we encounter the idea that it is only by a personal act, namely by a ↗ rebirth, that man becomes the child of god, ie, endowed with the divine nature.

2. *Old Testament and judaism.* The idea that man is the son of God by nature is alien to the religion of the Old Testament and judaism. The description 'sons of God' for the ↗ angels (Ps 29:1; Job 1:6; 2:1; 38:7; 1 Enoch 6:2; 13:8; 14:3; 101:1) has no physical or genealogical background, but is simply intended to express how closely these heavenly beings are attached to God, whose courtiers, servants, and messengers they are. Whether the phrase 'sons of God' in Gen 6:2-4 is likewise intended to refer to angels, or whether it designates men with special power

(see Ps 58:1; 82:6), is a disputed point. In other passages in which the appellation 'son of God' is applied to men it is not simply the generality of mankind that is in question. Again it is not usually applied to individual Israelites but to Israel as a people (Ex 4:22f; Deut 1:31; 8:5; 32:5f, 18; Is 63:16; 64:8; Jer 3:19; 31:9, 20; Hos 11:1; 13:13; Mal 1:6; 2:10; Wis 12:19, 21; 16:10, 26; 18:4, 13; 1 Enoch 62:11; AssMos 10:3), or to the king as representative of Israel (Ps 2:7; 2 Sam 7:14; Ps 89:27; TestLev 17; TestJud 24). This sonship is based upon the election of Israel as the covenant people (Deut 14:1; Is 1:2, 4; 43:6; Mal 1:2f; 2:10). Even in those instances in which it is connected with the idea of creation, the underlying idea is not so much that God is the creator of men, but that he is the creator of Israel (Deut 32:6; Is 43:1; 64:8; see also 43:15; Mal 2:10). In view of this it should not be deduced from the fact that the designation 'firstborn son' is applied to Israel (Ex 4:22; Jer 31:9; 4 Ezra 6:58) that non-Israelites too were conceived to be sons of God. The Old Testament description of Israel as the son of God, as also its correlative, which is only found later and is used less frequently, namely the description of God as Father (Deut 32:6; Jer 3:4, 19; Is 63:16; 64:8; Mal 1:6; 2:10), are intended on the one hand to express the fact that Yahweh has chosen Israel before all the peoples as the object of his ↗ love, protection, and help, on the other hand the fact that Israel will and must respond to this election by showing reverence, faithfulness and trust in Yahweh (see Deut 14:1f), and by mutual brotherly love (Mal 2:10;

↗ brother). The idea of sonship, however, does not play a predominant part in the religion of the Old Testament. The relationship between Yahweh and Israel is for the most part conceived of as the relationship of a lord to his slave (both ideas are found together in Mal 1:6), often also as that of a king to his people, a married man to his wife, or a bridegroom to his bride (↗ marriage). In later times, and probably under hellenistic influence, an individualisation of the symbol of sonship gradually established itself. The devout individual is accounted a son of God (Wis 2:13, 18; Sir 4:10; PsSol 13:9; Jub 19:29; Philo, *De Vita Mosis* II 39 § 288; *De Spec. Leg.* I 11 § 318; *De Confus. Ling.* 28 § 145) and uses in his prayers the form of address 'my Father' (Wis 2:16; 14:3; Sir 23:1, 4; 51:10; Ps 73:15; see also Tob 13:4). Moreover the first signs appear of an eschatological use of the appellation 'son'. The following passage in Jub 1:24f treats of the age of salvation: 'I will be a Father to them and they shall be my children, and they shall all be called children of the living God, and all angels and all spirits shall know it, and shall recognise that they are my children, and that I am their Father in firmness and righteousness, and that I love them'. According to PsSol 17:27, the Messiah will 'recognise them, that they are all sons of their God'. It is possible that the use of the term in this sense is already to be found in Wis 5:5. Josephus does not apply the expression 'son of God' to anyone, nor does the term 'Father' used as a form of address in prayer occur in his writings, but he does use the title 'Father' of God, and, indeed, in a universalistic sense: God is 'Father of the whole human race' (*Antiq.* 4:262; see also 1:20; 2:152; 7:380). In the Qumran literature Ps 2:7 is several times applied to the people of God (as well as to the Messiah), not, however, to the whole of Israel, but only to the elect of Israel. At the same time the sectarians avoid any presentation of themselves as 'sons of God', and apparently do not use the title 'Father' of God either. The idea that the Israelites are sons of God and that God is their heavenly Father frequently recurs in the writings of rabbinical judaism (*Abot* 3:14; *Yoma* 8:9; *Sota* 9:15; b. *Taanit* 25f; also in the *Šemone Esre* and *Abinu Malkenu* prayers). In this, however, the eschatological use of the 'Father/son' image is virtually absent. Sonship is regarded as entailing the duty of following the pattern laid down by God in one's life, occupying oneself with the Torah and with the fulfilment of the commandments. On the other hand it was also a guarantee of God's unfailing ↗ mercy and compassion. For Rabbi Meir, the attribute of sonship was a gift bestowed upon the Israelites unconditionally and remaining valid even for the sinners among them. Admittedly Rabbi Yehuda ben Elai opposed this view. The title 'son of God' was not usually applied to the Messiah even in circles which interpreted Ps 2 as referring to him (PsSol 17:21-5; Qumran documents, late rabbinical tradition).

3. *The synoptics.* When Jesus describes God as the Father of mankind ('your Father': Mt 5:48; 6:32; 7:11 [all passages from Q!]; Mk 11:25; 'thy Father'; Mt 6:4, 6, 18), and when he trains the disciples to address God as

'(our) Father' in their prayers (Mt 6:9; Lk 11:2), he proclaims the universal Fatherhood of God in the sense that God's fatherly love, kindness, and protection is extended to every man, even to the sinner (Lk 15:1–32). This does not mean, however, that Jesus was now promising divine sonship to all men as well. The designation 'children of God' is altogether absent from the synoptics. That of 'sons of God' only occurs in three instances (Mt 5:9; 5:45 [=Lk 6:35]; Lk 20:36 [however, a comparison with Mk 12:25 shows that this is a secondary Lucan formulation]), and in fact with an eschatological force. According to these passages sonship of God is a gift which is neither bestowed upon all men as God's creatures, nor upon the disciples already here below, but one which will be imparted to the elect only in the future age of salvation, and one which goes together with eternal bliss, the sharing in the kingdom of God. A further fact which may be connected with the idea that the Father/son relationship will be revealed and will take effect only at the final consummation, is that Jesus's sayings concerning the final consummation lay special emphasis upon the Fatherhood of God (Lk 12:32; 22:29; Mk 8:38 and parallels; Mt 20:23 [otherwise in Mk 10:40]; 25:34), and speak of the kingdom of the Father for the most part in a strictly eschatological sense (Mt 13:43; 26:29 [otherwise in Mk 14:25]; 6:9f=Lk 11:2). Jesus claims divine sonship for himself in a unique and exclusive sense (Mt 17:24–7; 11:27=Lk 10:22; Mk 13:22). This claim to be a son of God by nature can also be recognised in the fact that Jesus never uses the designation 'our Father' in referring to himself together with others, but invariably confines himself to the designations 'my Father' or 'your (thy) Father'. In certain passages the terms 'son of God' appears as a messianic title (Lk 4:41; 22:70; see also Acts 9:20, 22). And it also appears to be used in this sense in Mk 14:62f and parallels, since there 'son of the Blessed One' is in apposition to 'Messiah'. In many cases we cannot arrive at a more certain conclusion on the question of whether 'son of God' is used as a description of Christ's nature or as designating his office as Messiah. For it is difficult to establish how far the terminology of the early Christian mission is present or absent.

4. *Paul.* In about forty passages God is called 'Father', mostly 'our Father' (Rom 1:7; 1 Cor 1:3; 2 Cor 1:2; Gal 1:3f etc), a few times 'Father of (our Lord) Jesus Christ' (Rom 15:6; 2 Cor 1:3; 11:31; Eph 1:3; Col 1:3), often too simply 'the Father' (Rom 6:4; 1 Cor 8:6; 15:24; Gal 1:1; etc). In this latter case it can be deduced, at any rate from the context, who is being thought of as the corresponding party to the relationship. The sayings which treat of divine sonship afford a clearer insight into the actual kind of 'father/son' relationship that is envisaged. In the nature of things Jesus Christ is the unique and only Son of God (Rom 8:3, 32; Gal 4:4; Col 1:13; see also 1 Cor 8:6; 2 Cor 8:9; Phil 2:6–8; Col 1:15f), but Paul also calls Christians 'sons of God', employing sometimes the expression 'sons of God' (Rom 8:14, 19; 9:26; Gal 3:26; 4:6f; 2 Cor 6:18; cf Heb 2:10; 12:5–8),

sometimes 'children of God' (Rom 8:16, 17, 21; 9:7f; Phil 2:15) without distinction. As applied to Christians sonship is based upon the fact that they have been accepted by God as his sons. The term *huiothesia*, which Paul uses to describe the Christian's status in Rom 8:15, 23; Gal 4:5; Eph 1:5, is used in Rom 9:4 of the Old Testament idea of Israel as son of God, a sign that Paul has transferred the concept in its eschatological fulfilment to the New Testament people of God. The word is a technical term for legal adoption, a practice which, while it was not general in judaism, was common throughout the hellenistic sphere, and was for this reason familiar to the apostle and his readers. 'The concept was entirely suitable to characterise the new and unique bond between men and God which had been effected by God's salvific work, while at the same time making due allowance for the special character of the "physical" sonship of God which was proper to Jesus Christ' (O. Kuss). The purpose of sending the Son of God into the world was to bring sonship to mankind as a whole, not merely to Israel (Gal 4:4f). To be a son or child of God in this developed sense is one of the benefits of salvation enjoyed in the present (Rom 8:16: 'We are children of God'; Gal 3:26: 'You are all sons of God'; 4:6: 'You are sons'), which man attains by ⁊ faith and by undergoing ⁊ baptism (Gal 3:26f). More specifically it is the pneuma (⁊ spirit) received in baptism by believers in Christ that brings about sonship (Rom 8:14f). Since this pneuma is 'the pneuma of his Son' (Gal 4:6), it imparts to the baptised person a quality which is analogous to that of true sonship of God (Gal 3:27; see also Rom 8:29), hence it can also be called 'the pneuma of acceptation into the status of son' (Rom 8:15). This condition, by which baptised persons become children of God, is a fact which can be experienced and recognised to the extent that the pneuma of the Son causes the believers in their prayers to break out into the spontaneous cry of enthusiasm 'Abba, Father!' (Rom 8:15f; Gal 4:6, where *hoti* should hardly be taken in a causal sense, but rather in an elliptic and declaratory one). The status of sonship implies a right to inherit. The ⁊ inheritance which God has bestowed upon those whom he has accepted as his sons consists in ⁊ 'life' (Rom 8:13) or in ⁊ 'glory' (8:17). Since Christ has already entered upon this heritage christians are 'co-heirs with Christ' (Rom 8:17). Basically Paul understands the sonship of God to signify the same reality which he elsewhere calls 'righteousness'. This is clearly expressed in Rom 8:13–17. The reason underlying the clause in v 13b, 'If by the Spirit you put to death the deeds of the body you shall live', is given in vv 14–17. Whereas elsewhere the connecting link between Spirit and life is righteousness (righteousness as an effect of the Spirit: Rom 8:10; 1 Cor 6:11; as a prior condition of life: Rom 5:17, 18, 21; 1:17; Gal 3:11, 21), here Paul introduces in its place the idea of divine sonship, because this is manifested as a fact of experience in the cries of 'Abba!'; and so, with the assistance of the idea of inheritance, it can serve as a proof of the fact that the Christian has received life. In Gal 4:1–7, on the other hand, the motif of sonship is presented in its own right. For in this passage Paul's aim is to establish the thesis enunciated in 3:29: 'You are heirs'. His point is that a prior condition of being an heir is being a son. Divine sonship and ↗ justification, or righteousness, complement one another in yet another respect. In both cases it is not a magical transformation of man that is in question, but rather a gift of grace which lays upon its recipient the duty of a moral life (at the same time equipping him to fulfil this duty). Thus the baptised man can be exhorted to 'walk in righteousness' (Rom 6:12–23 etc), as also to guard his state as a child of God (Phil 2:15; Eph 5:1; Rom 8:17). Both gifts appear sometimes as blessings of man's present state (righteousness or justification: Rom 3:21f, 24, 26, 28; 4:5; 5:5, 9, 16f; 6:18; etc; sonship: Rom 8:16; Gal 3:26; 4:6), sometimes as blessings to be hoped for in the future: according to Gal 5:5 'For through the Spirit by faith we wait for the hope of righteousness'; according to Rom 8:23 'We groan inwardly as we wait for adoption as sons, the redemption of our ↗ bodies', ie the moment when we shall be fully and definitively established as sons and heirs of God at the ↗ *parousia*.

John. In the fourth gospel and in the first two johannine epistles the title 'Father' as applied to God occurs more than 120 times. In this it is always God's relationship as Father to Jesus Christ that is being thought of, whether the word is being used absolutely ('the Father'), the most usual phrase, or otherwise ('my Father' [thirty-five times]). Jesus explicitly rejects the claim of the Jews that God is their Father (8:41–4). God is never referred to as Father of men. The only exception to this is Jn 20:17: 'I am ascending to my Father and your Father, to my God and your God'. What is expressed here by the fact that the risen Christ calls the disciples his brothers and God his Father and their Father is that by the resurrection the relationship between God and Jesus, on the one hand and the disciples on the other, has acquired an essentially more intimate character. But it is clear from the deliberate avoidance of the expression 'to *our* Father' that God is nevertheless Father of Jesus in another and a higher sense than that in which he is Father of the believing disciples. The uniqueness of God's relationship as Father with Jesus is made clear in numerous sayings of Jesus himself, and according to 5:18 is also recognised by the Jews, who wish to kill Jesus 'because he called God his Father, making himself equal to God'. This unique quality emerges no less clearly from those sayings of Jesus in John's gospel in which he refers to himself as the Son of God (3:18; 5:25; 10:36; 11:4), or as 'the Son' without further qualification (3:16f, 35f; 5:19–23, 26; 6:40; 8:36; 14:13; see too, 'thy Son': 17:1). There can be no doubt that the title of Son as used by John is not a paraphrase for Messiah, although both titles are closely connected with one another (11:27; 20:31). Rather this title of Son signifies the eternal (cf 1 Jn 4:14) Sonship of God by nature (see 20:28), in which the messianic function of Jesus is ultimately rooted. In some cases John underlines the uniqueness of the Sonship of Christ by affixing the adjective *ho monogenēs* (1:14, 18; 3:16, 18; 1 Jn 4:9), which signifies 'the only begotten, sole descendant, only one'. Whether this is intended to lend additional force to the idea that it is God who has caused this begetting (birth), and to characterise Jesus as the only one who has been begotten from the nature of God is disputed, and in point of fact makes little difference, inasmuch as in John the title 'son' is applied to Jesus unambiguously as a designation of his origin, and for this reason implicitly contains the idea of his eternal begetting by God. Finally, the uniqueness of the sonship of Jesus Christ appears in the johannine writings in the fact that he has a special terminology for it, the title 'Son of God' being reserved for Christ alone. Insofar as John speaks of men being sons of God at all he never employs the term 'sons', but invariably confines himself to the phrase 'children of God' to express this. This derivative childhood of God is for him, just as for Paul, a blessing of salvation which has already been imparted in the present life to those who believe 'in his name', that is, in Jesus as the Messiah and Son of God (Jn 1:12; 1 Jn 3:1f; 5:1). The Pauline idea that the relationship of child has been brought about by an act of adoption on God's part does not, however, appear in the johannine writings. According to them, being a child of God is brought about rather by a new birth (Jn 3:3, 7), or by being begotten (born) of God (1:13; 1 Jn 2:29; 3:9; 4:7; 5:1, 4, 18). The new birth is characterised in Jn 3:5 as a birth 'of water and the spirit', which can only mean that it is accomplished by↗ baptism, and takes effect through the↗ Spirit of God, who suffuses the subject in baptism, and re-creates him as a new being. The idea of↗ rebirth does admittedly occur elsewhere in the New Testament without any connection with the concept of being God's child (Tit 3:5; 1 Pet 1:3, 23; Jas 1:18). Again, when John speaks of 'being begotten (born) of God', in spite of the naturalistic overtones in this turn of phrase he means that the believer undergoes a purely spiritual process, by which the imparting of the Spirit to him gives him a new mode of existence which sets him in a wholly new and intimately personal relationship to God; and as with Paul the gift carries a task with it, and must bear fruit in the moral conduct of one's life (1 Jn 2:29; 3:9f; 4:7; 5:1–4, 18). Although the baptised believer enjoys the state of a child of God already here below, he still awaits its completion. This will only be revealed in the age of fulfilment ushered in by the↗ *parousia*, and will consist in being like God and seeing God (↗ vision). 'We know that when he appears we shall be like him, for we shall see him as he is' (1 Jn 3:2).

Bibliography: P. Baur, 'Gott als Vater im AT', *TSK* 72 (1899), 483–507; A. Dieterich, *Eine Mithrasliturgie*, Leipzig–Berlin 1903, 134–56; M.-J. Lagrange, 'La paternité de Dieu dans l'AT', *RB* 17 (1908), 481–99; S. Many, 'Adoption', *DB* I, 227–33; H. Lesêtre, 'Fils de Dieu', *DB* II, 2253–7; G. P. Wetter, *Der Sohn Gottes*, Göttingen 1916; A. von Harnack, *Die Terminologie der Wiedergeburt und verwandter Erlebnisse in der ältesten Kirche* (*TU* 42/3), Leipzig 1918; SB I, 219, 371–4, and 392–6; C. A. Bernoulli, 'Le Dieu-Père de Jésus d'après les Synoptiques', *Actes du Congrés international d'histoire des religions 1923* II, Paris 1925, 211–24; R. Gyllenberg, 'Gott der Vater im AT und in der Predigt Jesu', *Studia Orientalia* I (Helsingfors 1925), 51–60; M.-J. Lagrange, 'L'hermétisme', *RB* 35 (1926),

352–62; W. Bousset and H. Gressmann, *Die Religion des Judentums im späthellenistischen Zeitalter*, Tübingen 1926³, 377f; E. Wissmann, 'Gotteskindschaft', *RGG* II², 1394–6; M.-J. Lagrange, 'La régénération et la filiation divine dans les mystères d'Eleusis', *RB* 38 (1929), 68–81 and 201–14; A. L. Williams, '"My Father" in Jewish Thought of the First Century', *JTS* 31 (1930), 42–7; A. Bertholet and H. Seeger, 'Vatername Gottes', *RGG* v², 1442–5; W. F. Lofthouse, 'Vater und Sohn im Joh.-Ev.', *TB* 11 (1932), 290–300; G. Kittel, *TDNT* 1, 5f; J. Hempel, *Gott und Mensch im AT*, Stuttgart 1936², 170–78; J. Dey, *Palingenesia*, Münster 1937; W. Grundmann, *Die Gotteskindschaft in der Geschichte Jesu und ihre Religionsgeschichtlichen Voraussetzungen*, Weimar 1938; W. Twisselmann, *Die Gotteskindschaft der Christen nach dem NT*, Gütersloh 1939; A. Oepke, *RAC* 1, 105–9; J. Leipoldt, *Jesu Verhältnis zu Griechen und Juden*, Leipzig 1941, 124–44; F. Büchsel, *TDNT* IV, 737–41; Haag 914f; J. Bieneck, *Sohn Gottes als Christusbezeichn. d. Syn.*, Zurich 1951; A. Oepke, *TDNT* v, 650–54; S. Zedda, *L'adozione a figli di Dio e lo Spirito Santo*, Rome 1952; S. V. McCasland, 'Abba Father', *JBL* 72 (1953), 79–91; P. Winter, 'Monogenês para patros', *ZRG* 5 (1953), 335–65; R. Schnackenburg, *Die Joh.-Briefe*, Freiburg 1953, 155–62; G. Schrenck and G. Quell, *TDNT* v, 946–1015; J. Schmid, *Das Ev. nach Mk (RNT 2)* 1954³, 17–20; J. Schmid, *Das Ev. nach Mt (RNT 1)*, 1956³, 124–8; W. Grundmann, *ZNW* 47 (1956), 113–33; A. Wikenhauser, *Das Ev. nach Joh. (RNT 4)*, 1957, 91–4; O. Bauernfeind, *RGG* II³, 1798–1800; J. Giblet, 'Jésus et "le Père" dans le IVe Evangile', *Recherches Bibliques* 3 (1958), 111–30; O. Kuss, *Der Römerbrief*, Regensburg 1959, 596–608; P. Schruers, 'La paternité divine dans Mt 5:45 et 6:26–32', *ETL* 36 (1960), 593–624; O. Michel and O. Betz, 'Von Gott gezeugt', *Judentum, Urchristentum, Kirche* (Festschrift J. Jeremias), Berlin 1960, 3–23; E. Pax, *LTK* IV², 1114–16; I. Hermann, *Kyrios und Pneuma*, Munich 1961, 94–7; W. Grundmann, 'Zur Rede Jesu vom Vater im Joh.-Ev.', *ZNW* 52 (1961), 213–30; B. M. F. van Iersel, *'Der Sohn' in den syn. Jesusworten*, Leiden 1961; E. Lövestam, *Son and Saviour*, Lund–Copenhagen 1961; G. Cooke, 'The Israelite King as Son of God', *ZAW* 73 (1961), 202–25; F. W. Danker, 'The *huios* phrases in the New Testament', *NTS* 7 (1961), 94; T. de Kruiff, *Der Sohn des lebendigen Gottes*, Rome 1962; F. Hahn, *Christologische Hoheitstitel*, Göttingen 1963; W. Kramer, *Christus, Kyrios, Gottessohn*, Zurich 1963; M. W. Schoenberg, 'St Paul's Notion on the Adoptive Sonship of Christ', *Thomist* 28 (1964), 51–75.

Josef Blinzler

Spirit

A. *The Spirit of God in the Old Testament.* The concept of spirit occupies a prominent place in the theology of the Old Testament. As a rule the word *rûaḥ* in the Hebrew text should be translated 'spirit', and there are about 380 occurrences to which this would apply. LXX, with only 355 instances, falls somewhat short of the Masoretic text. It usually renders *rûaḥ* as *pneuma* (264 times).

I. *Spirit in the Old Testament.* The Arabic words corresponding to the Hebrew *rûaḥ* (the verb, occurring only in the hifil, = 'to smell', hence the noun *rēaḥ* = 'odour') are *riḥ* = 'wind' and *ruḥ* = 'spirit', both being derived from *raha* = to blow.

1. *rûaḥ* = wind. (a) *Concept.* In the earliest passages *rûaḥ* probably means the 'stream of air' which manifests itself in the movement of the wind, the soft 'current of air' (Gen 3:8[J]; 1 Kings 19:11; Job 4:15; 41:16; Is 57:13); the wind (Gen 8:1[P]; Num 11:31; 2 Sam 22:11; 2 Kings 3:17; Is 27:8; 57:13; Jer 2:24; 10:13; Ezek 17:10; 19:12; Hos 8:7; Amos 4:13; Hab 1:11; Zech 5:9; Job 28:25; 41:13; Pss 1:4; 83:13; 103:16; 104:3f); the tempest (Ex 10:13; 14:21; 1 Kings 18:45; 19:11; Is 32:2; 41:16; Jer 4:11; 13:24; 18:17; 22:22; 49:36; Ezek 1:4; 13:11; Hos 4:19; Jon 1:4; Job 1:19; 21:18; Ps 11:6; 18:11; 35:5; 55:8; 107:25; 135:7).

This sense is encountered in all areas of Hebrew literature, most frequently in Jeremiah and the Psalms. As the places whence the wind comes, the quarters of the heavens are called *rûḥôth* (1 Chron 9:24; Ezek 37:9; 42:20; Zech 2:6; 6:6; Dan 7:2; 8:8; 11:4). Since the wind, which man can neither see nor grasp (see Jn 3:8), is a suitable image for all that is vain and empty, *rûaḥ* comes to acquire the metaphorical sense of a vain, empty, and futile matter. 'All is vanity and a striving after wind' (Eccles 1:14; 2:11, 17; 4:6, 16; 5:16; 6:9; Is 26:18; Jer 5:13; Hos 12:1; Mic 2:11). Hence the idioms 'to speak words of wind' (Job 16:3), 'to sow the wind', and 'to reap the whirlwind' (Hos 8:7; Prov 11:29).

(b) *The effects of 'rûaḥ'*. Man in the ancient Near East experienced a reverent awe for the mystery of the wind. (i) For him the wind is equivalent to an overwhelming and mysterious power, which the gentile peoples honour as a divinity of nature, but which the Israelites, thanks to their superior monotheism, value only as an instrument for putting into effect God's purposes in salvation history. The *rûaḥ* represents a force of nature, of which God avails himself at all critical turning-points in the tempestuous history of salvation for carrying out his plans. The tempest is able to rend the mountains and shatter the rocks (1 Kings 19:11). At God's behest it brings an end to the flood (Gen 8:1[P]). At the time of the Egyptian plagues the east wind carried the assembled swarms of locusts into the land of Pharaoh, and the west wind threw them into the sea (Ex 10:13, 19). At the Exodus from bondage a strong east wind provided the people of God, hard-pressed as they were, with a way to safety through the Red Sea (Ex 14:21f; see also 15:10f; Is 11:15). David describes, with a high degree of poetic imagination, how the Lord 'bowed the heavens and came down. . . . He flew hither, hovering upon the wings of the wind. The channels of the sea were seen' (2 Sam 22:10–16 = Ps 18:10–16). In the wilderness wanderings a strong wind drove a host of quails in from the sea, and a rain of manna down from heaven for the hungry people (Num 11:31f; Ex 10:19; 16:13–16; Ps 78:24ff). At the covenant institution at Sinai a strong wind, together with the loud blast of a trumpet ushered in the thunder and lightning which were the precursors of the divine Lawgiver (Ex 19:16; see also Acts 2:2f). At the Lord's command a strong wind will execute the divine sentence upon the unfaithful people which he pursue into the exile: 'The wind shall shepherd all your shepherds, and your lovers shall go into captivity' (Jer 22:22; see also 4:11ff). A terrible desert wind will come against Ephraim, a wind of the Lord which arises out of the wilderness and brings in ruin (Hos 13:15; Ezek 13:13). Again in the name of God the tempest carries out its destructive work upon the peoples (Is 57:13; Jer 51:1). At the return from Babylon the purified 'remnant' will be able to cross the Euphrates in sandals by the power of the wind sent by God (Is 11:15).

(ii) In certain passages, relatively few in number and late in date, a creative force is also ascribed to the wind sent by God. The oriental, with his close ties with the processes of nature, observed how the wind brings in clouds with the rain which fertilises the desert parched for water (see 1 Kings 18:45; 2 Kings 3:17; Hos 13:15; Job 1:19). According to the Priestly author (P) 'the earth was without form and void, and darkness was upon the face of the deep, and the wind (Spirit) of God was moving over the waters' (Gen 1:2), and then, by his word, God created heaven and earth and all that they contain (Gen 1:3–30). In the messianic era 'a *rûaḥ* from on high' will be poured out, and will transform the land into a garden of paradise (Is 32:15). The Hebrew, who judges by appearances, thinks of the wind, which is located in space (Ezek 37:9), as intimately connected with the word of God. The wind becomes, so to say, the bearer of the creative word. It is striking how in poetic passages the 'wind' is represented anthropomorphically as the 'breath of God', which instils life into creation and nature (Ex 15:8, 10 with Ex 14:21; 2 Sam 22:16=Ps 18:15; Is 11:15; 27:8; 30:28; 33:11; 34:16; 40:7; 59:19; Hos 13:15; Job 4:9; 26:13; 37:10; 147:18). Even if this idea, based as it was on the sensible appearance of material things, was mitigated in the course of time, still it was never altogether discarded. 'By the word of Yahweh the heavens were made, and all their host by the breath of his mouth' (Ps 33:6; see also Gen 1:2; Judith 16:14). Even in the most recent book of the bible it is stated that 'the spirit of the Lord has filled the whole world' (Wis 1:7).

(iii) The wind is not an independent force, but a power controlled and directed by God for the furtherance of salvation history and creation. God

'has created the wind' (Amos 4:13). He 'brings forth the wind from his storehouses' (Jer 10:13; 51:16; 135:7). On account of this dependence of the wind upon God the wind is often depicted in poetic passages as 'the breath of Yahweh' or as 'the breath of Yahweh's nose' (Ex 15:8; Is 40:7; Ps 18:15; etc).

(iv) Just as man is unable either to see or grasp God, so too he is unable to see or grasp his messenger. He does not know whence it comes or whither it goes. The wind is shrouded in mystery (see Jn 3:8). Thus the properties of the wind are power and mystery. Because the God of the Old Testament is a God of power and mystery, the authors of sacred scripture appropriately describe the nature and attributes of God by the image of the wind, mysterious in its origin and powerful in its effects.

2. *'rûaḥ' = breath.* Just as in the context of nature *rûaḥ* is 'wind', so in man and beast it becomes 'breath' or 'respiration'. This sense is already attested in very early passages (Gen 45:27: Judg 15:19). (i) In the grandiose vision of the dry bones the *rûaḥ* is commanded to blow from the four quarters of the wind and to blow upon the bones so that they come to life (Ezek 37:9). The *rûaḥ* is a life-giving entity. Man lives precisely so long as he breathes in and breathes out. 'Dum spiro spero!' Hence the 'breath' becomes the seat and supporter, the source of life for man and beast (Gen 7:22[J]; Num 16:22; 27:16; Is 42:5; Job 34:14f; Ps 104:29f; Eccles 3:19). God blew into the nostrils of the first man the 'breath of life' (*nišmat ḥayyîm* = the *rûaḥ ḥayyîm* of Gen 6:17[P], 7:15, 22[P], both paralleled in Is 42:5;

57:16; Job 4:9; 27:3; 34:14; etc), so that he became a living being (Gen 2:7[J]; cf Gen 6:3[J]). The whole *span of man's life* depends upon the *rûaḥ*. All life must dissolve in death when God withdraws his breath of life (Job 27:3f; 34:14f; Ps 104:29f; 146:4; Eccles 3:18–21; 12:7). The 'breath of life', however, is only 'lent' for the short period of his earthly days. He cannot dispose of it as he wills (see Wis 15:8, 16; Lk 12:20). Yahweh alone is 'the Lord of the breath of life' (Num 16:22; 27:16; see also 2 Macc 14:46), which he imparts to man from motives of divine love and solicitude (Job 10:12).

(ii) It is entirely in harmony with the idea of the *rûaḥ* in men, both according to the senses and the intellect, that physical exhaustion or recuperation are represented as the withdrawal or the return of the breath of life (eg, Judg 15:19; 1 Sam 30:12; Ps 143:7; Job 17:1). At joyful tidings the breath of life is thrown into agitation. Intense astonishment renders one 'out of breath' (1 Kings 10:5; 2 Chron 9:4).

(iii) On the occurrence of some misfortune or under the impact of some strong emotion the 'breath' comes more quickly or more slowly, more strongly or more weakly. Because of this *rûaḥ* is used to describe the different emotions of the irascible appetite, such as anger (Judg 8:3; Job 4:9; 15:13; Prov 1:23; Eccles 7:9; Is 25:4; Zech 6:8); disquiet (Gen 41:8; 2 Kings 19:7); trouble (Gen 26:35; 1 Sam 1:15; 1 Kings 21:5; Job 7:11; Ps 34:19; Prov 15:4; Is 54:6; 66:2); despair (Ps 77:4; Is 61:3; Ezek 3:14); courage (Josh 2:11; 5:1; Sir 48:12; patience (Prov 17:27; Eccles 7:8; Sir 5:11); impatience (Ex 6:9; Job 21:4; Prov 14:29; Mic 2:7); jealousy (Num 5:14, 30; 1 Sam 16:14f, 23; 18:10; 19:9); and discord (Judg 9:23). Animal functions and the movements of the lower senses are invariably ascribed to the *nepeš* (normally = 'soul'), not to the *rûaḥ*, which in fact comes from above and has an element of nobility in it.

(iv) *rûaḥ* can also be used to describe those ways of conducting one's life which give expression to an interior attitude of mind. Here any sensible basis which we can apprehend vanishes more and more. Instances of this are humility (Prov 16:19; Is 57:15; Dan 3:39); pride (Ps 76:12; Prov 16:18; Eccles 7:8; Dan 5:20); faithfulness (Num 14:24; Ps 51:10, 12; 78:8; Prov 11:13); or quite in general, a 'disposition' (Ezek 11:19; 36:26; see also Prov 16:32; 25:28).

(v) Finally *rûaḥ* is considered the source of the higher, spiritual life from which stem aims and ideas (Ps 77:6; Job 32:8; Prov 1:23; Is 19:3; Jer 51:1; Ezek 11:5), as well as plans and decisions (Ex 35:21; 1 Chron 5:26; Hag 1:14).

The primary meaning of *rûaḥ* may be taken to be *wind*, the mysterious and irresistible power of which Yahweh avails himself in the execution of his designs in salvation history and creation. On the human plane it designates the *breath* with all its concomitant manifestations which permeates the lives of men (and beasts) from the first moment of their existence to the last. This breath of air and of life comes from on high, from God, and it permeates, brings to life and maintains all the inhabitants of the world together (see Wis 1:7; Acts 17:28). In this sense it is omnipresent (Ps 139:7).

II. *The Spirit of the Lord in the Old Testament.* Just as extraordinary events in nature are attributed to the power of the wind, so too astonishing feats performed by men in order to save the chosen people are attributed to the 'spirit of the Lord'. It is that mysterious force which proceeds from God and takes powerful effect in the history of the covenant people. It constitutes an historical phenomenon, which brings about the *magnalia Dei* through figures who are empowered by the spirit.

1. In the earliest passages what is attributed to the spirit of the Lord is transitory phenomena in the physical or psychological order, all of which have an element of the tempestuous and the violent in them. The spirit of the Lord 'impels' (Judg 13:25) or 'falls upon' someone (Ezek 11:5), 'carries him away' (1 Kings 18:12; 2 Kings 2:16), 'comes mightily upon him' (Judg 14:6). It arouses in a subject chosen by it for the benefit of the people of God gigantic physical strength (Judg 13:25; 14:6, 19; 15:14); heroic feats of arms (Judg 6:34; 11:29; 1 Sam 11:6f); prophetic raptures and ecstasies (Num 11:24–30; 1 Sam 10:5–13; 19:20–24), which seize upon Saul himself and even the messengers of Saul (1 Sam 10:10; 19:19–24; see also 1 Kings 22:10ff); physical as well as spiritual transports (1 Kings 18:12; 2 Kings 2:16; see also Acts 8:39; Ezek 3:12; 8:3; 11:1; 37:1; 43:5); the power to perform stupendous wonders (1 Kings 17:14, 17ff; 2 Kings 2:15; 4:1ff); an amazing gift of prophecy (Num 24:2; 1 Chron

12:18; 2 Chron 20:14; 24:20); and interpretation of dreams (Gen 40:8; 41:16, 38; Dan 4:5; 5:12; 6:3). In the passages referred to, the bestowal of the spirit is a free gift of God's grace. The Lord 'gives' the spirit (Num 11:25; 2 Kings 19:7). It is of divine origin. The spirit comes 'upon' the man concerned (Judg 3:10; 1 Sam 16:16). The *rûah* of Yahweh manifests itself as a mysterious, supernatural, and miraculous force (Is 31:3).

2. In later passages particularly, charismatic leaders and prophets are endowed with the spirit of the Lord no longer in a tempestuous and intermittent manner, but continuously. It 'rests' upon Moses, the prototype of the leader of the people and of prophets (Num 11:17, 25; see also Is 63:11); upon the seventy elders (Num 11:25, 29); upon Joshua (Num 27:18; Deut 34:9); upon Saul (1 Sam 16:14); upon David (1 Sam 16:13; 2 Sam 23:2), whose hereditary form of kingship superseded the dominion that was charismatic and theocratic in character (1 Sam 16:13); upon Elijah (2 Kings 2:9); and upon Elisha (2 Kings 2:15).

But it is the prophets who are considered bearers of the spirit of God *par excellence*. It is correct to say that those belonging to the pre-exilic period never explicitly claim the spirit of the Lord as the source of their inspiration. What they appeal to is rather the word of God. This is probably because the frenzied ecstatic bands of prophets and the false prophets call upon the spirit of the Lord although these false prophets are only 'wind' (Jer 5:13). Yet there are sufficient passages to show that these true prophets were conscious of being endowed with the spirit of the

Lord. According to Hos 9:7 the ↗ prophet is in popular parlance simply called 'the man of the spirit'. Those who merely seem to be prophets are indeed equipped with a *rûaḥ*, but this is only 'wind', and so falsehood and deceit (Mic 2:11). In contrast to these Micah acknowledges: 'I am filled with power, with the spirit of the Lord and with justice and might to declare to Jacob his transgression and to Israel his sin' (Mic 3:8). For Isaiah the act of making a covenant which is not according to Yahweh's spirit is equivalent to acting against Yahweh's spirit or will, which is revealed in the prophet as the 'mouth' of the Lord (Is 30:1f; see also 48:16). After the exile all possible emphasis was laid upon the idea that it was through his spirit that Yahweh sent his instructions through the medium of the earlier prophets (Zech 7:12; Neh 9:30). Often in place of the 'spirit of the Lord' we find the parallel expression 'the hand of Yahweh', to which the same effects upon the spirit and will of the prophet are ascribed (1 Kings 18:46; 2 Kings 3:15; Is 8:11; Ezek 1:3; 3:14; 8:3; 37:1; 40:1; and compare Lk 11:20 with Mt 12:28). From the exile onwards the spirit of the Lord is clearly considered as the soul of prophetic inspiration (Ezek 2:2; 3:24; 11:5).

Through the spirit of the Lord the prophets receive first and foremost Yahweh's 'instructions' (Is 30:1; Zech 7:12), divine directives for the religious and political guidance of the people (2 Sam 23:2; 2 Chron 15:1; 20:14; 24:20; Is 11:2; 42:1; 61:1), as well as 'prophecies' in the strict sense (Num 24:2; 1 Chron 12:18). It is the spirit of the Lord too which imparts to

the prophets the 'power' to preach boldly and to suffer heroically (Mic 3:8; 2 Chron 24:20f). The spirit of God transforms the prophet into 'a fortified city, an iron pillar' (Jer 1:18; see also 1:8; 20:11), makes his brow like 'adamant, harder than flint' (Ezek 3:9; see also Is 6:6–9).

3. It is noteworthy that in the earlier period only physical and psychological effects were attributed to the spirit of the Lord. It is only from the exile onwards that the *rûaḥ* Yahweh is also conceived of as a moral force in human life, though only for the just. The author of Ps 51 prays for the 'holy spirit', which is able to dwell lastingly in the soul of the just man, and to bestow upon him power to live a holy life (Ps 51:12). In a moving psalm of repentance (Is 63:7–19) from the time of the return from the exile the prophet extols the 'spirit of holiness' (vv 10, 11) which God has set in the inmost heart of Moses. Since the spirit is made parallel to the 'arm of Yahweh', which divided the water of the Reed Sea before them (v 12), he is probably referring primarily to a divine power which was bestowed on Moses to enable him to lead the people (see Num 11:17). This is all the more probable if the Jews have perhaps replaced the phrase 'spirit of Yahweh' by that of 'spirit of holiness' from motives of reverence for the tetragrammaton. A teacher of wisdom prays for the 'holy spirit of discipline' (Wis 1:5), or for the 'holy spirit' (Wis 9:17), which is identical with Wisdom (Wis 1:4ff; 7:14, 22–5) and which, in the last analysis, does not so much initiate the religious and moral life as maintain it and guard it from the dangers of sin

(Wis 1:5; 9:17; see also 1:3f, 6; 7:14, 23, 25). From this it becomes clear that only the just are endowed with this power to lead a virtuous life (Wis 1:4; 7:25; TestSim 4:4; TestBen 8:2; Jub 1:21), exactly as in Ps 51:12.

In other passages the phrase 'the good spirit' of God means not, strictly speaking, the power to live a moral life, but rather a teacher who guides and strengthens the just (Ps 143:10), or the chosen people (Neh 9:20; Zech 7:12) so as to bring them to a life that is pleasing to God.

Up to the exile the spirit of the Lord is not conceived of as a source of religious and moral living. But since this period it undoubtedly is so, although only for the just. The transformation of the sinner into a 'new creature' in the messianic period is promised by Ezekiel, and fulfilled in the New Testament.

For the doctrine of the 'evil spirit' in the sense of a personal being, a demon, the Old Testament affords only adumbrations. The 'spirit of jealousy' (Num 5:14, 30), of 'harlotry' (Hos 4:12; 5:4), of 'uncleanness' (Zech 13), of 'confusion' (Is 19:14), of 'stupefaction' (Is 29:10)—these are nothing but vivid personifications of an evil power or passion. It is probable, however, that when the men of those ancient times speak of the 'evil spirit' which Yahweh sent between Abimelech and the men of Shechem (Judg 9:23), or which at God's command came upon Saul (1 Sam 16:14ff, 23; 18:10f; 19:8f), they have in mind some obscure idea of a personal being which sowed 'dissension' or stirred up Saul's diseased jealousy. This conception is still more clearly expressed in 1 Kings 22:19–23, where Yahweh sets a 'lying spirit' (*rûaḥ* in the masculine) in the mouth of the prophets, that is a spiritual being distinct from and subordinate to God, a demon.

4. The spirit of the Lord in the messianic age. The finest of the writings of the great prophets have been devoted to the spirit of the Lord which will produce the most marvellous effects both in the psychic and the religious and moral orders in the Messiah, in the messianic community of the saved, and in its members.

(a) In an age which rejoiced in its kings first Isaiah presents a masterly portrayal of the future ideal ruler, who is to be endowed *lastingly* with the spirit of the Lord. On the messianic king 'rests' all the fullness (the single spirit of the Lord with its three spirit-pairs = the sevenfold gift in which this fullness consists) of the most precious and most variegated gifts of a ruler: the proverbial wisdom and understanding of Solomon, the counsel and strength of David, the knowledge and fear of the Lord of the patriarchs Abraham, Isaac, and Jacob (Is 11:1f). The Lord will equip the closest collaborators of the messianic king with the 'spirit of righteousness', so that 'the Lord of hosts will be a crown of glory and a diadem of beauty to the remnant of his people' (Is 28:5f). After the downfall of the royal house, Deutero–Isaiah portrays the coming redeemer with the traits of the compassionate 'servant of God' who, in the fullness of the prophetic spirit, will proclaim the true religion to the heathens, and will lead the Israelites home from the exile (Is 42:1–7). From the historical background of the post-exilic community arises the moving figure of the unknown prophet who in the power of the spirit of God will proclaim the good tidings of salvation to the *ʿānāwîm* (=the poor), and will restore justice (Is 61:1–3).

(b) According to the earlier passages the spirit of the Lord will renew the face of the messianic community of the saved. The great prophets now present us—and this is the element that is new—with a universal outpouring of the spirit of God, a divine power which will transform and make glorious nature and people alike. The 'spirit of judgement and of purification' will purify the daughter of Zion from all sin (Is 4:4–6). The 'spirit from on high', like a warm rain, will bring forth paradisal fruitfulness in nature, and perfect righteousness in the hearts of the people so that overflowing peace will issue forth (Is 32:15–20). In his Book of Consolation, Deutero–Isaiah promises that Yahweh will 'pour out' his spirit, the breath of life upon the seed of Israel, and thereby rouse the people who are dying out to a new life (Is 44:3ff; see also Ezek 37:1–14).

(c) After the return from the exile the small 'remnant' awaits the most glorious of all the gifts of the spirit, which will actually bring about a new creation in the members of the community. Then Yahweh will pour out his spirit 'upon all flesh', upon young and old, high and low, so that all will be thrown into prophetic ecstasy and will have both dreams and visions (Joel 2:28). The 'spirit of grace and of weeping' will wipe out every sin in the inhabitants of the Jerusalem of the final age, and will remove every cause

of sin from them, for the Lord 'pours it out', or lets the 'fountain' stream forth (Zech 12:10–14; 13:1–6). Ezekiel, the priestly prophet, leads us to a plane as exalted as that of the New Testament. According to him the Lord will no longer 'pour out' his spirit as rain, but will 'sprinkle' it as the water of a cultic purification upon all the members of the community (Ezek 36:25), so as to purify them from all moral pollution. Then Yahweh will replace the 'heart of stone' in them with a 'heart of flesh', that is, he will give them a 'new heart' and will put a 'new spirit' (another disposition) within them; he will make them into a 'new creature' (Ezek 11:19; 18:31; 36:26; see also 2 Cor 5:17; Gal 6:15). Finally the Lord will fill the hearts thus transformed for ever with his spirit, with a superhuman power to lead a holy life according to God's 'commandments and precepts' (Ezek 36:27; 39:29; 37:14; see also Is 61:1–4; Jer 31:31–4; 32:38ff). From this point onwards it is only one step further to the mystery of the indwelling of the holy spirit in the souls of the just, which is rightly considered as the climax of the process of grace.

It is evident that neither the New Testament nor the present Church have completely exhausted the depths of these divine prophecies in all their richness. Their complete fulfilment will be achieved only with the true consummation of all, with the resurrection of the dead (Ezek 37:1–14) and with the 'new heaven and the new earth' (Is 65:17; 66:22).

5. *The nature of the Spirit of God.* From what has been said it will be seen that throughout the entire Old Testament the spirit of the Lord is conceived of not

yet as a person but merely as a force, as a physical reality, as a kind of extremely fine matter. The original interpretation is echoed more or less strongly in this. In the classic formula, 'The Egyptians are men and not God, and their horses are flesh and not spirit' (Is 31:3), it is not the 'spirit' that is in some sense contrasted with matter, the immaterial with the material, but rather the weak, mortal human nature with the powerful, immortal breath of God. When we are told of the spirit of the Lord that it is sent, that it envelops, breaks in upon, falls upon, guides and leads, sanctifies . . ., this means merely that an impersonal divine power receives a living human form, a form which can be recognised as the person of the Holy Spirit only in the light of New Testament revelation.

B. *The Spirit of God in the New Testament.* The New Testament terms corresponding to *ruah* in the Old Testament is *pneuma*. It is found some 375 times, and exhibits the same range of meaning, though with a notable shift of emphasis. The synoptics mention *pneuma* seventy-nine times (Matthew nineteen times, Mark twenty-three, and Luke thirty-seven). The Acts of the Apostles has sixty-eight passages referring to the Spirit, far more than any of the other books. *Pneuma* also constitutes a major element in the earlier pauline letters: Romans thirty-two times, 1 Corinthians forty, 2 Corinthians seventeen, and Galatians sixteen (1 Thessalonians five times and 2 Thessalonians twice). Among the captivity epistles, the Letter to the Ephesians, with fourteen references, stands out from the others (Philippians five, Colossians two, and Philemon one), whereas there is hardly any mention at all of *pneuma* in the pastoral epistles (1 Timothy three times, 2 Timothy three times, and Titus once). Among the catholic epistles 1 John comes first with twelve references, and is followed by 1 Peter (ten), 2 Peter (one), James (two), and Jude (two). The Letter to the Hebrews contains twelve passages on the Spirit. John's gospel (with twenty-three references) and the Book of Revelation (with twenty-four) are evenly balanced. The development of the idea of the Spirit from the Old Testament to the New proceeds in a directly ascending line: the meaning 'wind' disappears almost completely. While, in the synoptics and Acts, the psychic effects of the Spirit predominate, the major epistles and John's gospel, with their teaching on the mystery of the new creation or rebirth, attain to a high point in the New Testament theology of the Spirit. The anthropological sense of *pneuma* receives peripheral mention, especially in the pauline writings.

I. *The Spirit in the New Testament.* 1. *Pneuma* in the original sense of 'wind' is only found in Jn 3:8 and Heb 1:7 (= Ps 104:4). While the basis in sense experience also disappears almost completely, so that the only surviving trace of it occurs in the episode of the mighty wind of Pentecost, still the characteristic quality of the tempest, namely mysterious and irresistible power, is permanently ascribed to the working of the Spirit of God.

2. *'Pneuma' in man.* Far more numerous are the passages in which *pneuma* is used to designate the spirit of man: the breath (2 Thess 2:8; see also Is 11:4; Jn 20:22; Acts 17:25): the

breath of life or the principle of life which comes from God and returns to him (Mt 27:50; Lk 8:55; 23:46; Jn 6:63; 19:30; Acts 7:59; Heb 4:12; Jas 2:26; Rev 11:11; 13:15); the spirit as the seat of perceptions and feelings (Lk 1:47; Jn 11:33; 13:21; 1 Cor 4:21; Gal 6:1; Eph 4:23; 1 Pet 3:4); of thought (Mk 2:8; 8:12; Lk 1:80; Acts 18:25; Rom 1:9; 2:29; 7:6; 1 Cor 2:11; 5:3, 4, 5; 6:17; 14:2, 12, 14, 15, 16, 32; 16:18; 2 Cor 2:13; 7:13; 12:18; 2 Tim 4:22; Phil 4:23; Philem 25), and of decisions of the will (Mt 26:41; Acts 20:22); a state of mind, an attitude of the spirit (Lk 1:17; Mt 5:3; Jn 4:23f; Rom 12:11; 1 Cor 2:12; 4:21; 2 Cor 4:13; 6:6; 7:1; 2 Tim 1:7; Phil 1:27; 2:1; 1 Jn 4:1f; 1 Pet 3:4); the 'spirit of truth and spirit of error' (1 Jn 4:6); the human personality (Gal 6:18).

3. *Evil spirits.* The New Testament very seldom speaks of spirits in general (Acts 23:8f), of good spirits or of angels (Heb 1:14; Rev 4:5), but far more frequently, especially in the synoptics and Acts, of the 'evil spirits', for which it has various designations: 'spirit' (Mk 9:20; Acts 16:18; Eph 2:2); 'spirits' (Mt 8:16; 12:45; Lk 10:20; 11:26; 1 Cor 12:10); 'evil spirits' (Lk 7:21; 8:2; Acts 19:12f, 15f); and 'dumb spirits' (Mk 9:17, 25). The term 'unclean spirits' is encountered particularly often. Of twenty-three passages referring to *pneuma* in Mark, fourteen are concerned with the 'unclean spirits' (or similar expressions Mk 1:23, 26f; 3:11, 30; 5:2; etc; Mt 10:1; Lk 8:29; 11:24; Acts 5:16; 8:7; Rev 16:13; 18:2). The 'spirits in prison' are also called *pneumata* (1 Pet 3:19), as are the souls of the de-

parted (Heb 12:23). The expressions 'deceitful spirits' (1 Tim 4:1) and 'spirit of stupor' (Rom 11:8; ↗ Spirit of God in the Old Testament, ↗ Demon) have a wholly Old Testament ring.

II. *The Spirit of God in the New Testament.* With the new covenant the 'marriage' of the Spirit of God is inaugurated. The choice of the Greek and Latin adjectives—*pneuma hagion* (not *pneuma hieron*), *Spiritus sanctus* (not *Spiritus sacer*)—is enough by itself to show this. The full and lasting possession of the Spirit constitutes the great and blessed experience of newness for Jesus Christ. His glorified body constitutes the unquenchable source of the Spirit for the apostles, the church, the faithful—in fact, for the whole of creation.

1. *The Spirit of God and Jesus Christ.* In the person of Jesus Christ the most glorious bearer of the Spirit appeared, he who had been promised by the prophets (Is 11:2; 42:1; 61:1), and who was awaited by contemporary judaism (PsSol 17:42; Enoch 49:3f; TestLev 18:7; TestJud 24:2).

From his miraculous conception onwards, Christ is under the influence of the Spirit of God. The angel dispels the hesitation of Mary with the words: 'The Holy Spirit will come upon you, and the power of the Most High will overshadow you' (Lk 1:35; Mt 1:18, 20; see, too, the equivalent ideas in Acts 1:8). The angel attributes the miracle of the conception to the creative power of the Spirit of God (see Gen 1:2; Ps 104:30; Wis 1:7), who will descend upon Mary like a cloud, the sign of the divine presence (see Ex 13:21; 19:16; 24:16; 40:34). In the Old Testament every child born under miraculous circumstances was dedicated in a special manner to God. Thus for example Isaac (Gen 18:14; 21:1), who was born according to the Spirit (Gal 4:29), Joseph (Gen 30:22f), Samson the Nazirite (Judg 13:2f, 7), Samuel (1 Sam 1:19f). In the same way the miraculous conception of Jesus represents the matchless masterpiece of the Spirit of God, who cannot increase his presence in Christ as he does in the Baptist (cf Lk 2:40 with 1:80), and who consecrates him as holy and as Son of God.

The Holy Spirit had already 'rested' (Jn 1:32; see also Is 11:2; Zech 3:8) upon the Son of God 'without measure' (Jn 3:34; Lk 4:1) from the moment of his birth. But at his baptism God 'anointed him with the Holy Spirit and with power' (Acts 10:38), ie, God revealed him and attested him in the eyes of all the world (see Lk 1:41, 44, 67; 2:25ff, and 37f) as the longed-for Messiah. The new creation begins with Christ filled with the Spirit, and yet the Baptist beheld the Spirit descending as a dove from heaven and hovering upon Jesus (Mt 3:16; Mk 1:10; Lk 3:21f; Jn 1:32f), just as on the morning of the first creation the *rûaḥ ᵉlōhîm* flew to and fro like a bird above the primordial waters as a power of fruitfulness and life (Gen 1:2), or as after the Flood the dove bore a fresh olive-branch in its beak as a sign of peace for the new humanity embodied in the Messiah (Gen 8:11).

At the beginning of his public ministry the Spirit of God drove Jesus, the 'new man', into the wilderness, where, like Moses (Ex 34:28) and Elijah (1 Kings 19), he fasted and prayed for forty days. And just as the first man was tempted by the devil, so too the second Adam was tempted by Satan. Triumphantly he overcame by power from above the subtle suggestions of the devil that he should build the messianic kingdom on the foundations of money, honour and power (Lk 4:1; Mk 1:12; Mt 4:1). Jesus ushered in once more the peace between man and beast which prevailed in Paradise (Gen 2:19; ApocMos 16). For according to Mk 1:13, when he had conquered temptation he sojourned 'among the wild beasts', and the evangelist may probably have intended to indicate by this that the paradisal conditions of the final age had been inaugurated (see Is 11:6–8; 65:25). And just as, according to the Midrash, in paradise food was prepared for Adam by the angels, so here angels provided heavenly food for the new man.

After this the Holy Spirit led him back to Galilee (Lk 4:14), where he prepared himself for his prophetic mission. (a) As he proclaimed for the first time the good tidings of the kingdom of God, as also throughout all his later preaching activity (Mt 12:18–21 = Is 42:1–4), he knew that he was endowed with the Spirit of the Lord (Lk 4:18f = Is 61:1f). (b) All the miracles which he performed were a sign of the Spirit of God, in whose power he drove out devils (Lk 4:36; Mt 12:28 = Lk 11:20: 'with the finger of God'; see also Ex 8:19; Deut 9:10), heals the sick and infirm, and raises the dead to life (Lk 5:17; 6:19; 8:54f; 13:32; Mt 12:18, 20). He prays in the Holy Ghost (Lk 3:4; 5:16; 6:12; 9:18, 9:29; 11:1; 22:32; 23:34–46), and is overflowing with joy in him (Lk 10:21). (c) In a further episode, while a radiant cloud upon the mountain, the 'majestic glory of God' (2 Pet 1:17), the symbol of the Spirit of God, over-shadowed Jesus, Moses, and Elijah, a voice proclaimed: 'This is my beloved Son' (Mk 9:2–13; Mt 17:1–13; Lk 9:28–36). Baptism and transfiguration reveal the divine sonship of Jesus. In his redemptive sacrifice upon the cross, through the 'eternal Spirit', Christ overcame (Heb 9:14) the weakness of his *sarx*, the mortality and limitations of his human nature (Mt 26:41). Then the 'Spirit that gives life' (Jn 6:63), ie, the creative power of God, raised Jesus to glory: 'If the Spirit of him who raised Jesus from the dead dwells in you, he who raised Christ Jesus from the dead will give life to your mortal bodies also through his Spirit which dwells in you' (Rom 8:11; see also 1 Pet 3:18).

The act of raising from the dead which the Father has accomplished through the mediation of the Holy Spirit as the executive organ is also attributed by Paul to the *dunamis* (lit. = power) which is equivalent to the Holy Spirit: 'Having the eyes of your hearts enlightened, that you may know . . . what is the immeasurable greatness of his power, which he accomplished in Christ when he raised him from the dead and made him sit at his right hand in the heavenly places' (Eph 1:18–20; cp 1 Cor 6:14; 2 Cor 13:14).

When Paul writes, 'Christ was raised from the dead by the *doxa* (*kābod*, ↗ glory) of the Father' (Rom 6:4), he is thinking of the cloud of light and fire, the shekina, which reveals the glory, presence and power of God (see Ex 24:17; 40:34; Num 10:34; Ezek 10:4), and in this respect the role of the cloud

has, with the passage of time, been transferred to the Spirit of God (see Is 63:10–14).

In his resurrection Christ also be-came transfigured by the Spirit. Above all he became, according to the law of the Spirit, designated Son of God (Rom 1:4). Thus he who on earth lived according to the psyche became in the Resurrection, in accordance with the nature of the Spirit, a spiritual being (1 Cor 15:45), so that from that time onwards he is pulsating with the over-flowing and life-giving power of the divine Pneuma: 'The Lord is himself the Spirit' (2 Cor 3:17; see also v. 6). So totally is the glorified Christ filled with the all-embracing and life-giving reality of the Holy Spirit that according to Paul it is justifiable to say that a man is in Christ (Gal 2:17) or in the Spirit (1 Cor 6:11), sanctified in Christ (1 Cor 1:2) or in the Spirit (1 Cor 6:11), sealed in Christ (Eph 1:13) or in the Spirit (Eph 4:30). And yet Paul does not regard the glorified Christ and the Holy Ghost as interchangeable. For while the believer is still sojourning in alien surroundings 'far from the Lord' (2 Cor 5:6), the Spirit of Christ is already dwelling within him (Rom 8:9).

In the power of the Holy Spirit Christ descended after his death to the 'spirits in prison', ie, in limbo, where he proclaimed the good tidings of sal-vation to those men who had perished in the flood, or announced to the devils the fact that they were finally bound and subjected to his power as *Kurios* (1 Pet 3:18–20).

It is the spiritualised and exalted body of the Lord, which is no longer subject to the laws of gravity, that the believer consumes in the ⁊ eucharist. In other words, he eats the flesh of Christ, not in its earthly mode of existence, but as it is when transfigured by the Spirit. 'It is the Spirit that gives life, the flesh is of no avail' (Jn 6:63). This is Jesus' rejoinder to the Jews when they murmur against him and take scandal at the realism of his demands (Jn 6:52–63). The glorified body is a 'spiritual' food (1 Cor 10:3).

2. *The Spirit of God and the apostles.* During his earthly life Christ was the unique bearer of the Spirit, if we abstract from the charismatic figures who appear in the infancy narrative of Jesus (Lk 1:15, 41, 67; 2:25ff) and do not regard the power of working miracles extended to Jesus' disciples as an effect of the Spirit (Mt 17:19; Mk 16:17; Lk 21:15). It is with the Resurrection that the great mission of the glorified Lord begins, in which he pours out the Holy Ghost on all believers, the ⁊ apostles first of all (see Is 28:6). According to the synoptics and the Acts of the Apostles it was not until Pentecost that Christ bestowed on the apostles (Acts 2:4, 33; see also 2:17) that 'baptismal fire', the Spirit of God which the Baptist had promised (Mt 3:11; Mk 1:8; Lk 3:16; see also Jn 1:22, 23), of which he himself had held out the prospect (Lk 24:49; Acts 1:2, 4, 5, 8; 11:16) and which he had ardently desired (Lk 12:49). For John, on the contrary, the sending of the Spirit is connected with the resurrection: 'If anyone thirst', says Jesus at the feast of Tabernacles, 'Let him come to me and drink, he who believes in me. As the scripture has said, "Out of him (Christ) shall flow rivers of living water"' (Zech 14:8; Ezek 47:1f; see

also Jn 4:1). The evangelist interprets this saying of the Lord: 'Now this he said about the Spirit which those who believed in him were to receive. For as yet the Spirit had not been given because Jesus was not yet glorified' (Jn 7:37–9; see also 16:7; 3:14f; 10:10). From the wound in his side when he was crucified (Jn 19:34; see also 1 Jn 5:6ff), from the glorified body of Christ as the messianic temple (see Jn 2:19; Ezek 47), the Spirit was indeed to be poured out over the whole earth and to the end of time. On the evening of the day of his resurrection he breathed (breath, exhalation!) upon the disciples with the words: 'Receive the Holy Spirit!', and by this gift he imparted to them the power to forgive sins (Jn 20:22f). The two authors do not contradict, but rather supplement, one another. Luke is concerned with the charismatic effects which he sees as deriving from the gift at Pentecost. John, on the other hand, has primarily in mind the sacramental graces which he sees as proceeding from the gift at the first Easter.

On the festival of Pentecost the apostles were assigned the charismatic function of prophets and leaders. They were equipped by the gift of the Spirit of God for preaching the word of God and for leading the church. Just as the Spirit of God had spoken through the mouth of the prophets (see Mt 22:43; Mk 12:36; Acts 1:16; 4:25; 28:25; Heb 3:7; 9:8; 10:15; 2 Tim 3:16; 2 Pet 1:21), so too he speaks through the mouth of their successors the apostles (Acts 5:39; 11:12; 1 Cor 12:28; 1 Pet 1:11f). The tongues of fire (Acts 2:3) point on to the preaching of the *magnalia Dei* (Acts 2:11) and also of the divine instructions (Rev 2:7, 11, 17, 28; 3:6, 13, 22). The Holy Spirit imparts divine authority and dignity to their inspired words (see 2 Tim 3:16; 2 Pet 1:21; Rev 14:13). Once the Holy Spirit has descended upon them they realise the immense significance of the message of the risen and exalted Lord (Acts 1:8; 2:33; 4:8; 6:5, 10; see also Rev 19:10) for obtaining a deeper insight into the mystery of Christ (1 Cor 2:10–14; 12:3; 2 Cor 4:13f; Eph 3:5, 16ff). The Holy Spirit does not reveal any new truths to the disciples, but reminds them of the teaching of Christ (Jn 14:25f; 15:18, 25f), which hitherto they have not understood (Jn 16:12). The reverential title 'Spirit of truth', which is accorded to him, is appropriate (Jn 14:17; 15:26; 16:13). Under the promptings of the Holy Spirit the christological meaning of the messianic prophecies of the Old Testament is disclosed (Acts 2:17–21 = Joel 2:28–32; 2:25–8 = Ps 16:8–11; 2:34f = Ps 110:1; 3:22f = Deut 18:15, 19; 4:25f = Ps 2:1f; etc).

At the same time the Holy Spirit equips them with superhuman power in order that in spite of opposition and persecution they may preach the 'word of God', ie, the message of Jesus Christ, with unflagging courage and burning zeal (Acts 2:29; 4:20, 29–31; 5:29; 9:27f; 19:8; 26:26; 28:31; 1 Cor 2:3f; 2 Cor 3:4–6; 4:1; 1 Thess 1:5), in 'the power of Christ' (2 Cor 12:9).

The success of their preaching is powerfully promoted by a whole series of impressive gifts of the Spirit such as inspired speech (Acts 2:4, 11, 15; ↗ charisma); the performance of major miracles (Acts 9:39–42; 12:5–17; 13:9–11; Rom 15:19); physical (Acts 8:39) and spiritual transports (Rev 1:10; 4:2; 17:3; 21:10); and prophecy in the strict sense (Acts 9:17; 20:23; Rev 2:1 = 8, 7 = 11; 2 Thess 2:2; 1 Tim 4:1; Jud 18; see also Lk 1:41, 67).

Like the leading figures of the chosen people, such as Moses (Num 11:17) or David (1 Sam 16:13), so too the apostles are equipped with charismatic gifts to exercise the functions of leader or pastor. By means of the ↗ laying on of hands they impart these to their disciples also (Acts 6:3; 20:28; 2 Tim 1:6; see also Num 8:10f).

The Spirit of God directs the young church through them (Acts 1:8; 13:2; 15:28; 20:28–31). In the Acts of the Apostles the chief protagonist is neither Peter nor Paul, but the Holy Spirit, by whose assistance the church grows (Acts 9:31). By the choice of Matthias (Acts 1:15–26) he brings the apostolic college to its full complement, making it the counterpart of the group of the twelve patriarchs of Israel. He determines who are to be the seven deacons (Acts 6:3, 5, 6; compare the seventy elders in Ex 24:1; Num 11:16), and who are to be the servants of the church (Acts 13:2). He institutes bishops (Acts 20:28; 1 Tim 4:12; 2 Tim 1:6); breaks down the inveterate prejudice against receiving gentiles into the church (Acts 10:19; 11:12; 15:28); guides and strengthens the 'apostles' (Acts 1:8; 5:3; 8:14–17) and the 'evangelists' (Acts 2:18; Eph 4:11; 2 Tim 4:5) on their hard missionary journeys (Acts 4:8; 6:10; 8:29; 10:19; 13:2–4; 16:6f; 20:24).

3. *The Spirit and the church.* According to the evidence of the Acts of the

Apostles, both the young church at Jerusalem, the 'Israel of God' (Gal 6:16), and also the gentile world (Acts 10:44f, 47; 11:15; 15:8f) celebrated a miniature Pentecost (Acts 4:31; see also 5:32; 8:17; 9:31; 19:2, 6) which was after the pattern of the prophecy of Joel (Acts 2:17=Joel 2:28).

With the exaltation of Christ and the sending of the Spirit (see Mt 16:18; Jn 7:39) the kingdom of God has begun (Acts 2:33; see also 1:3, 6; 2:20–36; 4:10f). The time of the church is essentially the time of the Spirit of God. Church and Spirit belong to each other inseparably as body and soul. According to Paul, the church is the glorified body of Christ, which is permeated by the living power of the Holy Spirit (1 Cor 12:13; Eph 4:2f). By him the believer's surrender of himself to Christ and his incorporation in the mystical body is sealed as a pact is sealed by the stamping of the seal upon it (Eph 1:13; 4:30). When Paul compares the church to a temple in which the Spirit of God dwells (1 Cor 3:16; Eph 2:22; cf 1 Pet 2:4f), this is another way of expressing the same truth.

The Holy Spirit was imparted to the individual members of the church by the imposition of hands (Acts 6:6; 8:17ff; 19:6; 1 Tim 4:14; 2 Tim 1:6; cp Deut 34:9). Since the charismatic gift of the Spirit of God was customarily bestowed only in view of a specific task, one who is already 'full of the Holy Spirit' by baptism is still open to further strengthening by the charismatic gifts of the Spirit (Acts 6:3, 10). The Samaritans had already received the baptism in water and the Holy Ghost, but it was only through the ⁊ laying-on of hands by the apostles

that the charismatic manifestation of their possession by the Spirit was granted to them (Acts 8:14–19; cf 19:5–7).

The Spirit of God breathed most powerfully through the young church, in which the primary result of his presence was the accomplishment of certain effects which were quite out of the normal course, and were most closely connected with the mission of the church. The church itself had abundant experience of being strengthened by the Holy Spirit (Acts 9:31), and it was due to him that the time of flowering in the christian life was so full of promise. Wholly characteristic of the Spirit of God was the aim of conquering the world for Christ. One expression of this aim was the courageous preaching of the word of God (Acts 4:31; 5:32; 6:5, 10; 11:24); others were the charismatic inspiration of the spoken and chanted liturgy (Acts 2:47; Eph 5:18–20); the gift of prophecy (Acts 8:19; see also Lk 1:15, 41, 67; 2:25ff); illuminations and inward promptings of the will (Acts 11:12); visions (Acts 7:55); prophecies in the strict sense (Acts 11:28; 21:4–11); miracles (Acts 3:1–8; Heb 2:4; 6:1f); ecstatic speech (Acts 10:44ff; 19:6; 1 Cor 12:10; 14:2–28; 1 Thess 5:19f) and its interpretation (1 Cor 12:10; 14:13, 27f); the ability to distinguish between spirits (1 Cor 12:10; 14:29; 1 Thess 5:21; 1 Jn 4:1); and the amazing wisdom and boldness of speech of the persecuted christians when they were brought to judgement (Mt 10:20; Lk 12:12; Jn 14:26; Acts 6:5, 10).

4. *The Spirit of God and the faithful.* It is above all the pauline letters and the

fourth gospel which bring us into what is properly the domain of the Holy Spirit. According to these, with the resurrection of Christ the miracle of religious and moral transformation promised by the prophets (Ezek 36: 25ff; Jer 31:31, 34) has been accomplished. One day this work will be crowned by an act of glorification of mankind and of nature which will be absolutely comprehensive in its effects. In the pauline letters extraordinary feats have only a subordinate part to play, while in the 'spiritual' gospel of the beloved disciple they go unmentioned altogether.

(a) The Holy Spirit dwells in the souls of the faithful as in a temple (1 Cor 3:16f; 6:19; Eph 2:22), but this is achieved no longer by the laying-on of hands, but rather by ↗ baptism (Mt 28:19; Mk 16:16; Acts 8:12f, 16, 38; 9:18; 16:14f; 18:8f; Eph 4:5; Col 2:12), or by baptism in the name of Jesus (see Acts 2:38; 10:48; 19:5; 22:16; Rom 6:3ff; 1 Cor 1:13).

(b) The transformation accomplished by baptism is depicted by Paul as a new creation. Recalling the water of purification used in the cult (see Ezek 36:25; see also Is 4:4; 31:9; 66:15; Amos 7:4), he tells us how the soul is washed, sanctified and declared justified in the 'washing of the water' (Eph 5:26; Heb 10:22) of baptism from all guilt. This means that in fulfilment of the prophetic promise (see Ezek 36:27; 37:14) it is changed by the Holy Ghost into a new creature (cp 1 Cor 6:11; 2 Cor 5:17; Gal 3:27; 6:15; Eph 4:24; Rom 15:16; 1 Thess 1:5ff; 4:7f; 2 Thess 2:13; 1 Pet 1:2).

For this reason once they have been baptised the Jewish christians no longer observe the ↗ law 'of the letter', which was written on stone, but the law 'of the Spirit', which is inscribed in the hearts of christians (2 Cor 3:2–11). He who is free from the 'old written code' of the law 'serves in the new life of the Spirit' (Rom 7:6); but he who conducts himself according to the law fulfils the requirement of the law (Rom 8:4). The letter of the law now grown obsolete kills; only the 'new Spirit' brings about new life, the life that is in Christ Jesus, a new creation (see Rom 7:6; 8:1ff; Gal 6:8). Paul then goes on to draw this conclusion: '. . . walk not according to the flesh but according to the Spirit . . . To set the mind on the flesh is death, but to set the mind on the Spirit is life and peace' (Rom 8:4, 6; see also vv 7ff, 13). 'Walk by the Spirit and do not gratify the desires of the flesh' (Gal 5:16), ie, 'you shall not do the works of the flesh' (see Gal 5:19ff, 24), 'but will bring forth "the fruit of the Spirit"' (see Gal 5:22f, 25f). In this struggle against corrupted nature the christians are not alone. In the power of the Spirit they put to death the deeds of the flesh (cp Rom 8:13; Gal 5:13).

John conceives of the interior transformation of man achieved in baptism as a ↗ rebirth, which is, in the last analysis, another way of expressing the same truth. According to the proclamation of the Baptist (Jn 1:33; see also Ezek 36:25f), in baptism the believer is born 'of God' (Jn 1:13), 'of the Spirit' (3:5, 6, 8), 'from above' and 'anew' (3:3: in John *anō* has both these senses). This is a divine new birth which is set in contrast to the birth 'from below' (8:23) 'of the flesh' (3:6), 'of the devil and the world'

(8:42–7; 15:19; 17:14, 16). In the 'bath of rebirth' we have been renewed by the Holy Spirit whom the Father, of his compassion, has poured out upon us in rich measure through Jesus Christ our Saviour in order that we, justified by his grace, may become heirs according to the hope of eternal life (see Tit 3:5ff).

(c) What effects do the pauline new creation or the johannine rebirth entail? Above all, sonship of God, the victorious act of faith, burning love for the brethren and the bearing of inspired witness.

In baptism the believer is in a mysterious manner 'baptised into' (see Rom 6:3ff) the dying and rising Lord, so that together with this newness of life his Spirit too is bestowed upon him, the Spirit of the Son, the Spirit of ↗ sonship: 'And because you are sons God has sent the Spirit of his Son into our hearts crying "Abba, Father", so through God you are no longer a slave but a son, and if a son then an heir also' (Gal 4:6f). In baptism 'the flesh', that is the bondage of the earthly sinful man (Rom 8:1–8), is overcome by the 'Spirit' through whom God, together with his Son, has raised up us also to the new life of sonship (Rom 8:9–14). Henceforward the 'Spirit of God' (Rom 8:9), the 'Spirit of Christ' (Rom 8:9), the 'Holy Spirit' (Rom 5:5), or simply the 'Spirit' (Rom 8:11), dwells for ever in us and bears witness to the fact that we are sons of God (Rom 8:14–17). This Spirit of divine sonship obliges the christian as a son of God to persevere, 'to let himself be led by the Spirit of God' (Rom 8:14), 'to walk according to the Spirit' (8:4), 'to set his mind on the things of the Spirit' (8:5), 'on life and peace' (8:6), 'on ↗ righteousness' (8:10), that is true holiness.

The Spirit bestows upon us in ↗ prayer a sureness of the fact that we are sons of God (Gal 4:6). He also teaches the christian the right manner in which he should pray to the Father in heaven (see Phil 1:19). Indeed he himself intercedes for him with sighs too deep for words (Rom 8:16, 26f; Jude 20; Phil 3:3). During the time 'when our Redeemer is absent', the Spirit of Christ arouses in us a prayerful longing for the return of our Lord (Rev 22:17, 20).

The Holy Spirit instils in us that ↗ faith in Christ which does not derive from the works of the flesh (Gal 3:14; 5:5). It arouses in us an unshakeable faith in the person of the exalted *Kurios* (1 Cor 12:3).

In the power of the Spirit the christian maintains a superabundant ↗ hope (Rom 15:13), and in this power he emerges victorious (Rom 8:1–7; Gal 5:16ff) over the desires 'of the ↗ flesh', the 'old nature' (Gal 6:8).

The Spirit strengthens the interior man in faith and love (Eph 3:14f). The Spirit of the Father, 'a Spirit of power' (2 Tim 1:7), is efficacious in a quite special degree when he speaks through the mouth of his persecuted children (Mt 10:20; Mk 13:11; Lk 12:12; Jn 14:26), imparts strength to the martyrs to suffer and to lay down their lives for the sake of Jesus' name (1 Pet 4:14), the greatest possible proof of a love of Christ that is genuine (cp Jn 15:13).

According to Paul the spirit of brotherly love (↗ brother) flows from the risen Christ into the soul of the baptised: 'God's love has been poured (perfect tense = lasting effect) into our hearts through the Holy Spirit which has been given to us' (aorist = initial occurrence: Rom 5:5; see also 15:30; Gal 5:22; Col 1:8; 2 Cor 6:6; Eph 3:16f) ↗ Love coincides so closely with the new life of the Spirit that 'to walk in the Spirit' is virtually synonymous with 'to love one another' (Gal 5:16, 18; see also Rom 8:4; Eph 5:2); to fulfil 'the law (of Christ)' (Gal 5:14; 6:2; 1 Cor 9:21) is virtually equivalent to 'to bear one another's burdens' (Gal 6:2).

The Holy Spirit watches with special care over the development of the beloved church. He instils daily brotherly love, ↗ joy, patience, friendliness, ↗ goodness, faithfulness, and gentleness (Gal 5:22; cp 1 Cor 13:4–7; Eph 4:2; Col 3:12), and ↗ humility (Eph 4:2). When the Spirit of love and the holiness of God is present in someone, through that love the law is fulfilled in the most perfect possible manner (Rom 13:10; Gal 5:14; Col 3:14).

Love is enthroned in the church as a queen. In the body of Christ it occupies the first place, for it has the same part to play as the Spirit (see Eph 4:16; Col 2:2). It immeasurably exceeds all other gifts of the Spirit (1 Cor 13:1–3, 8–10, 13; 14:1; see also 1 Jn 5:7), and includes them (Rom 15:30; Col 1:8; Gal 5:22). All charismatic feats performed in the service of the church are, in the last analysis, services of love for the brethren (see Acts 6:3). Without the Spirit of love the church would no longer be the church of Christ, but only a dead structure, a caricature of a church.

For John, too, the Spirit is so closely connected with love that he uses the words *Spirit* or *love* without distinction (1 Jn 4:13–17). When one compares 1 Jn 4:13–17 with Jn 17 one is tempted to discern in the love of the 'priestly prayer' the Spirit of the Lord himself who makes actual the unity of the faithful in the single Body of Christ (Jn 17; see also 1 Cor 12:4–12). The Holy Spirit draws the faithful into that relationship of love which unites the Father with the Son. Thus through the Holy Spirit man's encounter with God is made personal and living.

The Holy Spirit imparts a superhuman strength to the disciples of Christ in order that the ↗ witness which they bear to the exalted Lord shall be an inspired one.

5. *The Spirit of God and the glorification of creation*. In the 'new creation' or in the 'new birth' the entire man, and so the body too, takes part in the transformed life of glory. Paul explicitly enlightens us upon this: 'God has made *us* alive together with Christ . . . and raised us up with him and made us sit with him in the heavenly places' (Eph 2:5f [verbs in the perfect]; see also Col 2:12f).

The approaching ↗ resurrection, as foretold in the great vision of the dead bones (Ezek 37:1–14), is essentially and in principle already entered upon in holy baptism. There the Spirit is given to us as a 'pledge' of the physical resurrection (Rom 5:5; 8:11; Gal 3:2; 4:1; 1 Thess 4:8; Eph 1:13). More than this, indeed, the reception of the Spirit is the gift of first fruits (Rom 8:23), a 'down payment' or deposit on the part of God which guarantees the full outpouring of glory which will transfigure all without exception (2 Cor 1:22; 5:5; Eph 1:14).

In one passage, however, the raising of the body is regarded as the achievement of the Father, who will restore it through the power of the Spirit with its creative effect: 'If the Spirit of him who raised Jesus from the dead dwells in you, he who raised Christ Jesus from the dead will give life to your mortal bodies also through his Spirit which dwells in you' (Rom 8:11; see also 1 Cor 6:14). The Spirit is the miraculously life-giving force which will bring about the resurrection of the flesh (2 Cor 3:6; Gal 6:8; see also Jn 6:63).

Paul does something to throw light upon the question of 'how' the resurrection is to be effected (see 1 Cor 15:35–53). The earthly body, which is subject to the conditions of sense-experience, will then be raised into a 'spiritual body' which will be wholly permeated with and dominated by the life-force of the divine Spirit (1 Cor 15:44). Just as up to that point we shall have been conformed to the image of the 'first Adam', the earthly man, so then we shall be conformed to the image of the 'new Adam', the heavenly man, Christ (1 Cor 15:44–9; see also Rev 21:5). This is the image of 'incorruptibility' (1 Cor 15:42, 52f), of 'immortality' (1 Cor 15:53), of 'glory' (1 Cor 15:43; see also Rom 8:18; 2 Cor 4:17; Phil 3:21; Col 3:4).

The Spirit of God was at work in the first creation (Gen 1:2; cp 2:7). Through the ↗ sin of man, to whom creation was handed over for better or for worse (cp Gen 3:17), it was thrown into 'the bondage of decay' (Rom 8:21), 'has been groaning in travail together until now' (v 22). But once the bodies are glorified, then the smitten world of creatures will also take part in the 'glory of the children of God' (v 21) through the creative power of the Spirit of God. Then it will find its redemption in the glorified Body of Christ and in that of man (Rom 8:18–23; see also Col 1:20; Eph 1:10; 2 Pet 3:13; Rev 21:5), 'in the new heaven and on the new earth' (Rev 21:1; Is 65:17; 2 Pet 3:13). Thanks to the living power of the divine Spirit, the paradise belonging to the beginning of time will break out once more in the glory of the eschatological new creation.

6. *The Spirit of God as person.* It may be concluded from the passages adduced that in most cases the Spirit of God is conceived of wholly in the sense of the Old Testament *rûaḥ*, as a divine power. Only in this sense can we understand what is meant by such expressions as the outpouring of the Holy Spirit, baptising, anointing, sealing, filling, etc with the Holy Spirit. Often Spirit and power are found as parallel terms (Lk 1:17, 35; Acts 1:8).

Just as in the Old Testament, the Spirit of God is personified. He speaks through the mouths of the apostles (Acts 8:20; 13:2; etc) as he spoke through those of the prophets (Acts 4:25); he sends the disciples out (Acts 13:4); he leads the church (Acts 20:28). The Spirit can be found in place of ↗ wisdom or power (1 Cor 2:4f, 13), and Paul means for the most part the supernatural presence and activity of God. For this reason 'God', 'Lord', and 'Spirit' can be used in parallelism to one another (1 Cor 12:4ff).

In the synoptics explicit reference to the three divine persons is found only in a single passage: the baptismal formula of Mt 28:19, which probably bears the stamp of later liturgical usage. In the Acts of the Apostles the passage: 'It has seemed good to the Holy Spirit and to us' (Acts 15:28), should probably be interpreted in the same sense. In the pauline letters certain passages point to the activity and presence of a distinct person of God. Among these passages are the trinitarian formulae in 1 Cor 12:4–6 and especially in 2 Cor 13:14. The fourth gospel and the Book of Revelation leave nothing to be desired in point of clarity. The Father sends the 'Supporter' (Jn 14:26) who proceeds from him (15:26) so that he can take the place of Christ in instructing the disciples (14:26) in order to bear witness to Jesus (15:26), in order to convince the world of sin (16:8–11; etc). The Holy Spirit occupies the place of Jesus Christ among the disciples and represents him (7:39; 16:7) during the long interval which must elapse before the return of the Lord (14:16). Again in Revelation, John the theologian envisages a person who is distinct from the Father and the Son. The Spirit speaks as a person to the community (Rev 2:7, 11, 17, 29; 3:6, 13, 22; 14:13). With John the theology of the Spirit of God as person achieves its definitive form.

Bibliography: On A: apart from the Old Testament theologies, see in particular: A. Westphal, *Chair et Esprit*, Toulouse 1885; J. Köberle, *Natur und Geist nach der Auffassung des AT*, Munich 1901; H. Gunkel, *Die Wirkungen des Heiligen Geistes nach der populären Anschauung der apostolischen Zeit und der Lehre des Apostels Paulus*, Göttingen 1909³; P. Volz, *Der Geist Gottes und die verwandten Erscheinungen im AT und im anschliessenden Judentum*, Tübingen 1910; J. Hehn, 'Zum Problem des Geistes im alten Orient und im AT', *ZAW* 43 (1925), 210–25;

P. van Imschoot, 'L'action de l'esprit de Yahvé dans l'AT', *RSPT* 23 (1934), 553–87; P. van Imschoot, 'L'esprit de Yahvé, source de vie dans l'AT', *RB* 44 (1945), 481–501; P. van Imschoot, 'L'esprit de Yahvé et l'alliance nouvelle dans l'AT', *ETL* 22 (1936), 201–26; P. van Imschoot, 'Sagesse et esprit dans l'AT', *RB* 47 (1938), 23–49; P. van Imschoot, 'L'esprit de Yahvé, principe de vie morale dans l'AT', *ETL* 16 (1939), 457–67; P. van Imschoot, 'L'esprit selon l'AT', *Bible et Vie Chrétienne*, 2 (1953), 7–24; P. van Imschoot, 'L'esprit de Yahvé, source de piété dans l'AT', *Bible et Vie chrétienne* 6 (1954), 17–30; A. R. Johnson, *The Cultic Prophet in Ancient Israel*, Cardiff 1944; H. W. Robinson, *Inspiration and Revelation in the Old Testament*, Oxford 1946; B. W. Miller, *The Holy Spirit, What the Bible Teaches about Him*, 1950; R. Koch, *Geist und Messias. Beitrag zur bibl. Theologie des AT*, Vienna 1950; R. Koch, 'La théologie de l'Esprit de Yahvé dans le Livre d'Isaïe', *SP* 1 (Paris–Gembloux 1959), 419–33; R. Koch, 'Der Gottesgeist und der Messias', *Bbl* 27 (1946), 241–68; K. Galling, 'Der Charakter der Chaosschilderung in Gen 1:2', *ZTK* 47 (1950), 145–57; K. Prümm, 'Israels Kehr zum Geist', *ZKT* 72 (1950), 385–442; T. Maertens, 'Le souffle et l'esprit de Dieu', *Evangile* 14 (1954), 9–49; D. Lys, '*Ruach*', *Le Souffle dans l'AT*, Paris 1962; D. Lys, '*Nephesh*', *Histoire de l'âme dans la Révélation d'Israël*, Paris 1959; E. Haulotte, 'L'Esprit de Yahvé dans l'AT', *L'homme devant Dieu* (Mélanges H. Lubac 1), Paris 1964, 25–36; I. Herrmann, *HTG* 1, 642f; P. van Imschoot, Haag 527–35; M. J. Le Guillou, *Catholicisme* IV, 474–7; *TDNT* VI, 332–89 (=*BKW* IX); *RGG* II³, 974–6 and 1270–72.

On B: see the well-nigh exhaustive details supplied in *TDNT* VI, 332–4. See also: H. Wendt, *Die Begriffe Fleisch und Geist im bibl. Sprachgebrauch*, Gotha 1878; J. Gloël, *Der Heilige Geist in der Heilsverkündigung des Paulus*, Halle 1888; G. Weinel, *Die Wirkungen des Geistes und der Geister im nachapostolischen Zeitalter bis auf Irenäus*, Freiburg 1899; M. Goguel, *La notion johannique de l'Esprit et ses antécédents historiques*, Paris 1902; E. Sokolowski, *Die Begriffe Geist und Leben bei Paulus*, Göttingen 1903; K. Deissner, *Auferstehungshoffnung und Pneumagedanke bei Paulus*, Leipzig 1912; H. B. Swete, *The Holy Spirit in the New Testament*, London 1912; H. Bertrams, *Das Wesen des Geistes nach der Anschauung des Apostels Paulus*, Munster 1913; W. Reinhard, *Das Wirken des Heiligen Geistes im Menschen*, Freiburg 1918; H. Leisegang, *Der Heilige Geist*, Leipzig–Berlin 1919; E. Scott, *The Spirit in the New Testament*,

London 1923; H. von Baer, *Der Heilige Geist in den Lukasschriften*, Stuttgart 1926; F. Büchsel, *Der Geist Gottes im NT*, Gütersloh 1926; R. B. Hoyle, *The Holy Spirit in St Paul*, London 1926; P. Gächter, 'Zum Pneumabegriff des heiligen Paulus', *ZKT* 53 (1929), 345–408; W. Michaelis, *Reich Gottes und Geist Gottes nach dem NT*, Basle 1931; E. Fuchs, *Christus und der Geist bei Paulus*, Leipzig 1932; W. Grundmann, *Der Begriff der Kraft in der ntl. Gedankenwelt*, Stuttgart 1932, 92–106; E. B. Allo, 'Sagesse et Pneuma dans la première Epître aux Corinthiens', *RB* 43 (1934), 321–46; N. A. Waaning, *Onderzoek naar het gebruik van 'pneuma' bij Paulus*, Amsterdam 1939 (dissertation); H. E. Dana, *The Holy Spirit in Acts*, Kansas City 1943; K. L. Schmidt, 'Das Pneuma Hagion als Person und Charisma', *Eranos-Jahrbuch* 13 (1946), 187–235; J. Loncke, 'Liber Actuum apte vocatur Spiritus Sancti Evangelium', *Collationes Brugenses* 46 (1946), 46–52; C. K. Barrett, *The Holy Spirit and the Gospel Tradition*, London 1947 (see also *Expository Times* 67 [1956], 142–5); F.-M. Braun, 'L'eau et l'Esprit', *RT* 49 (1949), 5–30; K. Prümm, 'Die katholische Auslegung von 2 Kor 3:17 in den Letzten vier Jahrzehnten', *Bbl* 31 (1950), 316–45 and 459–82; and 32 (1951), 1–24; J. Schmid, 'Geist und Leben bei Paulus', *GL* 24 (1951), 419–29; J. Michl, 'Der Geist als Garant des rechten Glaubens', *Vom Wort des Lebens* (Festschrift M. Meinertz), Münster 1951, 142–55; E. Schweizer, 'Geist und Gemeinde im NT und heute', *Theologische Existenz heute*, Munich 1952; E. Schweizer, 'The Spirit of Power: The Uniformity and Diversity of the Concept of the Holy Spirit in the New Testament', *Interpretation* 6 (1952), 259–78; H. D. Wendland, 'Das Wirken des Heiligen Geistes in den Gläubigen nach Paulus', *TLZ* 77 (1952), 457–70; S. Zedda, *L'adozione a figli di Dio e lo Spirito Santo*, Rome 1952; B. Schneider, 'The Meaning of St Paul's Antithesis of the Letter and the Spirit', *CBQ* 15 (1953), 163–207; *LV* 10 (June 1953); *LV* 1 (January 1953); T. Maertens, 'Le souffle et l'esprit de Dieu', *Evangile* 14 (1954), 9–49; T. Maertens, 'L'Esprit qui donne la vie', *Evangile* 17 (1955), 7–64; O. Cullmann, *Life After Death or Resurrection of the Body*, London 1958; E. Schweizer, 'Röm 1:3f und der Gegensatz von Fleisch und Geist vor und bei Paulus', *ET* 15 (1955), 563–71; E. Schweizer, 'Die sieben Geister in der Apokalypse', *ET* 15 (1955), 502–11; E. Schweizer, 'Gegenwart des Geistes und eschatologische Hoffnung bei Zarathustra, spätjüdischen Gruppen, Gnostikern und den Zeugen des NT', *The Background of the New Testament and its Eschatology* (Studies in honour of C. H. Dodd), Cambridge 1956,

482–508; M.-E. Boismard, 'La révélation de l'Esprit Saint', *RT* 55 (1955), 5–21; *Bible et vie chrétienne* 14 (May–July 1956); M. Dibelius, *Der Herr und der Geist bei Paulus*, Tübingen 1956; J. Goitia, *La noción dinámica 'pneuma' en los libros sagrados*, Madrid 1956/7; Neil Q. Hamilton, *The Holy Spirit and Eschatology in Paul* (*SJT* occasional papers no. 6), Edinburgh–London 1957; A. Dietzel, 'Beten im Geist', *TZ* 13 (1957), 12–32; P. Bonnard, 'L'Esprit Saint selon le NT', *RHPR* 37 (1957), 81–90; M. A. Chevallier, *L'esprit et le Messie dans le Bas-Judaisme et le NT*, Paris 1958; F. X. Durrwell, *The Resurrection: A Biblical Study*, London 1969³; D. E. Holwerda, *The Holy Spirit and Eschatology in the Gospel of John. A Critique of Rudolph Bultmann's Present Eschatology*, Kampen 1959; R. Padberg, 'Pneuma und christliche Wirklichkeit', *Kaufet die Zeit aus. Beiträge zur christlichen Eschatologie*, (Festschrift T. Kampmann), Paderborn 1959, 73–91; O. Kuss, *Der Römerbrief*, Regensburg 1959², 540–95; R. T. Fortna, 'Romans 8:10 and Paul's Doctrine of the Spirit', *ATR* 151 (1959), 77–84; P. Bläser, 'Lebendigmachender Geist', *SP* II (Paris-Gembloux 1959), 404–13; J. Hermann, *Kyrios und Pneuma*, Munich 1960; P. Biard, *La Puissance de Dieu*, Paris 1960; T. Blatter, *Macht und Herrschaft Gottes*, Fribourg 1962; K. Stalder, *Das Werk des Geistes in der Heiligung bei Paulus*, Zurich 1962; O. Betz, *Der Paraklet*, Leiden–Cologne 1963; R. Koch, 'L'aspect eschatologique de l'Esprit du Seigneur d'après Saint Paul', *Stud. Paulin. Congressus Internat. Cath.* I, Rome 1963, 131–41; H. Schlier, 'Zum Begriff des Geistes nach dem Johannesevangelium', *Festschrift J. Schmid*, Regensburg 1963, 233–9; C. Huyghe, *Conduits par l'Esprit. Une école de la foi*, Paris 1964; K. Niederwimmer, 'Das Gebet des Geistes, Röm 8:20f', *TZ* 20 (1964), 252–65; E. Stauffer, *Theologie des NT*, Gütersloh 1948⁴, 144–7; Bultmann I, 153–64, 203–10, and 336–40; and II, 88–91; P. van Imschoot, Haag 535–40; M.-J. Le Guillou, *Catholicisme* IV, 477–82; R. Haubst, *LTK* v², 108–13; V. Hamp, *LTK* VIII², 568–70; J. Guillet, *DBT*, 499–505; I. Hermann, *HTG* I, 643–7; *TDNT* VI, 332–455 (=*BKW* IX); *RGG* II³, 976f, 1272–9, and 1283–6; P. H. Menoud, Allmen 168–72; W. D. Davies, 'Paul and the Dead Sea Scrolls', *Flesh and Spirit: The Scrolls and the New Testament*, 1957, 157–80; F. Nötscher, 'Geist und Geister in den Texten vom Qumran', *Mélanges A. Robert*, Paris 1957, 305–15; D. Flusser, 'The Dualism of "Flesh and Spirit" in the Dead Sea Scrolls and the New Testament', *Tarbiz* 27 (1958), 158–65 (in Hebrew).

Robert Koch

Suffering

A. *Old Testament.* 1. *Terminology:*
The Hebrew word for suffering in the
objective sense, ie, as an evil, is *ra*ᶜ
(= 'that which is evil'), but this can
mean both moral evil, that which is
vicious, and that which is harmful.
Besides this, the Old Testament expresses evil by means of paraphrases
based on the roots ᶜ*tsb* (= 'injure') *ḥly*
(= 'be sick'), *kᵓb* (= 'find oneself in a
terrible, desperate situation'), etc. The
Hebrew language has no term for
'pain' as a physical sensation, but can
only give a description of the external
appearance and behaviour of one
suffering pain, and so permit one to
deduce indirectly what the sensation of
pain is like, as well as the effect which it
has upon the spirit: *ᵓēḇel* and *tsyrîm* are
the symptoms of birth-pangs, but are
also used of pain and anguish in
general. *ḥîl* denotes the shuddering and
quaking of a body tormented with pain
and anguish; *kaᶜas* is the vexed, sullen
disposition of one suffering; *ᵓēḇel* is the
attitude of mourning; *mispēd* the lamentation and sorrowful behaviour of one
in mourning. Various expressions for
injuries, wounds, sickness, hard toil
(ᶜ*āmāl*), unpleasant sensation (*mar* =
'bitter'), etc, serve to indicate pain and
suffering, with the result that in a given
case it can only be decided with difficulty whether the pain referred to in the
passage concerned is physical or mental,
whether the expression is to be understood literally or metaphorically. This
must be borne in mind in interpreting
Lamentations, and passages such as
Is 53.

2. *Physiological and psychological concepts.* The following kinds of physical
suffering are mentioned in the Old
Testament: injuries, sicknesses, physical
chastisement, and birth-pains. Chastisement and birth-pains are considered as
so painful that they are the chief
images used to describe the extreme
anguish of mental suffering. The following causes of mental suffering are
mentioned in the Old Testament:
danger of death (2 Kings 20:1ff; Is
38:1ff); the death of children, whether
this is presumed, impending or has
already taken place (Gen 21:15f;
37:31–5; Judg 11:35; 2 Sam 19:1–5;
Tob 10:1–8), especially the death of a
first-born child or an only son (Jer
6:26; Amos 8:10; Zech 12:10).
Further causes of mental suffering are:
childlessness (Gen 15:2; 1 Sam 1:9ff);
homesickness (Ps 43; 61; 84; 137);
persecution and hostility (Num 16:15;
Jer 20:14–18; Ps 22; 38:13; 39:2f);
mockery and malicious gloating at one's
misfortunes on the part of enemies (Jer
20:7; Ps 22:7f, 13f; 31:11, 13; 42:10f;
55:3f; Job 19:18; 30:1–10); loneliness
and the sense of having been abandoned
(Ps 22:2; 31:12f; 38:10f; 88:9, 18; Is
53:3; Jer 15:17); ingratitude and
faithlessness on the part of one's own
friends and relations (2 Sam 13:19;
Jer 18:20; 20:10; Ps 41:9; 55:13ff;
Job 16:20; 19:17, 21f; Prov 10:1;
17:25; Sir 3:16; 30:9, 12); and also
the misfortune of friends and acquaint-
ances (Ps 35:13f; Job 2:11; 30:25;
42:11; Sir 7:34f)—the devout man
suffers especially when his own people
are in need (Ex 5:22; 32:11f; 2 Sam
1:11–27; Is 22:1–4; Jer 4:8, 19–31;
6:24f; 8:18–23; 13:17; 14:17f; Ezek
9:8; 21:12; Mic 1:8–16; Bar 4:9–20; Ps
44:10–23; 60:3–7; 74; 77:2–11; 79;
80:5–15; 89; 137; Lam; Neh 1:4;

Esther 4:1ff; 6:12; 2 Macc 3:16–22).

The oriental's capacity for suffering is such that any deeply felt suffering affects the entire body/soul compositum. Pain is connected with specific parts of the body: with the bones (Is 38:13; Jer 23:9; Ps 31:10; 42:10; Job 30:17); the kidneys (Ps 73:21; Job 16:13; Lam 3:12f); the liver and gall (Job 16:13; Lam 2:11; Prov 7:23); the bowels (Is 16:11; Jer 4:19; Job 30:27; Lam 1:20; 2:11); and the heart (1 Sam 1:8; Jer 4:19; 8:18; 23:9; Lam 1:20, 22; Ps 38:10; 55:4). Suffering impels the subject to outbursts of anger and cursing (Jer 11:20; 15:15; 17:18; 18:18–23; Ps 35:4–8, 26; 69:23–29; 109:6–15; 137:7ff; Job 3). It can make one physically sick (Neh 2:2; 1 Macc 6:8; 2 Macc 3:16f) and lead to despair and disgust with life (Gen 37:35; Jer 15:10; 20:14–18; Job 3; 6:8ff; 7; Lam 3:1–20; Tob 3:6). Old Testament man does not conceal his pain, but expresses it in weeping and pitiful lamentations. Such behaviour is not considered unworthy of a man. Suffering is avoided as far as possible. Any attitude of asceticism such as might in some sense lead one voluntarily to embrace suffering in order to bridle the lower instincts or to strengthen the body or the will is alien to the Old Testament. At the same time, however, the devout member of the Old Testament people does understand how to bear unavoidable suffering, especially when the service of God requires it, with exemplary fortitude.

3. *How suffering is judged of from a religious point of view*. The Old Testament considers the deeper cause of suffering to be any disturbance of the relationship between God and man through sin, and the anger of God thereby incurred. Pain in bearing children, various kinds of troubles, hardships and suffering, sickness and death, came into the world as a result of the first sin (Gen 3:16–19; Wis 2:24). In spite of this 'aetiology of the origins' of suffering not all the actual sufferings recorded in the Old Testament are interpreted as the direct effects of sin or of the divine anger, as is the case in the Babylonian Laments. At the same time suffering is in many cases considered to be punishment for sin (Gen 42:21f; 44:16; Lev 26:14–40; Num 12:9–12; 21:6; Deut 28:15–68; Judg 2:1–4, 11–18; 3:7ff; 4:1ff; 6:1–7; 10:6–16; 2 Sam 12:11–18; 24:11–17; Is 57:17; Jer 4:18; Ezek 23:33; Ps 32:3ff; 38:4f, 19; 39:12; Lam 1:18–22; 3:40–7). Other factors which were regarded as painful experiences were remorse (Zech 12:10–14; Ps 51; Is 53:1–4), the incomprehensibility of the disposition of good and bad order in the world, ie, the prosperity of the wicked and the misfortune of the devout (Ps 35; 73), disappointments encountered in the service of God (Ex 5:20f; Num 11:11–15; Is 49:4; 50:6; 52:13–53:12; Jer 1:8, 17ff; 12:5f; 20:7–13; Ezek 2:6; 24:15–18), and above all the misfortunes of the people of God (see under 2 above).

Suffering always implies temptation, and even the devout man turns against God for a time and rebels under it (Ex 5:22; Num 11:11; Jos 7:7; Is 38:17; Jer 12:1; 15:18; 20:7; Ps 79:5; 85:6; Job 7:12; 9:22; 19:6–12; 30:17–22; Lam 3:10f), so that bitter reproaches against God are wrung from the sufferer, leading to the pressing questions: 'Why?', 'How long?'. But suffering also breaks down resistance against God, so that the sinner and rebel is brought to reflect and repent (Ps 32:3ff; 34:19; 51:19), and to acknowledge his fault (Ps 32:3ff; 38:4, 18; 39:2–12). It is precisely in the hour of bitterest suffering that the longing for union with God makes itself felt (Ps 17:15; 22; 42; 84:2f; 120; 123:2; Job 19:27ff; 29:2ff).

Even when it is the ↗ wrath of God that brings suffering upon man, still God is moved to compassion by man's suffering so that he forgives and comes to his aid (Gen 21:17f; Ex 2:24; 3:7; 2 Kings 19:6f; 20:5; 22:19; Tob 3:16f; Ps 3:4; 17:6; 22:24f; 86:12–17). God richly rewards his devotees when they are faithful in enduring suffering (Gen 22:16; 1 Sam 2; 2 Macc 7:11, 36; Is 49:5; 52:13; 53:10ff; Wis 3–5; Job 42:10–17).

Thus the Old Testament achieves a rational explanation of suffering which goes far beyond all the futile attempts of other and earlier peoples and religions to find some meaning in suffering. According to the Old Testament conception suffering is intended to compel a man to decide which position he will take up, for or against God, and so to prove the faithfulness and devotion of the man concerned (Gen 22; Ps 30; Job 1:11; 2:5). It is intended to draw him out of his self-confidence, to remind him of his fault against God, and so to introduce the process of healing needful after sin (Ex 15:26; Deut 32:39; Is 19:22; 30:26; Jer 30:17; 33:6; Hos 6:1; 14:4). Suffering is indeed often a means of chastisement, but it is a chastisement that comes not from the hand of a heartless tyrant, but from God as loving Father (Jer 10:24;

30:11; 31:18; 46:28; Lam 3:33; Ps 30; 31; Wis 3:5). Suffering purifies devotion and deepens man's union with God (Sir 2:5; Wis 3:5). The Old Testament revelation on the meaning of suffering reaches its climax in Is 53; Zech 12:10–14; Dan 3:23(6)f; 2 Macc 7:37f): the suffering of the devout is a means of atonement which, by a process of substitution, takes away the guilt of the sinners and of the whole people, and so mediates salvation to others.

Already, then, in the Old Testament we find a realisation that suffering is a prior condition for the attainment of salvation on the part of sinful humanity. It is through suffering that man must enter into the joy of the kingdom of God. Between suffering and salvation there is a connection similar to that between a mother's birth-pangs and her joy (see Is 66:9f; Jer 30:6f; Mic 4:10). The most effective motive prompting the devout adherent of Old Testament religion to transcend his suffering inwardly is the thought that in suffering man draws closer to God, and contributes to the salvation of God's people. By contrast the hope of resurrection or belief in the after-life as a motive of consolation in suffering becomes a significant factor only at a very late stage (Dan 12:1f; Wis 3–5; 2 Macc 7; ↗ resurrection).

It is only for the obdurate and finally reprobate (Dan 12:2; Judith 16:17; cf Is 66:24) that suffering has the function of punishment without the further significance of salvation. So long as man is not altogether cast off from God, suffering always continues to be a grace for him, because it can still bring about his 'contrition', and thereby his forgiveness also.

The Old Testament manner of speaking, which ascribes human feelings to God, also recognises a suffering on God's part. This is the suffering of disappointed love (Gen 6:6; 1 Sam 15:11, 35; Is 1:2–5, 21; 5:1–7; 39; 65:1–4; Jer 3:6–10, 19f; Ezek 16; Hos 10:1ff; 11:1–5; 12:14f; Mic 6:1–8), or of merciful sympathy with men (Is 49:15; 66:12f; Jer 31:20; Hos 2:16f), but it never ascribes to God the kind of suffering that comes from weakness.

Bibliography: E. Balla, 'Das Problem des Leidens in der Geschichte der israelitisch-jüdischen Religion', *Festschrift H. Gunkel*, Göttingen 1923, 214–60; N. Peters, *Die Leidensfrage im AT*, Münster 1923; L. B. Paton, 'The Problem of Suffering in the Pre-exilic Prophets', *JBL* 46 (1927), 111–31; J. J. Stamm, *Das Leiden des Unschuldigen in Babylon und Israel*, Zürich 1946; J. Scharbert, *Der Schmerz im AT*, Bonn 1955; J. Scharbert, *HTG* II, 37–44; J. L. McKenzie, 'Divine Passion in Osee', *CBQ* 17 (1955), 287–99; J. A. Sanders, *Suffering as Divine Discipline in the Old Testament and in Post-biblical Judaism*, Rochester 1955; E. F. Sutcliffe, *Providence and Suffering in the Old and New Testament*, Edinburgh 1955; H. Frey, 'Zur Sinndeutung des Leidens im AT', *Wort und Dienst* 6 (1959), 45–61; O. Garcia de la Fuente, 'El Problema del dolor en la religion babilonica', *La Ciudad de Dios* 174 (1961), 43–90; J. S. Croatto, 'El problema del dolor', *RB* 24 (1962), 129–35; C. T. Francisco, 'Evil and Suffering in the Book of Hosea', *Southwest Journal of Theology* 5 (1962/3), 33–41; A. R. C. Leany, 'The Eschatological Significance of Human Suffering in the Old Testament and the Dead Sea Scrolls', *SJT* 16 (1963), 286–301; J. Salguero, 'Finalidad del dolor segun el AT', *Ciencia Tomista* 90 (1963), 369–97; R. Bultmann, *TDNT* IV, 313–24; W. Michaelis, *TDNT* V, 904–39.

Josef Scharbert

B. *Later judaism*. The attitude of later judaism to suffering is determined by the concept of ↗ retribution. At the same time it is involved in a quest for a rational solution to the problem confronting theodicy, and it hopes to achieve this by recourse to this same idea of retribution. It takes as its starting-point the idea that all men are sinners, and goes on to assert that all sufferings are connected with sin. For the devout, who are likewise not free from sin, suffering is a means of divine discipline. Sufferings are intended to compel man once and for all to examine his course, and thereby to bring him to repentance. Thereafter suffering becomes a means of atonement which obliterates sin in the sight of God. In this way God gives the devout man the opportunity of atoning for his sins in this world so that in the world to come he may be preserved from punishment (Bar [Syr] 78:6), whereas he lets the wicked go unpunished and thus withholds from him this possibility of atoning for his sins. Moreover God rewards such minor acts of virtue as he performs by prosperity in order to allow him to feel the full weight of his punishment in the world to come. This principle applies to peoples and individuals alike (2 Macc 6:12–17). The sufferings of the devout, therefore, are the chastisements of love, and their purpose is to increase merit and reward. Finally, judaism also recognises suffering endured in atonement on behalf of others (↗ mediation), which serves the purpose of atoning for the sins of the entire people. The patriarchs, Moses, David, the prophets, and Job are counted as men who have suffered on behalf of the entire people in this way. But above all it is the death of the just and of martyrs which has this power of atonement, and so benefits the entire people. On the other hand no evidence is to be found in the literature of later judaism for the idea of the Messiah undergoing atoning suffering on behalf of others (as a development of the idea contained in Is 53). This is to be explained by the fact that the concept of the Messiah which prevailed in later judaism did not admit of the idea of a suffering Messiah.

C. *The New Testament.* For the New Testament suffering has a still greater significance than for judaism. Almost all the books of the New Testament speak of suffering in numerous passages. On one occasion Jesus designates the power of Satan as the origin of suffering (Lk 13:10–17; similarly Paul in 2 Cor 12:7; see also Acts 10:38). Nor is it disputed that suffering can be punishment for sins decreed by God. According to Lk 13:1–6 when Jesus encounters special cases of misfortune he sees in them on the one hand punishment that is deserved, on the other a warning to others. According to Jn 9:1, however, we should not enquire after the cause of the suffering of the man born blind, but rather its purpose. It is an opportunity for the works of God to be made manifest. The Jewish idea that sickness can be the result of sin and so punishment also finds expression in one passage of Paul (1 Cor 11:30–32). On the other hand, both Jesus (Lk 16:19–31) and the New Testament in general altogether deny the prevailing doctrine of the Pharisees that all suffering is retribution.

In order to understand the attitude of Jesus and of the New Testament towards suffering we must take as our starting-point the fact of his own suffering and what he has to say about it. His entire messianic work consisted of suffering in manifold forms. Jesus has neither home (Mt 8:20 = Lk 9:57), nor family (Mk 3:31–5), and as he journeys through the towns and villages of Galilee the works he performs there are exhausting. Yet he encounters a complete absence of understanding on the part of the people and bitter hostility from their leaders. The result is almost total failure and his death on the Cross. He has not only predicted this, but actually emphasised that it is willed by God (Mk 8:31; 9:31; 10:33; 14:21; Lk 13:32f). He is the suffering ↗ servant of God, who must lay down his life vicariously on behalf of the many (Mk 10:45; Lk 22:17). It is through suffering that he must enter on his glory (Lk 24:26). And just as suffering belongs to Jesus' own fate, so too it belongs to the life of his disciples. To be a disciple is to follow him in his suffering. It is to carry the cross after Jesus (Mk 8:34ff; Mt 10:38f = Lk 14:27). It is to tear oneself away from the most cherished human ties (Mt 8:19–22 = Lk 9:57–62). It implies a renunciation of life's enjoyments, of worldly esteem and repute (Mt 10:43f). It entails slander, hatred, persecution and even death as its consequences (Mk 13:1–13), and for this reason demands self-abnegation to the point of laying down one's life (Mk 8:34; Mt 10:39 = Lk 17:33; Jn 12:24f). Blessed is the disciple whom the Lord finds worthy to follow him even to a martyr's death! (Jn 11:28f). Only he who loses his life for Jesus' sake will save it (Mk 8:35). Jesus has come to bring division upon the earth, to introduce discord even into families (Lk 12:49ff = Mt 10:34–6), and this because he compels men to decide whether they are for him or against him. The reason for this manifold suffering consists primarily in the condition of this world, for which the gospel is a scandal and a folly, and which therefore hates and persecutes Jesus' disciples even as it hated and persecuted Jesus himself. But the ultimate reason for all this suffering is to be found in the will of God. It is precisely for this reason that the cross which the disciples must carry after Jesus is also the mark of election, and therefore reason for joy. Jesus pronounces those blessed who suffer slanders, calumnies, and persecutions for his sake (Mt 5:11f=Lk 6:22f).

The ↗ passion of Jesus represents a special problem, which is not confined merely to early christian apologetics. For in it the element of the divine is wholly hidden under weakness and deepest degradation. Here suffering becomes a problem of christology. What took place on Good Friday was not only a stumbling block to Jew and a folly to gentiles (1 Cor 1:23), but has appeared to christians also as incomprehensible and shocking (see Mk 8:31–3). There is one passage in which, in order to overcome this shock to faith, Paul views the passion in connection with the resurrection (1 Cor 15:3f), and then, connecting it further with Jesus' own words concerning the fact that his suffering was willed by God, goes on to explain it in the light of Old Testament prophecies, especially the Messianic interpretation of Ps 22. For the Jews, who demand signs (proofs of divine power), and for the Greeks, who seek wisdom, the preaching of Jesus crucified is indeed folly, but for those who are called it is precisely in him that the power and wisdom of God

stand revealed (1 Cor 1:22–4). It only seems that it is by his human adversaries that Christ has been laid low. In reality it was God who 'delivered him up' (Acts 2:23; 3:13–18; 4:10; 5:30f; 13:27–30; Rom 4:25; 8:32), and thereby made atonement for the world through him (2 Cor 5:19).

The words of Jesus concerning the necessity of suffering are also echoed throughout the entire New Testament in the life of the faithful. Probably the Jewish idea is also present, namely that suffering is a means of divine chastisement or ↗ discipline (Heb 12:4–11; Rev 3:19), that it is a test by which the believer must prove himself (Rom 5:3f; 1 Pet 1:7), and for this reason the christians should rejoice over their sufferings (Jas 1:2–4; 1 Pet 1:6). But this is not the specifically christian understanding of suffering, the theology of which has been developed above all by Paul. The many sufferings which the christians encounter they endure 'for the sake of the name of Jesus' (Acts 5:41), and in imitation of his example (Heb 12:1f; 1 Pet 2:20f). Suffering falls especially upon the preachers of the gospel (Acts 9:16). God has 'set them in the world as the last of all, like gladiators sentenced to death' so that they have become a spectacle for the the world, for men and for angels (1 Cor 4:9ff). But Paul does not only suffer *like* Christ, in accordance with his example (1 Pet 2:20f), and *'for* him', that is for the sake of Christ (2 Cor 4:11): he also suffers *with* him (Rom 6:3ff). His sufferings proceed from the fact that he 'exists in Christ'. In what he has to endure day by day he continually bears the death of Jesus in his own body (2 Cor 4:10). Because in baptism, as Rom 6:2ff lays down, he has died with Christ and risen to a new life, he can and must also 'become like Christ in his death' (Phil 3:10). In suffering he takes the Cross of Christ upon himself (Gal 6:14), experiences what it is to have a share in the sufferings of Christ (Phil 3:10). Therefore he can call his sufferings 'the sufferings of Christ' (2 Cor 1:5; Phil 3:10; Col 1:24) and the marks of the wounds which have been inflicted upon him in the exercise of his apostolic ministry, the marks of the wounds (*stigmata*) of Jesus (Gal 6:17). Suffering brings the christian to an awareness of his own weakness and nothingness, and guards him against the self-presumption of relying on his own strength instead of the strength of God (2 Cor 1:9; 12:7). But Paul also knows that he does not suffer as an isolated individual for himself alone. The sufferings which come so copiously upon him are for the benefit of the church, and that too not only in the sense that they cannot be thought of apart from his work as an apostle (2 Cor 11:23-9), or that he, having been consoled by God in his sufferings, can also console others (2 Cor 1:4-7), but they contribute directly to the salvation of the church, the formation of the body of Christ (Col 1:24). If death is at work in him, this is in order that life may be at work in others (2 Cor 4:12-16). And because it has this significance for him he has overcome suffering inwardly. So far as he is concerned it no longer represents any problem of theodicy, nor is there any element of harsh compulsion in it. Rather it is a grace (Phil 1:20; see also 1 Pet 2:20), so that he can say: 'I rejoice in my sufferings'

(Col 1:24). This does not mean that he is in any sense a Stoic who meets the afflictions that come upon him from without with the strength of some immovable *ataraxia* or calmness. On the contrary he is acutely aware of the reality of suffering and experiences it for what it really is. But the strength which preserves him from breaking under the burden of his sufferings is the strength of Christ who lives in him. But for Paul, as for the New Testament in general (Acts 14:22; 1 Pet 4:13; Heb 2:10; 2 Tim 2:11ff), suffering is transcended by eschatology, and that too in a sense quite different from that which it bears in later judaism. The law, 'Through suffering and death to life and glory' does not apply to Christ alone. 'Provided we suffer with him in order that we may also be glorified with him' (Rom 8:17). Viewed in the light of the glory that is to come, Paul's present sufferings seem to him 'not worthy of mention' (Rom 8:18). 'For this slight momentary affliction is preparing for us an eternal weight of glory beyond all comparison. Because we look not to the things that are seen, but to the things that are unseen. For the things that are seen are transient, but the things that are unseen are eternal' (2 Cor 4:17).

The theology of suffering of the fourth gospel appears from the teaching concerning the ↗ 'world' which is peculiar to this gospel. Because the disciples called by Jesus out of the world have been chosen from the rest (15:19), they no longer belong to the world, even though they still exist in it. And for this reason they incur the hatred of the world, and participate in Jesus' own fate (15:18-21). The suffering which they must bear is a necessary corollary of their belonging to Jesus; therefore it is the beginning of that joy which, since it does not derive from the world, lasts for ever (16:21f).

Bibliography: On B: S. Büchler, *Studies in Sin and Atonement*, London 1922; SB II, 274–82; *TDNT* v, 617f; W. Wichmann, *Die Leidenstheologie*, Stuttgart 1930.

On C: A. Juncker, *Jesus und das Leid*, Berlin 1925; R. Liechtenhan, 'Die Überwindung des Leidens bei Paulus und in der zeitgenössischen Stoa', *ZTK* 3 (1922), 368–99; J. Schneider, *Die Passionsmystik des Paulus*, Leipzig 1929; A. Wikenhauser, *Die Christusmystik des Apostels Paulus*, Freiburg 1956[2]; K. H. Schelkle, *Die Passion Jesu in der Verkündigung des NT*, Heidelberg 1949; Bultmann (see Index); *TDNT* IV, 313–27; *RGG* III[2], 1563–5; J. Coste, 'Notion grecque et notion biblique de la souffrance éducatrice', *RSR* 43 (1955), 481–523; E. F. Sutcliffe, *Providence and Suffering in the Old and New Testament*, Edinburgh 1955; J. Carmignac, 'La théologie de la souffrance dans les hymnes de Qumran', *RQ* 3 (1961/2), 365–86; *RGG* IV[3], 297–300.

Josef Schmid

Taking up

References to bodily 'taking up' or ascension into heaven are to be found in the Old Testament where they are expressed by means of the technical term *lāqah*.

1. According to the early passage of Gen 5:23 (P), after 365 years (one for each day of the solar year) Enoch, the seventh (the number of perfection, fullness) of the antediluvian patriarchs, was taken away (*lāqah*) by God by reason of the holiness of his life. What is this 'taking away' or 'up' intended to convey? Probably the primary intention of the priestly writer is to emphasise that the prophet of cosmic religion (Jude 14) could not fall victim to the penalty of the flood. This is why God took him to himself. Does this mean, then, that it was by a death that was in some sense premature? When he died he would not yet have attained the great age of the rest of the patriarchs. Nevertheless the fact that the years of his life were so immense in number was regarded in ancient times as a special sign of divine favour. It is only in the last century BC that death at an early age is ascribed to God's special favour (see Wis 4:7–20). Others envisage a physical taking up to heaven, so that Enoch would have provided a type of the resurrection and ascension of Jesus Christ. But until the resurrection of Christ heaven remained closed to unredeemed mankind (see Mt 27:52f). Medieval theologians, therefore, thought that it was a 'taking up' into paradise that was meant (this idea is already to be found in Jub 4:23; see also Gen 2:15). Others contend that the phrase signifies an 'ecstasy'.

Surely, however, the literary form in which the description is couched points in another direction. According to the Epic of Gilgamesh the hero Utnapishtim is taken up (*leqû*) by the gods together with his wife, and is admitted to their fellowship (Gressmann, *AOT* I, 1908, 55). The biblical author must have adapted this mythological idea to his monotheistic beliefs. After a life of great holiness Enoch would have been admitted into blessed fellowship with God without descending into Sheol, where man had to endure a diminished and shadowy form of existence far from God. But the sacred author does not go into any closer detail as to the manner in which this would have taken place.

However this may be, the mysterious fate of Enoch gave rise to an immense wealth of speculation in the literature of later judaism, eg, Sir 44:16; Wis 4:10f. In addition to the references here, which are relatively sober in character, the figure of Enoch became the centre of a whole group of legends in the apocrypha, and traces of these legends have survived in the New Testament as well. In Enoch (Eth)—from the first half of the first century BC—the 'taking up' of the patriarch does seem to approximate to an 'ecstasy' similar to that in which Paul was 'caught up' into the third heaven (2 Cor 12:2). In the course of his ecstasy Enoch is inaugurated in the mysteries of the heavenly cosmology and the plans of God (Enoch (Eth) 14:8-11, 70-71). Enoch (Slav), from the first century AD, describes the taking up of Enoch and his journey through the seven heavens, the purpose of which is that he may live there for ever (1–21; 22:4–10; 23:6; 33:8f; 47:2; 48:6; 50:4; 68:2; Jub 10:13. See *TDNT* ii, 554f).

In the New Testament Heb 11:5 repeats ideas which have often been expressed in Enoch (Eth) and in Jub 10:17. Jude 14 appears to be taken word for word from Enoch (Eth) (60:8).

2. *Elijah* is separated from his disciple by a fiery chariot, and taken up (*lāqaḥ*) to heaven in a tempest (2 Kings 2:3, 5, 11). This too has been taken as referring to an 'ecstasy'. According to the context, however, this was the occasion on which Elijah bade farewell to Elisha for ever. Henceforward he no longer appears on the scene. The ancient tradition is that this great zealot for Yahweh's cause, like Enoch, escaped the fate of descending into Sheol and instead went straight to God. The fiery horses and the fiery chariot, like the pillar of fire at the Exodus and other examples, served merely to symbolise the fact that God was present in a special sense. According to the ancient popular conception the place for a man of such outstanding quality could only be close to God.

This background of mystery and the prophecy of the return of the prophet after he had been taken up (Mal 3:23f=LXX 4:4f) were still arousing lively interest in later times (see Sir 48:9, 12; 1 Macc 2:58; Enoch (Eth) 89:52; 93:8; Josephus, *Antiq.* 9:28) among the Jews of the New Testament period (Mt 16:14 and parallels; Mt 17:10–13=Mk 9:11–13; Mt 27:47–9 =Mk 15:35–6; Lk 9:8=Mk 6:15; Jn 1:25). According to Mt 17:12 the return of Elijah before the day of judgement as foretold in Mal 3:23 is probably to be understood, not in the sense that Elijah was to return in person, but rather of the advent of a man in the spirit and power of Elijah. Late judaism added further details to the miracle story. From the fact that Elijah was 'taken up' it was deduced that he was without sin. He was elevated to angelic status, and regarded as an intercessor for Israel, the friend of the poor and the deliverer of the oppressed. No less than three late apocalypses of Elijah were in circulation (see Haag 380f).

3. In the fourth of the 'Servant of Yahweh' poems we are told that after his atoning suffering on behalf of others this mysterious figure was 'taken up' (*lāqaḥ*) (Is 53:8), probably in glory to

898

God like Enoch and Elijah: 'By reason of his sufferings he shall look upon the light' (Is 53:11), ie, experience resurrection and glorification in his own body.

Thus the biblical concept of 'taking up' contained within itself, however obscurely, the germ of belief in the resurrection and ascension. A similar idea is to be found in two of the psalms. The pious suppliant hopes to be 'taken up' from his state of dire need into glory by means of an extraordinary intervention on the part of God: 'But God will ransom my soul from the power of Sheol. For he will take me up (*lāqaḥ*)' (Ps 49:15). 'Thou dost guide me with thy counsel and afterwards thou wilt take me up (*lāqaḥ*) into thy glory' (Ps 73:24). This hope, faint echoes of which are to be discerned in the ancient texts and the two psalm passages (see von Rad I, 406f), is developed further in the post-exilic period (see Ezek 37:1-14; Is 26:19; Dan 12:2-3; 2 Macc 7:9, 11, 14, 23).

In this sense the ancient idea of 'taking up' remotely foreshadows and prepares for the ascension of Christ into heaven, the climactic event of salvation history.

Bibliography: Apart from the commentaries on Genesis and 2 Kings, see esp.: W. Bousset, 'Himmelsreise der Seele', *ARW* 4 (1901), 136–69 and 229–73; P. Billerbeck, 'Der Prophet Elias nach seiner Entrückung aus dem Diesseits', *Nathanael* 30 (1914), 43ff, 93ff, and 112ff; H. Bietenhard, *Die himmlische Welt in Urchristentum und Spätjudentum*, 1951; W. Reiser, 'Eschatologische Gottessprüche in den Elisa-Legenden', *TZ* 9 (1953), 327–38; J. Daniélou, *Holy Pagans in the OT*, London 1956, 45–59; *Elie le Prophète* I–II (*Etudes Carmélitaines*), Bruges 1956; K. Galling, 'Der Ehrenname Elisas und die Entrückung Elias', *ZTK* 53 (1956), 129–48; J. Steinmann, *Le prophétisme biblique des origines à Osée*, Paris 1959, 112–15; *TDNT* II, 556–60 and 928–41; Haag 380f, 399, and 688f; *RGG* II³, 424–7; *RGG* III³, 334f; *LTK* III², 905 and 806–10; *EKL* II, 159f; SB IV, 764–98.

Robert Koch

Temple

As with all religions, so too in the Old Testament the cult, the external worship paid to God, and the place of cult are located where this worship is manifested to the divinity, and where it hearkens to the believers and, at least during the actual cultic ceremonies, is thought to be present in a special way. The choice of the sanctuary does not depend upon human caprice, but is determined by God, who manifests himself to man for the purpose (Ex 20:24; Judg 6:24–6; 2 Sam 24:16–25). This place is sacred, and must be respected as such by man (Ex 3:5). The Old Testament traditions have preserved the memory of various shrines from the time of the patriarchs: Shechem (Gen 12:6f; 33:18–20), Bethel (Gen 12:8; 28:10–22), Mamre (Gen 13:18), and Beer-sheba (Gen 21:33; 26:23–5; 46:1–4). The sacred tabernacle employed during the sojourn in the wilderness is represented as conforming to the pattern of the Jerusalem temple (Ex 25:16; 40:20). It was used for Moses to speak with God (Ex 32:11), and for the encounter of God with Moses and the people (Ex 29:42f; 30:36). Before the temple was built at Jerusalem there were shrines at Gilgal (Josh 4:19), Shiloh (Josh 18:1; 21:2), Mizpah (1 Sam 7:5–12), Gibeon (2 Sam 21:1–14), Ophrah (Judges 6:11–32), and Dan (Judg 17–18).

The building of the temple of Solomon at Jerusalem was completed in the tenth century (1 Kings 6f). David had paved the way for this by transferring the ark to Jerusalem (2 Sam 6) and by the building of an altar there (2 Sam 24:16-25). The temple was built on the rocky outcrop at the north of the Ophel (2 Chron 3:1), where at a later date the temples of Zerubbabel and Herod were also built. It consisted of a vestibule (*'ûlām, 'êlām*: 1 Kings 6:3; 7:19), the Holy Place (*Hêkāl* = the principal division of the temple: 1 Kings 6:3), and the Holy of Holies (*Debîr*: 1 Kings 6:5, 19-23, also called *qōdeš qadašîm*). In front of the entrance to the temple were placed two bronze pillars (1 Kings 7:15-22, 41f), which are reminiscent of the steles which stood before the ancient Canaanite sanctuaries. The names by which they were called, *Jākîn* (='he erects') and *Bōʿaz* (='with power') suggests that they were built after the model of the Egyptian Jed pillar, a symbol of permanence (of temple and dynasty) familiar throughout the ancient Near East at that time. In the forecourt were placed the altar of whole burnt offerings (2 Kings 16:14), the 'bronze sea' (1 Kings 7:23-6), and the ten lavers (1 Kings 7:27-39). In the Holy Place stood the altar of incense (1 Kings 6:20f), the table of shewbread and the ten lamps (1 Kings 7:48f). The Holy of Holies where the ark was enshrined (1 Kings 6:23-8) was separated from the Holy Place by a dividing wall of wood with a door to which five steps led up, and which corresponded to the 'thin walls' of Ezek 41:3, and the veil of the tabernacle (Ex 26:33) or in the temple of Herod (Josephus, *Bell.* v,

5, 5). In comparison with non-biblical temples this temple does exhibit certain similarities in detail, but there are differences also. The similarities are to be explained by the sacral architecture which was general at that time, and by the fact that non-Israelite builders were engaged for the work (1 Kings 5:6, 18). In the Assyrian temple there was no dividing wall separating the Holy Place from the Holy of Holies, so that the cultic image which stood upon the podium (Holy of Holies) was constantly visible. Unlike the immense temple tower at Babylon, which was likewise divided into three parts, the Holy of Holies did not constitute a temple situated at the summit.

Since the temple was built and maintained by the kings (1 Kings 15:15; 2 Kings 12:19; 15:35; 16:10-18), it was a royal sanctuary (Amos 7:13), but it was also essentially more than that, because David had intended a house for Yahweh (2 Sam 7:1f), and Solomon actually did build this and, together with all Israel, consecrated it (1 Kings 8:1-5, 13, 62-6).

The temple of Solomon was destroyed in 587 BC, and its equipment was carried off to Babylon (2 Kings 25:13-17; Jer 52:17-23). In the exile Ezekiel had his vision of a new temple (Ezek 40:1-44:9). This was not in fact ever realised in practice, but the prophet had known the temple of Solomon, and he ascribed the same proportions to his visionary temple, so that his description of it could have influenced both Zerubbabel and Herod. After the exile, under Sheshbazzar (Ezra 5:16), the rebuilding of the temple began, and it was completed under Zerubbabel in 515 (Ezra 4:24-5:2; Hag 1:1-2, 9;

Zech 4:7–10). The temple of Herod was begun in 20 BC and completed in all essentials ten years later. The building may not have been wholly completed, however, right up to the time of the destruction of Jerusalem in AD 70.

The temple of Solomon was the religious centre of Israel and continued to be so even after the division into two kingdoms, in spite of the schismatic sanctuaries of the northern kingdom at Dan and Bethel (see 1 Kings 11:32). After the ark of the covenant had been brought into the temple God took possession of it as his house, and the cloud filled the temple (1 King 8:10). It is recognised that a cloud is repeatedly mentioned as a type and symbol of the presence of God (see Ex 33:9; 40:34f; Num 12:4–10; Is 6:1–4; Dan 7:13; Mt 24:30; 17:5; Acts 1:9; 1 Thess 4:17), and the darkness in the Holy of Holies was also intended to recall this (1 Kings 8:12). The temple as the dwelling place of God for all eternity (1 Kings 8:13), combined with faith in the special presence of God in the temple, constitutes the basis for the temple cult and the honouring of the temple on the part of the believers (see Ps 27:4; 42:4; 76:2; 84; 122:1–4; etc). In spite of their alleged hostility to the cult the prophets shared this conception (see Amos 1:2). From the time of Isaiah onwards the name 'Zion' has a religious significance, for by reason of the temple it is the 'mountain of Yahweh' (Is 2:2; etc;↗mountain), the 'glorious throne' of Yahweh (Jer 14:21). Admittedly the prophets preached that the presence of Yahweh in the midst of his people is a free gift of grace which can be forfeited by the people's own unfaithfulness (Jer 7:1–

15; 26:1–15). Ezekiel saw the withdrawal of God's glory from the temple, which was profaned by sin (Ezek 8–10), but the Lord will return to a new temple in order to have his throne in the midst of the children of Israel for ever (Ezek 43:1–12). The idea that the temple is Yahweh's dwelling-place was also the principal motive which hastened the rebuilding of the temple after the Exile (Zech 2:13; 8:3).

This conception of the presence of God in the temple led, however, to theological difficulties. If Yahweh utters his voice from Zion (Amos 1:2; Is 2:3 = Mic 4:2) his presence still appears to be in some way connected with the material temple. How can the transcendence of the cosmic Lord be reconciled with his historical presence in Israel? The Deuteronomist editor of the Books of Kings puts this question on the lips of Solomon (1 Kings 8:27), and as the solution to it he lays down that the believer prays in the temple and Yahweh hears him in heaven (1 Kings 8:30–40). In other words, if we follow the meaning of the Deuteronomist way of putting the matter, the idea of the presence of God is mitigated to the extent that it is the 'name of Yahweh' which dwells here (1 Kings 8:17, 29; see also Deut 12:11; 14:23; 16:2, 6, 11; 26:2; Jer 7:12). Since the name represents the personality of its bearer, the presence of the 'name of Yahweh' means that God is present in a special sense. This theological speculation arrives at its logical conclusion in the conception of the *shekinah* in judaism, the idea that God is graciously present in the midst of Israel without his character as transcendent being thereby impugned.

The temple is above all a sign of the free and gracious election of God, who has himself designated the site for the temple by means of a theophany (2 Sam 24:16; 2 Chron 3:1), and thereby has chosen his dwelling-place (Ps 68:17; 76:2; 78:68; 132:13; Deut 12:5). In this connection the election of David and the endurance of his dynasty are often set in parallelism (see 1 Kings 8:16; 11:13, 32; 2 Chron 6:5f). The unexpected raising of the siege of Jerusalem by Sennacherib in the year 701 BC was greeted as an historical ratification of the promises of God (2 Kings 19:34; Is 37:35), and an unshakeable trust emerged in the inviolability of the temple (Jer 7:4). After the people's faith had been put severely to the test in the year 587, faith still arose once more during the post-exilic period in a new election of Jerusalem as the dwelling-place of the 'name of Yahweh' (Neh 1:9; Zech 1:17; 2:12; 3:2).

Under the influence of hellenism Jewish thinkers, in a manner similar to many of the fathers of the church and theologians of the Middle Ages, sought to discover a cosmic symbolism in the temple. Now it is true that the temple was built after the pattern of temples not mentioned in the bible which belonged to non-Israelite peoples. These, therefore, could have had symbolic meanings in mind when they built it, but this cannot be proved, and still less can it be shown that Israel would have known of these symbolic meanings and would have taken them over. Nowhere in the biblical text do we find mention of the temple having a cosmic significance, or of any intention to make the three divisions of the temple correspond to the three cosmic spheres (heaven, earth, underworld), or of the bronze pillars being connected with the sun and the moon, or the lamps with the five planets, or the lavers with rain-clouds, or the 'bronze sea' with the primordial ocean and more alleged correspondences of the same kind. Only the darkness in the Holy of Holies has a symbolism, but this is stated in the text, and is not cosmic in character, for the darkness symbolises the cloud with which God veiled his presence (1 Kings 8:12). Obviously the temple did have a symbolic significance, but one which can be deduced not from myths, but only from the history of the Old Testament. Just as the great cultic festivals recalled the liberation from the Egyptian bondage, and as the ark of the covenant recalled the covenant of God with his people, so too the temple constituted a token of the election of Jerusalem and of the Davidic dynasty by Yahweh.

The prophets had a positive attitude towards the temple, but resisted any over-emphasis on the cult of the temple at the expense of religious morality. When Nathan explains that in earlier times Yahweh neither possessed a house nor required one (2 Sam 7:5-7), this did not mean that the building was to be postponed until the time of Solomon —as the gloss to 2 Sam 7:13 and the redactor of 1 Kings 5:5 suggest—but that he absolutely refused to have a temple. In fact the building of a temple seemed to many Israelites tantamount to a breaking of faith with the bridal time of Israel in the wilderness, and a concession to pagan forms of cult. Moreover this negative attitude to the temple continued to survive even later, even if it was not always apparent on the surface. After the exile there were protests against the rebuilding of the temple on the grounds that Yahweh had no need of any temple (Is 66:1). Stephen too refers explicitly to this (Acts 7:48). When Jesus utters the prediction of the destruction of the temple and the rebuilding of another temple not built with human hands, (Mk 14:58) the material temple is transformed into a spiritual one; the living stones of this spiritual temple are the members of the New Testament people of God (1 Pet 2:4f), who are firmly knit together through Christ as their cornerstone (Eph 2:20–22). As *verbum incarnatum* he *is* the presence of God for ever, and it is through him that salvation is mediated. ↗ Cult.

Bibliography: K. Galling, 'Das Allerheiligste in Salomons Tempel', *JPOS* 12 (1932), 43–6; W. F. Albright, *Archeology and the Religion of Israel*, Baltimore 1942, 142–55; J. Daniélou, *Le Signe du Temple ou de la Présence de Dieu*, Paris 1942; J. Daniélou, 'Le symbolisme cosmique du Temple de Jérusalem', *Symbolisme cosmique et Monuments religieux*, Paris 1953, 61–4; M. Schmidt, *Prophet und Tempel. Eine Studie zum Problem der Gottesnähe im AT*, Zollikon–Zürich 1948; A. Parrot, *Le Temple de Jérusalem*, Neuchâtel–Paris 1954; L. H. Vincent and A. M. Steve, *Jérusalem de l'AT* II–III, Paris 1956, 373–610; L. H. Vincent, 'Le caractère du Temple de Salomon', *Mélanges A. Robert*, Paris 1957, 137–48; S. Yeivin, 'Jachin and Boaz', *Eretz-Israel* 5 (1958), 97–104; E. L. Ehrlich, *Die Kultsymbolik im AT und im nachbiblischen Judentum*, Stuttgart 1959, 24–33; W. Kornfeld, 'Der Symbolismus der Tempelsäulen', *ZAW* 74 (1962), 50–57; de Vaux, 312–440.

Walter Kornfeld

Temptation

A. *The Old Testament*. The verbs *nāsâh*, *peiran*, and *peirazein*, 'to make an

attempt, have experience of' etc (see 1 Sam 17:39; Eccles 7:23; Wis 2:24; etc), 'to prove, test' (1 Kings 10:1; Dan 1:12, 14; etc), are used in the profane sense, but they can also have a religious meaning, and it is this that is primary in the biblical usage. As used in this sense they can have either God or Satan or man himself as their subject.

1. The classic example is the temptation of Abraham (Gen 22:1–19). The result of this is expressed in v 12: 'Now I (God) know that you fear God'. By the use of his free will in taking a decision (↗ freedom) the man proves himself to be godfearing, obedient to God. In exactly the same way God also puts the entire people to the test (Ex 15:25f; 16:4; 20:20; Deut 8:2; Judg 2:22) as to whether they keep his commandments, do not fall into pagan practices etc. This testing is part of his work of salvation, for his commandments are designed to show the way by which salvation can be attained.

2. This continues to be the basic purpose of testing even in cases in which (in later passages) ↗ Satan appears as the tester or tempter, as in Gen 3:1–19; 4:1–16(?) or in the narrative framework of the Book of Job. This precise point is illustrated in Gen 4:7 in the words which God addresses to Cain: 'If you do well, you will be accepted, and if you do not do well, sin is couching at the door. . . .' Cain's testing consists in the fact that God, by a free decision of his will (see Ex 33:19), accepts Abel's offering, but refuses Cain's—no reason is assigned in the text for God acting thus—whatever the circumstances may be in which this has been made known

(perhaps in the success or lack of attained by the two brothers respectively).

In the Wisdom books Abraham is held up as an example of how to behave in temptation (Sir 44:20; see also Judith 8:25f; 1 Macc 2:52), although here (see especially Sir 2:1; 4:17; 33:1; Wis 3:5f) the idea of educating also has a part to play. God disciplines (↗ discipline) and educates man through ↗ suffering. This idea, characteristic of the Wisdom literature, also occurs in Philo, although in his case, as also in that of Josephus, the word *peirasmos* is not used. *nāsâh* is also absent from the Qumran texts, even though the reality being treated of there is testing or tempting. The 'sons of darkness' seek to lead the 'sons of light' into apostasy (1 QM), the angel of darkness and his wicked spirits strive to seduce the just (1 QS 3:21–5; 4:15–18; cp CD 14:5).

3. Man 'tempts' God when he doubts his will to save or his power to deliver. Wis 1:2: 'He is to be found by those who do not put him to the test, and shows himself to those who do not distrust him' (see Ex 17:1–7; Num 14; Ps 78:17f, 40f; 95:8f; 106:14; Is 7:12). The requirement not to tempt God (Deut 6:16f; Sir 18:23) is a requirement to exercise ↗ faith. The New Testament too recognises this kind of culpable want of faith and disobedience (compare 1 Cor 10:9 with Ps 78:18, and Heb 3:8f with Ps 95:8f), which constitute rebellion against God and incur severe punishment (Acts 5:9; 15:10).

B. *The New Testament.* 1. *peirasmos* is that alien factor in man's life by which he is brought into a state of wavering and instability so that he has already almost fallen into the power of the evil one. We do not often find it stated who brings this about. In Jas 1:13 objections are raised against describing God as tempter (in order to make him responsible for one's own sins). In Paul the 'tempter' is Satan (1 Thess 3:5; cp 1 Cor 7:5), as also in the saying of Jesus about Peter being 'sifted as wheat' (Lk 22:31). In 1 Cor 10:13 we find a reference to 'human temptation', that is, to one which human nature is able to endure. Clearly there is also one in which fall and sin are already implicitly present. As used in this sense it must be said that 'God himself tempts no man' (Jas 1:13), ie, he does not *seduce* anyone (into sin). The admonition to 'take heed to yourself lest you are led astray' in Gal 6:1 has the same basic meaning, and there is a parallel passage to this in 1 Cor 10:12: 'Let anyone who thinks that he stands take heed lest he fall'. Again, Mt 6:13 (Lk 11:4) is not a prayer for total immunity from temptation, but a cry for help in case of attack. It represents a negative formulation of the same idea which is expressed positively in the second half of the verse (parallelism): 'Deliver us from evil', ie, from the power of Satan. (The phrase *apo tou ponērou* is masculine and should be taken as referring to the evil one, see J. B. Bauer, *VD* 34 [1956], 12–15). The English words *tempt* and *temptation* are still too neutral in import. Like our term *seduce*, the New Testament word sometimes, as in the passages referred to above, of itself carries the implication of the evil outcome (precisely as opposed to any possible good outcome) of the temptation.

2. The ⁊ sufferings which christians must take upon themselves for Christ's sake are also called *peirasmoi*. Since these are, basically, tests of faith and constancy one should actually rejoice at them (Jas 1:2f, 12; 1 Pet 1:6; 4:12f, 17). Rev 3:10 and 2:10 contain references to the eschatological affliction, in which the devil makes special efforts to lead the faithful into apostasy. In this connection also we may mention the references to Jesus being tempted in Heb 2:18; 4:15. These are to be related not to the temptation stories in the synoptics, but (as can be seen from Heb 5:7–9) to the terrible sufferings of Gethsemane. He became 'in every respect tempted as we are' (Heb 4:15; cf Lk 22:28), ie, he endured all the sufferings which men have to endure (cf Lk 22:28), but without sin.

Sufferings do indeed constitute 'temptation' in that they can become the occasion of unbelief and lack of trust (as in the case of Cain); but they can also, as in the case of Job, become the occasion of boundless trust in God; see Heb 5:8, of Jesus.

At this point too it may be appropriate to recall a non-biblical saying attributed to Jesus: 'No-one can attain to the kingdom of heaven without being tempted' (Tertullian, *De baptismate* 20). See, too, Lk 24:26, in which *edei* (lit. = 'it was necessary') as used of Christ's sufferings is to be understood as implying, not that these constituted his unavoidable lot, but rather that they represented the task which God had laid upon him (see E. Fascher, *BZNW* 21 [1954], 228–54). See also Lk 22:28f (and on this again NmRabbah 15 [179a], SB I, 136, and Ex Rabbah 31 [91c], SB I, 822).

3. The temptation of Jesus (Mk 1:12f; Mt 4:1–11; Lk 4:1–13) is a repetition of the temptation of the chosen people in the wilderness. The Messiah must, as it were, undergo once more the great experiences of the history of Israel, must undertake these once more, and so bring that history to its consummation. Jesus emerges victorious from those temptations to which Israel succumbed in the wilderness, applying to himself certain readings from Deuteronomy (Mt 4:4; cf Deut 8:3; Mt 4:10; see also Deut 6:13). The essential significance of the temptation stories of Jesus is that they show: (a) that Jesus is the Son of God in that sense in which the title had been applied to him just before at his baptism; and therefore (b) not in the sense expected by his contemporaries. He remains true to the mission laid upon him by God in spite of the seductive ideas of a temporal and worldly messianism suggested to him by Satan (⁊ scandal, ⁊ sin B 1).

Bibliography: H. Seesemann, *TDNT* vi, 23–36; E. Lohmeyer, *Das Vaterunser*, Göttingen 1946, chapters 8f; K. G. Kühn, *ZTK* 49 (1952), 200–22; S. Lyonnet, *Bbl* 39 (1958), 27–36. On A2: M. Buber, *TZ* 7 (1951); J. B. Bauer, *Die Biblische Urgeschichte*, Paderborn 1956, 37–54; J. B. Bauer, *TPQ* 103 (1955), 126–33; J. B. Bauer, *Der Seelsorger* 24 (Vienna 1954), 226–9 and 328–30. On Qumran: K. Schubert, *TLZ* 78 (1953), 495–506; Nötscher, esp. 82f and 171–4. On B2: W. Nauck, *ZNW* 46 (1955), 68–80. On B3: R. Schnackenburg, *TQ* 132 (1952), 297–326; J. Dupont, *NTS* 3 (1957), 287–304; J. Guillet, *Leitgedanken der Bibel*, Lucerne 1954, 26–8; M. J. Sykes, *Expository Times* (1961/2), 189f.

Johannes B. Bauer

Thanksgiving

In the bible far more references are to be found to thankfulness towards God than to thankfulness towards men. Indeed, in the New Testament, the only instances of the latter are in Acts 24:3 —the words of one who is not a christian—and Rom 16:4. The thought of the bible is theocentric, and thanksgiving is the response to the freely offered gifts of God. In the Old Testament, thanksgiving towards God is expressed in the praises offered to him. Hebrew has no special word for thankfulness and thanksgiving, but expresses these periphrastically by the verbs 'to praise' and 'to glorify' (*yādâh, tôdâh*: see P. Joüon, 'Reconnaissance et action des grâces dans le NT', *ETL* 29 [1939], 112-14). Israel expresses its thanks in the form of thank-offerings (Amos 4:5; Jer 17:26; 33:11; Ps 56:12; 100:4), and in psalms of thanksgiving (Ex 15:21; Ps 48; 66; 118; 124; 135). Some of these psalms were sung as accompaniments to thank-offerings (100:1; 50:14, 23; 107:22), others betray their cultic origin by the fact that they are designed to be sung by cantor and choir or by two choirs (Ps 107; 135).

In the later books of LXX the word-group *eukharistein, eukharistia* was introduced (Judith 8:25; then Esther 8:12; 2 Macc 1:11; 2:27; 10:7; Wis 18:2). Philo ascribes the greatest significance to *eukharistein*. For him thanksgiving is the highest form of honour paid to God, the highest virtue, an effect produced by God in the soul (see P. Schubert, 122-31). In the New Testament the word-group occurs only in authors affected by hellenistic influence (in Luke twice,

Acts twice, Paul thirty-four times, John once, Revelation three times—never in the synoptics or the catholic epistles). Paul is not the creator of the word-group in the New Testament field. It was already established among the Greek-speaking Jews. Apart from brief interjections (Rom 1:25; 9:5; 2 Cor 11:31), only two of his prayers begin with the Jewish expression of praise 'Blessed be God' (2 Cor 1:3; Eph 1:3).

Jesus expresses his thanksgiving by praising his Father (Mt 11:25; Lk 10:21: *exhomologoumai*). Zechariah, too, begins his canticle in the manner of the Old Testament (Lk 1:68; see Lk 1:46–55; 2:29–32). Luke records that one of the ten lepers whom Jesus had healed returned and 'thanked' Jesus. Jesus expected this thanksgiving, and expressed his sorrow that only this single one had 'given honour to God' (Lk 17:18). The one who did so return was a foreigner (Samaritan). Acknowledgement, praise, and thanksgiving to God for benefits received is the most elemental and basic of religious acts. Lk 6:35 replaces 'the just and the unjust' (Mt 5:45) by 'the ungrateful and the selfish'. The prayer of thanksgiving becomes merely external and formal unless the attitude of thankfulness directs one's vision away from oneself to God. The self-righteous prayer of thanksgiving of the Pharisee in the temple becomes an obstacle to repentance and true righteousness (Lk 18:11). John says that Jesus 'thanked his Father for having heard him when he was preparing to raise Lazarus to life' (11:41).

'Thanksgiving' is a characteristic feature of the accounts of the institution of the eucharist: Mt 26:27; Mk 14:23

(Lk 22:17); Lk 22:19; I Cor 11:24, whereas the expression used in Mt 26:26; Mk 14:22 (see also 1 Cor 10:16) is 'to pronounce a blessing' (*eulogein*). According to the custom of his people, Jesus said the grace before and after the meal (*eulogēsen*: Mt 14:19; Mk 6:41; Lk 9:16; Mk 8:7 [the multiplication of loaves]; Lk 24:30; *eukharistēsas*: Mt 15:36; Mk 8:6; Jn 6:11, 23 [the multiplication of loaves]; Acts 27:35). The fact that the original *eulogein* ('to pronounce a blessing') has been replaced by *eukharistein* ('to give thanks') in the institution passages would have been due, not to the hellenising of the earlier word *eulogein*, but to the fact that it represents ancient 'eucharistic' terminology. Probably in his prayer over the third cup Jesus had already departed from Jewish custom in respect of form and content alike (see Mt 14:19 and parallels: 'to lift up the eyes', which was not a Jewish custom; Lk 24:30). Jesus would have been thinking with thankfulness of God's deeds of salvation of the New Testament era (see the interpretative elements). Following Jesus' example the apostolic communities were able to use at the celebration of the Eucharist a form of thanksgiving which was free and christologically motivated in place of the Jewish thanksgiving formula. Thus by reason of the special character of the eucharistic prayer of christians the eucharistic act comes to be designated as *eukharistia* at a very early stage. The episodes in the New Testament in which meals are described (such as the multiplication of loaves) became heavily coloured with this eucharistic terminology (see Meinertz 1, 132; H. Schürmann, *Der Paschamahlbericht Lk 22:[7–14], 15–18*

[*NA* 19/5], Münster 1953, 53–60). In Did 9:1–5; 10:1–4; Justin Dial 41:1; 70:4; Apol 1 65:5; 66:1f; Ignatius, *Eph* 13:1; *Smyr* 8:1, in which the prayer recited, the action performed, and the sacramental elements employed at the Lord's Supper are together called ↗ 'eucharist', the subject of thanksgiving is the mighty deeds of God, and it renders these present, so that at a very early stage it may have come to be thought of as a suitable form of *anamnēsis* (J. Betz, 158f). In the pauline communities the 'thanksgiving' in the liturgy is directed to be acclaimed by the members responding 'Amen' to it (1 Cor 14:16f; Just, *Apol* 1 65:3; see *TDNT* 1, 337). Such thanksgiving (also found in 1 Thess 5:18; Eph 5:20; Col 4:2; 3:16; 1 Tim 2:1–4) found expression in 'psalms, hymns, and spiritual canticles' (Eph 5:19f; see H. Schlier, *Der Brief an die Epheser*, Düsseldorf 1957, 246–50). Col 1:12–22 must represent a fragment of a liturgical eucharistia (G. Harder, 38ff). The celestial hymns recorded in Revelation are an echo of the eucharistic prayers of thanksgiving (Rev 4:9–11; 11:17; see also 5:9f, 12f; 7:12).

The apostle and theologian of thanksgiving is Paul. He adopts the epistolary form customary in the hellenistic world (see 2 Macc 1:11; A. Deissmann, *Licht vom Osten*, 145–50), but almost always—with the exception of Galatians, 1 Timothy, and Titus—inserts an expression of thanksgiving to God after the prescript (Rom 1:8f; 1 Cor 1:4–6 (2 Cor 1:3–4); Eph 1:15f; Phil 1:3–5; Col 1:3; 1 Thess 1:2–4; 2 Thess 1:3; Philem 4f; 2 Tim 1:3). The prescript has a special structure of its own: (a) an allusion to Paul's prayer on

behalf of the recipient; (b) commend-
ation of the community (2 Cor 1:2);
(c) the thanksgiving formula; and
(d) a transition to the eschatological
perspective (1 Cor 1:4–9; Phil 1:3–11;
Col 1:3–23; 1 Thess 1:2–4; 2 Thess
1:2–10). For Paul these introductions
to his letters are not mere formal
expressions of courtesy: rather, they are
genuine prayers of thanksgiving. (This
element emerges in a particularly
cordial form in Philippians.) At the
same time they represent a *captatio
benevolentiae* in which Paul expresses his
praise and appreciation of the communities, and so of God for having
made them worthy of praise.

Thanksgiving is a duty. It is God's
will in Christ Jesus that we should be
thankful in all circumstances (1 Thess
5:18). To give 'honour and thanks' to
God is among the basic acts by which
we acknowledge God and show our
devotion to him (Rom 1:21). Ingratitude is the vice characteristic of men in
the last days (2 Tim 3:2). Just as
eulogein (to praise or bless) is man's
response to God's *eulogia* (blessing), so
too *kharis, eukharistia* (thanksgiving) is
his response to the *kharis* (grace or
gracious gift) of God. *kharis* (in the
sense of the grace of vocation to the
apostolate) must bear fruit in the
eukharistia (thanksgiving) of those who
have been converted by the apostle
(2 Cor 4:15). In thanksgiving God is
given back what he himself has bestowed (1 Thess 3:9). Paul does not
wish to be alone in giving thanks for the
charisma of his redemption. Rather,
many individuals must join in expressing this prayer of thanks; a choir
of thanksgiving must proclaim God's
praise (2 Cor 1:11).

Thankfulness is a motive for ethical
conduct. The underlying motive of
Paul's apostolic work is that the thanksgiving of men may overflow more and
more to the glory of God (2 Cor 4:15).
Apostolic grace (here personified) seeks
constantly to extend its sphere of
influence. The ultimate goal of this
activity is that God shall be glorified.
The medium of expression in which the
first of these, apostolic grace, becomes
fruitful in the second, the glorification
of God, is that chorus of thanksgiving
which is sent up to God from the
growing number of believers in the
liturgical assemblies. Charity is to be
practised in order that by the prayers
of thanksgiving resulting from it God
may be glorified (2 Cor 9:11). Through
the apostle who has brought about the
assembly the gift which the Corinthians
give, and which itself is a gift of God,
causes God to be glorified by thanksgiving. The collect has two effects: the
relieving of need at Jerusalem, and the
copious thanksgiving by which the
recipients of it praise God. The second
of these effects quite overshadows the
first. The work of external and material
succour ('liturgy') leads on to the
further work of liturgical worship
('liturgy' also). There is no mention of
thanks being given to men. Even where
thankfulness to the human givers does
appear, it is inseparably united to an
awareness that behind all stands the sur-
passing ↗ grace of God (9:14). Through
thanksgiving, activities which are indif-
ferent in themselves become consecrated
for the most exalted aim of life. This
applies both to words and deeds (Col
3:17), and also to eating and drinking.
Paul presupposes that the Christians
say their grace in the manner strictly

prescribed among the Jews. Once it has been pronounced the entire meal becomes an expression of divine praise (*TDNT* II, 760f). Paul treats of this grace as a prayer of thanksgiving (thus Rom 14:6; 1 Cor 10:30; 1 Tim 4:3f). He himself recites it also (Acts 27:35). It is through his prayer of thanksgiving that food and drink are consecrated. 'For everything created by God is good, and nothing is to be rejected if it is received with thanksgiving. For then it is consecrated by the word of God and prayer' (1 Tim 4:4f). It is by this attitude of thankfulness that the christian acquires his decisive orientation towards the glorifying of God (1 Cor 10:31). All that the christian says or does he shall do in the name of the Lord, in that through him he gives thanks to God the Father (Col 3:17). It is the prayer of thanksgiving that provides the criterion for deciding the questions of diet: the question which arose at Rome about the strong not giving scandal to the weak in this matter (Rom 14:6), the question of the Corinthians as to whether flesh offered to idols should be eaten (1 Cor 10:30), and the question of the dietary rules laid down by heretical teachers, against which 1 Timothy is directed (1 Tim 4:3f). Thanksgiving certainly does not exempt one from paying due heed to the conscience of the weak (1 Cor 10:29f; Rom 14:20).

Paul constantly exhorts his hearers to express their thanksgiving in act. They must do this in communal worship (1 Cor 14:6f; Eph 5:20; Col 1:12; 3:17; 1 Tim 2:1) as well as in private (2 Cor 4:15; 9:11f; 1:11; Phil 4:6; Col 2:7; 4:2; 1 Thess 5:18). Christians must not pray for themselves alone, but

must offer thanksgiving and prayers on behalf of all men (1 Tim 2:1). At all times (Eph 5:20; 1 Thess 2:13) and in all things (1 Thess 5:18) thanksgiving must rise up to God. The christians are 'givers of thanks' (Col 3:17). Thanksgiving is of the very essence of the christian life. The christian must show himself 'abounding in thanksgiving' (Col 2:7) because the graces which he has received are likewise superabundant (2 Cor 9:14; 1 Tim 1:14; Eph 2:7; Phil 4:7; 2 Cor 7:4; Eph 3:19; 2 Cor 12:7; see also 2 Cor 1:5; 11:23). Prayers of petition must be constantly intermingled with thanksgiving (Phil 4:6; Col 4:2). The christian's conversation is to be characterised not by stupid chatter and unseemly levity, but by thanksgiving (Eph 5:4). Joy and thanksgiving go together (Col 1:12). Both have their basis in the gift of salvation. Paul himself is a man of thankfulness. He utters prayers of thanksgiving for himself (1 Tim 1:12) and for his communities (Rom 1:8; 1 Cor 1:4; Phil 1:3 [Philem 4]; Eph 1:16; Col 1:3; 1 Thess 1:2; 2:13; 3:9; 2 Thess 1:3; 2:13; 2 Tim 1:3). He does not know how to find an adequate expression of his thankfulness (1 Thess 3:9). Exclamations of thankfulness are interspersed through the text of his epistles (in these cases the word used for thanks is always *kharis*: Rom 7:25; 1 Cor 15:57; 2 Cor 2:14; 8:16; 9:15; see also 2 Ezra 7:17).

God's deeds of salvation constantly occupy the centre of Paul's thought. He gives thanks for ↗ faith, ↗ hope and ↗ love (Rom 1:8: faith; Eph 1:15; 2 Thess 1:3; Philem 4f: faith and love; 1 Thess 1:3: the works of faith, the self-sacrifice of love, the steadfastness of hope; 2:13: acceptance of the word of God in faith). Paul also gives thanks for the grace of God and the charisms (1 Cor 1:4–6), for joy over the believers (1 Thess 3:9), for redemption and the fruits of redemption (Col 1:12–23), for redemption from the body of death through Christ (Rom 7:25), for his fellow-workers (2 Tim 1:3), for the guidance of God in apostolic work (1 Cor 1:14), for the conquest of death (1 Cor 15:57), for the vocation to apostolic work (1 Tim 1:12), for rescue from danger of death, because thereby the apostle can go on to convert many more individuals (2 Cor 1:11), for triumph in his apostolic work (2 Cor 2:14), for the zeal of Titus (2 Cor 8:16), for the inexpressible gift which God gives to the Corinthians, and which urges them to the work of charity (2 Cor 9:15). The gifts for which Paul gives thanks pertain to eschatological salvation. The final age has no further need of the prayer of petition, but only recognises the jubilation of thanksgiving (Rev 4:9; 7:12; 11:17). The prayer of the new aeon is a prayer of thanksgiving (see G. Harder, 128f and 184).

Prayers of thanksgiving are as a rule directed to God: to God (1 Cor 1:4; 1 Thess 1:2; 2:13), to 'my God' (Rom 1:8; Phil 1:3; Philem 4), to God the Father (Col 1:12; 1 Thess 1:3), to God the Father of our Lord Jesus Christ (2 Cor 1:3; Eph 1:3; Col 1:3). The ultimate source of all gifts is God the Father. Only in one single passage is thanksgiving directed to Jesus Christ (1 Tim 1:12). Paul gives thanks for having been called to be an apostle, for this too he habitually ascribes to the Father. In this connection he takes

occasion to emphasise that he, like the rest of the apostles, has been called by Christ. Prayers of thanksgiving are uttered 'through Christ' (Rom 1:8; Col 3:17). The 'pneumatic' Christ is the mediator of thanksgiving (Rom 1:8; Eph 5:20; see G. Harder, 173–84). Thanksgiving returns to God by the same way by which his grace to men went forth from him. Through Christ the christian must hope that he can give thanks to God fittingly. Christ represents the 'solution to the crisis in prayer of antiquity' (G. Harder, 187). The Ephesians are to thank God the Father 'in the name of our Lord Jesus Christ' (Eph 5:20). This formula (and this is the only passage in the New Testament in which it is connected with 'thanksgiving') often points to the context of cultic worship as the situation in which it arose (1 Cor 5:4; 6:11; Phil 2:10; Col 3:17; 2 Thess 3:6). Thanksgiving is to be offered by the community which has assembled in the name of Jesus, and which is his mouthpiece (H. Schlier, *Der Brief an die Epheser*, 249). In the name of Jesus the fullness of those divine gifts of grace for which christians must give thanks is summed up (*TDNT* v, 272f).

Bibliography: J. Wobbe, *Der Charisgedanke bei Paulus* (*NA* 13/3), Münster 1932; G. Harder, *Paulus und das Gebet*, Gütersloh 1936; J. M. Nielen, *Gebet und Gottesdienst im NT*, Freiburg 1937; P. Schubert 'Form and Function of the Pauline Thanksgivings', *BZNW* 20 (1939); E. Kalt, *BRL* 1, 354f; E. Mócsy, 'De gratiarum actione in epistolis paulinis', *VD* 21 (1941), 193–201 and 225–32; Osterloh 81f; J. Betz, *Die Eucharistie in der Zeit der griechischen Väter* 1/1, Freiburg 1955, 156–62; H. Schürmann, *LTK* III², 158f; C. Westermann, *BHHW* 1, 320–22; B. Rigaux, *Paulus und seine Briefe*, Munich 1964, 171f.

Alois Stöger

Three

A. A ceremonial declaration or legal formula is repeated *three times* before witnesses in order to bring a legal enactment formally into force. This is what took place at the purchase of the cave of Machpelah by Abraham (Gen 23). This is still the custom in Palestine for the drawing up of a marriage contract or at the declaration of a divorce in accordance with Islamic law. In a cultural milieu where memory and the oral pronouncements of men have to be relied upon instead of written contracts, the part played by this legal form becomes immediately comprehensible.

When Jesus tells Peter that he is to be the pastor of his people (Jn 21:15–17) he employs the same form of *threefold repetition* because his words have the force of just such a legal enactment. From this it is clear that Jesus did in fact found a church with legal norms, in that by a solemn act of handing over legal authority he gave it a visible representative of himself.

Likewise in the vision of Peter (Acts 10:10ff [see also 11:10]) the *threefold* repetition of the declaration that the unclean food was clean probably has a similar purpose, being a formal legal guarantee that this declaration of God had full force.

In this connection *thrice*-repeated prayer should perhaps be mentioned. In Mt 26:39–44 Jesus solemnly submits himself to the will of the Father *three times*. In 2 Cor 12:8 Paul declares that *three times* he besought God with tears to take the sting from his flesh, but that he received the answer (*three times?*): 'My grace is sufficient for you'.

B. Like the English phrase 'a couple of', *three* can stand for a small number, 'some', 'several'. 'Three days' or 'on the third day' (both terms are materially identical) is equivalent to 'a few days', and this is a relative expression for what may be felt to be an extremely short period or, on the other hand, a long period, according to the point of view of the speaker or hearer. 'Three days' is a long time for looting to last (2 Chron 20:25), for a slaughter (2 Macc 5:14), for passing through a city (Jon 3:3), for a man to remain in the belly of a fish (Jon 1:17), for the disciples expecting some kind of sign (Lk 24:21), for parents seeking their lost child (Lk 2:46). On the other hand it represents a very brief interval for mobilisation of an army (Josh 1:11; 2 Sam 20:4), for a sickness to last until it is healed (2 Kings 20:8; Hos 6:2), for a temple to be built anew (Mk 14:58; 15:29; etc), for remaining in the realm of the dead ('resurrection in three days').

Bibliography: P. Gächter, *Petrus und seine Zeit*, Innsbruck 1957, 11–30 (on A); J. B. Bauer, *Bbl* 39 (1958), 354–8 (on B). For a more detailed treatment, see R. Mehrlein, *RAC* IV, 269–310.

Johannes B. Bauer

Time

The bible has hardly any speculations to offer on the nature of time such as are found in philosophy, at least from the time of Plato and Aristotle onwards. Hence there is no one unified concept of time in the bible and no single term for time. Instead we find various conceptions of time which find expression in the Hebrew words (or their Greek equivalents) for 'day', 'hour', 'eternity', 'aeon', 'end', 'moment', 'decisive point in time', 'now', 'today', 'festal time', etc. The biblical conceptions of time which lie behind these terms are different, in the first place, from mythological ideas of time in the ancient Near East, for these are determined by the cycles of the stars and the yearly seasons. In other words, in these mythological conceptions time is thought of in terms of cycles of time and cycles of history returning endlessly to their starting-points. But no less alien to the bible is the present-day conception of 'linear' time. In this, time is thought of as a straight line of limitless extent which, viewed from the present, extends backwards through past events and forwards through future ones. The bible, on the other hand, knows nothing of the idea of time as 'empty' space, as a prior entity which is subsequently filled out with the ordered succession of temporally distinct events. Yet it is precisely the history writing of Israel which orders the various traditions and occurrences of its own past as a people into an historical sequence so as to show their extent in time, and at the same time attaches them to cultic celebrations which are constantly and recurrently entered upon anew. On a simplified view of the matter, therefore, the biblical idea of time seems to lie between the mythical and cyclic on the one hand, and the 'linear' and accumulative on the other.

A. *Old Testament ideas of time.* The most important characteristic of the biblical idea of time is that of time which is 'filled', time 'for' something. It is based on the underlying psychology of the two Semitic or Hebrew tenses, which appears to recognise only two kinds of past, namely that of the completed event (perfect, *factum*) and that of the still uncompleted event (imperfect, *fiens*), in addition to the present and the future. Time, therefore, is conceived of subjectively from the standpoint of the beholder of history, who divides it according to the events which he himself regards as significant. These important times, referred to in Hebrew as *ʾēth* and *yôm*, were brought into connection with the periodic acts of revelation and salvation performed by God, and it is only from these that they derive their specification. They are never thought of as having any significance in themselves apart from these events, or purely as chronological points in the flow of time. Instances of this basic idea of time as specified by its content are, for example, the time for driving the flock (Gen 29:7), the time of Harvest (Joel 3:13; Mk 4:29), the time for giving birth (Mic 5:3; Lk 1:57; 2:6), the proper season for the tree to bear fruit (Ps 104:27; Acts 14:17). Thus there is a time for every matter under the sun (Eccles 3:1), which man has to use, and which imparts a rhythm to his life. The individual history of a man's life is made up, therefore, of the total sum of these rhythms in time (in the plural), and it is this history of his own life as an individual that the psalmist is referring to when he says in his prayer, 'My times are in thy hand' (Ps 31:15; see also Ezek 12:27; 24:1). The sum total of the salvific deeds of God in the life of the chosen people constitutes the time of salvific history in its total extent (see the summaries in Deut 26:5–10; Josh 24:2–13), considering these events in their relevance to the present life and worship of the individual Israelite. The word ʿōlām, which is translated 'eternity', means the time of God as extending away into invisible distances consisting of a vaguely imagined pre-history on the one hand, and an endless future on the other. As applied to mankind, however (1 Kings 1:31; Ps 73:12), it can also stand for a period which, though subjectively long, is objectively speaking of short duration, provided that the content of the period in question is of corresponding importance. As applied to God this is, of course, undoubtedly the case. Thus ʿōlām itself too is, in the last analysis, not a temporal but a qualitative concept. The Israelite experiences the impact of God's intervention upon him with special intensity at festal times, in which the salvific event which has taken place in Israel's history is rendered present in such a way that it is as though the times of the patriarchs are in some sense synchronised with those of the participators in the celebrations, who think of themselves as identical with their own forefathers (compare the later synchronisation in the Gospel of John). The events which took place at the time of the exodus from Egypt have in some sense so strongly specified that period that the individual who is engaged in commemorating them cultically believes himself to be carried back to that time, and in this way renders present the earlier salvific event (cf Mish Pesa 5:5, 10 and Ex 13:8; Deut 6:23). The idea of the 'corporate' or 'collective person' (Adam: see Rom 5; or Abraham: see Gal 4),

in whom the fate of all subsequent generations is determined, is the corresponding factor in the spatial dimension to this fusing of present and past in the temporal one. Thus from its temporal aspect salvific history is not to be equated with a process whereby the individual salvific deeds of God are assigned a place in an extent of time previously given. On the contrary the temporal sequence results, to some extent, as a byproduct, from the arrangement in a series of the events embodying God's gracious leadership of the people, which constitute times filled with salvific power.

In the prophets and in apocalyptic circles of later judaism the idea of time that is constituted by its own content, as upheld by earlier generations and in the traditions of the patriarchs, is transformed into a future hope of the judgement and fulfilment that is awaited. This now becomes as important as history for life in the present—indeed it takes the place of history. The future crisis is already making itself felt. And finally apocalyptic introduces the idea of periods by combining the mythological idea of cycles with the ancient and indigenously Israelite image of 'this-worldly' history in such a way that world history in its total extent is divided into two aeons (see 4 Ezra 7:26ff), and the approaching post-messianic aeon is presented as transcending the entire past (Enoch [Eth] 65:7f). The end to which time is directed begins to outdo its origins.

B. *The New Testament ideas of time* are based upon those of the Old Testament and judaism. With the event of Christ the new aeon, the aeon which is 'to come' has commenced (Eph 1:21;

2:7), though this does not mean that the present evil aeon has already been deprived of its power (Gal 1:4; Heb 6:5). Of special importance in the message of the New Testament is the idea of the *kairos*, the time which has as its content the work of Jesus (Mt 26:18; Jn 7:8) and the decision of man to accept or to reject this salvific event (2 Cor 6:2). In the *kairos* the gift of God and the demand that man shall lay hold of this offering of salvation on God's part is brought home to men in a definitive and unrepeatable manner (Lk 19:44; Jn 7:6), and this *kairos* of God gives certainty. In this it is unlike cosmic or human *kairos*, which has to remain in a constant state of readiness for all possible opportunities even when these are only remote. In the preaching of the kingdom of God by Jesus in the present the hour of decision has been ushered in (Lk 12:54ff), for now the turning-point of the ages has arrived. This hour of decision will remain as an enduring 'now' and 'today' until the approaching consummation, and scarcely admits of the further survival of salvific history after the Old Testament pattern, or in the sense of profane, chronological history. But in spite of its abiding expectation that Jesus' message of the kingdom of God is about to be realised, the primitive church does maintain a genuine openness to the possibility of a further stage in the revelation of God's salvific will, and for fresh acts mediating salvation to men to be performed, for a fresh beginning in the preaching of salvation, for a new 'now' of salvation history (A. Vögtle). New Testament eschatology, therefore, makes it possible for statements about the future and the present to stand side by side. Thus the present salvation is 'redemption in hope' (Rom 8:24), hope that is entertained in a dynamic present which is imbued with the approaching end (1 Cor 7:29ff). The problem of the delay of the ↗ *parousia*, which arose from the fact that at first the return of Christ was expected in the imminent future, hardly arose as a problem at all in New Testament times, but nevertheless the post-Easter expectation of the end was based particularly upon the facts, events and truths of the revelation of Christ, though not on the knowledge of any definite appointed time at which the end was to come. In spite of this the eschatological ideas on time in Paul (R. Bultmann), the lukan conception of time in terms of salvation history (Old Testament: time of the promise; gospel: Jesus as the centre of time; Acts: the time of the church; see O. Cullmann), and the johannine historicisation of eschatology cannot be reduced to a single common denominator. What is common to them all, as also to the Book of Revelation, is the revelation of the 'time of grace', the 'day of salvation' (2 Cor 6:1f) and the 'today' of God (Heb 3:7ff), which, as the time of the Holy Spirit, is to be used by those to whom the message of the bible is addressed. But the power to transcend time for all those who are in the world can only come from Jesus Christ, 'Yesterday, today and for ever', and therefore in the last analysis only from God.

In that God himself fixes the time and brings it once more to an end, he shows that he is the Lord who transcends time, and who, in spite of the fact that his work is fitted into the time process, never undergoes a temporal dissolution, or remains imprisoned by it, but maintains his being independently of the human form of existence which is of its nature temporal, in a perfection that is eternal. [W. Eichrodt, p 123.]

Bibliography: O. Cullmann, *Christ and Time*, London 1962; O. Cullmann, *Heil als Geschichte*, Tübingen 1965; R. Bultmann, *History and Eschatology*, London 1957; R. Bultmann, *Glauben und Verstehen* III, Tübingen 1960; T. Boman, *Hebrew Thought Compared with Greek*, 1960; W. Eichrodt, 'Heilserfahrung und Zeitverständnis im AT', *TZ* 12 (1956), 103–25; G. Delling, *Das Zeitverständnis des NT*, Gütersloh 1940; E. Dinkler (ed.), *Zeit und Geschichte*, Tübingen 1964; E. Fuchs, 'Das Zeitverständnis Jesu', *Zur Frage nach dem hist. Jesus*, Tübingen 1960; W. G. Kümmel, *Promise and Fulfilment*, 1957; P. Neuenzeit, 'Biblische Zeitvorstellungen', *Geschichtlichkeit und Offenbarungswahrheit*, ed. V. Berning, P. Neuenzeit, and H. R. Schlette, Munich 1964, 37–65; E. Vögtle, 'Zeit und Zeitüberlegenheit in biblischer Sicht', *Weltverständnis im Glauben*, ed. J. B. Metz, Mainz 1965, 224–53.

Paul Neuenzeit

Tradition

Tradition derives its importance from the very nature of our religion, which is wholly the outcome of a revelation. This is not constantly recurring anew, but was imparted once and for all at a specific point in human history. All men remain bound by this privileged *kairos*.

1. The fact that the concept of tradition has so many aspects often makes theological discussion of it difficult. It is therefore essential to gain a clear idea of the complexity of the concept. First, then, the word can be used in an active, an objective, or even in a documentary sense. Tradition in the active sense is the human activity of 'handing on', or even—for activities can exist only as the accidents of substances—the author of such activity, the 'tradent'. But the word can also signify the object of the 'handing on', that which is 'handed on'. The handing on of a piece of tradition is made possible chiefly by means of certain material aids drawn from the past of the individual man. These are the *monumenta traditionis*, the witnesses, whether written or otherwise, to the past.

A further division is also important, that namely which is based on the distinction between the broader and more comprehensive use of the word tradition and a narrower sense which it can also bear. In the more comprehensive sense tradition stands for all methods of handing on, including therefore the 'handing on' (in an extended sense of the term) which is the function of sacred books. In this sense holy scripture is one form, one aspect, one part of tradition. In the narrower sense, on the other hand, tradition is confined precisely to those kinds of 'handing on' which do *not* constitute the 'handing on,' in this extended sense, of the sacred scriptures or, regarded objectively, to those matters alone which have *not* been passed down from one generation to the others by means of sacred writings.

The two divisions already mentioned must now be viewed in their bearing upon a third and still more important distinction, that namely between apostolic and ecclesiastical tradition. By apostolic tradition we mean that which derives from the apostles as its active bearers or 'tradents'. This may apply either to traditions which are of divine origin or to traditions which actually originated with the apostles. The church is obviously the bearer and source of traditions, and these too can be of various kinds. The church can hand down apostolic traditions. It can also itself be the author and originator of fresh traditions.

Obviously the theology of the church, as essentially bound by revelation, is primarily interested in apostolic tradition. The distinctions drawn above give rise to the following division at this point: I. Tradition as the act of handing down or as the subject who hands down. II. Tradition as material content and as document: (a) in the broader sense, (b) in the narrower sense: the *sine scripto traditiones*, *scripta* here being understood to apply solely to the inspired scriptures.

2. In the connection between scripture and tradition three main aspects are to be distinguished. The most important, and for many christians today the most perplexing, aspect arises from the fact that scripture, regarded from the human aspect, is itself a product of tradition. But what kind of tradition? One which is principally preservative or one which is creative and gives birth to new stories? It is the second aspect which emerges from the bible's own statements about tradition, which constitute a theme. This aspect is not, of itself, identical with the first. It is not always that one can experience the mystery of a personality from the statements which the individual concerned makes about himself. It is no less difficult to deduce the nature of the tradition of the New Testament merely from a survey of the

thematic statements upon this subject contained in the bible. Finally, there is a third aspect, which has a direct relevance to the current teaching of theology on our knowledge of God. The post-apostolic christian is indeed guided by the Spirit of God, but he no longer has any direct access to the act in which God reveals himself. Instead he is told to rely upon holy scripture and on non-biblical tradition to mediate this knowledge to him. Both can be called sources in the sense in which this term is employed in scientific history, and with reference to the knowledge of faith. But how are these sources of our knowledge in faith related one to the other? In considering the problems indicated here let us confine ourselves to the difficulties which arise in connection with the New Testament.

3. The problems which arise from the nature of scripture as tradition are admittedly not apparent in the thematic statements which scripture makes about tradition. In their presentation of these statements contemporary exegetes show hardly any perceptible divergence of view.

To express the phenomenon of tradition the New Testament employs the verb *paradidonai* and the substantive *Paradosis*. For the manifold use of these terms, which occur frequently in the New Testament as also throughout the Greek language, we may refer to the article of F. Büchsel, *TDNT* ii, 169–73.

'The religion of the Old Testament and judaism is a religion of tradition, and indeed of the revelation imparted to the fathers by Yahweh, which was set down in writing in the Torah. Side by side with this in later judaism oral tradition ("the tradition of the fathers") acquires an ever increasing importance. By it the "law" is interpreted, supplemented and applied to fresh situations' (F. Mussner, 'Tradition', *LTK* x, 291). In his controversies (Mk 7; Mt 15) Jesus takes issue with the *paradosis tōn presbuterōn* (= 'the tradition of the elders': Mk 7:3, 5; Mt 15:2), with the *paradosis tōn anthrōpōn* (= 'the tradition of men': Mk 7:8), or with the *paradosis humōn* (= 'your tradition': Mk 7:9, 13; Mt 15:3, 6).

In Mt 11:27 and Lk 10:22 *paradidonai* is used in connection with the supreme power of Jesus as Messiah or Son of God: *panta moi paredothē* (= 'all things have been delivered to me'). Considerable use of *paradidonai* is also made in the passion narrative, where the frequency of its occurrence is equalled only by the frequency 'which is usual elsewhere too in accounts of trials or martyrdoms' (F. Büchsel, *TDNT* II, 172).

According to Jude 3, christian teaching is the *hapax paradotheisē tois hagiois pistis* (= 'the faith which was once for all delivered to the saints'); according to 2 Pet 2:21 it is the *paradotheisē hagia entolē* (= 'the holy commandment delivered [to them]'). 'In reality the church is aware right from the outset that the event of Christ and its abiding impact on the life of its community exercise a decisive influence on its very nature'. *paradidonai, paradosis* and *paralambanein* (= 'to receive [tradition]') are from the very outset terms which designate the manner in which tradition is developed (1 Thess 2:13; 4:1; Gal 1:9; 1 Cor 11:2, 23; 15:1, 3; Phil 4:9; see also Col 2:6; 2 Thess 2:15; 3:6; Jude 3; 2 Pet 2:21; 1 Clem 7:2; Did 4:13; Barn 19:11), and *parathēkē*

as used in the pastoral epistles is the term used for the deposit of teaching provided by tradition (1 Tim 6:20; 2 Tim 1:12, 14; see also 2:2), having been chosen, perhaps, as a juridical term in order to avoid using *paradosis*, which had been rendered suspect by the gnostics (von Campenhausen). The content of *paradosis, parathēkē* is normally right teaching as opposed to erroneous teaching. It can, however, also mean that which is ethically required (Did 4:13; Barn 19:11; 1 Clem 7:12; and in 2 Pet 2:21 probably moral requirement and teaching both together). 'The apostles' proclamation founded the tradition, and in the apostle concept the idea of tradition becomes the dominant factor' (R. Bultmann, *Theology of the New Testament* II, 119).

Already in the New Testament itself the dispute as to the authentic form and the rightful bearers of tradition is apparent (*successio apostolica*). In the post-apostolic church this goes further, and leads, among other things, to the establishing of the canon of scripture.

4. In the controversy between catholics and reformed christians concerning the theory of *sola scriptura*, the principal point of difference consists not in the acceptance or rejection of *sine scripto traditiones* (ie, traditions not contained in scripture), but in the basic religious orientation of the individual; in how he conceives of tradition in the active sense, what he thinks of the role of the church and of private judgement. This has been brought out very clearly by Newman in his *Lectures on the Prophetical Office of the Church*. In practice, for the reformed christian of the continental type, the individual conscience as enlightened by the Holy Spirit, and in

solitary engagement with the bible, probably always remains the ultimate court of appeal. He rejects every *sacrificium intellectus* of his historical or speculative understanding which 'the church' could possibly demand. The Anglican constantly commits himself to a *via media* position, which Newman unsuccessfully attempted to translate into terms of practical living. The distinctive element in the catholic's position derives from his doctrine of the church. This must never, indeed, suppress the historical or speculative understanding of the individual. In other words it must never demand an acknowledgement of the truth of propositions which are contrary to reason. But it certainly can go beyond the historical and speculative reason. Guided by the Spirit of God and of Christ, the church claims authority to interpret the will of God in applying revelation to the particular concrete situations as they arise, and it claims that its power to do this exceeds the clear reflexive understanding of the original recipient of the revelation concerned, and likewise the powers of our individual historical and speculative reason.

All this has, of itself, nothing to do with the question of the sufficiency or insufficiency of scripture in terms of its content. When and how did this question come to occupy the central point in the teaching of theologians on our knowledge of God?

The question of the *sine scripto traditiones* scarcely played any significant part before the late Middle Ages. *Sacra pagina* and *sacra doctrina* were almost synonymous terms. The concept of oral tradition is almost totally absent from the writings of Aquinas.

Admittedly, Aquinas does recognise that the apostles of the church have handed on certain prescriptions which were not set down in their writings. In practice, however, according to Aquinas, these directives are confined to the sacraments and other questions of the liturgy. He teaches, on the one hand, the sufficiency of sacred scripture with regard to subject-matter, and on the other hand that this subject-matter does include a definition of what is necessary for salvation, and that the truths necessary for salvation are not *ipso facto* identical with revelation in its entirety.

The view according to which sacred scripture contains all the truths necessary for salvation was still to be upheld by the catholic theologians of the sixteenth century. Thus, for example, Driedo and Robert Bellarmine. Again, many of the reformation theologians gave their allegiance to this idea in order to restrict the sphere of authority of the magisterium of the church. Soon the truths necessary for salvation came to be known as a fundamental article of faith, and in order to substantiate them the theologians took up the criterion formulated by Vincent of Lerins: *Quod semper, quod ubique, quod ab omnibus.* In the concrete these truths necessary for salvation were identified with the articles of the credal confession of faith interpreted in a comprehensive sense in the light of christian antiquity. In anglicanism the concept of the *fundamentals* is found in the works of G. Cassander, Hooker—the classic theologian of the *via media*—and after him many other anglican theologians, especially Bishop Laud (in his controversy with the Jesuit Fisher), G.

Calixt, and Jurieu. Not the least of those who upheld this doctrine was the anglican Newman. The doctrine of the *fundamentals* and the sufficiency of scripture and infallibility of the church as confined to this occupied the central point in his teaching on the *via media*.

In the late Middle Ages a shift of emphasis took place in the teaching of theologians on the knowledge of God. Aquinas was chiefly preoccupied with the material object of faith, and more particularly with its salvific content. By contrast the theologians of the later Middle Ages preoccupied themselves increasingly with the external formal object of theology, and it was at this point that the ambiguous nature of the concept of truths necessary for salvation was borne in upon them, and led to a gradual abandonment of the theory of the sufficiency of sacred scripture, for the formal object of theology is not the eternal salvation of man but the authority of God who reveals. As a result of this the necessity of doctrines for salvation had to be measured not so much by their direct bearing upon eternal salvation as by their common character as revelation. The development of theology brought with it a multiplication of the doctrines which were regarded as revealed, and also an increase in the number of those doctrines which it was not believed possible to discover in sacred scripture. And when they reverted to the teaching of the past the theologians established that the idea that sacred scripture was insufficient in terms of content was traditional in the church. For instance, in their teaching on the nature of baptism, the fathers of the church too had derived this from tradition alone.

Yet to deny their teaching on this point was condemned as heretical and punished by excommunication from the church.

The polemics of the counter-reformation introduced an emphasis not merely on the formal insufficiency of sacred scripture but also on its insufficiency in terms of content. According to the definition of the Council of Trent concerning revelation (*DS* 1501 [=DB 783]), the gospel message is accessible to us *in libris scriptis et sine scripto traditionibus*, and the believer must adopt an attitude towards the apostolic traditions which are still in force in the church today defined as *pari pietatis affectu*, that is, he must treat them with the same reverence as sacred scripture itself. 'In consequence of this, the conception of tradition as a second material source side by side with sacred scripture came increasingly to the fore in post-tridentine theology' (J. Ratzinger, 'Tradition', *LTK* x, 297). In recent times the true significance of the tridentine decree, and the value of the post-tridentine development, have become the subject of numerous and impassioned discussions which we cannot pass over without drawing attention to certain facts.

According to the teaching of the Council of Trent the catholic must obviously accept *in principle* that the fact that a doctrine is not contained in sacred scripture is not a sufficient ground for refusing to recognise it as a revealed truth. But the council does not solve the question of whether *in fact* there are any important doctrines not contained in any way at all in scripture. For, however we interpret the statement of the council, it does not contain any information at all with regard to the number and the nature of the *sine scripto traditiones*, apart from the fact that they constitute elements in the gospel message. Let us take the extreme case of a theologian who, on concrete historical grounds, maintains that no document known to him justifies him in asserting that the apostles were explicitly aware of some particular point in our *fides divina et catholica* which was not contained in sacred scripture. Let us further suppose that this same theologian goes on to say, again on concrete historical grounds, that he would be unjustified in asserting that the point in question does in fact fulfil the necessary conditions for inclusion in this *fides divina et catholica*. In making this twofold assertion he would in no way be controverting the teaching of the Council of Trent.

It is possible to regret the 'two-source theory' of revelation of post-tridentine theology. At all events, one must be on one's guard against a mythical presentation of this theory. Its adherents have never presented the sources as separate and partial sources with differing contents, somewhat in the manner in which the power to govern may be divided between two parties, each having his own proper sphere of authority. The upholders of the theory have never maintained that what we today call 'tradition' in the church, that is, the handing down of the gospel message in word and deed from generation to generation, would not always have contained the whole of this gospel message. They have never denied that tradition *in sensu activo* has always been formed in the first instance as a commentary on and an explica-

tion of the content of sacred scripture. And it is surely difficult to perceive why the assertion—whether true or false—that scripture does not contain all the teaching and all the supplementary material which together make up the gospel must lead to the assumption of two bodies of tradition with two quite different contents, each incomplete in itself and parallel to the other.

Moreover the adherents of the so-called 'two-source theory' have scarcely left the catholic doctrine of the *analogia fidei* out of their considerations. They have for the most part emphasised the indirect evidence, the arguments *ex convenientia* that scripture offers in support of the theory of *sine scripto traditiones* which they maintain, and they have done this in fact better than many theologians of today, for whom everything is contained in scripture 'somehow'. The question may be asked whether the protestants of today do not often require a still greater *sacrificium intellectus* than was demanded in the centuries of the two-source theory.

Actually, the position of contemporary catholic and reformed christians with regard to the dogmas proclaimed in the previous century differs only in one important respect from the position of the post-tridentine christians with regard to the dogmas defined at the Council of Trent. The earlier generations had greater trust in the possibilities of finding theological solutions with the speculative reason, as well as in the possibility of direct historical proof, than most theologians of today. Progress in the methods of historical research since the middle of last century has probably been one of the most important factors in the development of the new theology. It has led to a prudent evaluation of direct historical arguments in theology, as well as of the premisses on which the arguments in speculative theology are based. Not least, it has also provided a better insight into the traditio-historical character of sacred scripture. It has shown that arguments from sacred scripture are often just as difficult to adduce as the so-called arguments from tradition. The effect of this has been to emphasise to an increasing extent the role of indirect proof, through the medium of the life of the church and its magisterium. So strongly, indeed, has this been emphasised that the magisterium itself has been forced to react against an exaggerated emphasis on its role and a corresponding neglect of directly historical and speculative methods of argument.

Apart from the progress in historical and other sciences, a further factor which led to a change of attitude towards the problem of tradition was the oecumenical atmosphere, borne of an altered situation of the world, in the relations between christian confessions. This has recently borne fruit in the *Dogmatic Constitution on Divine Revelation* of the Second Vatican Council.

5. 'The debates of the Second Vatican Council were characterised by a dialogue of a type which is classical in post-tridentine scholastic theology, and by efforts to achieve a deeper understanding of tradition on the basis of the heritage of the early Church. In this the legitimate concerns of reformation thinking were duly taken into consideration'. This is J. Ratzinger's

accurate estimate (*LTK* x, 298). The efforts mentioned above were crowned with success.

Of the twenty-six paragraphs of the *Constitution on Divine Revelation*, no less than nineteen are concerned with sacred scripture. Sixteen are devoted to it exclusively. The apostolic preaching, it is stated, is 'expressed in a special way in the inspired books' (§ 8). The Council numbers sacred scripture, together with the Holy Eucharist, as among the most precious treasures of the church: 'The church has always venerated the divine scriptures, just as it venerates the body of the Lord, since from the table of both the word of God and of the body of Christ it unceasingly receives and offers to the faithful the bread of life' (§ 21). The sacred scriptures 'contain the word of God, and since they are inspired, really are the word of God; and so the study of the sacred page is, as it were, the soul of sacred theology' (§ 24).

The constitution devotes hardly more than three paragraphs to tradition. It presents sacred scripture as a privileged form of tradition. The council fathers again reiterate the tridentine teaching on the formal insufficiency of sacred scripture. Thus, 'it is not from sacred scripture alone that the church can draw its certainty about everything which has been revealed' (§ 9). The council takes up once more the *pari pietatis affectu* of the tridentine decree: 'Therefore both sacred tradition and sacred scripture are to be accepted and reverenced with the same sense of devotion and reverence' (§ 9).

In yet another respect emphasis is laid upon the formal insufficiency of sacred scripture: 'Sacred tradition and sacred scripture form one sacred deposit of the word of God which is committed to the church. Holding fast to this deposit the entire holy people, united with their shepherds, remain constantly steadfast in the teaching of the apostles. . . . The task of authentically interpreting the word of God, whether written or handed on, however, has been entrusted exclusively to the living teaching office of the church, whose authority is exercised in the name of Jesus Christ. This teaching office is not above the word of God, but serves it, teaching only what has been handed on' (§ 10).

In the *Constitution on Divine Revelation* the fathers of the council do not show an excessive concern to arrive at a precise analysis of the concept of tradition. In those passages in which they provide a statement of what the true function of tradition and of the teaching office of the church is they take this function to be, on the one hand, in the active sense, what J. Geiselmann calls 'living tradition', and on the other hand, in terms of content, or objectively regarded, what Y. Congar calls 'tradition in the comprehensive sense'. The question of the sufficiency or insufficiency of sacred scripture in terms of content, on the other hand, which has been at the centre of the controversies between confessions ever since the Council of Trent, is simply set aside. It is not treated of *ex professo* at all. All the statements on the relationship in content between the two basic types of the 'handing on' of divine revelation are kept neutral. There is no mention whatsoever of 'sources' of revelation.

The council leaves the question open.

It teaches neither the sufficiency of what is contained in sacred scripture nor its insufficiency. It is probably clear from the text that the doctrine of the insufficiency of what is contained in sacred scripture with reference to the content of revelation should not be regarded as the binding doctrine of the church. The question as stated pertains to the area of free theological and historical research. It can only be decided *a posteriori* in terms of particular cases, and on the basis of concrete evidence. It should no longer provide reasons for division between the confessions as such. The crucial point of difference in fundamental theology is to be sought elsewhere.

Bibliography: N. Appel, *Kanon und Kirche. Die Kanonkrise im heutigen Protestantismus als kontroverstheologisches Problem*, Paderborn 1963; P. Asveld, 'Ecriture et Tradition', *ETL* 41 (1965), 491–529; J. Beumer, 'Die mündliche Überlieferung als Glaubensquelle', *Handbuch der Dogmengeschichte* 1/4, ed. M. Schmaus and A. Grillmeier, Freiburg 1964; H. Beintker, *Die evangelische Lehre von der Heiligen Schrift und von der Tradition*, Lüneburg 1961; G. Biemer, *Überlieferung und Offenbarung. Die Lehre von der Tradition nach J. H. Newman*, Freiburg 1961; Y. M. J. Congar, '"Traditio" und "Sacra Doctrina" bei Thomas von Aquin', *Kirche und Überlieferung*, ed. J. Betz and H. Fries, Freiburg 1960, 170–210; Y. M. J. Congar, *La Tradition et les Traditions* I, Paris 1960; and II, Paris 1963; G. Ebeling, *Wort Gottes und Tradition*, Göttingen 1964; J. R. Geiselmann, 'Das Konzil von Trient über des Verhältnis des Heiligen Schrift und der nichtgeschriebenen Traditionen', *Die mündliche Überlieferung*, ed. M. Schmaus, Munich 1957, 123–206; J. R. Geiselmann, *Die Heilige Schrift und die Tradition*, Freiburg 1962; J. R. Geiselmann, *HTG* II, 686–96; H. Holstein, *La Tradition dans l'Eglise*, Paris 1960; W. Kasper, *Die Lehre von der Tradition in der Römischen Schule*, Freiburg 1962; P. Lengsfeld, *Überlieferung. Tradition und Schrift in der evangelischen und katholischen Theologie der Gegenwart*, Paderborn 1960; P. Lengsfeld, 'Tradition innerhalb der konstitutiven Zeit der Offenbarung', *Mysterium Salutis. Grundriss heilsgeschichtlicher Dogmatik*, I, Cologne 1965, 239–

88; and 'Tradition und Heilige Schrift. Ihr Verhältnis', *Mysterium Salutis*, 463–96; J. L. Murphy, *The Notion of Tradition in John Driedo*, Milwaukee 1960; F. Mussner, *LTK* x², 291–3; K. Rahner, *Inspiration in the Bible*, London 1961; K. Rahner, 'Schrift und Tradition', *Das Zweite Vatikanische Konzil*, ed. K. Forster, Würzburg 1963, 69–91; K. Rahner and J. Ratzinger, *Offenbarung und Überlieferung*, Freiburg 1965; J. Ratzinger, *LTK* x², 293–9; P. Rusch, 'De non definienda illimitata insufficientia materiali Scripturae', *ZKT* 85 (1963), 1–15; H. Schauf, *Die Lehre der Kirche über Schrift und Tradition in den Katechismen*, Essen 1963; *Schrift und Tradition. Mariologische Studien*, ed. Der deutschen Arbeitsgemeinschaft für Mariologie, Essen 1962 (this work includes certain articles previously published elsewhere, which are important for our understanding of the most recent discussions); B. Decker, 'Sola scriptura bei Thomas von Aquin', *Universitas* (Festschrift A. Stöhr) 1, Mainz 1960, 117–29; *Schrift und Tradition. Untersuchungen einer theologischen Kommission*, ed. K. E. Skydsgaard and L. Vischer, Zurich 1963; G. H. Tavard, *Holy Writ and Holy Church. The Crisis of the Protestant Reformation*, London 1959; M. Thurian, *L'unité visible des chrétiens et la Tradition*, Neuchâtel 1961.

Paul Asveld

Transfiguration

The motif of being changed into another form recurs frequently in the conceptual and imaginative milieux of the ancient religions. Sometimes it occurs in the form of stories about gods appearing to men in earthly guise (the metamorphoses of Greek mythology); sometimes the change is in the opposite direction, of man into a divine being by acquiring heavenly form (hellenistic mystery religions). The account of the transfiguration of Jesus on the mountain as recorded in the bible represents a metamorphosis which is totally different in character from these. Of the four accounts of this episode, that found in Mk 9:2–9, which is manifestly based upon the tradition handed down by Peter, must be considered the earliest. This in turn provides a basis for the parallel account in Mt 17:1–9, which differs from it only in inessentials, while Lk 9:28–36 has drawn not only upon the markan account, but upon another one as well, one which derives, perhaps, from John the son of Zebedee. Independent of the gospels a further version, admittedly only fragmentary, is to be found in 2 Pet 1:16–18.

In the interpretation of this event opinions have been, and continue to be, widely different. First, it is clear that what is in question here cannot be a revelation directed to Jesus himself. Baltensweiler's theory to the effect that the transfiguration would have been a subjective experience on Jesus' part, arising from his temptation to conceive of his messianic calling in political terms and in terms of the Zealot movement, cannot be reconciled with the accounts. These leave no possibility of doubting that, in the first instance at least, it was for the sake of the three apostles who were present as witnesses that the event took place. To them the true dignity of their Lord, hitherto concealed, was revealed by means of a vision which they saw and words which they heard. The only questions that arise are in what precisely this dignity is to be regarded as consisting, and why it was momentarily unveiled to the three witnesses. The answers which have been suggested to both these questions are extremely divergent (see Höller, 206–28). Recently attempts have been made to interpret the transfiguration as an anticipatory vision of the ⟋ *parousia* (Boobyer) or as the inauguration of Jesus as messianic king presented after the pattern of the

Old Testament enthronement sequence (Riesenfeld). Notable arguments can be advanced in favour of both these theories. At the same time a theory in which every individual element in the story falls into place convincingly and without strain has yet to be discovered. The recognition of this fact has led some to doubt the unity of the narrative. Lohmeyer believed that Mk 9:3 was a fragment from a hellenistic myth which had been applied to Jesus. It could be separated from the rest of the narrative, in which transcendence of Jesus over the heroes of the Old Testament was depicted in the hues of Jewish eschatology. H. P. Müller finds two distinct sequences of ideas, an earlier one in which Jesus is proclaimed eschatological king after the pattern of Ps 2 as interpreted messianically (9:2ab, 7, [9]), and a later one in which Jesus appears as the heavenly Son of Man and as a divine being (9:2c–6, 8). But these hypothetical reconstructions give the impression of being far too artificial to be convincing. Moreover Lohmeyer later abandoned his hypothesis.

In any attempt at determining the theological import which the narrative would have borne for the community which handed it down, we must take the *vox interpretativa* of Mk 9:7 as our starting-point. Unlike the voice at the baptism, the voice here resounding from the clouds, the symbol of the divine presence (Ex 16:10; 19:9; 24:15f; 33:9; Num 11:25; 2 Macc 2:8), is clearly addressed to the disciples. Echoing Ps 2:7, it declares Jesus to be the beloved (=only) Son of God, ie, the Messiah, and thus provides *divine* confirmation of Peter's confession (8:29), to which, therefore, the interval

mentioned as having elapsed in 9:2 must, at least originally, have referred. Admittedly, for Mark and the primitive community the title 'Son of God' would not merely have designated Jesus' status as Messiah, but would have carried the further implication of his sonship of God in the metaphysical sense as well. In the second part of the utterance from heaven Jesus is indirectly declared to be the eschatological prophet promised in Deut 18:15, whose words are to be hearkened to and obeyed. With regard to the appearance of Moses and Elijah, some have regarded these as representatives of the law and the prophets; in spite of the paucity of the evidence, however, it is more probable that they were intended as forerunners of the Messiah (see Jeremias, *TDNT* II, 938f; IV 859f and 871). The presence of these figures, then, appears to have had the same significance of bearing witness to the messiahship of Jesus. By the transformation of his appearance and the unearthly whiteness with which his garments shone Jesus appeared for a moment in the state appropriate to the heavenly mode of existence (see Dan 7:9; 10:5; Acts 1:10; Rev 3:4f; 4:4; 7:9; Bar [Syr] 51:3, 5, 10, 12). Thereby he unveiled himself to the witnesses as the heavenly Son of Man (Dan 7:13f; I Enoch 46:1–3; [62:5; 69:29]; Mk 8:38; 13:26; 14:62; Rev 1:13f). In the mind of Mark the reason for this epiphany being imparted to the apostles precisely at this point is probably to be found in the passion prediction which precedes it in 8:31f. In that case the significance of the revelation which they received can be stated as follows: the fact that Jesus takes the path of a servant in lowliness and suffering, and not the path of a king in the acquisition of earthly power, as was generally expected, in no way alters the fact that he is the messianic Son of God of Ps 2:7, the eschatological prophet and teacher promised in Deut 18:15, the Son of Man endowed with heavenly glory as depicted in Dan 7:13. The fact that only the three closest of his disciples were privileged to receive this revelation, like the enjoinder to silence recorded in 9:9, is connected with the 'messianic secret'. In the parallel accounts in the other synoptics, and specifically in Matthew, the transfiguration has in all essentials the same meaning. The reference back to the passion prediction, which is only to be inferred in Mark, is in Luke stated plainly and explicitly. For according to him the conversation of the two Old Testament figures with Jesus was concerned with his 'departure' at Jerusalem (9:31). Furthermore, by introducing the term *doxa* (=glory) and applying it both to Jesus (9:32), and also to Moses and Elijah (9:31), Luke, even more than Mark, imparts to the vision of the three figures features which are characteristic and definitive of the heavenly mode of existence (see also 2 Pet 1:17).

Bibliography: J. Höller, *Die Verklärung Jesu*, Freiburg 1937 (with bibliography of the earlier literature); J. Blinzler, *Die ntl. Berichte über die Verklärung Jesu*, Munster 1937; E. Dabrowski, *La Transfiguration de Jésus*, Rome 1939; P. Dabek, '"Siehe, es erschienen Moses und Elias"', *Bbl* 23 (1942), 175–89; G. H. Boobyer, *St. Mark and the Transfiguration Story*, Edinburgh 1942; T. F. Torrance, 'The Transfiguration of Jesus', *Evangelical Quarterly* 14 (1942), 214–29; H. Riesenfeld, *Jésus transfiguré*, Lund 1947; B. Zielinski, 'De Doxa transfigurati', *VD* 26 (1948), 291–303; B. Zielinski, 'De Trans-figurationis sensu', *VD* 26 (1948), 335–43; J. Schildenberger, 'Die Verklärung des Herrn', *BM* 24 (1948), 23–9; A. M. Ramsay, *The Glory of God and the Transfiguration of Christ*, London 1949; F. X. Durrwell, 'La Transfiguration de Jésus', *VS* 35 (1951), 115–26; P. Bonnard, Allmen 429–30; G. B. Caird, 'The Transfiguration', *Expository Times* 67 (1955/6), 291–4; J. R. Macphail, *The Bright Cloud. The Bible in the Light of the Transfiguration*, London 1956; A. Kenny, 'The Transfiguration and the Agony in the Garden', *CBQ* 19 (1957), 444–52; M. Sabbe, 'De Transfiguratië van Jesus', *Collat. Brugenses et Gandavenses* 4 (1958), 467–503; A. Feuillet, 'Les perspectives propres à chaque évangeliste dans les récits de la Transfiguration', *Bbl* 39 (1958), 281–301; H. Baltensweiler, *Die Verklärung Jesu*, Zurich 1959; A. M. Denis, 'Une théologie de la Rédemption. La Transfiguration chez S. Marc', *VS* 41 (1959), 136–49; A. George, 'La Transfiguration (Luc 9:28–36)', *Bible et Vie chrétienne* 33 (1960), 21–5; H. P. Müller, 'Die Verklärung Jesu', *ZNW* 51 (1960), 56–64; J. Larisis, *Hē metamorphōsis tou Sōtēros hēmōn Iēsou Khristou*, Athens 1960; C. E. Carlston, 'Transfiguration and Resurrection', *JBL* 80 (1961), 233–40; P. Miquel, 'Le mystère de la Transfiguration', *Questions Litug. et Paroissiales* 42 (1961), 194–223; M. Sabbe, *La rédaction du récit de la Transfiguration. La venue du Messie*, Paris–Louvain 1963, 65–100.

Josef Blinzler

Transitoriness

The transitoriness of all earthly existence is a theme which is not confined to the bible alone. It pervades a major part of the literature of the ancient Near East.

The Old Testament has no abstract term for it. It depicts transitoriness by means of comparisons. All earthly existence seems like a dream (Job 20:8), like a garment devoured by moths (Is 51:6; Job 13:28), like smoke (Ps 102:3; Is 51:6), like grass and flowers (Ps 90:5–7; Job 14:1f; Is 40:6). The generations of mankind pass away and are succeeded by others (Eccles 1:4). Even memory vanishes (Job 18:17). All is vanity (Eccles 1:2). In all this evanescence there is only one who remains and whose years have no end, namely God (Ps 102:27; Dan 12:7). But this is not a fact in which man can *ipso facto* place his reliance, for his sins have drawn down the anger of God upon him, and with it death and liability to corruption (Gen 3; Is 6:5; Ps 90:7). Only in fear and trembling does the devout man attempt to trust in the eternity of God. He reminds God of the fact that in Sheol no-one can serve him (Ps 6:5; 30:9). He steeps himself in the Torah as a wellspring of life (Ps 119:92), he relies on the compassion of God. Only very seldom does he envisage an association with God which enables him to transcend the power of death (Ps 73:26). Only in the latest books do we find the consoling light of the idea of ↗ resurrection (Dan 12:2; Is 27 [later interpolation]).

In the period of the deutero-canonical and pseudepigraphal literature faith in the resurrection was universal. In the New Testament it appears to be taken for granted. But it does not yet signify the overcoming of death and transitoriness. There is the second death (Rev 20:6, 14; 21:8). One can perish (*apollumi*: Mt 5:29; 8:32; 10:39; etc). ↗ Death is the wages of sin (Rom 6:23). It is Paul who sees the importance of the fact that death, hell, and the devil belong together. It is not merely a man's individual sins but his whole being, which is in a state of alienation from God, that sets him in a condition of lostness, makes the 'flesh' transitory, threatens that he will pass away beyond all hope of return.

Because of sin the 'flesh' (ie, the natural, human existence, both spiritual and physical) is *phthartos* (= 'mortal', 'perishable': Rom 1:23; 8:21; Gal 6:8; 1 Cor 15:42; see also 2 Pet 2:12, and we are the slaves of corruption (2 Pet 2:10). But the New Testament is no longer devoid of hope as it confronts this transitoriness and liability to death on the part of creaturehood, which is the outcome of sin and the anger of God. The ↗ hope which is tentatively hinted at in the Old Testament, that God can give ↗ life which is no longer subject to death, has become a certainty. The Gospel of John is full of this message (5:21, 24; 6:58, 63; 11:25; 14:6). The Book of Revelation in its very first chapter shows us Christ as possessing the keys of hell and of death (1:18). It knows that death will be no more (21:4), and knows also of the tree of life, the fruits of which give life to those who were formerly alienated from God (22:2). Again Paul rejoices over the victory of Christ (1 Cor 15:55; 2 Tim 1:10). The cosmos which continues to exist apart from Christ does indeed remain *phthartos*. It is moving towards its end (1 Thess 4:17; Rom 13:11ff), but only in order to give place to a new world at the ↗ *parousia*. Christ is the *arkhēgos* of this new world. He who is baptised in his death and resurrection, and who has his Spirit—he also has life, and no longer stands under the curse of transitoriness (Col 3:3; Rom 6:3, 8, 23; 5:12, 17; 10:9; Heb 2:14; Rom 8:10; Gal 6:8). Hence for christians there is no longer any mourning (1 Thess 4:13). What was transient has become intransient (1 Cor 15:53).

Bibliography: T. C. Vriezen and H. Conzelmann, *RGG* II³, 799ff (with bibliographical references); E. Lohse, *BHHW* 623; B. Reicke, *RGG* VI³, 912–21; *TDNT* I, 394–6.

Georg Molin

Truth

The biblical concept of truth is something quite different from that conveyed by the term 'truth' in popular parlance. This appears primarily from the Hebrew word ʾ*ēmeth* which lies at its root. Originally and basically concrete in conception, this term has come to have a wide range of meaning attached to it, a range of meaning which has subsequently been taken over by the corresponding word in Greek, *alētheia*. ʾ*ēmeth* (appearing in the Old Testament 132 times) is derived from ʾ*āmint*, a part of the verb ʾ*āman*, meaning 'to be firm, stand firm, be reliable, unchangeable'. The opposite of ʾ*ēmeth* is *šeqer*, 'instability, nothingness, lie' (see Prov 11:18). Instances of this basic meaning of stability and sureness are to be found in 2 Kings 20:19 = Is 39:8 and Jer 14:13 ('peace and security', 'assured peace'). Again the phrase *beʾēmeth*, 'in truth', 'truly', 'really', clearly implies the element of lastingness. Only that which has firmness, that which will not vanish in the next moment is real and true. In Is 16:5 *beʾēmeth* should actually be translated 'for ever' (see Sir 37:15; 51:15).

Frequently—in more than half the passages, in fact—ʾ*ēmeth* has a religious meaning. Either alone or in conjunction with *ḥesed* (↗ grace) it is often referred to as an attribute of God or of the divine law.

1. *As an attribute of God*: in this sense ʾ*ēmeth* is connected with ↗ covenant and promise. (Sir 41:19 LXX [Vulg 24] is hardly the result of an accident, even if the verse seems out of place in the context; see 1 QH 10:30f). In Ex 34:5–7 Yahweh is said to be 'rich in *ḥesed* (grace, loving-kindness) and ʾ*ēmeth*', and this is explained by the statement that he 'keeps this same *ḥesed* for a thousand generations'. ʾ*ēmeth*, therefore, is the attitude of God by which he makes his kindness last and be stable. ʾ*ēmeth*, therefore, must be translated literally as 'faithfulness'. In this sense the promises to David in Ps 89 constantly invite comparison with the declarations of Yahweh's ʾ*ēmeth* (see Mic 7:18–20; Zech 8:8; etc). In this sense too Ps 132:11 is particularly enlightening: 'Yahweh swore ʾ*ēmeth* to David, an oath from which he will not turn back . . .'. The object of the oath that is sworn is not some abstract entity such as faithfulness; rather it is connected with objects in the concrete. The *Liber Psalmorum* gives the appropriate rendering *promissum firmum*, 'a sure promise'. The basic connotation of stability contained in ʾ*ēmeth* is applied in the context of the oath and the promise. The fact that ʾ*ēmeth* is found side by side with the justice of God (Zech 8:8; Hos 2:21f [Vulg 19f]; Neh 9:33; ↗ righteousness) or with his holiness (Ps 71:22) shows that the word does not merely mean faithfulness as such, but carries the further connotation of permanence. In the passages referred to this permanence consists precisely in the favourable attitude and behaviour of God towards his own.

2. Another side of the concept ʾ*ēmeth* appears in contexts in which it is used

to express the faithfulness of God inasmuch as this constitutes the refuge and sure protection of the just, and hence is often presented under the images of shield, rock and fortress (Ps 91:4; see also Ps 54:7). It is not the covenant faithfulness of Yahweh that is referred to in such passages, but his reliability and unwavering readiness to help quite in general (Ps 40:11; 42; 43; 54:7; 60:4; etc.).

3. In four passages in the Old Testament the faithfulness of God is explicitly referred to: in the address of Moses (Deut 7:9) concerning his covenant faithfulness; Deut 32:4 and Is 49:7 in a general sense: God is faithful towards his people; in its most sublime form in Ps 31:6: God's faithfulness is the hiding-place, the refuge of the just; all his trust is based upon him (see also Sir 41:19 LXX; Vulg 24).

4. What does the combination *ḥesed weʾēmeth* signify? Are the two words used (a) synonymously, (b) as a hendiadys, that is, as signifying lasting kindness, unfailing benevolence, or (c) simply as signifying 'kindness and faithfulness'? Ps 138:2–4 shows that both terms express the two aspects of the realities referred to (covenant and promise) inasmuch as these promises are expressions of the kindness and love of God (*ḥesed*), and inasmuch as God remains faithful to these promises (*ʾēmeth*) (see Gen 24:27; 32:10; 2 Sam 2:6; 15:20; etc.).

5. *ʾēmeth* is also used of men, whether in respect of the relations of men to each other or in their religious life. 'Men such as fear God, men who are trustworthy', *ʾanšê ʾēmeth* (Ex 18:21; Neh 7:2). While in both these passages the aspect of faithfulness which the author

primarily has in mind is loyal obedience, nevertheless the connection with the virtue of fearing God shows that the religious aspect is also included. This is also apparent in Hos 4:1f, where the synonyms show us that *ʾēmeth* here is a social virtue, which applies to the whole range of duties towards one's neighbour. Far more frequently *ʾēmeth* is used of duties towards God. This can also be deduced from the various similar expressions with which it is set in parallelism: 'Serve the Lord in total self-surrender and faithfulness (*ʾēmeth*)' (Jos 24:14; see also Judg 9:16, 19). 'I have walked before thee in faithfulness and with a whole heart' (2 Kings 20:3; Is 38:3). 'Hezekiah did what was good and right and faithful (*haʾēmeth*) before Yahweh' (2 Chron 31:20). 'Jerusalem shall be called the faithful city and the mountain of the Lord of hosts, the holy mountain' (Zech 8:3). Two particularly noteworthy usages are 'to walk in truth' (1 Kings 2:4; 3:6; 2 Kings 20:3; Is 38:3; Pss 26:3; 86:11; Tob 3:5), and 'to do *ʾēmeth*' (2 Chron 31:20; Sir 27:9; Tob 4:6; 13:6; Is 26:10 [LXX]). In both usages it is faithfulness to God's law that is meant (see especially Tob 3:5) in attitude and in act. Again the phrase 'to practise *ḥesed weʾēmeth*' is in some instances used of men (Gen 24:49; 47:29; Josh 2:14; Prov 3:3; 14:22; 16:6; 20:28). Here it is precisely steadfastness and faithfulness that *ʾēmeth* adds to the idea of the exercise of kindness and favour. In some few passages we can even establish a juridical aspect of *ʾēmeth*, as in Prov 29:14; Ezek 18:8; Zech 7:9: 'to judge in *ʾēmeth*' is to judge truly because the judgement is immutable.

It can neither be influenced beforehand by corruption, nor retrospectively revised on the grounds that it was unjust. It is only a short step from the idea of *ʾēmeth* as faithfulness and reliability to the further significance of integrity. This comes out very clearly in Prov 12:19: 'Truthful lips endure for ever, but a lying tongue is but for a moment'.

6. Truth in the narrower sense is neither a human nor a divine attribute, but simply a quality of speech: 'Truth (*ʾēmeth*) is something spoken' which proves to be genuine and reliable even after it has been put to the test, an assertion which does not evaporate into nothingness upon closer examination (see the passage just quoted above from Prov 12:19). Thus the queen of Sheba, when she has seen everything with her own eyes, can confirm what she has heard of Solomon: 'The report was true which I heard ...', or in a freer translation (Stenzel): 'What I have been told in my own land about your condition of life and your wisdom is in conformity with the facts' (1 Kings 10:6). When Micaiah, against the probabilities, predicts that Achab will be victorious, the king asks him: 'How many times shall I adjure you that you speak to me nothing but the truth in the name of the Lord' (1 Kings 22:16), in other words 'that which really will come to pass'. From these texts alone it can be seen that in Hebrew truth and reality are one and the same—*ʾēmeth*. Not to speak the truth is the same as not to express the real state of affairs (see Jer 9:5; 23:28; Zech 8:16). What applies to statements and words also applies to realities. *ʾēmeth* in the sense of reality, of a certain genuineness, can be used of these too: eg, Jer 2:21: 'I

planted you (Israel) a choice vine, wholly of pure seed (*zerʿa ʾēmeth*). How then have you turned degenerate ...?' (see also Is 5:2). *ʾēmeth* is also used in the sense of the way (Gen 24:48), of a sign (Josh 2:12), of God (2 Chron 15:3; Jer 10:10), always in order to emphasise the genuineness and rightness of the object thus qualified, and to distinguish it from the false or deceitful way, sign or god.

7. Truth as a religious expression: 'The sum of thy words is *ʾēmeth*, every one of thy righteous ordinances endures for ever' (Ps 119:160, cf 43), 'thy words are *ʾēmeth*' (2 Sam 7:28). The usage 'to walk in *ʾēmeth*' adduced above (§ 5) is also found in the form 'to walk in thy *ʾēmeth*'. No basic difference is to be inferred from this. The second of these two usages adds only the element that the *ʾēmeth* in question comes from God, is taught by him and commanded by him (thus as we find: 'Show me your way, teach me your law', etc). At this point, however, a development is introduced which leads to an identification of *ʾēmeth* with the law of God, his revelation or his will: 'Teach me thy way, O Yahweh, that I may walk in thy *ʾēmeth*' (Ps 86:11). This manner of speaking attains its full development in the Wisdom books and Daniel: 'For my mouth will utter truth; wickedness is an abomination to my lips' (Prov 8:7; see the verses following and Prov 22:21; Eccles 12:10). A striking combination of synonyms is apparent in Prov 23:23: 'Buy truth and do not sell it; buy wisdom, instruction, and understanding'. 'Truth' (*ʾēmeth*) in this context is the teaching of the book as a whole (see 4:5, 7; 16:16; Sir 4:25). In Daniel *ʾēmeth* comes to have a purely religious

meaning, for it is used in the sense of the revelation of God: 'In the place of the daily burnt offering transgression was laid down, and truth was thrown down to the ground' (8:12). The transgression here is the form of cult introduced by Antiochus, while the truth is the monotheistic religion of Israel (see also 8:26; 9:13; 10:1, 21; 11:2).

B. *Later Judaism*. In rabbinic judaism and in the Qumran texts *'ēmeth* is a term frequently used, and it reappears here with all the nuances and shades of meaning familiar to us from the Old Testament. Let us concentrate primarily on the specifically religious meaning (see A7 above): 1. God himself is the truth; 2. his *tôrâh* is truth; and 3. those who practise it are men of truth, are his faithful ones, the observers of his law, who are in covenant, in union with him.

1. 'As thou, God, art *'ēmeth*, so too thy word is *'ēmeth*' (Ex Midrash 29:1). God 'is the truth itself' (CD 2:10 [2:11f]), is a God of truth (1 QH 15:25).

2. The *tôrâh* likewise, therefore, as the utterance of the divine word, is *'ēmeth* (Midrash Ps 25 § 11). One can speak of a 'law of thy truth' (1 QS 1:15), as also of the 'truth of the law of God' (1 QS 1:12; CD 9:51 [20, 29]). In this case truth and law appear so interchangeable that it amounts almost to an actual identity between the two. Finally *'ēmeth* embraces the whole sphere of the divine in general; it designates true religion and the practice of religion, and contrasts these with the attitude of aversion from God and irreligion as expressed by the terms 'wickedness' (*ršᶜ*, *ᶜwl*) or lies (*kzb*, *šqr*).

3. Men are repeatedly said to 'do the truth' (see Tob 4:6; 13:6; Is 26:10 [LXX]; Sir 27:9b—In TestRub 6:9 and TestBen 10:3 it is required that man shall 'practise the truth' towards his neighbour). An equivalent usage (*ᶜabad kûštâ*) is found in Targ. Hos 4:1, and here the moral conduct which is so designated is clearly thought of as connected with the attitude of true religion. The people of Qumran are called 'men of truth who fulfil the law, whose hands do not slumber in the service of truth' (1 Qp Hab VII 10–12). This is synonymous with the service of God (1 QH 2:36). The opposite of it is 'the service of deceit' (*ᶜbwdt šww*), or the works of lies, to which the preacher of lies seduces many (1 Qp Hab x 9–12). Thus on the one side stand the 'men of truth who fulfil the law' (1 Qp Hab VII 10f; 1 QH 9:35), on the other all evil-doers and 'men of deceit' (1 QH 14:14) or 'violent men who rebel against God' (1 Qp Hab VIII 11).

In the Qumran texts, furthermore, much is said of the struggle between truth and perversity, truth and lies, between the 'sons of truth' and the 'sons of perversity'. The spirits are divided into spirits of truth and spirits of perversity (1 QS III 18f), that is into the groups of spirits of life and spirits of darkness. Two hierarchies of spirits, those of truth and light and those of perversity and darkness, are engaged in a struggle with each other, and carry this struggle actually into the hearts of men by the influence which they exercise over them. The whole world is subject to this dualistic influence until the end, the final victory of truth (1 QS IV 19). The 'judgement that is decreed' brings this struggle to an end, and with his 'truth' God purifies the deeds of men. He sprinkles 'the spirit of truth' like lustral water upon all the abomination of lies (*šqr*), (1 QS IV 20).

C. *The New Testament.* Recently doubts have once more been cast, not unjustifiably (von Friedländer), upon the etymology of *alētheia* as meaning a state of affairs which is unconcealed, unveiled, open to view. Here, however, we can leave this question aside, together with the further question of how the concept of *alētheia* was represented in Greek culture—the more so since, in terms of meaning, *alētheia* in the New Testament follows on from the corresponding term in the Old Testament and later judaism, *'ēmeth*.

1. In this connection it is not always easy to discern the precise aspect on which the emphasis is laid in any given instance. In Eph 4:21; Gal 2:5, 14; Rom 2:8 *alētheia* can be taken in the sense of 'validity', a 'valid norm'. But the fact that the opposite of it is mentioned (see Gal 1:6 and above A6) implies that there is an emphasis on genuineness here as well.

2. In Rom 3:7 *alētheia* means the 'faithfulness and reliability' of God (see the preceding phrases *pistis theou* = 'faithfulness of God' [Rom 3:3] and *theou dikaiosunē* = 'God's justice, righteousness' [Rom 3:5]). Exactly as in the Old Testament, it means his faithfulness to his promise (Rom 15:8).

3. In 2 Cor 7:14; 11:10; Phil 1:18; 1 Tim 2:7; 2 Jn 1; 3 Jn 1 *alētheia* means human integrity and honour.

4. In Rom 1:18 it is that which is manifest, well-known that is expressed by *alētheia* (similar to the usage in Wis 6:22). The subject here is the revelation of God which is made known even among the heathens. A little

further, in v 25, the *alētheia* of God is opposed to *pseudos* (= lie, falsehood). Thereby the aspect of *alētheia* which is brought to the fore is that of reality as opposed to deceitfulness, and of genuineness as opposed to falsehood (idols), a contrast which is wholly dependent upon the opposition between *'ēmeth* and *šeqer*.

Thus usages such as *en alētheia(i)*, etc signify *truly* (Col 1:6; see also Acts 4:27; 10:34; Rom 2:2; and especially 1 Jn 3:18).

5. In Acts 26:25; Mk 12:14, 32; Lk 4:25 it is the truth of a statement that is meant.

6. True doctrine (see above A7; see also Philo, *Spec. Leg.* IV, 178, where the proselyte is described as 'changing over to the truth'). Perhaps Gal 2:5, 14 (to which 2 Cor 13:8 is related), passages which have already been mentioned above under 1, should more appropriately be placed under this heading. In 2 Cor 4:2 ('the open statement of the truth') truth stands for the 'word of God' which has just been mentioned. In Rom 10:16 'to hearken to the gospel' has exactly the same significance as the expression 'to follow the truth' in Gal 5:7. Christian faith is 'obedience to the truth' (1 Pet 1:22). The preaching of the gospel is 'the word of truth' (Eph 1:13; Col 1:5; 2 Cor 6:7; etc). 'To arrive at a knowledge of the truth' (2 Tim 3:7 and frequently elsewhere) means nothing else than to become like Christ. In this phrase the words *epignōsis alētheias* (lit. = 'knowledge of the truth') mean 'christian knowledge' deriving from the true teaching, and bearing fruit in the subject's life. Hence in Titus 1:1 the term can appear side by side with

pistis (faith). Here, too, the word *sōthēnai* (lit. = 'to be saved')—as used specifically in the context of conversion to christianity, as it is, more or less, in Rom 8:24—can be made parallel to *eis epignōsin alētheias elthein* (= 'to come to the knowledge of the truth': 1 Tim 2:4). For the same reason, in 1 Tim 4:3, a passage intended to point to the true christians, these can be referred to as *tois pistois kai epegnōkosi tēn alētheian* (= 'those who believe and know the truth'; see Dibelius, 177). In this, too, the connotation of the genuine and unfalsified state of the christian teaching is repeatedly present (see 1 Tim 6:5; 2 Tim 2:18; 3:8; 4:4; Tit 1:14). Bultmann is justified in his apposite statement: 'As the concept of *pistis* [↗ faith] is determined by the thought of obedience, so *alētheia* is 'authoritative teaching'. The way is thus prepared for the historical development which fashions the concept of dogma, in which truth and law are conjoined.' (*TDNT* 1, 244.)

7. It is only at this point that we are in a position to combine the two usages *peripatein en alētheia(i)* (= 'to follow the truth': 2 Jn 4; 3 Jn 3f) and *poiein tēn alētheian* (lit. = 'to do the truth': Jn 3:21; 1 Jn 1:6), although we have already pointed out the precise correspondence between the two above in A 5 and B 3. What the phrase expresses is that true integrity which loyalty to the law involves. And it is precisely the Qumran texts which show that this had been perceived. In this sense the corresponding elements in the New Testament cannot be understood otherwise than as referring to the way of life inspired by christian teaching: to do the truth no longer means loyally to observe the law of the Old Testament (and the tradition of the fathers), but to fulfil the law of Christ.

8. John shows a special predilection for the word *alētheia*, though he uses it in a wide variety of senses, and, in fact, frequently combines all the various shades of meaning which it has come to acquire. In addition to these a fresh shade of meaning comes to be expressed by *alētheia* and *alēthinos*, namely, 'that which alone really exists, the transcendent and eternal'. This fresh shade of meaning is acquired under the influence of the hellenistic and dualistic mentality as exemplified in Heb 8:2 (see Philo *Leg. All.* 1, 32f; *Vit Mos* 1, 289; etc). As it appears in the New Testament, however, it is not altogether unmodified, but is radically conditioned by revelation (as, for instance, in Jn 4:23, where 'the true worshippers' are those who worship in spirit and in truth, that is in the divine reality revealed through Jesus, and not merely through an understanding of God that is purged of anthropomorphisms and spiritualised). Likewise the 'true light' (1 Jn 2:8; Jn 1:9) is 'the light of life' (Jn 8:12). Thus in the johannine *alētheia* three elements are present simultaneously: the truth of the actual statement (in which the underlying reality is expressed), this reality itself, and the revelation of it through and in Christ (Jn 8:40–47; cp v 33 and 18:37). From this we can understand the functions ascribed to the 'truth': it sets free (Jn 8:32), and that not merely as the truth of the spoken word (in the formal sense) but as the reality of divine salvation, as saving knowledge and redemption from sins (Jn 8:33f).

It sanctifies (Jn 17:17–19; see also Jn 15:2f and 1 QS IV 19f; see above B 3). Christ is 'the way, the truth and the life' (Jn 14:6), that is, he has essentially made possible and inaugurated that which the Spirit will carry on, namely, 'he will guide you into all the truth' (Jn 16:13). This means further that in the revelation which Christ brought, word and deed constitute a single entity (one might say a sacramental entity): the word is not the means to an end, but a sign of the divine deed which is inseparable from it. What this 'truth' means for men is nothing less than entry into the sphere of the divine in terms of knowledge and in terms of existence (cf the striking exposition in 1 Pet 1:3–11). It means that they belong to God. 'To be of the truth' (Jn 18:37; 1 Jn 3:19) is the same as 'to be of God' (Jn 8:47). Here we may notice the emphasis which John lays upon the fact that those who are of God hear his word, while those who do not hear it are not of God. What he means by this is to specify the two spheres of influence in which the two groups which he mentions respectively stand. For it is the Christian form of existence, abiding in this truth (considered as the divine deed of salvation), which begins with the preaching and acceptance of the message of this truth; and this must go on to find expression in the conduct which corresponds to this new existence (1 Jn 3:11–20). In fact it must take the form of co-operating with the divine truth (considered as message and as work of salvation) in bringing it to unbelievers (3 Jn 8). Thus the truth 'abides in us and will be with us for ever' (2 Jn 2) because this existence in

the truth is itself precisely the true and eternal life (Jn 14:6).

Bibliography: M. Dibelius, *Festschrift G. Heinrici*, Leipzig 1914, 176–89; R. Bultmann, *ZNW* 27 (1928), 113–63; R. Bultmann, *TDNT* I, 238–51; G. Quell, *TDNT* I, 232–7; G. Kittel, *TDNT* I, 237f; M. Zerwick, *VD* 18 (1938), 338–42 and 373–7; F. Asensio, *Misericordia et Veritas*, Rome 1949; I. de la Potterie, *VD* 27 (1949), 336–54; 28 (1950), 29–42; J. C. C. van Drossen, *De derivata van den stam ᵓmn in het Hebreeuwsch van het OT*, Amsterdam 1951; E. T. Ramsdell, *Journal of Religion* 31 (1951), 264–73; F. Nötscher, '"Wahrheit" als theologischer Terminus in den Qumran Texten', *Festschrift V. Christian*, Vienna 1956, 83–90; A. Wikenhauser, *Das Evangelium nach Johannes* (*RNT* 4), 'Exkurs zu Joh 8:39ff'; R. Schnackenburg, *Die Johannesbriefe*, Freiburg 1953 (*ad loc.*); W. Luther, 'Der frühgriechische Wahrheitsgedanke im Lichte der Sprache', *Gymnasium* 65 (1958), 75–107 (against Friedländer); J. H. Vrielink, *Het waarhedsbegrip*, Nijkerk 1956; I. de la Potterie, 'L'arrière-fond du thème johannique de vérité', *Studia Evang.*, Berlin 1959, 277–94; F. Moritz, *Die Wahrheit tun*, Rome 1960 (dissertation); H. Boeder, 'Der frühgriechische Wortgebrauch von Logos und Aletheia', *Arch. f. Begriffsgesch.* 4 (1959), 82–211; E. Heitsch, 'Die nicht-philosophische Aletheia', *Hermes* 90 (1962), 24–33; D. J. Theron, *Aletheia in the Pauline Corpus*, Princeton Theol. Sem. 1950 (dissertation); A. Vögtle, '"Die Wahrheit" als geoffenbarte Wirklichkeit und wirkende Gotteskraft', *Oberrhein. Pastoralblatt* 62 (1961), 1–8; J. Blank, 'Der johanneische Wahrheitsbegriff', *BZ* 7 (1963), 163–73.

Johannes B. Bauer

Vengeance

A law which is to be numbered among the earliest principles of justice known to the ancient Near East is the *lex talionis*. This lays down that when somebody has been wronged or deprived of his rights in any way the recompense which has to be made must be equal in value to the rights of which the injured party has been deprived ('ox for ox', Ex 21:36; 'Eye for eye, tooth for tooth', Ex 21:24); this principle finds its ultimate application in the law of blood vengeance ('life for life', Ex 21:23). The practice of exacting blood vengeance is rooted in the sense of corporate unity which manifests itself in various forms among the peoples of the ancient Near East according to the various ways of life prevailing among them. Some led a nomadic existence, while others had become sedentarised and had developed a peasant culture. These factors had a decisive influence upon the form in which this sense of corporate unity manifested itself. In nomad cultures the tribes living together constitute a unity based on a common 'mind' and 'soul' in which each individual is the representative of the whole, and conversely depends for his basic attitude and outlook upon the whole. This sense of belonging together is based upon a social structure which is patriarchal in character. The consciousness of common descent, whether real or imagined, constitutes a blood bond, and unites the individuals concerned into a community. And it is this community alone which makes it possible to lead a life which is in any sense fruitful. For outside this fellowship the individual has no rights to safeguard his well-being. Hence as a basic principle of justice blood vengeance implies that the tribe takes collective responsibility for the transgressions of any one of its members, and conversely that the community champions the cause of any member who suffers injury at the hands of those outside the tribe. In sedentarised cultures, on the other hand, the exclusive unity of the tribe is dissolved, and local communities take the place of the tribe. These are based upon particular families, and it is to these that the sense of corporate unity is now transferred. In the sphere of justice and law, in place of blood vengeance we now have the *lex talionis*, in which the transgressor against justice is answerable to a greater extent for his own personal crimes, and individual responsibility progressively takes the place of tribal responsibility even though remnants of the nomadic conception of justice still exercise an influence here and there. In ancient Israel the nomadic heritage continued to survive long after the stage of sedentarisation, and for this reason the custom of blood vengeance was still recognised right into the period of the monarchy (Gen 4:23f; 9:6; 34; 1 Sam 25:33). The community was responsible for the acts of the individuals belonging to it (Judg 20:13f; see also Judg 15:9–13), just as, conversely, an entire family could obtain exemption from punishment because of the merits of one of its members (Josh 6:22–5; Judg 1:24f). Hence it was felt to be an obvious expression of divine justice that children were punished for the sins of their fathers (Ex 20:5). Nonetheless, after the sedentarisation of Israel, the village community became increasingly prominent, and urban culture more and more loosened the earlier communal ties. The protection of the individual became the responsibility of the local court, and the awareness of corporate unity was transferred from the tribe to the family. As a result of this the individuality of the particular member of the family was strengthened. Collective responsibility disappeared, the transgressor was held personally responsible for his own misdeeds, and those related to him remained unaffected by his punishment. True, in the grave cases of violation of the sacral law and high treason the family was included in the punishment of the offending member (Josh 7:24ff; 1 Sam 22:12ff; 2 Kings 9:26), but even here the aim of confining punishment to the offender alone is already apparent (2 Kings 14:6). Blood vengeance was already restricted by the prescriptions of the Book of the Covenant, which attached a different degree of guilt to deliberate assassination and manslaughter (Ex 21:13, 14), and, furthermore, made provision for the individual who had done manslaughter to take asylum in a sanctuary (Ex 21:13f). This right of sanctuary certainly also survived till a later stage, for many expressions in the psalms undoubtedly recall this (Pss 5:7–8; 27:2–5; 61:4f). In the nature of things the cities of refuge represented a more permanent institution (Josh 20:1–9; Deut 19:1–14; Num 35:9–34). It was here that the transgressor had to submit himself to the judgement of the elders of the community. In the case of premeditated murder he was delivered up into the hands of the *goʾel*, the closest responsible relative of the victim, who incurred the duty of exacting blood vengeance. In the case of unpremeditated killing the perpetrator had to remain in the city of refuge until the death of the high priest. This was probably because the official accession of a new high priest was accompanied by a general amnesty. Since the disappearance of the earlier tribal solidarity entailed fresh dangers for the

individual, from now on special emphasis was laid upon the protection of his rights by the reminder that God was his covenant Lord. The oppression of the poor and weak, which is attested in the prescriptions of Deuteronomy and in passages in the prophets and Proverbs (Deut 24:17; 27:19; Is 10:2; Jer 7:6; 22:3; Zech 7:10; Prov 23:10 etc), calls down the vengeance of Yahweh upon the oppressors (Deut 32:35; Is 34:8; 61:2); ie, in place of the earlier solidarity of the tribe, that of religion came to the fore as a determining factor in the people's lives, together with the sense of corporate unity entailed by the covenant with God. Already in the story of David we can discern a certain tendency to aim at meekness in the face of injury and to renounce vengeance for Yahweh's sake (1 Sam 24:7, 11, 19f; 25:31ff). Again, the message proclaimed by the prophets to the effect that the relationship with God was of its nature with the individual as distinct from the community had the effect of finally driving out the idea of collective sharing in guilt (Ezek 18). Finally it was possible for the New Testament to require a complete renunciation of private vengeance (Mt 5:38–42) because of the progressive perfecting of the official concept of justice and the growing sense of an interior moral code. ↗ Enemy, ↗ love, ↗ hate.

Bibliography: E. Merz, *Die Blutrache bei den Israeliten*, Leipzig 1916; H. Cazelles, *Etudes sur le Code de l'Alliance*, Paris 1946, 117–20; J. Scharbert, *Solidarität in Segen und Fluch im AT und seiner Umwelt* (BBB 14), 1958; Eichrodt II–III, 1964⁵, 157ff.

Walter Kornfeld

Victory

Victory and defeat exist as the outcome of ↗ contest, strife, and ↗ war in this world; and defeat exists as the consequence of finite limitations, ↗ sin and ↗ death. Victory is the expression of power (see Hebrew *geḇûrâh*), strength, and might. The strong and mighty triumphs in the victory. The weak or he who has been deprived of his power succumbs in the defeat. God's compassionate emptying of himself has overthrown the rulers of this world in the paradox of the Cross; eschatological victory appears in the guise of defeat in this world.

A. The *Old Testament* contains accounts both of the victories of Israel and of the victories of her enemies, defeats suffered by the people. In the interpretation of Israel's history, which is focused upon Yahweh's powerful and gracious leadership, the victories and military successes (Ex 15:1–18; 17:8–16; Josh 6:16; 10:10; Judg 7:15; 1 Sam 14:6; 2 Chron 14:10f) are ascribed to HIM who fights on his people's behalf (Ex 14:14; 2 Chron 20:15). 'To conquer' (=$yš^c$ in the Hiphil) in Hebrew means 'to obtain help from God'. Yahweh himself fights for his people and makes them rich in victories (Deut 33:29; see also Hab 3:8). Yahweh, who alone is truly powerful (Ps 44:4; 48; Is 49:24–7), gives the victory (Deut 20:4; Josh 22:4; 1 Sam 14:45; 2 Sam 8:6). In their battles the people entreat Yahweh for victory (Ex 17:11). Victory depends upon him (Prov 21:31), and they receive it from him as a gift (Ps 18:32ff; 20:7–10; see also Ps 118:15f). It is not ascribed to their own power in battle

(Ps 33:16f; 1 Macc 3:19; 2 Macc 10:37f; 13:15; 15:8ff; Eccles 9:11; Judg 7:2ff; see also 1 QM III 5:8f; IV 13; XI 4f). But even though Yahweh is the unconquerable covenant partner of the people (Deut 32:22–43; Is 30:27–33; Nah 1:2–8; Hab 3; Judg 6:13ff), he can also give the victory to the enemies of the people and assign defeat to themselves (2 Chron 21:14; 24:20; 25:8–20; Jer 15:1–9; 27:6; Ezek 22). Moreover the people are aware as a matter of experience that in their victories, or in the victory of individuals among them, the power of evil is not finally broken. These factors keep alive their awareness, especially in the message of all the prophets, that every victory in this present age is subject to the ambiguity of that which is provisional and which merely foreshadows the final eschatological victory of God. This will take place in the final age, when God, either in person or through his Messiah, will enter into conflict, battle, war, as in the primordial age he waged war against the chaos dragon (Ps 74:13; 89:10; see also Is 51:9f; Job 26:11f), will overcome all the 'victories' of this world, of sin, death and Satan, and will finally set up his kingdom (Gen 3:15; Ps 51:62 [LXX]; see also Zech 14; Ezek 38f; Is 63:1–6) and usher in everlasting peace (Is 9:1–7; 11:1–9; Jer 23:5f; Ezek 34:23ff; etc).

B. According to the *New Testament*, in ↗ Jesus the one who is stronger has come, the one who conquers Satan and his accomplices (Lk 11:22; Col 2:15), the servant who brings justice to victory (Mt 12:20), the conqueror of the 'world' (Jn 16:33). In his preaching by word and deed, the victory of

God over the 'world', over the devils, sin, sickness, and death (see the miracle stories in the gospels), is accomplished. The victory gained in the death of Jesus (1 Cor 15:55)—in the world's eyes an ignominious defeat—has been confirmed by God through the resurrection. Jesus is the lion from the tribe of Judah who has conquered (Rev 5:5), the victor who has set out to conquer (Rev 6:2), the Lamb who was slain (Rev 5:12), who conquers the kings of the earth because he is the Lord of lords and the King of kings (Rev 17:14). The victory of Christ, won in death and resurrection, is only temporary, hidden (in defeat), and it is not until his ↗ *parousia* that it will finally be revealed for what it is. The victory of Satan and his forces (Rev 11:7; 13:7), which is now to be seen in the forefront of affairs, will have no enduring future because this 'victory' is only a 'constantly being on the point of' victory (Schlier), which is in despair of being able to hide the real defeat, and seeks to postpone the unveiling of the final victory of Christ.

Taken with Jesus in his failure, the christian has already in the present a share in the victory of Christ in faith, hope, and love (Rom 8:37; 1 Jn 2:13f; 5:4f; Rev 12:10f; 15:2), but he still remains engaged in the struggle (1 Cor 9:24; Phil 3:14), must show patience, steadfastness, and faithfulness (Rev 2-3), must fight against the 'world', against the forces of infidelity and immorality (1 Jn 2:13f; 5:4), in order that he may, as victor, be given a share of the kingdom with Christ (Rev 2:26; 3:21) and eternal life (Rev 2:7) in the blessed state of union with God (Rev 21:7). In faith and in love (especially as proved in the ordeal of martyrdom) the christian extends the victory of Christ in history already here below, the victory of Christ which consists in the fact 'that it is no longer the self-will which dominates history from within that prepares the immediate and the final future for itself, but the love of God, which has come to reign in Jesus Christ' (H. Schlier, *Besinnung auf das NT* II, 361). The christian can celebrate the victory of Christ already in the here and now in the words of the hymn: 'Thanks be to God who gives us the victory through our Lord Jesus Christ' (1 Cor 15:57).

Bibliography: TDNT IV, 942–5; F. Rienecker (ed.), *Lexikon zur Bibel*, Wuppertal 1960[2], 1295–6; *DBT* 553–5; R. Völkl, *Christ und Welt nach dem NT*, Würzburg, 1961, 430 and 454–63; H. Schlier, 'Jesus Christus und die Geschichte nach der Offenbarung des Johannes', *Besinnung auf das NT* II, Freiburg 1954, 358–73; H. Schlier, *Principalities and Powers in the New Testament*, London and New York 1961; R. Schnackenburg, *Die Johannesbriefe*, Freiburg 1963[2], 253–5.

Rudolf Pesch

Vigilance

The English concept of 'being awake' is used to cover several ideas which in biblical theology are distinct. What is common to them all is the emphasis on paying special heed. The most important of the aspects covered is that of preparedness or vigilance, which is particularly emphasised in the New Testament. At the same time, however, the other aspects must not on this account go altogether disregarded. Above all it is necessary to recognise which groups of ideas are mutually overlapping or even, in certain cases, synonymous.

A. *Old Testament*. The demand of God that his commandments, words and ways must be exactly observed is found in numerous passages in the Old Testament, together with warnings of punishment for non-observance. (Among the great number of these passages, see especially Ex 12:17, 24f; 13:10; 23:13, 15; Lev 8:35; 18:4f, 26, 30; 19:37; 20:8, 22; 22:9, 31; 25:18; 26:3; Deut 4:2, 6; 6:2, 17; 10:13; 12:28; 28:13; etc). Next among the prophets we find the Israelites reproached with having failed to maintain this observance, on which so much stress had been laid (see Mal 2:9; 3:7; Jer 16:11). Together with the more general exhortations we also find exhortations to maintain the same exact observance of individual commandments, especially the sabbath commandment (see Ex 31:13f; Lev 19:30; 26:2; Deut 5:12, 15; Is 56:2), but also the commandment prescribing unleavened bread for the Passover (see Ex 12:17; 23:15). The necessity of keeping guard over that which proceeds from the mouth is the subject of a special exhortation (Deut 23:23). In return for paying due heed to his will in the manner thus commanded God promises a reward (Ex 15:26; 19:5; 23:22; 1 Kings 6:12; etc). The greatest reward of God for loyal adherence to his commandments is the assurance that he in his turn watches over the devout (Ex 23:20: his angel goes before Israel; Ps 121:4, 7; 12; 17:8; 34:20; 89:28). The devout entreat God for this benevolent watchfulness over them (see Ps 16:1; 86:2; Jer 5:24; Ps 141:9). The idea of watchfulness (for the *parousia*) hardly occurs in the Old Testament.

B. In the *New Testament* also exact observance is referred to and required, and those who do not obey will be punished. The rich young man boasts of his observance of the law (Mt 19:20 and parallels). Stephen reproaches his adversaries with deficiency in this loyalty to the law (Acts 7:53; see also Gal 6:13). Blessed are they who keep the word of God exactly (Lk 11:28). He who keeps the word of Christ will not be judged by him (Jn 12:47). The clauses of the apostolic decree must be observed exactly (Acts 21:25). Timothy must hold firm to the teaching which has been handed down to him (1 Tim 6:20; 2 Tim 1:14).

Christians must guard themselves from devils (1 Jn 5:21) and in general pay great heed to themselves lest they lose the stability which they have acquired (2 Pet 3:17). Again, according to the teaching of the New Testament, God watches over the men who remain loyal to him (2 Thess 3:3; Jude 24). Christ has kept those who have been entrusted to him; the only exception is the son of perdition (Jn 17:12). The elders of Ephesus are exhorted to watchfulness over the flocks of God which have been entrusted to them (Acts 20:31). The same applies to the 'angel' of Sardis (Rev 3:2). The leaders of the churches watch over those who are under their authority and must render an account for them (Heb 13:17). By far the most significant statement concerning vigilance in the New Testament is the exhortation, which is so much stressed, to be ready for the *parousia*. Since we know neither the day nor the hour we must be ready and watch (Mt 24:42; 25:13). Just as a householder would watch if he knew at what hour the thief was to come, so we would watch if we knew the hour of the *parousia* (Mt 24:43). But the Father has hidden the day and the hour from us in this way (Mk 13:32 and parallels) in order that he might lay vigilance upon us as a task (Mk 13:34). This command to watch applies to the apostles, but likewise to 'all' (Mk 13:35, 37). Blessed are those servants whom when the Lord comes he shall find watching; the Lord himself will be their servant (Lk 12:37f).

The episode of the Garden of Olives shows how closely the prayer and the vigilance required of Christ are connected (Mt 26:38–41 and parallels). It is necessary (physically) to watch in order to pray; through prayer we keep watch in expectation of the coming of Christ. Clearly this impressive exhortation of the Lord has been taken up by the apostles (1 Cor 16:13; Col 4:2: 'Be watchful in prayer'; see also Eph 6:18; 1 Thess 5:6; 1 Pet 5:8).

In this case, as in so many others, the mysterious Book of Revelation takes up this exhortation of the Lord and unites many of his different sayings in a single one, that namely in which he is represented as saying: 'Blessed is he who is awake, keeping his garments that he may not go naked and be seen exposed' (Rev 16:15).

Bibliography: Meinertz I, 64f; A. Oepke, *TDNT* II, 338f; Bultmann 79; G. Friedrich, Osterloh 66of; M. Didier, *DBT* 563–5.

Wolfgang Beilner

Virgin birth

There can be no mistaking the special interest with which Matthew and Luke record, at different points in their respective infancy narratives, the mysterious manner in which Jesus was conceived by his virgin mother Mary (Mt 1:18–25; Lk 1:26–38). This was achieved by the Spirit of God without the intervention of a human father. Even if we accept the generally admitted position that both narratives are independent of each other from the literary point of view, still they do both derive from an earlier tradition which is common to them both. A further indication of this from the form-critical point of view is that the two accounts agree in all essentials in the basic structure and plan of the revelation episode: the imparting of the mystery— difficulties and ponderings on the part of the recipient—explanation by the angel—willingness and acceptance on the part of her to whom it is addressed. Thus the tradition reaches back beyond the stage at which the gospels were written to the first age of the Jewish–christian community, a fact which is confirmed in Matthew and Luke alike by the religious and linguistic colouring of the narrative.

In Matthew the uniqueness of Jesus' conception is already indicated at the conclusion of the genealogy of Joseph (1:16), and that too by means of a formula which he has probably employed of set purpose: 'the child and his mother' (2:11, 13f, 2of). Likewise in Lk 3:23 the immediate significance of the parenthesis *hōs enomizeto* (='as was supposed') is that it is an indication of the fact that it was only in the judgement of those among whom he lived that Joseph was counted as the father of Jesus, whereas the real mystery of Jesus' birth is imparted in Lk 1:26–38. Here a further point is indicated, namely that whereas the incarnation of Jesus was brought about miraculously by the Holy Spirit, at first this remained unknown to the generality of men, and the true facts were preserved only in the narrow circle of the initiated. In view of this, those who regard the silence of the rest of the New Testament as an argument against the historical truth of the virgin birth find that their objections are deprived of their force. The virgin birth was not included as an urgent and vital element in the early christian preaching because, according to Acts 1:22; 10:37 and according to the general outline and the content of Mark (see 1:1), this consisted essentially in the 'words and deeds' of Jesus (Acts 1:1) in the course of his public work. It began, therefore, with his baptism and continued up to the witness to the resurrection. So far as judaism was concerned, it was more important that the messianic characteristics of Jesus should be pointed out than the fact of his virgin birth, and first and foremost among these messianic characteristics was the proof of his Davidic descent as demonstrated by both the family trees of Joseph (Mt 1:1–17; Lk 3:23–38). This was all the more true in view of the fact that any idea of a virgin birth was quite unfamiliar to the Jews. Thus Paul too has no reason to speak of the virgin birth in connection with his message of redemption. Indeed his primary concern throughout was the preaching of salvation, and his interest in the history of Jesus was

secondary and subordinate to this. The phrase *genomenon ek gunaikos* (='born of woman') in Gal 4:4 is an expression for the birth of a man which also occurs in the Old Testament (see Job 14:1; compare Mt 11:11 with Lk 7:20). Again, 'without father, without mother' in Heb 7:3 is not meant to refer to the virgin birth, and the variant readings for Jn 1:13f (b, Iren., Tertul. have *natus est* in the singular), which might be adduced in support of the virgin birth (in the apocryphal Letter of the Apostles 3 the phrase is taken in this sense), cannot be maintained from the point of view of textual criticism. From the fact that the virgin birth is not included among the themes and statements regarded as essential from the outset in the early christian preaching, it can be deduced that it was not a 'creation' of the community belief, and that the idea of the virgin birth could not have been an assumption deriving from this.

While, therefore, the attestation of the virgin birth in the New Testament is relatively scanty, still no statement can be found in it which is opposed to the possibility or the actuality of the virgin birth. It is true that Jesus is described by his countrymen as 'the carpenter's son' (Mt 13:55; in the parallel passage of Mk 6:3 he is called simply 'the carpenter, the son of Mary' without any mention of Joseph), or as 'the son of Joseph' (Lk 3:23; 4:22; Jn 1:45; 6:42). Again in Lk 2:27, 41ff there is mention of his 'parents'. In Lk 2:33 we find a reference to 'his father and his mother', and in Lk 2:48 'your father and I'. But these references apply to the legal fatherhood of Joseph in the sense attested in Mt

1:1–17, and from this it is to be concluded that in the popular estimation Jesus was also regarded as the son of Joseph by physical descent (see Lk 3:23). It must be observed that neither Matthew nor Luke has felt that these statements represent any contradiction of what they have recorded in their infancy narratives concerning the conception of Jesus by the miraculous intervention of the Spirit, and without any human father. In fact this is expressed particularly clearly in the manner in which the generations follow strictly one upon another in the human genealogy recorded in Mt 1:1–17, and also in the revelation concerning the part played by the Holy Spirit in the conception of Jesus (Mt 1:18–25). From Mk 3:21 inferences have sometimes been drawn to the effect that when the 'friends' of Jesus took measures to restrain him Mary did not behave like a mother who was conscious of the miraculous and mysterious circumstances of his birth. But no argument can really be adduced from this passage, for it has nothing whatever to tell us either about whether his mother was present at all, or about her behaviour on this occasion. On the other hand we should maintain an equal reserve with regard to the exact meaning of the saying of Mary in the episode recorded in Jn 2:1–11. For apart from the unique style of the johannine presentation we cannot conclude with any certainty that the reference to his mother implies that it was her awareness of the mystery of the birth of her son that made her expect him to give miraculous assistance on this occasion.

It is equally impossible to establish that the infancy narrative, together with the tradition of the virgin birth, must represent a secondary embellishment subsequently prefixed to the earlier account of Jesus' public ministry. As has been mentioned above, from the aspects of religion and language alike various elements in the narrative evince a judaeo–christian character present in them from the outset, and this tells against any such assumption. This is true not only of Luke but equally of Matthew. On examining his work we can discern exactly the same methods of presentation and composition in the infancy narrative as in the main part of the gospel, so that the first two chapters must have grown up together with the gospel as a whole.

A. von Harnack attempted by means of arguments based on literary criticism to strike out the passages referring to the virgin birth from the lukan narrative (1:27 with its two mentions of *parthenos* (=virgin, young woman); 1:34f with its clear assertion of the miraculous conception; 3:23: *hōs enomizeto*) on the grounds that they are secondary additions. In this way he sought to arrive at an account in which the virgin birth was omitted. This attempt, though misguided, has not yet been wholly recognised as obsolete. From the text-critical point of view this approach involves an indefensible arbitrariness with regard to the clear and unambiguous assertion of these passages, but apart from this the erasures which it involves would deprive the narrative of its underlying point and consistency, and would fail to do justice to the significant difference between the proclamation of the birth of Jesus here, and that found in Jn

1:8–25. The very fact that the angel was sent not to Joseph—as might have been expected from his prior apparition to Zechariah—but to Mary, the bride, shows that there is a mystery here which primarily affects Mary. A further point which can be noticed in the narrative of the prediction of the birth of John is that the great age of Zechariah and the barrenness of Elizabeth up to this point is stressed, so that the intervention of God here is brought into line with the Old Testament episodes affecting women such as Sarah, who were favoured by God with the power to conceive naturally even though circumstances had seemed to rule it out. The same point is implicitly conveyed in the story of Zechariah and Elizabeth as told in Lk 1:23f. In Mary, on the other hand, as presented in Lk 1:27, 34, we are confronted with a young, chaste maiden who received a promise and a guarantee that she would conceive a child who was the Messiah by reason of a special intervention on God's part. In this no reference whatever is made to any human father, and in fact it can plainly be seen that any such father is excluded. The evangelist's reserve with regard to the fact of the conception and the miraculous incarnation of the child is palpable, and he says nothing of this.

These considerations, drawn as they are from the intrinsic content of the narrative, tell strongly in favour of the position that the virgin birth was intended from the first to belong to the gospel narrative of Luke. But apart from this we have the witness of Matthew, which is incontestable on either literary or text-critical grounds. And this, as has been said, must derive from the same original tradition as that which lies behind Luke.

The miraculous intervention of God transcending the process of natural generation is described in Lk 1:35: *pneuma hagion epeleusetai epi se kai dunamis hupsistou episkiasei se* ('the Holy Spirit will come upon you, and the power of the Most High will overshadow you'). Again, in Mt 1:18, 20 the words *ek pneumatos hagiou* ('of the Holy Spirit') make God the agent of the virginal conception. 'Holy Spirit' here can hardly be intended in a trinitarian sense, but rather in accordance with Old Testament usage, for which the synoptics show a preference, so that it is used to designate the special intervention of God. It is apparent that the two relevant clauses stand in synonymous parallelism to one another, and from this it can be deduced that the words 'power of the Most High' is an alternative expression of the same idea. The two expressions 'come upon you' and 'overshadow you', which are likewise to be taken as synonymous, are hardly intended as analogous to the natural processes of generation. Such an interpretation cannot be maintained either on grounds of linguistic usage or in terms of the Old Testament and Jewish idea of God. In view of the religious tone of the narrative, characterised as it is throughout by an atmosphere of deep reverence, it is more probable that the term *overshadow* is calculatedly reminiscent of the 'glory of God' descending upon the Tabernacle as described in Ex 40:34f. The term used for this in LXX is *epeskiazen*. The clause in 1:35b can be translated in various ways, but the reference to the 'Son of God' which it contains is certainly not intended to imply that it was only through the virgin birth and by reason of it that the child who was conceived was to be called 'Son of God'. The references to the 'Holy Spirit' and the 'power of the Most High' point rather to the mystery of the Son of God from all eternity, who by means of the virgin birth becomes man. Admittedly this indication is somewhat subtle, and, from a theological point of view, rather vague in the manner of its formulation (see the interpretation of 'Holy Spirit' and 'power of the Most High' in the earlier patristic exegesis of the *Logos*).

For critics of the gospels who have a rationalist approach, and who deny the reality of the supernatural as attested in biblical revelation, the question of how the idea of the virgin birth arose represents a much discussed problem. The passage from Isaiah (7:14) concerning the conception and birth of Immanuel through a 'maiden', which is cited in Mt 1:22f, plays a particularly important part in this discussion. Attention is especially focused upon the term *parthenos*, the LXX translation of the Hebrew *ʿalmâh*. It is held that it is possible to regard this prophetic oracle as the point of departure for the idea of a virgin birth. However the fact must be borne in mind that in LXX *parthenos* is also used to designate a young woman who has attained sufficient maturity to be ready for marriage (Gen 24:43; 34:3; Sir 30:20), so that it cannot be established that when the translator used *parthenos* in this passage of Isaiah he was thinking of a virgin in the strict sense, let alone of a virginal conception and birth. But over and above these considerations it must further be observed that the quotation,

which probably also underlies the lukan narrative, as used by Matthew has chiefly the force of a reflective commentary. He often inserts quotations of this kind by way of commentary in order to establish a connection between the facts which he has received and is handing down (and which are initially quite independent of the Old Testament records) and the salvific history recorded in the Old Testament. In the instance under consideration it should be borne in mind that, according to the present state of our knowledge of pre-christian judaism, Is 7:14 was never interpreted in the sense of a virgin birth, so that to the Jewish reader the account in Mt 1:18–25 must have appeared absolutely new and astonishing. Thus Is 7:14 cannot be taken as the point of departure for the idea of the virgin birth. Moreover the extent to which the contrary opinion was prevalent in judaism can also be gathered from the fact that in the later Greek translations of the Old Testament (second century: Aquila, Theodotian, Symmachus), which emerged in the time of the anti-christian polemic, the neutral word *neanis* (=young woman) was adopted in place of *parthenos* in Is 7:14.

Other attempts at explaining the virgin birth as recorded in the New Testament seek to establish influences of oriental and hellenistic myths according to which famous men such as Plato, Alexander, and Augustus were born of the union of gods with human women. In this connection the birth of a child promised in Virgil's Fourth Eclogue has been the object of special notice, as also have the ideas of the origins of divinised kings as children of the queen and the god Amon-Re, which are to be found especially in Egypt. These variations upon the *hieros gamos* (= 'sacral marriage') theme differ widely one from another, ranging from an extremely realistic and gross idea of sexual union to a sublimisation of the process. But however varied the individual versions may be, the idea always persists of a material union, and in this connection the expression *parthenos*, constantly recurring especially in these myths, is used in a very broad sense. Thus Ishtar, the Babylonian goddess of love (as also her counterparts Aphrodite, Hathor-Isis, or the mother of Helios), is often called 'virgin' although she appears as 'the *hierodoulē* (= temple courtesan) of all the gods'. This description is merely intended to convey the idea of unfading bloom and freshness, or that of the unwavering power of the goddess; it is not meant to contain the implication of being virginally intact. In this connection it should be noticed that in the earliest age of christianity these myths were no longer taken seriously as relating historical facts even among pagans. For this reason it is more than questionable whether the interests of christian preaching would have been served by ascribing virgin birth in this sense to men unless it was supported by the awareness of a revelation which was taken extremely seriously. Moreover such an assumption would utterly fail to do justice to the biblical concept of God, differing essentially as this did from that prevailing in the religions of antiquity. This idea of God as the absolutely spiritual being also falls to the ground if we assume that the conception of *pneuma* in the infancy nar-

rative is nothing else than a substitute for conceptions found in the accounts of 'sacral marriages' in hellenistic mythology. In that case one would be forced to assume that the idea of the spirit in the infancy narrative was different from that in the rest of the gospel. Besides this we should also notice that the infancy narrative emerged from the matrix of Jewish christianity, and this implies that it is the Hebrew word *rûaḥ* which lies behind the word *pneuma* (↗ spirit), and this Hebrew word has a feminine, not a masculine, force.

One further point remains to be added. It has sometimes been suggested that the idea of the virgin birth arose from theologising activities within the christian community as it sought to interpret its beliefs. But in what we have said above we have already made it clear that any such hypothesis is wholly superfluous. For the virgin birth is not necessarily postulated by the christian message, however much— once we have received the revealed truth—we may go on to educe ideas from it which are significant in their bearing upon the mystery of the incarnation of the eternal Son of God.

Bibliography: O. Bardenhewer, *Mariä Verkündigung*, Freiburg 1903; A. Steinmann, *Die jungfr. Geburt d. Herrn*, Münster 1926; J. Gresham, *The Virgin Birth of Christ*, New York and London 1930; M. Dibelius, *Jungfrauengeburt und Krippenkind*, Heidelberg 1932; J.-M. Vosté, *De conceptione virginali Jesu Christi*, Rome 1933; K. L. Schmidt, 'Die jungfr. Geburt Jesu Christi', *TB* 14 (1935), 289–97; K. Prümm, 'Empfangen vom Hl. Geiste, geboren aus Maria der Jungfrau', *Der christl. Glaube und die altheidnische Welt* I, 1935, 253–333; D. Edwards, *The Virgin Birth in History and Faith*, London 1943; R. Laurentin, *Structure et théologie de Lc 1–2*, Paris 1957; *R. Laurentin, *Queen of Heaven*, Dublin–London 1961²; E. Nroden,

Die Geburt des Kindes, Darmstadt 1958; E. Pax, *LTK* v², 1210f; G. Delling, *TDNT* v, 826–37; J. Bauer, 'Monstra te esse matrem, virgo singularis', *MTZ* 9 (1958), 124–35; K. H. Schelkle, *Die Mutter des Erlösers*, Düsseldorf 1958; J. Schmid, *Das Ev. nach Lukas (RNT* 3), 1960⁴, 44–50; O. Michel and O. Betz, *Von Gott gezeugt (BZNW* 26), 1960, 3–23; J. Gewiess, 'Lk 1:34', *BZ* 5 (1961), 221–34; A. Strobel, 'Der Gruss an Maria', *ZNW* 53 (1962), 87–111; G. Miegge, *Die Jungfrau Maria*, Göttingen 1962; M. Rehm, 'Almah', *BZ* 8 (1964), 89–101; A. Vögtle, 'Die Genealogie Mt 1:2–11 und die matthäische Kindheitsgeschichte', *BZ* 8 (1964), 45–58 and 239–62; and 9 (1969), 32–49; *L. Hermans, *The Bible on the Childhood of Jesus*, London 1965; *E. Schillebeeckx, *Mary, Mother of the Redemption*, London and New York 1964, 9–47.

Johannes Kürzinger

Virginity

A. The only reasons known to the *Old Testament* for setting a high value on virginity are, first, that maidens should be kept inviolate up to their marriage, and secondly, that virginity constitutes an element in cultic purity (↗ clean and unclean). For instances of the importance attached to maidens being preserved inviolate see Gen 34:7, 31 and also Gen 24:16, Judg 19:24. The loss of her virginity means that the maiden's marriageable value is diminished (Ex 22:15f; Deut 22:14–19). Indeed it entails the penalty of stoning (Deut 22:20f) or at any rate the loss of her honour (2 Sam 13:2–18; Lam 5:11; Sir 7:24; 42:9–11). The High Priest is forbidden to take any but a virgin in marriage (Lev 21:13f. This prescription applies to all priests in Ezek 44:22).

Virginity as a life-long state is unknown. So far from being a desirable condition it is counted as the greatest misfortune to die before marriage (Judg 11:37f. Moving scenes of funeral lamentations are known from Greek vase paintings, especially those appearing upon vessels destined for unmarried women: see K. Schefold, *Griechische Kunst als relig. Phänomen*, Hamburg 1959, 103), or even simply to remain childless when one has been married (Gen 30:23; 1 Sam 1:6, 11, 15). When the menfolk have been decimated by war the women actually decide to enter upon a marriage in which a single husband is shared by seven of them, and in which, moreover, they make themselves responsible for their own food and clothing, simply for the sake of being married and being able to bear the name of a husband (Is 4:1).

There are some indications that the unmarried state was prized in *later judaism*, in that it was considered honourable for a widow to remain unmarried after the death of her husband (Judith 16:22; cf Lk 2:36f). This is in line with the ideal of control of the instincts as pleasing to God, an ideal which finds expression in the prayer of Tobias: 'Not for fleshly lust do I take to wife . . .' (Tob 8:7). In Essene circles one repeatedly encounters a certain disdain for marriage, which is based first and foremost upon a contempt for woman, who is inclined to be dissolute and unfaithful (Josephus, *Bell. Jud.*, 2:8, 2), egotistical and immoderately jealous, shameless and arrogant, one who corrupts men's morals and would actually break up the monastic community of the Essenes (Philo in Euseb. *Praep. Evang.* 8:11). How far these reasons put forward by Philo and Josephus are the correct ones is incertain. Doubtless married

Essenes did occur, and in the Community Rule this is actually presupposed. But against this 1 QS is silent on the subject of marriage. Prohibitions such as that of not appearing naked before fellow-members of the sect or even allowing an involuntary exposure of the private parts (1 QS vii 12–14) visualise a community of men in that they are directed against homosexual tendencies. On the other hand, skeletons of women and children also have been found in the cemetery of Qumran, and celibacy is nowhere enjoined as a matter of precept. Still less is any motive adduced for such a prescription. Probably the solution is to be found in the fact that the members of the community thought of themselves as priests ministering at the true sanctuary, and it would have seemed obvious to them that sexual abstinence was required as a necessary condition for this cultic ministration (↗ clean; see also J. Maier, *Die Texte vom Toten Meer* ii, Munich–Basle 1960, 10f).

B. The *New Testament*. Mary, espoused as she was to Joseph, after she had brought the divine child into the world while still remaining a virgin (↗ virgin birth), chose the state of permanent virginity. Contrary to a long-established exegesis of Lk 1:34, however, she did not regard virginity in marriage as praiseworthy, or undertake it right from the first, for otherwise she would not have committed herself to entering upon any marriage at all. Mary's question in Lk 1:34 (in the context of the story of the annunciation the motive behind this is to provide an opening for the divine message) expresses nothing but astonishment at the fact that she is to become a mother at the time of her espousals, before actually being taken into her bridegroom's house (for a detailed exposition, see J. B. Bauer, *MTZ* 9 [1958], 124–35, and *Theologisches Jahrbuch*, Leipzig 1960, 257–70).

Jesus freely chooses the celibate state. We may recall the saying concerning those who disqualify themselves for marriage for the sake of the kingdom of heaven, a saying which it is not given to everyone to understand (Mt 19:10ff). J. Blinzler (*ZNW* 28 [1957], 254–70) is certainly right when he interprets this as Jesus' self-defence before the scribes and pharisees, who are precisely reproaching Jesus with this celibate life that he leads. In any case, the apostles did not take the saying as applying to themselves, as is shown by 1 Cor 9:5; for here we are told that they take their wives with them on their missionary journeys (see J. B. Bauer, *BZ* 3 [1959], 94–102). From this it may be deduced that Jesus' answer to Peter's question (Lk 18:28ff): 'There is no man who has left house or wife etc . . . for the sake of the kingdom of God who will not receive manifold more . . .', in no sense demands that marriage shall be completely given up. What Jesus is really concerned with here, as also in Mt 10:37f, is to define the priority of duties. As for the mention of the four daughters of Philip the evangelist in Acts 21:9, it may reasonably be doubted whether this is intended to imply anything more than simply that these '*virgins* endowed with the spirit of prophecy' were unmarried.

Paul, who is himself celibate (1 Cor 7:7), recommends the celibate state when it is a ↗ charisma (1 Cor 7:7), because then man can give undivided service to Christ (1 Cor 7:32–5), especially in the final age which has already commenced (1 Cor 7:26, 28), for this entails a certain emancipation from all earthly ties. We should keep our eyes fixed upon the ultimate, in which there will be no sexual union (1 Cor 7:29 cp Mk 12:35; Mt 22:30; Lk 20:35f; see further Mt 24:37ff; Lk 17:26f), no tears (1 Cor 7:30; see also Mt 5:4; Lk 6:21; Rev 7:17; 21:4), no earthly joy, no earthly gain, and no more commerce (1 Cor 7:30f; see also Lk 12:15–21; ⁊ riches).

The pastoral epistles require that he who undertakes an ecclesiastical office shall not have entered upon in the past, or enter upon in the future, any fresh marriage after the death of his first wife (1 Tim 3:2, 12; Tit 1:6). Again, only widows of one husband were admitted to the official status of widows in the early christian community (1 Tim 5:9). In both instances, proof of a well-balanced personality must be looked for, as manifested precisely by self-mastery in the matter of the instincts (see the conclusion of A above).

The 'virgins' (*parthenoi*) mentioned in Rev 14:4 are to be taken in a metaphorical sense. 'These have not defiled themselves with women, for they are chaste'. What is meant by this is faithful adherence to Christ, just as elsewhere: in the prophets, too, unchastity and adultery mean unfaithfulness to God as covenant partner. It cannot be intended to designate these chosen ones as virgins in the physical sense (as is still obstinately maintained in many commentaries, see Lohmeyer, Schick, etc, *ad loc.*), for in that case Peter himself and the other married

apostles would be excluded, and marriage would be stigmatised as 'defilement' (see Bonsirven and Karrer, *ad loc.*). Similarly in 2 Cor 11:2 virginity is an expression of total and exclusive adherence to Christ, to whom Paul has consecrated the community: 'For I betrothed you to Christ to present you as a pure bride to her one husband' (for the linguistic usage, see also Jer 18:13ff).

Bibliography: J. Fischer, *Ehe und Jungfräulichkeit im NT* (*BZF* 9) 1919, 3f; J. Dillersberger, 'Die Jungfräulichkeit nach der Lehre Jesu', *Anima* 7 (1952), 201–7; A. Löhr, 'Die Jungfräulichkeit als christliche Wesenshaltung nach Schrift und Liturgie', *Anima* 7 (1952), 207–20; J. Schneider, *TDNT* II, 765–8; G. Delling, *TDNT* v, 826–37; J. B. Bauer, *BL* 23 (1955/6), 8–13; Haag 875f; J. Michl, *LTK* v², 1213f; J. Leipoldt, *Griechische Philosophie und frühchristliche Askese*, Berlin 1961, esp. 31–8; J. Leal gives an enlightening treatment of 1 Cor VII in *VD* 35 (1957), 97–102, and especially also 1 Cor VII 36ff, where it is certainly a christian man (that is not 'father') and his bride (here *parthenos* manifestly has this meaning, just as in 2 Cor XI 2) that are in question (see also W. G. Kümmel, *Festschrift Bultmann*, (*BZNW* 21), 1957², 275–95; J. B. Bauer, *BL* 22 [1954/5], 143; and J. O'Rourke, *CBQ* 20 [1958], 292–8); L. Legrand, 'Fécondité virginale selon l'Esprit dans le NT', *NRT* 84 (1962), 65–75; L. Legrand, 'The Sacrificial Value of Virginity', *Scripture* 14 (1962), 65–75; L. Legrand, *La virginité dans la Bible*, Paris 1964; E. H. Maly, 'Virginity in the New Testament', *Marian Studies* 13 (1962), 41–61; R. Boon, 'Ontstaan, verbreiding en theologie der virginiteit in de vroeg-christelijke kerk', *TT* 16 (1961/2), 417–49; F. Wulf, *GL* 36 (1963), 341–52; *J.-P. Audet, *Structures of Christian Priesthood: Home, Marriage, and Celibacy in the Pastoral Service of the Church*, London and New York 1967, esp. 1–121.

Johannes B. Bauer

Vision of God

A. *The 'vision' of God on earth.*
1. References to 'visions' of God are

not infrequent in the *Old Testament*, but extremely varied in meaning. There are passages which are more primitive in outlook, in which God is thought of as present to the physical sight, that is in a divine apparition (theophany). By means of this, it is thought, God has willed to favour certain men with the privilege of holding converse with him and receiving his revelation. At the 'visit of God' to Mamre (Gen 18) Abraham sees three men (v 2). God comes to visit him with two companions (angels) in human form, promises him that a son will be born to him (v 10) and holds a discussion with him about Sodom (vv 20–33). His appearance is not described; instead the one point on which the narrative concentrates exclusively for its meaning is his coming and speaking with Abraham. Still more mysterious is Jacob's nocturnal struggle with God (Gen 32:25–33), after which the patriarch declares: 'I have seen God face to face, and yet my life is preserved' (v 30; see also 33:10), thus expressing the fact that he has had a direct personal encounter with God, who has confronted him as a human contestant of extreme strength, and yet who has remained hidden in the darkness of night and shrouded in mystery. At the same time we already find in the words of Jacob/Israel a hint of a conviction which is to be still more clearly expressed in later passages, namely that no man can see God and still remain alive (see also Ex 24:11; 33:20; Judg 6:22f; 13:22f—in the last two of these passages it is the 'angel of Yahweh' that is spoken of). The apparition imparted to Moses in the burning thornbush (Ex 3) has the sole purpose of revealing the God of the fathers and laying upon Moses the task of liberating the Israelites from Egypt. The idea of Yahweh making himself visible expressed in v 2 is mitigated—as so often elsewhere in the Old Testament—by the fact that it is the 'angel of Yahweh' who appears in the (or as the) flame of fire; Moses must not come any closer to see the burning thornbush (v 4f), and he veils his face, 'for he was afraid to look at God' (v 6). Again the seventy elders who ascend the mountain of God with Moses 'beheld the God of Israel', and this is regarded as a special proof of grace. Yet God himself is not described, only the flashing and glittering of light 'under his feet' is mentioned (Ex 24:10f). But the intention underlying the still naive language here is to express the close proximity to God of the parties involved. In the 'tent of meeting' where Moses put questions to God, 'the Lord used to speak to Moses face to face as a man speaks to his friend' (Ex 33:11). Yet God accedes to the request of his chosen mediator only to the limited extent of allowing him to see his 'back view' but not his 'face' (Ex 33:18–23). The prophet Elijah experiences the 'passing by of the Lord' without having any kind of vision, only by hearing him, and that too not in the storm, earthquake or fire but in the soft gentle murmuring (1 Kings 19:11f). Thus is expressed the religious conviction of those men who have had an experience of being in immediate proximity to God, or give accounts of this. 'Seeing' is only one of several possible ways of describing their experience. Many turns of phrase in which the 'face of God' is referred to are figurative or even formalised. 'To appear before the face of God' or to 'see' it means to visit the sanctuary (Ex 23:15, 17; 34:20, 23f; Deut 16:16; etc—a courtier's term for an audience). The 'face' of God is his attitude of attention to men, and thus signifies God's help (see Ps 11:7; 17:15; 24:6; 27:8; Job 33:26; Hos 5:15). It can be 'appeased' (literally 'stroked': see Ex 32:11; 1 Sam 13:12; 1 Kings 13:6; etc), and God 'lifts up' his countenance and lets it 'shine' (in the priestly blessing Num 6:25f; see Ps 4:6; 31:16; 67:1; etc). Prayer and cultic veneration in the sanctuary are ways of encountering God on earth, possibilities of 'seeing' him. The possibility of seeing God, supernatural and spiritual as he is, in actual physical fact continues to be denied.

This applies even to the 'visions' of the prophets. In Is 6:1, 5 the prince of the prophets, in speaking of the vision in which he received his vocation, says that he 'saw the Lord' (with his own eyes). But he does not describe his appearance, only that of his surroundings: the throne and seraphim and 'the train of his robe' which 'filled the temple'. For the rest he hears the voice of the Lord (6:8ff), and for all visionaries it is this revelation of the word that is the decisive factor (see 1 Kings 22:19-23, the prophet Micaiah son of Imlah; further on this Amos 9:1). Ezekiel's 'chariot vision' (Ezek 1), which played a major part in later Jewish mysticism for ecstatic experiences, (Merkaba mysticism) likewise mentions only 'something *like* the flashing of polished bronze, which looked *like* fire . . . and brightness shone all round him' (Ezek 1:27). The vision itself is full of similes and comparisons, and the attempt to put it into words is only a stammering and halting one. The description of the 'Ancient of Days' in Dan 7:9 is a figurative and symbolic mode of speaking about God, which is subsequently taken up in the New Testament revelation (see 1:12-17 on the 'one like a son of man'; c 4 on the 'throne'). These are similes and images for the indescribable glory of God in heaven. Right up to christian times judaism adopted an attitude of extreme scepticism towards ecstatic visions. The rabbis issued warning against such presumptuous approaches to God. Of the four rabbis who, according to the Jerusalem Talmud (*ḥagiga* 77a), entered paradise during their lifetime, only Rabbi Akiba survived the ecstatic experience unharmed. It was only later that the demand for a direct mystical experience of God developed.

2. In the *New Testament* complete clarity prevails on the point that a direct vision of God on earth is impossible. When Philip asks for a theophany he receives the reply from Jesus: 'He who has seen me has seen the Father . . . Do you not believe that I am in the Father and the Father in me?' (Jn 14:8-10). It is only in faith that we have the power to 'see' God, that is to attain to union with him. The incarnate Son of God is the perfect image of the Father, and the way to him. In faith the disciples beheld his glory (Jn 1:14), above all in the 'signs' which he performed (see Jn 2:11; 11:40). According to Paul the reason why it is impossible for us to see God is that we are still living in the body; 'we walk by faith, not by sight' (2 Cor 5:7). To believe is still 'to see

darkly in a mirror' (1 Cor 13:12a). Nevertheless in comparison with the old covenant, in which the glory of God was still veiled and limited, 'we behold with unveiled face the glory of the Lord (= Christ), and are being changed into the same image from glory to glory' (2 Cor 3:18). This passage, which has been rendered difficult to understand by Paul's 'midrash', is hardly intended to say more than what follows in 4:4–6, namely, that we can recognise the 'glory of God in the face of Christ' thanks to the fact that we have been endowed with the Holy Spirit and the inner enlightenment from God which illumines our hearts as light illumined darkness at the dawn of creation. Nowhere in the New Testament is any basis to be found for the possibility of a mystical or ecstatic vision of God upon earth. Paul adopts an attitude of extreme reserve towards visions and ecstasies, although he himself has been favoured with them (see 2 Cor 12:1–9). The present is still the time of afflictions and suffering in order that God's 'strength may be made perfect in (human) weakness'. John goes so far as emphatically to reject the idea of any man having seen God at any time (Jn 1:18; 5:37; 6:46; 1 Jn 4:12); only the only-begotten Son has brought us knowledge of God (Jn 1:18), and bears witness to that which he has seen and heard direct (from God) (3:32). It cannot be determined with certainty whether the point of this assertion is directed against the claims of the Jews to the effect that their history contains instances of men seeing God (Moses and the elders? see 1:18; 5:37), or against gnostics' assertions that they have experienced ecstatic visions of God (see 1 Jn 4:12; also 2:3; 3:6; 4:20; 3 Jn 11). In any case the principle of faith is expressed with all possible clarity: only by the revelation of the Son can we attain to knowledge of and communion with God.

B. *The direct vision of God in the world to come and in heaven.* So long as Old Testament religion had no clear light to throw on the possibility of bodily resurrection, and so long as it represented survival after death as a shadowy existence in the underworld (Sheol), it was also incapable of knowing anything of the blessing of a direct vision of God in the age to come. Job 19:26f, which is a difficult passage and textually uncertain, can be interpreted as referring to a vision of God in the next world. More probably, however, what it intends to convey is that God's favour and justification will be restored to Job anew when he has undergone extreme physical chastisement and dereliction of soul (see 14:13; 23:3–7). It is not until resurrection is understood as a participation in the glory of God that we find the idea of the just seeing that glorious world of God in which they themselves are endowed with 'radiance' (see Dan 12:3) and 'clothed with garments of glory' (Enoch [Eth] 62:16; Bar [Syr] 51:3, 5, 10). With loud cries of joy the just behold the 'glory of him who takes them to himself, and enter into rest with sevenfold joy' (4 Ezra 7:91). The seventh and highest joy is that they 'behold the countenance of him whom they have faithfully served in this life' (v 98). The idea of seeing God in heaven could also arise in connection with speculations about Paradise. Thus according to Enoch (Slav) 31:2 God opened heaven to Adam while he was still in Paradise 'so that he should see the angels and the light without darkness'. Reminiscences of the wilderness period also gave rise to the expectation of a direct vision of God: 'Whenever the Israelites saw God they became virtuous. They saw him at the (Red) Sea and became virtuous ... They saw him at Sinai and became honest ... They saw him in the tabernacle and became just ... and if they see him in the world to come then they will be virtuous' (Midr. Ps 149 § 1 [SB I, 213]). Finally the idea of God dwelling in the sanctuary gave rise to the idea of an unveiled vision of his glory in the time of salvation (see Sib v 420–28). In the New Testament description of the heavenly Jerusalem we find: 'They will see his face' (Rev 22:4). In the ApocAbr. 29:20 God promises the virtuous: 'But they see my face and rejoice with my people'. Similarly Jesus praises those men who are pure of heart, 'for they shall see God' (Mt 5:8). In all these passages it is the *eschatological vision* which is being thought of; but since in later Judaism the just were already considered to dwell in a (heavenly) Paradise (and no longer in the underworld), it cannot be excluded that each individual will receive a personal vision of God after his death (see Lk 16:22, 25; 23:42).

Paul and John teach us with all the clarity that could be desired that what is meant by this vision of God in the world to come (or in heaven) is a direct encounter with God, a knowing him, an apprehending him in blessedness, and a becoming one with him in love such as is not yet possible on earth.

Seeing God 'face to face' (1 Cor 13:12a) is contrasted with 'seeing him in a mirror darkly' here on earth. But it is not only our understanding that is affected by this knowledge of him which is no longer 'in part'. For 'knowing God' as conceived of in the bible implies finding union of life with God (see J. Botterweck), and to 'see God' is only one aspect among others of the nearness to God and the blessedness which is to be hoped for in the future kingdom of God (see Mt 5:3–10). 'We shall understand God even as we have been known (by God)' (1 Cor 13:12b), that is as God has embraced us with his gaze, has graciously chosen us and lovingly drawn us to himself. The graciousness of these prior acts on God's part is still more strongly thrown into relief in 1 Jn 3:2: although now we are already children of God in a wholly real sense (by baptism and godliness of life), 'it has not yet been revealed what we shall be, but we know that when it is revealed we shall be like him, for we shall see him as he is'. According to the views of the bible this likeness to God probably consists of glorification, the being adorned with divine and celestial glory (*doxa*), and this enables us too to see God as he is. On the other hand the vision of God assures us of our glorified existence which makes us like God. The promise of paradise is thereby fulfilled, and the longing, unsatisfied ever since paradise, to come near to God as far as any creature can come near to him at all, is brought to rest. But this gracious exaltation to God, in which we are filled and permeated with his nature, and the experience and apprehension of his divine riches which go with this, constitute the blessing of our direct vision of God. We will also see the glory of Christ (Jn 17:24), and Christ will then be able to complete his 'revelation of the name (nature) of God' (17:26). But in 1 Jn 3:2 what John has in mind is not his appearing (at the ⟋ parousia, see 2:28), and our likeness to Christ and vision of Christ; for the vision of God and being made like God correspond to the state of being God's children, and these constitute the ultimate fulfilment of that state and its eschatological elevation.

Bibliography: F. Nötscher, *Das Angesicht Gottes schauen, nach biblischer und babylonischer Auffassung*, Würzburg 1924; J. Botterweck, '*Gott erkennen' im Sprachgebrauch des AT*, Bonn 1951; G. Kittel, *Die Religionsgeschichte und das Urchristentum*, Gütersloh 1932, 95–106; J. Dupont, *Gnosis. La connaissance relig. dans les épîtres de s. Paul*, Lyons–Paris 1949; A. Brunner, 'Gott schauen', *ZKT* 73 (1951), 214–22; R. Schnackenburg, *Die Johannesbriefe*, Freiburg 1963², 172f; H. M. Féret, *Connaissance biblique de Dieu*, Paris 1955; W. Michaelis, *TDNT* v, 328–40 and 364–7; A. Wikenhauser, *Die Christusmystik des Apostels Paulus*, Freiburg 1956², 142–56. See also: W. W. Graf Baudissin, 'Gott schauen in der atl. Religion', *ARW* 18 (1915), 173–239; W. Bousset, *Kyrios Christos*, Göttingen 1935⁴, 163–72; R. Bultmann, 'Untersuchungen zum Joh-Ev', *ZNW* 29 (1930), 169–92; N. Hugedé, *La métaphore du miroir dans les épîtres de s. Paul aux Corinthiens*, Neuchâtel–Paris 1937; F. Amiot, 'Deum nemo vidit unquam (Jn 1:18)', *Festschrift A. Robert*, Paris 1957, 470–77.

Rudolf Schnackenburg

Visitation

A. *Old Testament*. English versions of the bible use 'visit' and 'visitation' to translate the term based upon the Hebrew root *pqd*, which in the Greek bible is rendered as *episkopeō* and *episkeptomai*, and in Latin for the most part as *visitare*. Throughout all its various shades of meaning this word retains the basic meaning of 'to prove somebody or something by testing', or 'to see that all is in order'. As predicated of God, visitation is an exercise of his ⟋ righteousness, and it implies salvation for the people of God, for the loyal and zealous, and even for repentant sinners, but ruin for the enemies of God and of his people. But whereas in most of the passages in which God's justice is mentioned it imports his faithful fulfilment of his promises of salvation, in most of the passages in which visitation occurs it is the connotation of punishment and misfortune that comes chiefly to the fore. As applied to the individual the visitation of God consists in the fact that he takes an active interest in the man concerned. Thus in Ps 8:5 we find a statement of the part played by God throughout in the fate of man. In passages such as Gen 21:1; 1 Sam 2:21 an individual man experiences the fact that God regards him benevolently and is ever ready to come to his help. In Jer 15:15 and Ps 106:4 it is one who is zealously devoted to Yahweh who experiences this; in Gen 50:24f; Ex 3:16; 4:31; 13:19; Ruth 1:6; Zech 10:3, it is the people of Israel; while in Is 23:17; Jer 27:22; 29:10; Zeph 2:7, it is sinners who have this experience after they have undergone their punishment.

God visits sinners and those who are his enemies, ie, he 'brings them to a reckoning' (Jer 6:15; 49:8; 50:32; Ps 59:5; probably also Job 7:18; Jer 32:5).

In Num 27:16; Is 62:6; Jer 1:10 it is a question of a demonstration of trust on God's part in that he 'entrusts' or commissions a chosen individual with a task of special importance in salvific history. This 'commissioning' can also be applied to the occasions when God uses profane forces as his instruments for punishing the people of God when they have broken the covenant (Lev 26:16; Jer 15:3), the enemies of God (Is 13:4), the enemies of the zealous and devoted (Ps 109:6). Yahweh visits the ↗ way of the sinner, ie, he 'puts him on trial', requites him (Hos 4:9). Above all he visits the sins, ie, he 'takes vengeance' for them, 'exacts a reckoning for transgression' (1 Sam 15:2; Jer 14:10; Hos 9:9; Lam 4:2, 22), as though 'with rod and scourges' (Ps 89:32). Frequently the person to whom God brings home his transgression is named (Ex 32:34; Is 13:11; 26:21; Jer 23:2; 25:12; 36:31; Hos 1:4; 2:15; Amos 3:2).

'The "vengeance" of Yahweh is no blind fury against the individuals or peoples concerned. Rather it always presupposes that their guilt has been established by "examination", or that it is notorious' (Scharbert, p 219). As used in this sense, visitation is closely connected with the ↗ judgement of Yahweh upon sinners and upon the powers which are hostile to God. In the prophets the noun occurs frequently in the sense of 'calling to account' and punishment (Is 10:3; Jer 8:12 etc; Ezek 9:1; Hos 9:7; Mic 7:4).

B. In the *Qumran texts* the verb *pqd* occurs in the sense of testing (1 QS 5:22, 24; 6:21; CD 13:11), of 'the ordination which results from this' (of annihilation 1 QS 2:6, of vindication 1 QS 16:5). God requites the guilt, ie, punishes it (1 QH 14:24); he requites the works of the evil-doer (CD 5:15f;

see also 7:9), visits the earth in order to exact requital from sinners (CD 19:6). He will visit all the members of his covenant who do not hold firm to his commandments, and consign them to destruction at the hands of Belial (CD 8:2; 19:14). CD 1:7 displays an awareness of visitation in the sense that God will pardon and bring help after he has chastised his people. The substantive appears to signify an eschatological visitation (this is numbered among the subjects in which the members must be instructed 1 QS 3:14), the time of which has been established by God (1 QS 3:18; 4:18; 1 QH 1:17; see also CD 8:3; 19:15). It will bring salvation, peace, life, blessing, joy to those who walk according to God's counsels (1 QS 4:6f; see also 1 QH 1:17); but to the obdurate, who walk in the way of darkness, it will bring affliction and destruction (1 QS 4:11ff). Only after this will the true world which is to last for ever emerge (1 QS 4:19). This visitation is to be expected at the end of the days (4 QpIs^b 2:2) by the 'generation of the visitation' (4 QpHos^b 1:10).

C. In the *New Testament* the idea of visitation comes to acquire, to a greater extent than in the Old Testament, the significance of a manifestation of God's benevolence and grace. Thus after Jesus has raised the young man of Nain to life the word goes round among the people 'that God has visited his people' (Lk 7:16), and certain manuscripts add the words 'for good', thereby attesting the fact that the word chiefly bore the significance of 'to punish'. In the Canticle of Zechariah (Lk 1:68, 78) the word under consideration acquires a messianic connotation from its connection with ↗ salvation and ↗ redemption. In Acts 15:14 James declares that Simeon has related how God was solicitous to take from among the Gentiles a people for his name. In this instance the word possesses its full salvific force.

Whereas in the Old Testament the 'day of visitation' (Is 10:3; see also Jer 6:15; 10:15; 11:23; ↗ day of the Lord) is a judgement day, on Jesus' lips the phrase 'time of visitation' is applied to his own coming, the time of the great visitation of grace (Lk 19:44). In 1 Pet 2:12 christians are exhorted to lead exemplary lives in the sight of the gentiles 'so that in case they speak against you as wrongdoers, they may see your good deeds and glorify God on the day of visitation', ie, when God of his grace calls them to the faith (see the exhortation of the Lord in Mt 5:16 and, by way of contrast, Rom 2:24; 1 Tim 6:1).

Bibliography: J. Scharbert, 'Das Verbum PQD in der Theologie des Alten Testaments', *BZ* 4 (1960), 209–26; H. W. Beyer, *TDNT* II, 590–608; J. Boan Hooser, *The Meaning of the Hebrew Root 'pqd' in the Old Testament*, Harvard 1962/3 (dissertation); see also *HTR* 56 (1963), 332.

Johannes B. Bauer

Vocation

Vocation and Election. The verb qr° ('to call', 'to give a vocation to') is one of the most significant and frequently recurring verbs in the Old Testament. It generally appears in constructions with a simple accusative, but is also found with the preposition b^e (= 'by'

or 'in'), as for instance in the expression qr° $b^e\check{s}m$ (= 'to call by name': Ex 31:2; 35:30; Is 43:1; 45:3–4). Apart from the profane usage, which is richly attested, the word is frequently employed with a religious connotation and in the following specific senses: 1. as a call to repentance and conversion, for instance in Jer 3:12ff; 2. as a personal summons which is at the same time a call to a specific office (Is 44:28; 45:3; 46:11; 48:15; 43:1; 51:2; Gen 12:1–3; Ex 3:1–12; 1 Sam 3:3ff; but also Is 6; Jer 1; Is 42:6; 49:1–9); 3. as a call to salvation, which may be directed to a single individual or to the people of Israel as a whole (Gen 12:1–3; 15:1–6; Is 41:8–9; 43:1; 48:12; 51:2; 54:6). This idea of vocation is often found combined with that of election, for God calls only those whom he has first chosen for a specific office or to have a share in his salvation (eg, Abraham, Moses, David). This appears particularly clearly in Deutero-Isaiah, where 'to call' and 'to choose' frequently occur in parallelism (41:9). However, a clear distinction must be borne in mind between the two acts of God involved. This can be gathered from the very fact that a different verb is used to express election, namely bhr (eg, Deut 7:6; 10:15; 14:2; 18:5; 21:5; Is 7:15; 41:8; 43:10; 44:1–2; 49:7; 65:9, 15, 22; etc). This verb appears 164 times in the Old Testament, ninety-two times with God as subject. In addition to this the verbal substantive $b\bar{a}\hbar\acute{\imath}r$ is also found. By comparison the roots $lq\hbar$ and $qbts$ appear only rarely. bhr is distinguished from qr° chiefly by the element of election and the act of the will involved.

Election is found throughout the Old

Testament as a key idea which is of decisive importance. Israel perceives God's act of election in episodes as early as his call to the patriarchs (Is 51:2). Indeed in their case it is especially clear that this election proceeds purely from God's sovereign will (Gen 12; 15; 25:22ff). It in no sense presupposes any prior quality on the part of the men concerned or in their relationship with God. Yet Israel is conscious of having been chosen and united to God as a whole in the persons of her patriarchs. From Abraham's time onwards the visible sign of this election is circumcision (Gen 17:9ff). From Sinai onwards it is the covenant relationship (Ex 19:5, etc) by which Israel becomes God's personal possession (Ex 19:5; Deut 7:6)—his people (Deut 4:20; 9:26; Ps 28:9 etc), his vineyard (Is 5:1-7), his firstborn son (Ex 4:22; Jer 31:9), his spouse or bride (Hos 2 etc), his community (Num 20:4; 16:3; Mic 2:4-5; Ps 74:2), his servant (Is 41:8; 42:19; Jer 30:10; Ezek 28:25; etc), as Deutero–Isaiah above all never tires of saying by way of consolation.

Such an election gives those concerned a claim to God's blessing, protection and solicitude, to his *šalôm* (Is 43:3f; 48:15), but at the same time it also entails heightened responsibilities towards him (Amos 2:9ff; 3:1ff). Since the people did not live up to this responsibility as a whole, the circle of the elect narrowed down to the 'holy remnant' (Isaiah, Jeremiah, Ezekiel, Zechariah) or, as it is expressed in the post-exilic literature, to the 'zealous'. As a result election in the strict sense is transferred from the people as a whole to individuals, whereas in earlier times

the election of individuals was only known in the case of kings, priests (Levi and Zadok), and prophets (1 Sam 10:17; 16:10; 2 Sam 16:18; 1 Kings 8:16; 11:34; 89:3; Sir 47:22). Admittedly, consciousness of having been chosen in the persons of the patriarchs continues to predominate in orthodox judaism. The deutero-canonical books display the same attitude as the rest of the post-exilic literature (Sir 46:1; Tob 8:10 [LXX]; Wis 3:9; 4:15). This results on the one hand in a significant narrowing down of the circle comprising the elect, on the other the possibility is opened up of extending it beyond Israel, a fact which is significant for our understanding of vocation and election in the New Testament.

The course marked out by the post-exilic writings of the bible is carried further by the literature of Qumran. References to election in all their various forms are here extraordinarily frequent. 'The elect' is a title of honour by which the community occupying the site from which these documents derive describe themselves (1 QpHab v 4; IX 12; X 13; CD VI 2; the hymns almost throughout; 1 QM III 13; X 9). 1 QpHab speaks of those who depend upon the *moreh tsedeq* as the 'elect of God'. 1 QS III 14ff refers plainly to the fact that the members of the community are chosen by God for the purpose of forming a 'holy community' to enter God's service as followers of the prince of light, and to gain for themselves a share of salvation. In 1 QH *bḥr* is not actually used. Nevertheless, references to the reality which it stands for constantly recur in the hymns, which lead up to the idea of being chosen by

God ('bound up in the bundle of life', 'not rejected', 'set upon an even basis', 'placed at the well-spring of life', etc: I 32; II 20; III 22; IV 5; VII 6ff; VIII 3). In CD, too, the word *qr⁾* occurs repeatedly, and there is a reference to the *qᵉri⁾ê šm* (2:9), that is, to those whom God has called by name, which in practice is equivalent to election. The 'teacher of righteousness' (I QpHab) and the Zadokite priests (CD VI 2; I QSᵇ III 23) are presented as the elect *par excellence*, while the rest of the members of the community participate in this election only by faith and obedience. The manner in which this election, as well as the possibility of obedience in this sense, applies to them is either not fully thought out or not yet altogether discernible to us in consequence of our knowledge of the distinctive theology of this community up to the present. Whereas in I QS and I QM the holy remnant can only be drawn from Israel, while I QH has nothing to say on this point, CD envisages proselytes as well. But wherever the idea of the remnant is used the Old Testament statements concerning the covenant people are transferred to the community, and indeed to it exclusively. Whoever does not belong to it is a mocker and a recreant. He belongs to the community of Belial, and is destined by God to the judgement.

Already in LXX the Greek word *kaleō* corresponds to the Hebrew *qr⁾*. It is used both in a profane and a religious sense. It becomes a religious term the moment it is predicated of God. For it means 'to call' (as in Abraham's case), or it can even mean the invitation to share in the blessings of salvation

sent out by God. Corresponding to *bḥr* and its derivatives, LXX has *eklegomai* (=to choose, elect) and the words deriving from its root, especially *eklektos* (=*bāḥîr*), which again is used to express God's freedom in choosing and with regard to the medium employed, but also his interest in those who are chosen.

In the *New Testament* John the Baptist appears as a personal summoner (Mk 1:3 and parallels), but the same applies to the apostles also (Mk 1:16–20 and parallels), that is to men who have been given an office, though admittedly this also includes their own call to salvation. They are under God's special protection (Lk 9:1ff; 10:1ff), but they also have a special burden to bear (Lk 9:57ff; Mt 8:19ff). In the New Testament all are called to participate in the blessings of salvation (Rom 8:20; 1 Cor 1:9; Gal 5:8; 1 Cor 7:15, 19; 1 Thess 2:12, 14; 1 Pet 1:15). But this presupposes repentance, renunciation of self, faithfulness, that is, the co-operation of man (Mk 1:15; Mt 22:12). In the case of the synoptics it is quite evident that they do not regard the call as a *verbum efficax*. Judas too is called (Jn 6:70; 13:18; 15:16), as too are the guests at the royal wedding-feast and the man without a wedding garment Mt 22:1–14). For the call as presented by the synoptics the following conclusions of Daumoser may be taken as established: 1. it is extended to all without restriction, except for the fact that it is so extended only through Jesus; 2. it derives its force from the free will of God himself, without any legal justification; 3. men must not arrogate it to themselves; 4. it confronts them inexorably with the fundamental decision; and 5. when rightly responded to it brings a reward as a direct consequence of this (↗ retribution, reward).

Among the synoptics, it is Luke in particular who makes frequent use of *kaleō*, which is less frequent in Matthew and rare in Mark. John likewise rarely employs the idea, while on the contrary Paul, Hebrews, and 1 and 2 Peter use it often. Abraham stands out as the type of the *kaloumenos*, the one who is called. To the extent that Jesus appears as the one who calls, it is precisely a divine function that he exercises when he calls men. Paul again is particularly interested in man's response to the divine call, that is, the act of *pisteuein* (↗ faith). In this connection it becomes clear that the call of God through Jesus and his apostles is an act of grace. On the basis of his own experience Paul interprets it as *efficax*, and is thereby brought to making statements of a predestinatory character (Rom). Similarly in Paul *kaleō* (= to call), *klēsis* (= calling), and *klētos* (= one called) have already become theological terms with a definite meaning. For him the *klētoi* are either the apostles (1 Cor 1:1; Rom 1:6) or, still more frequently, christians in general, so that *klētos* and christian become almost synonymous.

So far as *eklegomai* and the idea of election are concerned, they are found throughout the Old and New Testaments alike. It is nowhere denied that Israel is chosen (Mt 2:6; Lk 1:16, 32f; 13:16; Mt 8:12; 12:39; 15:24). Nevertheless Jesus, and with him the whole of the New Testament, decisively rejects those false claims which are based on the sense of election (Mt 3:7ff; Lk 13:23ff; 8:21; 16:19–31;

etc). It neither gives any exclusive rights nor is it a comfortable cushion on which to repose. It demands personal responsibility and obedience in faith in order to become established. Again the New Testament takes up the idea of the remnant, but unlike the Qumran sectarians, it does not take this in the sense of an esoteric group apart, but rather as the new people of God which every man can be called to join. In the New Testament election is always election to an office, whether that of the apostle (this also applies to the traitor), or deacon, missioner or elder (Acts 6; 15:22), or to the universal ↗ priesthood which glorifies God and proclaims his grace (1 Pet 2:9).

The motifs of free choice, of service, and of selection from a greater number (remnant) appear still more prominently in the substantive *eklogē* (= choice, election) than in the verb. Again it is the eschatological connotation attached to the adjective *eklektos* (= one chosen) that is noticeable throughout the entire New Testament. For the synoptics the *eklektoi* are the fine flower of those chosen by God (Mt 22:14) from Israel and the gentiles, the community of the eschatological age (Lk 18:7; Mt 24: 21–31; Mk 13:19–27). For them God shortens the period of eschatological affliction, guards them from Satan's temptation and redeems them in the new era (similarly too in 1 Pet 2:9). Paul, too, recognises the ultimate goal (1 Cor 1:27–9; Tit 1:1; 1 Tim 5:21). Again, 1 Peter lays the emphasis on the fact that election has already been made before time was (1:2ff). Only in virtue of the fact of having been chosen do the elect proclaim the mercy of God. For this reason they also bear the titles of honour belonging to the Old Testament people of God. The New Testament writings have little to say concerning the rival group of the reprobate, those who are not chosen.

One saying of Jesus in particular deserves special mention, that namely in which *klētoi* and *eklektoi* are set in contrast to each other. It is in Mt 22:14 that this saying is most firmly in place, although perhaps it was once an independent saying. Probably it should be set not merely in the context of the parable of the marriage-feast but in the whole group of parables (21:28–22:14) at the end of which it stands. Whereas in the Old Testament God's call affects those who are chosen, here the called appear as the greater group and the elect as the smaller. The latter are clearly those finally chosen from the circle of the called. Vocation can remain unavailing not only when the one called refuses it, but also when he supposes that he is able to evade the responsibility which it entails. Thus the logion is an emphatic reminder of the importance and urgency of vocation, and a summons to men to show themselves worthy of the ultimate selection which will be made.

Bibliography: K. L. Schmidt, *TDNT* III, 487ff; G. Schrenk, *TDNT* IV, 147ff; E. Egel, *Die Berufungstheologie des Apostels Paulus*, Heidelberg 1939; I. Daumoser, *Berufung und Erwählung bei den Synoptikern*, Meisenheim 1954 (with further copious bibliographical references); H. H. Rowley, *The Biblical Doctrine of Election*, London 1950; T. C. Vriezen, *Die Erwählung Israels nach dem AT*, Zurich 1953; E. Wright, *The Old Testament against its Environment*, 1950; Nötscher, 173–6; Eichrodt I (Index); M. Noth, *Amt und Berufung im AT*, Bonn 1958.

Georg Molin

War

A. *Old Testament*. From the outset it is important to remind ourselves that the Old Testament does not divide life into a religious and a profane sphere. So far from this, life as conceived of in the Old Testament is permeated and interwoven throughout by religion and faith. To one who bears this in mind, an idea which is alien to us of the present day will become comprehensible, namely, that according to the Old Testament even war is a religious event, so that one speaks of the 'holy war' as a religious institution. In this guise it figures in the Old Testament writings from Moses right up to the time of the Maccabees.

1. *Description of the 'holy war'*: the following specific elements can be laid down as characteristic of the holy war: Yahweh's anger is kindled against the enemy of the chosen people (1 Sam 28:18). The trumpets are sounded and the Israelites respond by voluntarily enlisting for military service (Judg 3:27; 6:34f; 1 Sam 13:3). The army thus assembled is called the people (host) of Yahweh (Ex 12:41; Judg 5:11; 20:2; 1 Sam 17:26), and is therefore under a strict obligation to preserve cultic and sexual purity, or alternatively to purify itself (1 Sam 21:6; 2 Sam 11:11). Sacrifices are offered (1 Sam 7:9; 13:9, 12). At a later stage, in the prophets, it is laid upon Israel as a duty to sanctify the war (Jer 6:4; Joel 1:9). Yahweh himself takes command in these wars (Is 13:3; Jer 51:27f). Hence he advances upon the ark at the head of the warriors of Israel (Num 14:42; Deut 20:4; 23:14; Josh 3:11; 10:14; Judg 4:14; 1 Sam

4:6; 2 Sam 5:24). He musters the army (Is 13:4). More than this, Yahweh raises up charismatic leaders to conduct the holy war (Deut 31:7; Judg 6:14). In consequence these wars are called 'Yahweh's wars' (1 Sam 18:17; 25:28). The enemies are Yahweh's enemies (Judg 5:31). It is Yahweh alone who conducts and decides the course of these wars (Ex 14:14, 18; Deut 1:30; Josh 10:42; 11:6; Judg 20:35; 1 Sam 14:23). Israel is required to conduct herself quietly, and to put her trust in Yahweh (Ex 14:13; Deut 20:3; Josh 8:1; 10:25; Judg 7:3; 1 Sam 23:17; 2 Sam 10:12; Is 7:4). The enemy, on the contrary, find their courage failing them (Ex 15:14ff; Josh 2:24; 5:1; 1 Sam 4:7f). Indeed they are filled with a panic that is divinely instilled (Ex 23:27; Deut 7:23; Josh 10:10f; Judg 4:15; 7:22; 1 Sam 5:11; 7:10; 14:15). The booty from the war belongs to Yahweh. It is consecrated to him by being 'put to the ban', and utterly destroyed (Num 21:2f; Josh 6:18f; 1 Sam 15:9). When victory has been achieved Israel renders her thanks to God, and rejoices before him. The laws of war are set forth in detail in Deut 20. Here we find exact directions of how the ↗ ban, the total destruction of all that survives, is to be carried out, and what is to be left as booty for the victorious army.

2. *History of the 'holy war'*. After the exodus of the twelve-tribe confederacy from Egypt, Israel was often compelled to engage in wars in the course of executing God's plan for the chosen people. In the episode in which the Egyptian army pursues Israel and is destroyed (Ex 14f) we encounter the earliest instance of the holy war, of which Yahweh himself decides the outcome (Ex 14:14). In the nature of things it must have acquired great importance for the period of the invasion of Canaan and the settlement in the land (Joshua, Judges). The following qualities may be laid down as characteristic of it.

(a) The wars in question are exclusively defensive in character; (b) the entire sacral confederation of tribes took part in the warlike event (at least in spirit). It is united in the consciousness of having Yahweh as its king even in the earthly sphere (Ex 19:5f). Hence it belongs to the exercise of Yahweh's dominion to bestow upon Israel the protection which she needs in wars as well as in peace. The victory which Israel obtains through Yahweh's intervention in her favour is therefore counted as one of the deeds of salvation which God has wrought for his people (Judg 5:11). Thus the holy war in Israel is not the same as the corresponding institution in Islam. For what Israel fights for is not her faith but her existence.

In the period of the Israelite monarchy the institution of the holy war acquires fresh forms. Since the earthly kings were called to be representatives of the divine king, one of the duties which was now laid upon them was the conduct of Israel's wars. The beginnings of a permanent army are already becoming apparent as early as the reign of Saul. It was to become one of the main preoccupations of the future rulers (see especially David's act of numbering the people, 2 Sam 24:1–9). In consequence of this God ceased to intervene directly as he had done hitherto in the waging of war.

Nevertheless certain elements of the holy war do persist and survive, as is to be seen, for instance, in the conduct of Uriah (2 Sam 11:11). It belongs to the ideal of Israelite manhood that it is trained for war (1 Sam 16:18). In David's dialogue with Goliath (1 Sam 17:43–7) the essential traits of the holy war reappear once more, but in a form which has been modified and conditioned by the introduction of earthly kingship. In the preaching of the prophets the idea of the holy war undergoes a fresh transformation. These are conscious of having been appointed guardians of the old sacral institutions, among them that of the holy war. In Samuel's dispute with Saul (1 Sam 15) we see the very first of the Israelite kings confronted with this claim. In the ensuing period this precedent is often followed by the prophets intervening in the warlike projects of the kings (1 Kings 15:13–21; 22:9–17; Is 7:1–9; 30:15; 31:1–3; 37:33–8). Indeed the prophets (Elijah and Elisha) count as the embodiment of God's protection against the enemies of Israel (2 Kings 2:12; 13:14).

The institution of the holy war lives on not merely in virtue of the fact that it has a part to play in the political life of the prophets' own times, but above all because they assign it a prominent place in their prophecies of the future. In their hands revelation as a whole undergoes a development, and with it the idea of the holy war also is transposed on to the new plane which has been attained in the unfolding of revelation, so that it may remain capable of expressing in deeper and more poetic terms the eschatological struggle of the kingdom of God against the forces hostile to him, a struggle which is to take place in the future. In other words, in the prophetic writings the institution of the holy war becomes *eschatologised*. It is transformed into the decisive struggle which is to take place at the end of time, and which is to be brought to its conclusion before the inauguration of God's dominion, which is to take place amid splendour and light, and to pervade the entire universe intensively and extensively. In Isaiah's overall picture of God's intervention in the course of world history he is especially inclined to present this in the form of the holy war. It is in this manner that God will execute his judgement against the people who are hostile to him. In his line of argument he passes on from God's historical intervention to his contest in the future, which gradually assumes meta-historical and typological traits such as appear in a very pronounced form, for instance, in Ezekiel. Not only the gentiles but Israel herself will have experience of this battle of God (Amos 2:4ff). In Mic 4:11–13 Israel is commissioned to conduct this final war against the assembled world of the gentiles as they conspire together to overthrow Zion and frustrate God's plan for Israel. The themes indicated here are projected wholly into the world of eschatology in Ezek 38f. Here we find described in hues that are in part apocalyptic the final onslaught of the gentile powers Gog and Magog, and their definitive destruction. In Ezek 38:19–22 nearly all the traditional traits of the holy war reappear in a form which has been transposed and adapted so as to fit the basic concept of this final contest. Zechariah too, like

Ezekiel, takes up the motifs of the holy war which have been handed down and transposes them so as to make them expressions of the eschatological strife in all its magnitude (4:6; 9:14).

In addition to these instances the holy war also finds an echo in the psalms. Here we find it in its original form, purged of its later developments (for instance, Ps 18; 20; 24:8; 33:16–18; 144). It is actually made the subject of petitionary prayer. Finally the institution of the holy war acquires a new lease of life in the community of the Dead Sea. This, wholly rooted as it is in the Old Testament, is, according to 1 QM (The Scroll of War), summoned as 'the sons of light' (a self-designation) to the historical, or more probably eschatological, struggle against the sons of darkness.

B. *New Testament.* In Lk 14:31; 1 Cor 14:8 the war is taken to be a fact of this present world. Heb 11:34 points back to the heroes of the Old Testament wars. In the apocalyptic sections of the New Testament the war appears to conform to the Old Testament prophecies concerning the final eschatological struggle. In Mt 24:6 and parallels wars are regarded as 'the beginning of afflictions'. They do not inaugurate the end. As events of the intervening period before the *parousia* they merely direct our attention to the fact that the end is coming, and they are intended to remind men of every age of that fact. In Rev 9:7, 9 war and chariots of war serve as images to describe the terrors of the fifth plague, which is expressed in images and motifs drawn from Joel 1–2 (the plague of locusts). The struggle of Michael with the dragon counts as a war (Rev 12:7–17). Again, the beast from the abyss (antichrist) will wage war against the Lamb and the 'saints' (Rev 11:7; see also Dan 7). Similarly with the beast in Rev 13:7. According to Rev 19:19–21 it will be overthrown and consigned to the lake of brimstone. Rev 20:8 takes up the motif of Ezek 38:2: Satan will bring Gog and Magog to wage the final war. But this eschatological enemy will be subjected to total destruction. Then war will be made to cease altogether (Is 2:4; Mic 4:3; Hos 2:18; ↗ peace), and will give place to the eternal peace of the final age in the 'new heaven and the new earth' (Rev 21:1).

Bibliography: A. G. Barrois, *Manuel d'Archéologie biblique* II, Paris 1953; 87–117; O. Bauernfeind, *TDNT* VI, 502–15; Haag 969f; H. Kruse, 'Ethos victoriae in Vetere Testamento', *VD* 30 (1952), 3–13, 65–80, and 143–53; F. Nötscher, *Biblische Altertumskunde*, Bonn 1940, 145–67; J. Pedersen, *Israel. Its Life and Culture* III–IV, Oxford–Copenhagen 1953, 1–32; de Vaux 247–67. See also: H. Fredriksson, *Jahwe als Krieger*, Lund 1945; G. von Rad, *Der Heilige Krieg im Alten Israel*, Göttingen 1958³; *G. von Rad, *Old Testament Theology* I and II (see Index); *G. von Rad, 'Deuteronomy and the Holy War', *Studies in Deuteronomy*, London 1953, 45–59; F. Schwally, *Semitische Kriegsaltertümer* I. *Der heilige Krieg im alten Israel*, Leipzig 1901; J. Comblin, *Theologie des Friedens*, Graz 1963, 84–110.

Heinrich Gross

Water

Beliefs, more or less vigorous in character, in local deities, spirits, and demons thought to inhabit springs, streams, lakes, etc are frequent. But, quite apart from any such beliefs, the findings of ethnology show how prominent a part water plays in the myths, cult, and rituals of peoples by reason of the use to which it is put and the symbolism attached to it. All the fullness of the various forces of life and the possibilities of existence are contained in the meaning of water. (In baptism the act of immersion signifies that one lays aside one's previous form, while to re-emerge from the water signifies to be restored to life.) It is intimately connected with fertility (primarily that of vegetation, but by extension the fertility of beasts and men as well), and as a means of cleansing it also becomes a cultic symbol for the attainment of purity and renewal (the blotting out of sins; ↗ clean and unclean).

As a monotheistic religion, Yahwism does not recognise any water spirits (↗ sea), but nevertheless water does figure prominently in the bible by reason of its importance for life, and also by reason of its manifold symbolic aspects both in the profane and the religious spheres. In the Near East, where water is scarce, it is accounted especially important and precious. Water was offered to strangers who were lodging for the night or passing through (Gen 18:4; 24:32). It was lack of water that brought the people of the Old Testament to murmur against Moses (Ex 15:22–5; 17:1–7; Num 20:1–13). David's bodyguard even put their lives into hazard to bring water for their king (2 Sam 23:16). Numerous miracles are recorded in the Old Testament (Ex 7:17ff; 14:16; 17:6; 2 Kings 2:8) and the New (Mt 8:23–7; 14:22–33; Jn 2:1–11) in which water is either the instrument or the object of miracles. In these God manifests himself as Lord of the elements so that the rituals employed

to obtain rainfall (1 Kings 17:1; 18:42–6; Job 38:34–6) always remain subject to Yahweh's will. Prayers for rain (1 Kings 8:35; 18:36f; Joel 1:20) are directed to God, who punishes the unfaithfulness of the people with drought (Amos 1:2; Joel 1:12; Zech 14:16f). But conversely he rewards faithfulness with fertility and rain (Lev 26:3f; Deut 11:13f; Is 30:23). The libation of water (1 Sam 7:5f) was clearly part of an atonement ceremony (water counted as a symbol of tears Jer 9:17; Ps 119:136), and served as a sign of the blotting out of sins (Ezek 36:25; in the course of the Feast of Tabernacles libations were made in the temple over the altar and the materials of sacrifice in order to entreat for rain, Succoth 4:9; 5:1).

The use of water in the service of the temple—eg 'the molten sea' (1 Kings 7:23–6, and the 'stands' (1 Kings 7:27–39)—had both a practical and a symbolic significance. The temple was accounted the most important manifestation of God's grace. It was the religious centre of the people, from which supernatural life radiated out. Hence in their descriptions of the messianic age the prophets sometimes use images in which God is presented as a 'source of living water' (Jer 2:13). In other passages it is the 'source of the temple waters' that is spoken of (Is 12:3; Ps 36:9; 46:4; see also Rev 22:1f), or the ideas of source and fertility (Joel 3:18), fertility, source, and blotting out of sin (Ezek 47; Zech 13:1; 14:8) appear in combination.

It is the association of water with the idea of purifying that lies behind the numerous ablutions prescribed in the

Old Testament as the means of obtaining cultic purity. 'Living' (ie, flowing) water had greater power and was necessary in cases of leprosy (Lev 14:5–7, 50–52), sexual emissions (Lev 15:13), as well as for the preparation of water of purification (Num 19). Those associated in the cult had to wash themselves before they were ordained (Ex 29:4; Lev 8:6), and also before (Ex 30:17–21; 40:31f; Lev 16:4) or after specific exercises of their office (Lev 16:24, 26, 28; Num 19:7f). Every member of the Old Testament people, for instance, must wash his clothes if he has been suffering from leprosy (Lev 14:8f), eaten carrion (Lev 11:40), experienced an emission due to sickness (Lev 15:5–11), a pollution (Lev 15:16–18) or menstruation (Lev 15:19–24), served in a war (Num 31:24). He must also do this after touching a corpse (Num 19:13, 18f), or the flesh of sin-offerings (Lev 6:20). The practice of washing the hands before meals (Mk 7:2ff) became in the course of time a symbol for interior purity (Ps 26:6; 51:2; 73:13) or innocence (Deut 21:6; Mt 27:24).

The use of water in ordeals as described in the Old Testament must also have originated from the property of water to cleanse in a symbolic as well as in a real sense. A woman who was suspected of adultery had to drink 'bitter water', that is water mingled with dust from the sanctuary, to the accompaniment of a formula of cursing (Num 5:12–31). The prophet Jeremiah recalls this when he announces that the whole of Israel is condemned to drink 'bitter' or 'poisonous' water (Jer 8:14; 9:15; 23:15). In the case of an unsolved murder (Deut 21:1–9) those living near the scene of the crime had to wash their hands over a cow that had been sacrificed in token of their innocence, a practice which was carried out in a manner analogous to that employed in the case of the scapegoat (Lev 16) or the ceremony involving a bird as prescribed for cases of leprosy (Lev 14:1ff).

Water is everywhere symbolically associated with the ideas of purifying, blotting out sins, and renewal, and it is this fact that justifies its use in ↗ baptism, the sacrament of rebirth in the New Testament (Jn 3:1–12; Acts 2:38; Rom 6:3–14; Col 2:8–15; 1 Cor 6:11f).

Bibliography: Art. 'Water' in *Encyclopaedia of Religion and Ethics* XII, 704–19; M. Eliade, *Patterns in Comparative Religion*, London and New York 1958, 188–215 (with extensive bibliography); P. Raymond, *L'eau, sa vie et sa signification dans l'AT* (Supplement to *VT* 6 [1958]); J. Hempel, *RGG* ²*IV*, 1665f; A. A. King, *Holy Water: the use of water for ceremonial and purificatory purposes in pagan, Jewish and Christian times*, London 1926.

Walter Kornfeld

Way

The Hebrew word *derek*, which is usually rendered by *hodos* in Greek, means primarily 'way' in the obvious and literal sense; but often, too, the word is used figuratively, and it is this that we shall be treating of here, even though it is often impossible to perceive the exact extent to which the idea of way as such may still have been conceived of in spatial terms (see Prov 1:31; Is 33:15; 1 Kings 8:32; etc).

In several Old Testament passages, however, *dērek* cannot mean way, but must have a force corresponding to the Ugaritic power, exercise of power, or dominion (thus Ps 110:7; Hos 10:13 [Hebrew]; Jer 3:13 AV; Prov 8:22; 31:3; Amos 8:14; Job 40:19; 26:14; see J. B. Bauer, *VD* 35 [1957], 222–7; *VT* 8 [1958], 91f with bibliography).

A. *Old Testament*. 1. The *whole of human life* is described as the way of man (Is 40:27; Job 3:23; 23:10; Ps 37:5): often this also contains the implication that God has the ways of man in his hands (=his power: Dan 5:23; Job 31:4; Jer 10:23; Prov 20:24; this idea is strongly in evidence in 1 QS XI 10ff, 17). Admittedly in this usage many additional shades of meaning may be derived from the context in which it occurs, such as the factor of human decision and purpose.

2. Way can also stand for man's *moral conduct*, how he 'walks' (Ex 18:20; Deut 5:32f; Jer 4:18; Job 21:31; etc).

3. Way in this sense is usually considered in connection with the will of God. The 'way of the Lord' is precisely *the course which God directs man to follow*, and in this sense 'way' is virtually synonymous with 'commandment' (we may notice the parallelism between way and commandment in Jer 7:23 and Ps 119:15). In this sense it can be said that men follow this way of God (as in Job 23:11; Ps 18:21; etc), or they may be reproached with failing to follow or observe or recognise the way of God (Mal 2:9; Jer 5:4f; Wis 5:7; Prov 2:13, 15; etc) and with going their own way (Is 56:11), which they persist in maintaining to be the right one (Prov 12:15; 14:12; 16:25). Hence the demand that they shall turn away from these ways, which God

punishes (Hos 4:9; Ezek 7:5–8 etc), and to turn back (Zech 1:4; Jon 3:8, 10; etc). In this manner it is particularly emphasised that God knows all the ways of men, that he sees them all, and that he scrutinises man's moral conduct (Jer 32:39; Prov 5:21; Sir 17:15).

4. In this connection a certain ambiguity sometimes arises. On the one hand we find reiterated prayers for God's help in showing the petitioner his ways, teaching them to him, leading him by these ways (the numerous turns of phrase with this general import in Ps 119 should be noticed; see also Ps 25:4; 86:11 etc). From this it is clear how much man needs the help of God's grace. On the other hand, entreaties are made again and again for man to be allowed to recognise the ways of God and to walk in, ie, follow them; and requests of this sort leave no possible room for doubt that man alone is answerable for his own way. Still more, the devout man recognises that he is in part responsible for the way of sinners, and he shows them the good way (Ps 51:13; 1 Sam 12:23).

B. *New Testament*. 1. *Access to the sanctuary*: 'The way into the [true] sanctuary was not yet opened as long as the outer tent [of the old covenant?] was still standing' (Heb 9:8; see also 8:2). To this we may attach the difficult passage of Heb 10:19f: 'We have the hope of entering into the sanctuary by the Blood of Jesus. This is the new [*prosphatos* = 'freshly slaughtered', new in this sense] and living way which he opened to us through the curtain, that is, [through] his flesh'. To what should the phrase 'that is, [through] his flesh' be attached? Certainly it cannot be the curtain, as though Jesus' physical nature was a separating element between Christ and God. On the contrary, according to Heb 2:14–18 men are enabled to stand in the relationship of children to God precisely by the human nature assumed by Christ. Philological considerations tell against taking the phrase '[through] his flesh' (ie, through his death) as connected with 'has opened'. In that case one would have expected an instrumental construction. The best course is to take the genitive '[through] his flesh' as epexegetical and so as qualifying 'the . . . way'. The explanation will then be that the new and living way consists precisely in Jesus' humanity. If *prosphatos* is allowed to retain its etymological sense of 'freshly slaughtered', then it can be understood as an oxymoron ('dead and yet living'). The underlying idea would then be similar to that in Rev 5:6, 9, 12; 13:8 (see also 1:18; 2:8). But on these difficult passages see the commentaries (of C. Spicq, and especially J. Héring and P. Teodorico da Castel S. Pietro). What connection can be established with Jn 14 remains obscure.

2. *Jesus as the way.* 'You know the way where I am going' (Jn 14:4). By this Jesus means not the way which leads to God by keeping his commandments, but the way of faithful discipleship. Thomas objects that they, the disciples, know neither the goal of Jesus' journey nor the way by which he is to arrive at it, but Jesus makes use of this objection to make a still deeper pronouncement: 'I am the way, the truth, and the life' (Jn 14:6). Grammatically speaking this sentence belongs to the class of noun clauses with two members (see C. Brockelmann,

Hebr. Syntax, Neukirchen 1956, 10 of § 14), as does Ps 19:10: 'The judgements of Yahweh [are] truth' (ie, 'are true', but in a most profound and exclusive sense! see also Ps 109:4: 'I [am] prayer', and 2 Sam 17:3: 'All the people will be peace' [ie, will to a unique extent live in ↗ peace and wellbeing]). Jesus' saying, therefore, is to be interpreted as follows: 'Not only do I know the way fully, I am the exemplar of it and manifest it in my own person: this is because I also not merely proclaim the ↗ truth, but it is inseparably connected with my person, and it is in my person that truth, and thereby life also, has appeared in the world (see Jn 1:18; 12:44f). Jesus is the life because it is only through him that true life can be obtained (Jn 1:4; 6:33, 51; 11:25).

3. A *figurative* use of way is to be found in Lk 1:79; Rom 3:17; Acts 2:28; 16:17; 1 Cor 12:31. Passages such as Acts 14:16; Rom 3:16; Jas 1:8; 5:20; 2 Pet 2:15, 21 speak of 'walking' (ie, the conduct of one's life). It is certainly the way of 'walking' commanded by God (see A 3 above) that is meant in Mk 12:14 and parallels; Mt 22:16; 1 Cor 4:17, and probably also in Acts 13:10; 2 Pet 2:21; Heb 3:10.

4. In Acts *hodos* has the force of *teaching*, as is shown especially by 24:14, where the reality thus designated is the same as that referred to as *hairesis* or sect (in this passage employed as *abstractum pro concreto*, a self-designation of the christian community; see also 9:2; 19:9, 23; 22:4; 24:22). This absolute use of 'way' in the sense of 'teaching', which in the New Testament appears only in Acts, may to some extent be paralleled in 1 QS IX 17

('to choose the way': notice the singular) and CD II 6 ('to depart from the way').

5. *hodos* is used of *the ways which God himself follows*, that is, of his plans for salvation and their accomplishment, in Acts 13:10; 18:25f; Rom 11:33; Rev 15:3.

6. *The teaching on the two ways*, which has its roots in the Old Testament (see Ps 1:6; Prov 4:18f; 15:19; and further TestAsh 1:3-5 etc) is to be found in Matthew's version of the logion concerning the narrow door (Lk 13:24), clearly an addition on the evangelist's part (Mt 7:13f). What is meant here in any case is that the decision for Christ which one is called upon to take costs toil, that the gift of the *basileia* (=kingdom) does not fall into one's lap without effort, and is not to be attained by the easy way. The emphasis is laid upon the earnestness of the decision involved. The saying must not be thought of as containing any element of gloom. Jesus is not answering the question which has been put to him: 'Will only a few be saved?'. Instead he demands: 'Do not ask such useless questions, but make efforts!' Jesus' words are a summons and an invitation, not the solution of a theological problem. In omitting this question (which is original, and which Luke has rightly retained) Matthew has in no sense put a false interpretation upon the logion. In fact it is he who has imparted to the two ways (or doors) that unique characterisation 'narrow or broad', ie, 'easy or difficult', which so powerfully underlines the element which has been mentioned (unless one may suppose that it is an independent though parallel logion of the Lord

which is recorded in this passage in Matthew).

Bibliography: W. Michaelis, *TDNT* v, 42-114; A. Gros, *La thème de la Route dans la Bible*, Lille 1954 (dissertation); J. Schmid, *Das Ev. nach Matthäus* (*RNT* 1) 1956³, 149f; Nötscher (see Index); J. B. Bauer, *VD* 30 (1952), 219-26; J. B. Bauer, *BL* 20 (1952/3), 321-7; F. Nötscher, *Gotteswege und Menschenwege in der Bibel und in Qumran* (*BBB* 15), 1958; P. Nötscher, *Recherches Bibliques* 4, 135-48; P. Nober, *VD* 37 (1959), 176-80 and 362f.

Johannes B. Bauer

Wine

Wine is one of the most ancient cultural benefits known to mankind. The very word for it is common to most languages. In Latin it is *vinum*, from which the Romance-language renderings *vin*, *vino*, etc are derived. In Greek it is (*w*)*oinos*, in Hebrew *yayin*, in Akkadian *inu*, in Ugaritic *yn*, but it is a non-Semitic word. A Babylonian tradition knows of the vine as the tree of life in the garden of paradise. The planting of the vine by Noah, therefore, may have been an attempt to awaken memories of paradise, and to regard the new beginning after the Flood as a kind of resumption of the creation. Noah began (again?) with vine-growing. . . . The relationship with the earth is no longer quite the same as that in which mankind stood before the Flood, when it was disrupted by a curse (Gen 5:29: 'And he called his name Noah, saying: "Out of the ground which the Lord has cursed this one shall bring us relief from our work, and from the toil of our hands"'). We find the fulfilment of this hope in Gen 9:20. Noah begins with vine-growing, and thereby brings relief to the earth. Through him God has bestowed upon mankind the vine, which, as conceived of in the Old Testament, is the noblest of plants known to nature (see Ps 104:15). To possess a vineyard, to enjoy its fine fruit, and to rest in peace under its shadow was the Israelite's idea of bliss and the object of his messianic longings (Gen 49:11ff; 1 Kings 4:25; 2 Kings 18:31; Hos 2:15; Mic 4:4; Amos 9:13). Utnapishtim, the Babylonian Noah, knows of the vine as the plant which prolongs life. It is understandable that the bible should regard the fruit of the vine as the most precious of all fruits, and one which Yahweh bestows upon his people. The product of the vine is the blessing of God, which Israel must learn by loyalty towards Yahweh (Deut 11:14). A bad harvest counts as punishment from God (Deut 28:39; Hag 1:11; Hos 2:14). When Israel returns once more, God reveals his favour towards the repentant sinners by bestowing afresh the fruit of the vine (Hos 2:22). At the time when Yahweh will restore the fallen booth of David the mountains will drip sweet wine and the hills shall flow with it (Amos 9:13; Joel 3:18). Is 25:6 describes how Yahweh will then prepare a feast for his own of 'fat things' and of wine on the lees. Hence in Mt 9:17 the new wine is the new covenant, and even in Jn 2 the two wines that are mentioned may each represent one of the two covenants. The Jews, drunk as they are on the old wine, can no longer realise the worth of the new, though this is far better than the old. All catholic exegetes are unanimous in holding that the wine at the marriage of Cana has a profound symbolic meaning. Gächter believes

that it can be regarded as a parallel to the miracle of the loaves. The latter foreshadows the bread of the eucharist, the former the blood.

From the outset, therefore, the situation is that bread maintains this present life, whereas wine permits man to gaze, at least momentarily, at another life and opens to him the door which is guarded by the angel with the flaming sword. This is the significance of 'eat, O friends, and drink; drink deeply, O lovers' (Song 5:1). 'What is life to a man who is without wine? It has been created to make men glad' (Sir 31:37).

Wine is also a symbol of the covenant and of the joy arising from it, a sign both of that covenant which men make with each other (such as that between Abraham and Melchizedek; there is no question of a sacrifice here), and also of the covenant which God makes with men. Wine is also found in sacrifices (Ex 29:38ff; Num 15:5). Moreover wine is closely associated with blood. For one thing the very colour is the same, for in Palestine it was for the most part black grapes that were planted. Then, too, wine is frequently described as the blood of the grape. Among the numerous images derived from the vine (Israel, the people of God as a vine, Christ as the true vine) there is hardly any more terrible than that of the treader of the wine-press. When divine retribution and the execution of divine judgement take place it is as though the treader in the wine-press was squeezing the blood from the grapes (Is 63:1–6; Jer 25:30; Lam 1:15; Rev 19:15). In Babylon, and probably also in Canaan, it was believed that the grape, in order to yield wine, has to lay down its life, and that too in a painful manner, so that— such was the belief—the wine of life comes from this painful death (compare Jn 12:24: 'Unless a grain of wheat falls into the earth and dies . . .'). In this way wine, the blood of the vine (Deut 32:14), could be substituted for the blood of sacrificial beasts (Deut 32:38). In Babylon libatior s of wine and blood offerings were identical, and the wine could be mingled with blood.

In spite of wine being so highly prized, however, abstinence from wine was practised. For the priests it was mandatory (Lev 10:9f; Ezek 44:21) to drink no wine when entering upon their sacred duties. Again the Nazarenes were obliged not to take any drink made from grapes (Num 6:3f; Amos 2:12), but only during the time of their novitiate. John the Baptist did the same. (For the Essenes, and the closely related sect of the Dead Sea, this practice was probably extended throughout the whole lifetime.) A sectarian community which totally renounced wine was that of the Rechabites, who continued to practise absolutely rigidly the nomad way of life handed down to them by their ancestor, Jonadab. They were opposed to cultural advances of every kind, and refused to practise cultivation or vine-growing. In Jer 35:12f God speaks through the prophet to the people who have despised his words, and points to the example of the Rechabites: they refuse to drink a single cup of wine (and reading between the lines one can sense how strange and unnecessary this was felt to be) because this has been enjoined upon them by their ancestor. They do this, so un-important, so idiosyncratic as it is,

because they obey. And Israel does not obey the words of her Father, God, in his wisdom.

We should perhaps draw attention to one further point. Wine figures as one of the chief of the messianic blessings, and in the messianic kingdom it will be drunk in profusion. Anyone who wishes to emphasise that this kingdom is not yet present, such as John the Baptist and his disciples with their asceticism, can demonstrate this fact by abstaining from wine. Jesus too will now drink no more from the fruit of the vine (notice the solemn manner of speaking here in Mt 26:29) until he drinks it once more in the kingdom of the Father.

The bible does not forbid us to enjoy wine. It cheers God and men alike (Judg 9:13). It is created to bring joy to men (Ps 104:15). One should, therefore, give strong drink to him who is perishing, and wine to him who is embittered in soul, so that he may drink and forget his misery (Prov 31:6f).

Warnings are given against excessive enjoyment of wine or drunkenness. With this, as with all other good things, it is a question of moderation. Man's virtue is to be gauged by the fact that he knows how to observe moderation. Thus wine actually becomes a touch-stone for testing the hearts of the proud (Sir 31:26). 'Drunkenness increases the anger of a fool to his injury, reducing his strength and adding wounds' (Sir 31:30). 'Wine drunk in season and temperately is rejoicing in heart and gladness of soul' (Sir 31:28).

Bibliography: E. Busse, *Der Wein im Kult des AT*, Freiburg 1922; J. Döller, 'Der Wein in Bibel und Talmud', *Bbl* 4 (1923), 143–67 and 267–99; L. Rost, *Festschrift Alt*, Tübingen 1953, 169ff; G. von Rad, *Genesis: A Commentary*,

London 1963², 132f; A. Maillot, *Allmen* 307; P. Gächter, *Maria im Erdenleben*, Innsbruck 1955³, 160–63; A. Penna, *Geremia*, Turin 1952, 256–60; G. Closen, *Wege in die Hl. Schrift*, Regensburg 1939, 101–15; H. Seesemann, *TDNT* v, 162–6.

Johannes B. Bauer

Wisdom

A. In the *Old Testament* wisdom is an idea with many shades of meaning, and a great many different qualities are grouped under this head and brought into association with it. For practical reasons we shall draw a distinction in the pages which follow between wisdom as teaching (1), as a human quality (2), and as a divine attribute and power (3).

Like all other peoples Israel too had a practical knowledge of the laws governing human life which was based on her own experience. She observed how many repetitions of an event produced the same or a similar outcome. Specific types of constantly recurring experience made a permanent impression upon her, which she then formulated in proverbs. Practical wisdom of this kind developed from prolonged observation is to be found, for instance, in Prov 16:18: 'Pride goes before destruction, and a haughty spirit before a fall'. It was inevitable that these maxims should have been assembled and handed on as teaching to those under instruction. This empirical and gnomic wisdom in the form of fixed sayings (see Prov 10:1–22:16), as also of counsel (see Prov 22:22–8), is to be found especially in the Book of Proverbs.

In the ancient Near East this wisdom was prized as a benefit of culture. Hence the kings in particular felt themselves responsible for maintaining and encouraging it. The fact that Solomon is mentioned three times in the Book of Proverbs (1:1; 10:1; 25:1) as its author justifies us in concluding that at an early stage the royal court of Jerusalem took over this tradition of the cultivation of wisdom. The wisdom of foreign peoples was known in Israel also: that of the Edomites (Jer 49:7; Obad 8), the Babylonians (Jer 50:35; 51:57) and the Egyptians (1 Kings 4:30), and among the Israelites foreign wisdom was drawn upon without restriction. In Prov 22:17–23:11 the hagiographer follows an Egyptian model (the Book of the Wisdom of Amenemope) and in the case of Prov 30, 31 it can be gathered from the title and the content alike that it presents us with non-Israelite wisdom. Nevertheless Israelite wisdom had a character of its own. Foreign wisdom was given a religious aspect and assimilated to faith in Yahweh. Whereas Egyptian wisdom is addressed only to scribes and officials, that is, is meant for one specific class, Israelite wisdom applies to the covenant people as a whole. This appears clearly in the Book of Proverbs: only a few verses are concerned specifically with court life (see 14:28; 16:12; 19:12), most of them are addressed quite in general to 'everyman'.

While this experiential wisdom also bears specifically Israelite traits, nevertheless when we compare it with the prophetic writings it becomes clear that it does not represent any typical Israelite form of thought. The prophets speak of Yahweh's sovereign *commandment*. The sage, on the other hand, with his *counsel*, intends his message rather for the intelligent consideration of man. Often he adduces motives for it of a utilitarian kind. Man's own interests are central to his message. The message of the prophets can be understood only against the background of salvific history. It is addressed to the covenant people or to individuals as members of the covenant people in their historical situation. The sage, on the other hand, addresses man as man, and thereby abstracts from his historical connections. The earlier experiential wisdom of Israel, therefore, has an international and universally humanist character.

Side by side with this universal and humanist wisdom drawn from experience, and at first not even connected with it, another idea is to be found in Israel, one which envisages wisdom not as acquired knowledge but rather as a gift bestowed by Yahweh. Eliphaz receives his teaching in the form of a nocturnal revelation (Job 4:12–16). For Elihu wisdom is not the fruit of age and experience alone, but an effect of God's spirit (Job 32:6–9), who forces the sage to speak as once he forced the prophets (Job 32:19f). Where wisdom is expected from God in this manner the whole of the Old Testament revelation already in existence could be summed up under the concept of wisdom. This identification of law and wisdom is actually made in Sir 24:23–34: law offers the fullness of wisdom. The wise man no longer forms his teaching on the basis of experience and observance. Now he steeps himself in the holy scriptures of Israel in order himself to become wise, and as one learned in the law to be of service to the uninitiated in speech and in

writing (see the prologue of the Greek translator of Sirach).

The author of the Book of Wisdom also incorporates profane knowledge into the wisdom bestowed by revelation. Divine wisdom has imparted all possible knowledge to 'Solomon' (Wis 7:21). He has been instructed by God in all branches of Greek science (7:17–20). 'Solomon', the prototype of the Wisdom teacher, thus owes all his knowledge to God and to the divine wisdom. The experiential wisdom which originally existed as an independent category side by side with religious wisdom is forced to give place increasingly to religious wisdom, until finally it becomes subsumed under it. The fact that Israel summed up religious and profane knowledge as a single whole under the concept of wisdom has its significance for the confrontation between her and the gentiles who surrounded her. Since this concept also occupied an important place in the hellenistic intellectual world, it could serve as a bridge for the encounter with hellenism.

2. Corresponding to the twofold character of wisdom as teaching we also find in the Old Testament a twofold understanding of wisdom as a human quality. It is (a) a gift of God which is imparted to individual men as an act of grace; but it is also (b) a natural quality which is *acquired by experience* and imparted through instruction.

(a) The first idea is to be found especially in the popular writings, in the prophets and in the later wisdom writings (Sir, Wis). There wisdom is the prerogative of God, and for this reason when it is imparted to men it appears in a manner similar to the spirit of God, as a mysterious power equipping the recipient for various kinds of task. Divine wisdom is veiled from man, he does not know the way to it (Job 28:12–27; Bar 3:15–35). To petition for this wisdom would be presumptuous, for it would make man like God (Gen 3:5, 22; see also Ezek 28:1–5). As the possessor of wisdom, however, Yahweh can impart it to men. It endows them with mysterious powers such as the interpretation of dreams (Gen 41:38f; Dan 1:17) and sorcery (Ex 7:11–13; see Wis 10:16), but also artistic skill and the cunning of the craftsman (Ex 28:3; 31:3, 6; 36:1f). But it is above all upon kings, rulers and judges that God bestows wisdom, in order to equip them to discharge their functions rightly. Thus he gives it to Moses (Num 11:17, 25) and his assistants (Num 11:25; Deut 1:13), to the king (Prov 8:15f; 16:10), David (2 Sam 14:17, 20; see 23:1f), Solomon (1 Kings 3:11, 28), and the messianic king of the future (Is 11:2–5).

Whereas in the earlier writings wisdom is imparted chiefly to rulers, later it is offered to all (Prov 2:6; see also 1:20; Ps 32:8; Sir 1:9). Wisdom has become more 'democratic'. Admittedly certain prior conditions are mentioned for the reception of wisdom. Only one who stands in God's favour (Eccles 2:26), who loves God (Sir 1:10), only holy souls (Wis 7:27) obtain wisdom. In the most recent texts Israel is mentioned especially as the possessor of wisdom (Sir 24:8; Bar 3:36; Wis 10:17). Israel reflects upon her long past and realizes the significance of being a chosen people.

Now that the circle of those who receive wisdom is changed, other effects produced by the possession of wisdom are mentioned also: knowledge of God (Job 11:6–9; Wis 9:17), righteousness (Prov 2:6f; Wis 9:17f), wisdom in speech (Job 32:8, 18–20, Sir 39:6; Wis 6:22–5), the spirit of prophecy (Wis 7:27).

(b) Even the most recent of the Old Testament writings recognises a twofold way of arriving at wisdom: prayer (Wis 7:7; 8:21) and instruction (Wis 6:9). Whereas the later writings regard wisdom predominantly as a gift of God, in the earlier stages it was regarded more as a natural quality to be gained through education and experience. For wisdom is first and foremost prudence in the affairs of life, the capacity to guide one's life into happy and prosperous channels. But manual skill is also described as wisdom. The craftsman counts as one who is 'wise of hand' (Sir 9:17). Even the carpenters, goldsmiths and weavers who fashion idolatrous images are called 'wise' (Is 40:20; Jer 10:9). Here wisdom has the force of 'skilfulness'. In a further usage it is the experienced and prudent counsellor who is accounted wise (2 Sam 13:3; 14:2; 20:16), the old man who has been able to accumulate experience throughout a long life (Job 8:8; 12:12; 15:10), the 'scribes' who are well versed in the law (Jer 8:8f). In the period of the monarchy 'scribe' designates the highest of state officials (see 2 Kings 25:19). There seems to have been a special class of 'sages', who enjoyed high repute (Is 3:3; 5:21; 29:14; Jer 8:8; 18:18). This class was probably identical with that of the scribes (Jer 8:8). These sages, together with the prophets and priests,

belong to the leading classes of intel-
lectuals in Israel from the eighth
century onwards. Probably it is they
who assembled the wisdom sayings and
employed them in instructing others.
In the post-exilic period the sages are
no longer royal officials, but those
learned in the scriptures who search the
law (Sir 39:1) and interpret it in the
'house of instruction' (Sir 39:8; 51:23).

He who possesses knowledge of men,
a sound understanding and prudence in
managing the affairs of life is accounted
wise. The object of behaving wisely is
to attain uninterrupted happiness in
one's personal life, and this is achieved
by regulating one's conduct in accordance with a prudence that is based upon
experience (see Prov 10:4, 8, 10, 14,
17). But the wise man also takes into
account a higher retribution, one
which rewards actions which are morally good in this present age, and
punishes evil behaviour (see Prov
10:3, 6, 22, 27, 29). The motive for
behaving wisely is to a large extent
personal happiness. The wise man does
what is morally good not because it is
good in itself, but because it obtains a
reward and because evil-doing brings
punishment upon itself (see Prov
5:1-20). But religious motivations are
also to be found, especially in the more
recent writings (Sir 7:36; 35:13-24;
Wis 9:8). The norms of wise conduct are
experience and insight into the consequences of one's actions (see Prov
16:18, 19, 21, 24, 26), the wisdom of
the elders and their experiences of life
(Prov 1:8; 2:1; 3:1), what is pleasing
to God (Prov 11:1; 12:22; 15:9), and
in the later wisdom writings the law of
Yahweh (Sir 6:37; 17:11; Wis 16:6;
18:4). In cases in which the law of

Yahweh is the norm of wise conduct the
sinner is accounted a fool, while the
righteous is wise and prudent. Sin is
then folly, while God's commandments
contain the highest wisdom (see Ps
14:1; Sir 1:26f).

(c) Yahweh is the wise. The prophets
praise the wisdom of God (Is 28:29;
31:2; 40:13f; Jer 10:12; 51:15; see
also Job 9:4; 12:13; 26:12). In other
passages wisdom appears less as an
attribute of God than as a distinct
entity with an existence of its own, the
way to which is known to Yahweh
alone, and which he has penetrated to
its depths (Job 28:23, 27; Bar 3:32).
In Prov 1:20-33; 8:1-21; 9:1-6 wisdom is personified in the feminine as a
preacher. She extols her prerogatives
and exhorts men to pay heed to her
instruction. In Prov 8:22-31 wisdom
speaks of her own origins. God possessed
her from the beginning and she was
already born before the beginning of
creation. When God created the world
she was at his side. A hymn to wisdom of
a similar character is to be found in Sir
24:1-22. Wisdom exalts herself because
of her origins and the blessings which
she confers. She went forth from the
mouth of Yahweh, sought for a resting-
place throughout the entire world, and
finally, at the behest of the Creator, who
formed her, pitched her tent in Israel,
where she grew and bore rich fruit. In
Sir 24:23 this wisdom is identified with
the law of Moses. Wisdom appears still
more as a subsistent entity in Wis
7:22-8:1. Wisdom is a being who is
understanding (7:22), who has come
forth from God (7:25) and is God's
image (7:26). Special works are ascribed to her. She penetrates and permeates
all in a manner similar to the Stoic

world reason (7:24; 8:1). She chooses a just one (10:5), leads men in their activities (9:11; 10:10), preserves (10:1, 5) and rescues them (9:18). She loves men (1:6), takes up her abode in them (1:4), and makes them friends of God and of the prophets (7:27). Divine qualities are ascribed to reason. She is immutable (7:27) and all-powerful (7:23, 27). She appears to subsist as a person in her own right, and as distinct from God. She lives with God; God loves her (8:3). She is initiated into God's secret knowledge, and is a chooser of his works (8:4). She is present at the creation of the world (9:9). She directs the course of the world (7:23, 24, 27; 8:1). She sits beside God's throne (9:4). She has come forth from God, and therefore participates in the divine nature (7:25f).

All these statements appear to point to a second divine person, but in view of the strict monotheism of the Old Testament this is extremely improbable. It is significant that in the Book of Wisdom (as also in Proverbs and Sirach) invocations in prayer are never directed to wisdom, but only to God, who can impart wisdom as his gift (Wis 9:4). On the other hand, in the Book of Wisdom wisdom is more than a mere poetic personification of a divine attribute. This appears especially from Wis 7:25f, where wisdom's connection with God is described. It can hardly be said of an attribute or quality that it proceeds from God, or that it is the image of his goodness. Wisdom, therefore, occupies an intermediate position between a subsistent person and a mere attribute of God. The concept of wisdom shares this intermediate position with the concepts of ↗ word and

↗ spirit. As dynamic concepts, they stand for a function of God in relation to the world in its concrete essence. These dynamic concepts are in conformity with a specific mode of thought which envisages in plastic and concrete terms a relationship which we are accustomed to represent to ourselves in abstract ones. Wisdom as described in Wis 7:22–8:1, therefore, is in the last analysis God himself in his work in and upon the world.

This representation of the divine activity under the image of wisdom is significant not only from the literary point of view, but also, and chiefly, from the theological one. In presenting divine wisdom in this form the Old Testament hagiographers have paved the way for the New Testament revelation concerning Christ.

B. In the *New Testament* wisdom does not appear to have the same significance which is ascribed to it in the Old. Only rarely do we find human wisdom referred to in commendatory terms (Acts 7:22; 1 Cor 6:5; Lk 16:8). Moral and religious wisdom (Lk 2:40, 52) and the wisdom of the scribes are attributed to Jesus who teaches with power (Mk 6:2; Mt 13:54; see also Lk 2:47). Paul wishes his christians to be 'wise as to what is good' (Rom 16:19). The human wisdom of self-will, which leaves no room for the divine wisdom, is rejected (1 Cor 1:17–29; 2:4ff, 13; 3:19; 2 Cor 1:12; Rom 1:22; Jas 3:15), for it derives from the flesh (2 Cor 1:12), the world (1 Cor 2:6; 3:19), and ultimately from the devil (Jas 3:15). In its self-sufficiency this human wisdom cannot apprehend the wisdom of God which is revealed especially in his mysterious plan of salvation (Rom 11:33). Thus the 'wisdom of the wise' sees in the message of the Cross only folly, whereas it is precisely the power of God that is revealed in it (1 Cor 1:18f). Human wisdom, which holds the wisdom of God for folly, thereby itself becomes folly (1 Cor 3:19). Yet the basic capacity for apprehending the revealed truth is not denied to the wise of this world from the outset. Always conscious that the mission with which he has been entrusted is for the wise and the foolish alike (Rom 1:14), in Corinth Paul actually wins over a few of the wise to faith (1 Cor 1:26). But he who is wise in the human and worldly sense, if he wishes to become truly wise, must first become a fool (1 Cor 3:18), ie, he must first recognise that the wisdom of this world is folly. True wisdom comes from above (Jas 3:17), from God (Jas 1:5), from the Father (Eph 1:17f), from Christ (Lk 21:15; Eph 1:9), from the Spirit (1 Cor 12:8). It explicates the knowledge contained in faith to ever clearer and broader apprehension. It reveals itself in a deep understanding of the event of salvation (1 Cor 2:7-9; Eph 1:8ff, 17-21), but also in the recognition of the divine will and the moral obligations arising from it (Col 1:9f; Jas 3:13, 17). This wisdom, far from consisting in pure and unrestricted speculation, is bound up with moral maturity (1 Cor 3:1-3). Thus there is a wisdom which is reserved to mature christians (1 Cor 2:6).

The explicit statements about wisdom to be found in the New Testament are relatively few in number. The influence of the Old Testament idea of wisdom on the portrayal of Christ in the New Testament is all the more significant on this account. Paul calls Christ the wisdom of God (1 Cor 1:24, 30). A comparison of pauline statements about Christ with the wisdom literature shows that Paul has transferred specific traits, which occur especially in the Book of Wisdom, as attributes of the divine wisdom to Christ. Christ is the image of the invisible God (Col 1:15; see also Wis 7:26), the firstborn of all creation (Col 1:15; see also Prov 8:22; Sir 1:4). Through him all things have come to be, and we too exist through him (1 Cor 8:6; see also Wis 9:1). It is due to him that the cosmos continues to be maintained in existence (Col 1:17; see also Wis 8:1; 7:27). Christ is the reflection of his (God's) glory, and the image of his being (Heb 1:3; see also Wis 7:25f). An approximation between Christ and the divine wisdom is already apparent in the synoptic gospels. In Mt 11:18f the works performed by Christ are compared with the works of wisdom. Mt 11:25-30 is still clearer on this point: in order to give a clear statement of his relationship with the Father and his significance for men Jesus avails himself of the hymnic expressions in which the Old Testament has described the relationship of the divine wisdom to God and to men (see Job 28:25-8; Prov 8:22-35; Sir 1:1-10; 24:18; Bar 3:27-38; Wis 6-9). But the influence which can be recognised most clearly of all is that of the divine wisdom of the Old Testament upon the portrayal of Christ in the fourth gospel. A comparison shows that the author of the prologue lays under contribution ideas which bear the stamp of the wisdom literature. Between the 'word' of the prologue and the divine wisdom of the Old Testament there exists a correspondence which cannot be overlooked (see Prov 1:29; 3:19; 8:22, 30, 35; Sir 24:6, 8; Wis 7:22, 25–30; 8:1). In the gospel itself Christ represents his relationship with the Father and with men in a manner similar to that by which the relationships between wisdom and God and wisdom and men are depicted in the wisdom literature.

Like wisdom Christ too has come forth from God (Jn 8:42; see also Sir 24:3; Wis 7:25). Both have been beloved by God from the very beginning (Jn 3:35; 17:24; see also Prov 8:27–31; Wis 8:3; 9:9). God has given all things into their hand (Jn 3:35; see also Wis 10:1–11:1). As God is at work, so too are the Son and wisdom (Jn 5:17, 19; Wis 11:17; 15:1; 7:22; 8:1; 7:27). In fact both live in intimate union with God (Jn 14:10f; (see also Prov 8:30; Wis 8:3), and are initiated into the knowledge of God (Jn 8:28; 14:24; see also Wis 8:4). Like wisdom, the Son too has been sent into the world in order to redeem it (Jn 3:17; see also Wis 9:17f). Wisdom takes up its abode in men and thereby draws down upon them the love of God (Wis 1:4; 7:27f). Likewise the Son lives in the men who love him and thereby establishes an inner relationship between God and mankind (Jn 14:20–23). In order to come to the Son or to wisdom man first needs God's grace (Jn 6:44; see also Prov 2:6; Sir 39:6; Wis 8:21). Men's destiny is decided according to the attitude which they adopt towards wisdom and to the Son (Jn 5:22, 27; see also Prov 8:35f; Wis 6:18; 10:1–11:1). For these can bestow and maintain life like God

himself (Jn 6:27, 51; see also Prov 8:35; Wis 16:26).

He who observes the commandments of wisdom and of the Son thereby obtains eternal life (Jn 8:51; see also Wis 6:18). He who takes these as his guide does not walk in darkness, for wisdom and the Son are light to men (Jn 8:12; see also Wis 7:26; 10:17; 18:3f). Since both derive from God they are free from sin (Jn 8:46; see also Wis 7:25, 30). Because they come from heaven they can bring a heavenly message to men (Jn 3:12; see also Wis 9:16f). Wisdom and Son alike bestow their friendship upon men (Jn 15:15; see also Wis 7:14, 27), preserve and protect them (Jn 17:12; see also Wis 9:11).

Thus the mysterious figure of the divine wisdom has great significance. The New Testament hagiographers found in the Old Testament presentation of wisdom apt concepts in which they could present the generation of Christ by God before the world began, the part he played in the creation of it, and his significance for mankind in a language that was current among the Jews. Surely we are justified in saying that in Christ it was the divine wisdom become man that they were contemplating.

Bibliography: P. Heinisch, *Die persönliche Weisheit des AT in religionsgeschichtlicher Beleuchtung* (*BZF* XI/1–2), Münster 1923; J. Fichtner, *Die altorientalische W. in ihrer israelitisch-jüdischen Ausprägung* (*BZAW* 62), Giessen 1933; C. Spicq, 'La vertu de prudence dans l'AT', *RB* 42 (1933), 187–210; W. Zimmerli, 'Zur Struktur der atl. Weisheit', *ZAW* 51 (1933), 177–204; P. van Imschoot, 'Sagesse et esprit dans l'AT', *RB* 47 (1938), 23–49; A. M. Dubarle, *Les sages d'Israël*, Paris 1946; R. Stecher, 'Die persönliche Weisheit in den Proverbien, Kap 8', *ZKT* 75 (1953), 411–51;

Witness

H. Windisch, 'Die göttliche Weisheit der Juden und die paulinische Christologie', *Ntl. Studien für G. Heinrici*, Leipzig 1914, 220–34; C. H. Dodd, *The Interpretation of the Fourth Gospel*, Cambridge 1953, 274f; A. Feuillet, 'Jésus et la sagesse divine d'après les évangiles synoptiques', *RB* 62 (1955), 161–96; G. Ziener, 'Weisheitsbuch und Johannesevangelium', *Bbl* 38 (1957), 416f; *RGG* 1800–03 and 1804–09; P. van Imschoot, Haag 1701–06; Eichrodt II, 38–45; von Rad I, 418–59; Bultmann I, 326f and II, 129–34; Imschoot I, 59f and 212–23; Heinisch (see Index); **Jerusalem Bible*, London and New York 1966, 723–8, 931f, 978f, 1004f, and 1034f (introductions to the Wisdom books); H. Gese, *Lehre und Wirklichkeit in der alten Weisheit*, Tübingen 1958; G. Fohrer, *TWNT* VII, 476–528.

Georg Ziener

Witness

The expression 'witness', 'to bear witness', 'testimony' are household words in the New Testament. The basic word for witness in Greek is *martus*. It occurs thirty-four times in the New Testament, most frequently in the Acts of the Apostles (thirteen times). In the epistles it occurs nine times in Paul, twice in Hebrews, once in 1 Peter, and five times in Revelation. The synoptics contain four instances of it, but in the johannine gospel and epistles it does not occur at all. The verb *marturein* (= to bear witness) is attested in seventy-six passages. The johannine writings, with forty-seven examples, far outstrip any of the other New Testament writings (John thirty-three times; 1 and 2 John ten times; Revelation four times). Luke has only two instances of it, and it is totally absent from Matthew and Mark. It is found eleven times in Acts, and Paul and Hebrews each have eight instances of it. The same is true of *marturia* (= testi-

mony), which is employed thirty-seven times in the New Testament. In the johannine writings alone it occurs thirty times (fourteen times in John, seven times in 1 and 3 John, nine times in Revelation), in the synoptics only four times (twice in Mark, twice in Luke, not at all in Matthew), in Acts once, and in Paul twice. The word *marturion* (also = testimony) is found twenty times: nine times in the synoptics, twice in Acts, six times in Paul, once each in Hebrews, James, and Revelation. These statistical findings reflect the development in terms of salvation history of the New Testament concept of witness as definitively established in Acts and in the group of writings attributed to John.

I. Concept. The word *martus* is derived from the law courts, and is already found in classical Greek and in LXX as a designation for one who has observed an event and can give an account of it, usually in court, by way of proof and to establish where liability does or does not lie (see Lev 5:1; Num 5:13; Deut 17:6f; 1 Sam 20:23; Is 8:2; Mal 3:5; Ps 89:37 [Heb]; Wis 1:6; Mt 26:65; Mk 14:63; Acts 6:13; 7:58; 2 Cor 13:1; 1 Tim 5:19).

Already in classical antiquity, however, the word means not only a witness to fact but also a witness to truth, a man who avows something to be true, that is a man who proclaims truths, stands up for his convictions, expresses his opinions and gives reasons for them (for examples from Greek literature, see *TDNT* IV, 481–4). In the Old Testament the word is found with this meaning only in a few passages (Ex 31:18; Deut 4:45; 6:17; Ps 19:7; 119:14, 24, 31, 46), but it is particularly frequent in the New Testament writings. According to Is 43:9–13 and 44:7–11, Yahweh summons the people of Israel to bear witness on his behalf in his cause against the gods of the gentiles in order that they may declare before all the world that Yahweh alone is the true God who controls the course of history (see, in the New Testament, Rom 1:9; 2 Cor 1:23; Phil 1:8; 1 Thess 2:5f, 10). They are to bear witness to him in this sense on account of his mighty deeds, which they have experienced and acknowledged by faith.

II. *Witness according to the Acts of the Apostles.* A. In the great confrontation which took place between the early church and judaism on the one hand, and the early church and the gentile world on the other, the idea of the *apostle* as witness to fact plays an absolutely primary role.

1. The apostles are first and foremost the eye- and ear-witnesses of the *risen Lord.* In the course of choosing a successor in place of Judas, Peter outlines the chief task of the apostle: 'So one of the men who have accompanied us during all the time that the Lord Jesus went in and out among us, beginning from the baptism of John until the day when he was taken up from us—one of these men must become with us *a witness to his resurrection*' (Acts 1:21f; see also 1:8). With inspiration and 'with great power the apostles gave *testimony of the resurrection of the Lord Jesus*' (Acts 4:33; see also Lk 24:46–8; Acts 2:32; 3:14f; 5:32; 13:31), with whom they had eaten and drunk after his resurrection from the dead (Acts 10:41).

Paul, too, lays claim to the title of 'witness to Christ', even though he has only seen the glorified Lord in a vision (Acts 22:15; 23:11; 26:9–20; Gal 1:11–2:10). Luke, however, draws a subtle distinction by which Paul is primarily 'a minister of the word' and only secondarily a 'witness' to the glorified Lord (Acts 26:16), whereas the converse is true of the eleven, namely that they were primarily 'eyewitnesses', and only secondarily 'ministers of the word' (Lk 1:2). The facts to which the apostles are to bear witness comprise not merely the resurrection and exaltation of Jesus, but also his life: baptism, miracles, healings, castings out of devils, preaching of the joyful message of the gospel. 'You know the word ... which was proclaimed throughout all Judaea beginning from Galilee after the baptism which John preached: how God anointed Jesus of Nazareth with the Holy Spirit and with power, how he went about doing good and healing all that were oppressed by the devil, for God was with him. And we are *witnesses* to all that he did both in the country of the Jews and in Jerusalem' (Acts 10:37–9; see also 1:22; 5:31–2a; 2:40; 3:13, 18, 26; 10:40a–43; 2 Pet 1:18). But the function of the apostles is not confined merely to bearing witness to the facts. They are also preachers who proclaim the significance of Jesus' resurrection as acknowledged by faith.

2. He alone could be a witness to Christ who was *chosen by God* for this purpose. The seventy-two disciples (see Lk 10:1–17; Acts 1:21–2), the five hundred brethren (1 Cor 15:6–7), and the two pilgrims to Emmaus (Lk 24:13–35) had all equally seen and heard the risen Christ. And yet Acts

recognises only the apostles as 'witnesses of Christ', the 'witnesses *chosen* by God from of old', who, moved by the gift of the Holy Spirit, realised the immense significance of this mighty deed of God (Acts 10:41-2; 13:31; 22:15; 26:16).

3. The apostles bore a *threefold* witness to the Lord: (a) It is the witness of the *word* that is primary. They were above all 'ministers of the word', that is of the good news of the risen and glorified Lord. According to the Old Testament a statement had probative force in the law-courts only if it was made by two or three witnesses (see Num 35:30; Deut 17:6; 19:15; Mt 18:16; Jn 8:17; 2 Cor 13:1; 1 Tim 5:19). For this reason, in the great cause for the rehabilitation of Jesus Peter always spoke in the name of the apostolic college when he brought evidence and laid it before the court of the Jews: 'God has raised the author of life from the dead. To this *we* are witnesses' (Acts 3:15; see also 2:32; 5:32; 10:39, 41, 42). Paul, on the contrary, customarily invokes the unique witness of his vision of Christ (see Acts 22:15-18; 23:11; 26:16) to prove his case to his hellenistic hearers.

Although 'unlettered and uneducated' (Acts 4:13), the apostles bore a powerful witness for Christ before a world which was ill-disposed because they had been equipped for the task with the *gift of the Spirit* at Pentecost (Acts 2:4), as had been promised by the Saviour (see Acts 1:8). This gift of the Spirit was a source of light and strength which could not be conquered. Exploring the mine of the Old Testament scriptures, Peter, guided by the Spirit of God, discovered Jesus'

messianic authority prophesied there (Acts 2:34-5 = Ps 110:1; 10:38 = Is 61:1), and also his prophetic mission (3:22-3 = Deut 18:15, 19), his passion under the figure of the mysterious Servant of God (3:13; 4:27, 30 = Is 52:13-53:12; see also Acts 8:32-3), his glorious resurrection (2:25-6 = Ps 16:8-11), etc, and he found these attested there 'with the certainty of divine truth' (*Summa Theologica* II-II, q 174, a 2 ad 2). The Holy Spirit filled the apostles with power as he had formerly filled the prophets, so that in spite of all difficulties, all dangers, all persecutions, they proclaimed the gospel tidings 'openly': 'For we cannot but speak of what we have seen and heard,' exclaims Peter proudly before the Sanhedrin (Acts 4:20; see also 4:31; 9:27-8; 13:46; 14:3; 18:9-10, 26; 19:8; and see the Old Testament precedents in Is 6:8; Jer 1:18; Ezek 3:8-9; Amos 3:4-8; Mic 3:8).

(b) Like their divine master (Lk 24:19; Acts 2:22), so too the apostles reinforce the witness of the word or of their preaching with 'signs' (*sēmeia*), that is, with miraculous power: 'And many wonders and signs were done through the apostles' (Acts 2:43; 5:12), above all by the hands of Peter 3:1-10; 5:15) and Paul (14:8-10; 19:11-12; see also 4:30; 14:3, 27; 15:4, 12; 21:19).

(c) Finally, the witness of the apostles is only genuine if it carries the stamp of persecutions and suffering, of oppression and the malice of conspirators plain for all to see. The lot of the disciple (Mt 10:17-22; Lk 21:12-15; Jn 16:1-2; 1 Pet 5:1) is the same as the lot of his master (Mt 23:34-5; Lk 11:47-51; Jn 15:20; Acts 3:22-3).

Under the influence of the Holy Spirit, the first christians regarded the condemnation of Jesus by the Roman authorities, the threats of the Sanhedrin and the fetters of the apostles, as the fulfilment of the messianic prophecy of Ps 2:1–2 (=Acts 4:25–6): 'For truly in this city there were gathered together against thy holy servant Jesus, whom thou didst anoint, both Herod and Pontius Pilate, with the gentiles and the peoples of Israel, to do whatever thy hand and thy plan had predestined to take place' (Acts 4:27–8). The power from on high had turned timid men into heroes who trod in the footprints of the servant of God: 'Then they left the presence of the council rejoicing that they were counted worthy to suffer dishonour for the name of Jesus' (Acts 5:41). The message of the beatitudes pronounced by Jesus had come true in their lives (see Mt 5:10–12; Lk 6:22–3). Indeed they were now ready for the ultimate test, to seal their witness to the master with their blood (see Acts 5:29; 6:15; 20:24; 21:13), although Luke in his account has not taken up the tradition of the violent death suffered by the prince of the apostles.

(B) Since the apostles alone were called to be witnesses to the fact of the resurrection, they are the witnesses to Christ *par excellence*. But their inspired witness to Christ has awakened an echo in the primitive community of christians which henceforward will not be silenced until the end of time.

1. If the christians of the early church no longer have any direct experience of the crucified and risen Lord they are none the less called to bear witness to him in word and deed.

This is witness in the broader sense, the indirect witness which is based upon the Easter preaching of the apostles. While, therefore, it does not rest upon the same foundations as that of the apostles, it has the same person as its subject, namely, the risen Lord.

2. The apostles sometimes refer to the fact of this indirect form of witness. Before the Sanhedrin Peter solemnly accounts for his actions in the following terms: 'We are witnesses to these things [the death and resurrection of Christ], and so is *the Holy Spirit whom God has given to those who obey him*' (Acts 5:32; see also 15:28), that is to say that the Holy Spirit also bears witness to the glorified Christ through the mouths of the Jewish and gentile christians who speak and act under his influence (see 2:4; 4:8, 31; 15:28). At Pentecost the Holy Ghost was poured out 'upon all flesh', that is, upon all members of the people of God (see Acts 2:17–21 =Joel 2:28–9, 32). After the liberation of the apostles Peter and Paul a 'miniature Pentecost' took place: 'And when they had prayed the place in which they were gathered together was shaken, and they were all filled with the Holy Spirit and spoke the words of God with boldness' (Acts 4:31).

The gentiles, too, received the gift of the Spirit of God, as, for example, in the case of the household of Cornelius: 'While Peter was still saying this the Holy Spirit fell upon all who heard the word, and the believers from among the circumcised [the Jewish christians] who came with Peter were amazed because the gift of the Holy Spirit had been poured out even upon the gentiles' (Acts 10:44; see also 11:15,

17). At the crucial council of Jerusalem Peter underlined this revolutionary fact of salvation: 'God who knows the heart bore witness to them [the gentiles], giving them the Holy Spirit just as he did to us' (Acts 15:8; see also 8:12, 17; 19:5–6).

Individuals, too, were endowed with the gift of the Holy Spirit, as, for example, Philip (Acts 8:29), Barnabas (Acts 11:24; 13:2), Stephen (Acts 6:5, 10; 7:55), Timothy (2 Tim 1:6).

3. The witness of the community, which was confined to the church at Jerusalem, as well as the witness of individual christians, which was spread through the whole world, brought astonishing effects in its train.

(a) The message of the apostles at Easter, in which they called upon men to become christians, exercised an overwhelming attraction upon the primitive church, in which a glorious spring of christian life sprang up, while unshakeable faith in the resurrection of Christ, the pledge of their own glorification, to be accomplished at the return of the Lord, kindled the spark of christian joy in the hearts of the first christians, a joy which sprang into flame chiefly at the liturgical celebration of the breaking of bread: 'Day by day . . . breaking bread in their homes, they partook of food with glad and generous hearts' (Acts 2:46; see also Eph 5:19), and praised the *magnalia Dei* (see also Acts 2:47; 3:8–9; 4:21; 11:18; 13:48; 21:20; Lk 24:52f). They gave vent to their overflowing joy in inarticulate cries and disconnected gestures according as the gift of tongues prompted them (see also Acts 2:4, 13, 17; 10:46; 19:6; 1 Cor 14; ↗ charisma).

The fiery Easter preaching of the apostles kindled in the hearts of the young communities the spark of an energetic brotherly love, the most winning element in the witness to Christ.

In the course of portraying the life of the early church from three distinct aspects (Acts 2:42–7; 4:32–5; 5:12–16), Luke has occasion to speak of the *koinōnia* (2:42), the 'brotherly fellowship' which welded the hearts and spirits of the believers into a unity: 'The company of those who believed were of one heart and soul' (4:32). In this happy period, in which many hearts beat as one, the faithful held all things in common. They sold property and possessions in order to distribute the proceeds among the starving brethren to each according to his need (Acts 2:44–5; 4:32, 34, 35). The name of Barnabas in particular shines out from the roll of honour of those who performed deeds of the most noble love, for he sold his field and laid the money at the foot of the apostles (Acts 4:37). This evidence of acts of brotherly love is more urgently relevant than ever before in our world, so rent as it is by social conflicts. Abbé Pierre, the apostle of the rag-pickers, testifies to the fact that in his brotherhood of Emmaus the order of the theological virtues is inverted. On their arrival the 'clochards' are given every kind of loving service. By degrees, under the rays of a heartfelt love, the ice of embitterment and cynicism melts. Hope is gradually generated in the hearts of these deprived ones, a hope which is at first purely at the natural level, and which is then directed, as it were spontaneously, towards the higher goods.

Finally faith in Christ is kindled in them.

(b) From Acts 6 onwards, the apostles, together with their disciples, priests and laymen alike, go out into the wide world in order to win over the gentiles to Christ above all by the preaching of the gospel message and by 'martyrdom'.

It was the chief task of the apostle to testify solemnly as in a trial in the law-courts to the fact of Jesus' resurrection, and thereby to his innocence. He was to do this before the Council of the Jews and the populace of Jerusalem. With the sending out of the apostles, the time of the *kērugma*, of the gospel, of the word of God is inaugurated—that is, the time when the good news of salvation in Christ is boldly proclaimed. Thus the function of the herald, the messenger who strives to win over Jewish and gentile hearers alike to Christ, comes to be associated with the task of bearing witness, and to be considered as an element of the highest importance in it.

So far as *believers* were concerned the great missionary campaign was inaugurated outside and beyond the holy city, whence they had been driven and scattered throughout the whole world by persecutions: 'They went from place to place and 'proclaimed' (*euangelizomai*) the 'word' (*logos*) (Acts 8:4; see also vv 12, 25, 35, 40; 11:19). Philip 'preached' Christ resoundingly (*kērussō*: Acts 8:5; see also 21:8). In these and other passages what is meant by *kērugma*, gospel, and word of God is nothing else than the indirect witness to Christ. The preaching of the Easter message awakened an unshakeable faith in the glorified Lord in the hearts of the first christians (see Rom 10:8–9, 14–17). They in their turn bore witness to the glorified Lord with burning inspiration. The modern apostle too, whether he be priest or layman, is called to bear witness to the risen Christ to a world which has grown pagan (see Lk 24:49; Acts 1:4, 5, 8; 2:33). We too ask for the gift of the Spirit, without which we can achieve nothing: when we humbly implore it from God he will open to us the immeasurable depths of holy scripture and will equip us with suprahuman power.

It is in persecutions and in the martyr's death that the christians' witness to their risen saviour shines out in all its purity. The *kērugma*, the message and word of God, represent a kind of preaching which is full of power to win men over to Christ; but they are devoid of any element of the forensic. They are the unalloyed expressions of convictions which are firm as a rock. But when christians stand before the bar of this world's courts they are no longer concerned to make attestations of their faith designed to win others over to it. Their preoccupation in this situation is simply to bear burning witness to Christ. It is witness in the juridical sense. The Holy Spirit will bear witness to the Lord through their mouths (see Lk 12:11; 21:12–15; Mt 10:17–20; Mk 13:11). First in the list of the unending procession of 'martyrs', Stephen the deacon stands out as 'a man full of faith and of the Holy Spirit' (Acts 6:5; see also vv 8, 10); 'But he, full of the Holy Spirit, gazed into heaven and saw the glory of God, and Jesus standing at the right hand of God'

(Acts 7:55–6). The Acts of the Apostles knows only this single one of those who bore witness with their blood: 'When the blood of Stephen thy witness (*martus*) was shed' (Acts 22:20; see also Rev 2:13; 11:3; 17:6). Since the deacon had no personal knowledge of the Lord either during his earthly life or in his risen state, he is not a witness to fact as the apostles were. On the other hand the expression does not signify 'martyr' in the sense which the term has acquired today, even though it is on the way to it. Towards the middle of the second century, when persecution and violent death for the sake of Christ became the daily bread of the church, the word *martus* came to be used solely as the technical term for the act of bearing witness by the shedding of one's blood—that is, martyrdom.

The prosecution of the faithful who remain true to Christ intensifies as the centuries unfold. The christians' witness by blood will be brought to an end only at the parousia by the witness of Jesus himself, the 'reliable and faithful witness' (Rev 1:5; 3:14) which he will then bear to all his own who have been faithful witnesses to him (see Lk 12:8–9).

III. In his gospel and epistles, *John* intentionally avoids the expression *martus*, but uses the verb *marturein* (forty-seven times) and the noun *marturia* (thirty times) all the more frequently on that account. This choice corresponds to the development of the idea of Christ which reached its culmination in John the evangelist. Like the apostles, John too had been a witness of Jesus' resurrection (see Jn 20–21; 1 Jn 1:1–3), but the time for

revising the trial of Jesus before the Sanhedrin and the people of Jerusalem through the witness of the apostles was long passed. It was pastoral considerations on a cosmic scale that burned in the soul of John the theologian. What he wanted was to bear witness to the person of Christ by his writings.

Seen through the eyes of the disciple whom Jesus loved, Christ developed his redemptive work in the setting of a hostile world. The hostility already indicated by the synoptics (see Mt 10:18; Mk 13:9; Lk 21:13) is still more powerfully emphasised by him. According to him the entire life of Jesus seems to develop in the form of a great trial at law in which Jesus himself and the world are the contestants. The various witnesses who are summoned to the bar of this court all pass on the word of revelation proceeding from the Father. Viewed in this light the johannine concept of witness acquires a juridical character. Hence John never uses the expression *kērugma*, current and frequent though this was in the tradition of the synoptics and Acts. What he is concerned with is not so much the preaching of the gospel message of divine salvation in Christ as the defence of Christ, the acknowledgement of Christ as Redeemer and Son of God. John's writings are not primarily intended to win over believers. Rather they have an apologetic character. They do not represent an avowal which is propagandist in character, as do the *kērugma*, the gospel or the word of God. Rather these writings constitute an ardent defence of Christ, and it is in this sense that they bear witness to him.

1. *On what is this witness based?* The witness is a statement concerning facts and events which are known from personal experience. In John the 'witness' is very often connected with the verb 'to see' (instances in 1:34; 3:11, 32; 19:35; 1 Jn 1:2; 4:14). The witnesses have seen with their bodily eyes an event which took place in Jesus' life. Therefore it is witness to fact (*martus*) which is meant, in the sense in which we have encountered this in the synoptics and Acts.

But according to John it is not to the facts as such of salvation history that the men who are called bear witness, but rather to the deeper reality hidden behind those facts. The baptist sees an event in the external world which points to the Messiahship of Jesus. He bears witness to this (1:32). John sees water and blood flowing from the side of Jesus; but it is not to the salvific fact as such that he bears witness, but rather to 'water and blood' as sacramental signs of baptism and the eucharist (19:36–7; 1 Jn 1:1–3). Behind the observed fact lies hidden a reality which is invisible, and which the earthly witness can only know through revelation. And it is to this that he bears witness. For this witness bodily vision of the fact in question was indispensable. For without it they would never have been able to bear witness at all (15:27). But their witness points on to that which revelation or faith has disclosed to them concerning the person of Jesus. For John witness is not primarily witness to fact, but witness to belief or to truth. Here, as in other instances, we are confronted with a special quality in the writing of this evangelist by which a given expression is used to signify a sensible experience and a mysterious spiritual reality both at the same time.

2. *To what does the johannine gospel bear witness?* From what has been said it will be clear that it is neither the resurrection of Jesus nor the events of his earthly life that constitute the subject of his witness. In his inmost heart stands the person of Christ (1:7, 8, 15; 5:31, 32, 36, 37, 39; 8:14, 18; 10:25; 1 Jn 5:9). In all these passages the question which the witness is intended to answer for us is: 'Who is Jesus?' The witness penetrates through the words and deeds of Jesus to the mystery of his being, to the spiritual reality of his person. The Baptist testifies to the Messiahship of Jesus, which is visible only to the eyes of faith (1:15, 32; 5:33;). The focal point of the witness is the person and the mission of Christ as revealed to believers alone. It is not the work of redemption that constitutes the central nucleus of the johannine theology but the person of the redeemer himself. It is this that gives his christology its special attraction.

3. *Who bears witness?* The evangelist records a whole series of witnesses. The baptist must bear witness to the light (1:7, 8, 15, 19, 32, 34; 3:26; 5:33, 36), to his messianic dignity (1:15), to the fact that he is the Son of God (1:30). The scriptures, in which God himself speaks, bear witness concerning Christ (5:39); hence one believes the word contained in them as one believes God himself, who speaks to us through his Son (5:24). The disciples bear witness concerning Christ (15:27; 19: 35; 21:24); so, too, Jesus himself bears witness concerning himself (5:31; 8:

13). Jesus' witness concerning himself is basically identical with the witness of the Father (5:32) who has sent him (3:34; 14:24). In immediate association with it is the witness of the 'works' which the Father has 'given' the Son power to perform (5:36). They are the works of the Father himself (9:3, 4; 10:37), who lives in Jesus as Jesus lives in him (10:38; 14:10–11). Later the Spirit of truth will bear witness in the church (15:26; 16:13). He will 'recall' to the disciples all that Jesus has said and done, that is he will disclose to them the deeper sense and the full significance of the words and deeds of Christ.

In the last analysis all of these distinct testimonies can be traced back to the single and unique testimony of the Father—to the Father's revelation which finds expression in the various earthly witnesses, is fulfilled in the witness borne by Jesus, and lives on in the witness of the Holy Spirit.

4. *What is the purpose of this witness?* From what has been stated so far it is evident that the witness in John is of its essence aimed at faith. It is meant to arouse and to deepen faith in Christ. The Baptist came to bear witness that all may believe (1:7). The evangelist gives testimony of the events of the crucifixion in order that all may come to believe (19:35).

According to 1 Jn 5:5–12 Jesus Christ constitutes the focal point of faith, and one which is based upon a threefold witness. Jesus Christ has come 'by water and blood', that is in the baptism at the Jordan and through death on the Cross. But there is also a reference to the 'water and blood' which flowed from Jesus' side (v 6ab).

Thus two distinct levels of significance for salvific history are to be found in 'water and blood', making them signs of baptism and the eucharist. To the historical witness of 'water and blood' (v 10 in the perfect) a third witness is added, that namely of the Spirit: the Spirit testifies to the reality and the presence of the Son of God in baptism and the eucharist (v 7: present tense).

According to Old Testament ideas of justice a statement is considered valid in law only if it is confirmed by two or three witnesses. For this reason three witnesses are called to testify that Christ is the Son of God: the Spirit, the water, and the blood. The witness of the Spirit evokes in us faith in Christ as Son of God (vv 5, 10). Baptism and eucharist admit us to a share in this divine life (v 11), life in the Son (v 11).

The witness of God (vv 9–10) combines all three witnesses in itself, the witness of the Spirit, the water and the blood. For through the threefold witness of faith and the two sacraments God himself gives testimony concerning his Son. But this witness of God finds a response only in the heart of the believer. Only for the believer can it become a source of life.

The apostles were called by God to be eye- and ear-witnesses of the risen and glorified Lord. The witnesses of the fourth gospel have plumbed revelation to its depths and there they have discovered the unfathomable mystery of the person of Christ and have borne witness to it. Their witness is a burning summons to believe in Jesus Christ, in the Messiah, in the word, and in the Glory of the Father.

May we, too, enlisted like the first christians in the corps of the risen and glorified Lord, and filled with the power which faith in the resurrection bestows, bear witness to the Lord by a life of true brotherly love and deep resignation to suffering! May the witness of the Father concerning his Son strengthen ever more in us faith in Christ! Pius XII summoned all christians to this task of bearing witness: 'Today more than ever, and as in the first centuries of her existence, the church chiefly needs *witnesses* . . . who by their whole way of life make the true countenance of Christ shine out before a world which has grown pagan' (*AAS* 39 [1947], 312).

Bibliography: General: H. von Campenhausen, *Die Idee des Martyriums in der alten Kirche*, Göttingen 1936; J. Smend, 'Der Zeugnischarakter der christl. Verkündigung', *ZST* 13 (1936), 489–517; E. Peterson, *Zeuge der Wahrheit*, Leipzig 1937; R. Asting, *Die Verkündigung des Wortes im Urchristentum*, Stuttgart 1939; E. Günther, *Martys. Die Geschichte eines Wortes*, Hamburg 1941; A. Verheul, 'Apostolaat en Verrijzenis', *Studio Cath.* 26 (1951), 171–84; M. Barth, *Der Augenzeuge*, 1946; E. Günther, 'Zeuge und Märtyrer', *ZNW* 47 (1956), 145–61; M. Lods, *Confesseurs et martyrs*, Neuchâtel–Paris 1948; N. Brox, *Zeuge und Märtyrer*, Munich 1961; H. Strathmann, *TDNT* IV, 474–514; S. de Diétrich, Allmen 456–8; A. Verheul, *DB* 1807f; *HTG* II, 903–11. On Acts: L. Cerfaux, 'Témoins du Christ d'après les Actes', *Receuil Cerfaux* II, 1954, 157–74; A. Retif, 'Témoignage et prédication missionnaire dans les Actes des Apôtres', *NRT* 73 (1951), 152–65; A. Rétif, *Foi au Christ et Mission*, 1953; R. Koch, 'Témoignage d'après les Actes', *Masses Ouvrières* 129 (1957), 16–33; 131 (1957), 4–25. On John: B. Trepanier, 'Contribution à une recherche sur l'idée de témoin dans les écrits johanniques', *Revue de l'Univ. d'Ottawa* 15 (1945), 5–63; C. Masson, 'Le témoignage de Jean', *RTP* 38 (1950), 120–27; A. Vanhoye, 'Témoignage et Vie en Dieu selon le quatrième évangile', *Christus* 16 (1955), 155–71; W. Nauck, 'Die Tradition und der Charakter des ersten Johannesbriefes', *Wissenschaftliche Untersuchungen zum NT*, ed. J. Jeremias and O. Michel, 1957; I. de la Potterie, 'La notion de témoignage dans S. Jean', *SP* II (Paris–Gembloux 1959), 193–208.

Robert Koch

Woman

A. *Woman in the Old Testament.* As the primeval history of the bible shows, the first woman was formed from the first man (Gen 2:21f); she was bone of his bone and flesh of his flesh (Gen 2:23). Hence she was called 'wo-man' by Adam since she was taken from man (Gen 2:23b). She was in the image and likeness of God (Gen 1:26f; ↗ likeness). The Hebrew words *ʾîš* and *ʾiššâh* are probably derived, etymologically speaking, from the same root, namely *ʾenāš*. The name in Hebrew designates the essence of a thing. Here it expresses with delicate artistry not only the complete conformity of nature between man and woman, but also the distinction of the sexes. In exploiting the similarity of sound between *ʾîš* and *ʾiššâh* in this way the biblical author has to a considerable extent followed the popular etymology based on the sound of words, which regarded the two terms as masculine and feminine forms of the same linguistic root. According to the account in Genesis it is the woman's function to be a helpmeet and, so to say, a complement to man (Gen 2:18), especially by joining with him in an indissoluble marriage (Gen 2:24). For it was not merely that she might be of the same nature that the first woman was formed from the first man—such identity of nature could equally well have been achieved if woman had been formed in the same way as man—but for the sake of unity between them. Woman, then, in spite of the secondary position she occupies in the order of creation, was called to live in a harmonious relationship with man, but not to be subordinate to him. Yet the very fact that woman was the more easily seduced (Gen 3:6) raises the question of whether woman was not considered the weaker partner. Finally we have that much disputed sentence in which a penalty is imposed upon the woman in Gen 3:16: 'He shall rule over you'. Many exegetes have concluded from this that henceforward woman is made subject to man as a penalty for having fallen into sin, and that the initial equality has been replaced by inequality, that is a reduction of woman's status. On the other hand, against this view the following factors may be pointed out: there can have been no intention to suggest that woman was juridically subordinated to man in the strict sense as a punishment for original sin, for man himself had been equally guilty. Likewise it cannot be a question of a subordination which is simply confined to family relationships, for this is already given in virtue of the original order of creation prior to original sin, and cannot therefore be a penalty arising from the first sin. 'He will rule over you' (16b) seems rather to represent a more specific application of the words: 'I shall greatly multiply your pain in childbearing' (16a), which means that in the marriage act woman must submit to the authority of her husband. For the purpose and the deeper meaning of the one being made subordinate to the other can only be that man and woman shall become one in a relationship of 'one flesh'. It cannot have been intended that woman should be abased or enslaved in either a juridical or a social sense (see J. Coppens and G. Reidick).

From the juridical point of view, the Israelite woman is not always accorded equality with man, but her position was probably far freer than that of women in the legal practice of other oriental peoples. The *marriage laws* are dominated by the principle of patriarchy. When she became married the woman passed from the authority of her father into that of her husband (1 Sam 18:17, 19, 27). The will and the inclination of the girl were, however, to a large extent taken into account (Gen 24:39, 58). The married woman and the espoused virgin alike were obliged to be completely faithful to their husbands. The husband only incurred the guilt of adultery if he intruded upon the marriage or espousals of another (Deut 22:22ff), a fact which is to be explained from the widespread practice of polygamy in Israel. The right of divorce belonged to the husband alone (Deut 24:1-4; ⁊ marriage). Virginity—that is, the lack of husband and children—carried with it a stigma in the Old Testament (Gen 30:23; Is 54:4; ⁊ virginity).

The highest happiness of which the Israelite woman was capable was that of *motherhood* (Gen 24:60; 30:1; 1 Sam 1:6f; Ps 113:9). When she became a mother she constituted the focal point of family life and as such was the object of honour on all sides and was highly prized. Several Hebrew women have won a place in history by reason of their true and immense motherly love: in particular the mother of Moses

(Ex 2:2–9), as well as Hannah, the mother of Samuel (1 Sam 1–2:21), Rizpah (2 Sam 3:7ff), the mother of the Maccabee brothers, who saw her seven sons die in a single day (2 Macc 7:1–41), and above all Mary, the mother of the Messiah. In Israel mother-love was of such great importance that it became a symbol of divine love on the lips of the prophet Isaiah: 'As one whom his mother comforts, so I will comfort you' (Is 66:13). As mother the Israelite woman enjoyed not only great honour but also equal authority with that of the father: 'Honour thy father and thy mother ...' (Ex 20:12; Deut 5:16). In Lev 19:3 the mother is actually mentioned before the father: 'Every one of you shall revere his mother and his father ...'. The breaking of the commandment to honour parents entails the severest penalty whether the offence is committed against the father or the mother (Ex 21:15–17; Lev 20:9).

In the sphere of *penal laws*, too, woman is made equal to man. According to Lev 20:10 the death penalty is prescribed for the adulteress as well as for the adulterer. Again in the case of a domestic animal which has killed someone, it makes no difference to the legal penalty which is prescribed whether its victim was a man or a woman. The owner of the beast is equally liable in either case. These juridical estimates show that for purposes of compensation, etc, man and woman were considered absolutely equal, which is not the case in other Oriental codes.

With regard to rights of inheritance the claims of the first-born alone take precedence over those of the wife. Where there are no sons, daughters have the right of inheritance (Num 27:1–11; 36:1–13). Admittedly in such a case they are obliged to marry within their own tribe in order that their family possessions may remain intact. In Job 42:15 on the other hand, a practice is referred to whereby the daughter shared with her brothers the possessions left by the father. In Ruth 4:3 and Judith 8:7 it is presupposed that a childless widow could inherit from her husband.

Women and girls in Israel were not only praised for their competence in household matters (Prov 31:10–31), they were also completely free to engage in daily affairs outside the domestic sphere (Gen 24:13ff; Ex 2:16; etc). At national festivals and also on religious occasions they appeared quite openly (Deut 12:12; Judg 21:21; 2 Sam 6:12ff), and certain Israelite women actually achieved great repute and influence in *political* life. Outstanding figures were: Miriam, the sister of Moses and Aaron, who under prophetic inspiration uttered the song of triumph at the overthrow of the Egyptians (Ex 15:21); Deborah, who in a period of the greatest religious and national decline acted as a judge of Israel in the mountains of Ephraim, and by her inspiring words guided the battle against Sisera to victory (Judg 4, 5); *Huldah* who prophesied in the name of the Lord like the great prophets of the old covenant, and whose counsel was sought by King Josiah (2 Kings 22); Judith, who freed her native city and the whole of Palestine from the enemy (Judith 15:9); and Esther, who, when confronted with the perilous situation in which her people stood, reacted with the words: 'If I must die, then let me die' (Esther 4:16).

With regard to religion, the woman takes second place to the man to the extent that she is excluded from all official acts of the cult. Israel, unlike other ancient peoples, had no priestesses. Nevertheless, women did perform specific services at the sacred tabernacle (Ex 38:8; 1 Sam 2:22). The woman no less than the man is bound to God by covenant (Deut 29:11). Together with her family she observes the great annual festivals, especially Passover (Ex 12:3), and also participates in the sacrificial meal prescribed in the cult (1 Sam 1:4f; Deut 12:12; 15:20). Sacrifices of purification are prescribed for the Israelite woman for various occasions (Lev 12; 15:19–33). Pious parents educated their daughters in accordance with the law of Moses (Dan 13:3). Women had to attend with the rest at the reading of the Book of the Covenant in order that they might learn to observe it exactly (Deut 31:12; Josh 8:35; Neh 8:2). They too are held personally responsible for transgressions (Amos 4:1; Is 3:16f).

Thus the portrayal of women in the Old Testament is on the whole not an unattractive one. It takes on more sombre hues in the period of post-exilic judaism. But this darkness is broken by the light of the day of redemption, in which man and woman appear once more equal in dignity as on the day of the creation.

B. *Woman in the New Testament.* In the course of his daily life Jesus is often occupied with the affairs of women, sick women whom he heals, sinners whom he forgives, woman disciples to whom he reveals himself. But it is chiefly Paul and Peter in their letters, and Luke in the Acts of the Apostles, who show us the official position accorded to woman in the christian way of life.

1. *Jesus and women.* For Jesus woman is just as much a person as man in the sight of God. For this reason he extended his salvific work to women too. He showed his compassion not only to Israelite women but to gentile women too. Even though he has been sent only to the lost sheep of the house of Israel, he fulfils the entreaty of a gentile mother because of her faith, the greatness of which he wonders at and praises. Then he heals her daughter with the words: 'Be it done for you as you desire' (Mt 15:21–8; Mk 7:24–30). He does not shrink from the touch of a woman who is unclean by reason of an issue of blood, but lovingly addresses her as his daughter (Mt 9:20–22; Mk 5:25–34; Lk 8:43–8). He heals the mother-in-law of Simon Peter, in whose house he is staying (Mt 8:14f; Mk 1:29–31; Lk 4:38f), as well as the daughter of Jairus, the leader of the synagogue (Mk 5:21–3 and 35–43). He strives for the soul of the Samaritan woman at the well of Jacob and turns her into a believer and a proclaimer of his name (Jn 4:1–42). He has a word of forgiveness for the unhappy adulteress. Full of compassionate love he bends down to the repentant sinner and forgives all her sins (Jn 8:1–11). In Galilee while at table in the house of a Pharisee, he allows his feet to be anointed by a woman sinner notorious in the city, and pronounces the judgement of divine pity: 'Your faith has saved you. Go in peace' (Lk 7:36–50).

Jesus stays in the house of the sisters of Bethany, and explains the word of God to them (Lk 10:38–42). It is to a woman that he reveals the deepest mystery of the hope of a resurrection, namely, Martha the sister of Lazarus (Jn 11:1–44). He accords the highest praise to the loving act performed by Mary of Bethany: 'Wherever this gospel is preached in the whole world, what she has done will be told in memory of her' (Mt 26:6–13; Mk 14:3–9; Jn 12:1–8). Finally he appears in his risen state to Mary Magdalene *before* appearing to the apostles, and it is to her that he gives the task of bringing the news to the disciples that he is alive: hence the title of honour 'apostola apostolorum' has rightly been bestowed upon her (Jn 20:1–18; Mk 16:9–11).

It can plainly be seen, then, that Jesus fulfilled his vocation as Saviour by helping many women as well as men. Often a section of tradition which has to do with men is counterbalanced by a corresponding parable about a woman: the lost sheep—the lost drachma, the parable of the mustard seed taken from husbandry—the parable of the leaven taken from the domestic sphere.

Women are found among the followers of Jesus (Lk 8:2f; see also Mk 15:40f), and these often minister to him as far as they are able. They follow him right up to his death and watch this from afar (Mt 27:55f; Mk 15:40f; Lk 23:49). They also see the grave and watch while his body is buried.

2. *The official position of woman in the New Testament.* Paul in particular shows in his letters how the early Christian community interpreted Jesus' acts. For those who have become children of God there is no difference between man and woman. 'There is neither male nor female (a reference to Gen 1:27); you are all one in Christ Jesus' (Gal 3:27). Hence woman is made equal to man in the hope of eternal life (1 Pet 3:7). From the outset women belong to the church as fully enfranchised members (Acts 1:14; 12:12). This appears particularly clearly from the lists of those to whom Paul extends greetings in his epistles, where women are addressed as sisters and fellow workers (Rom 16:1, 3; 1 Cor 9:5, etc).

On the other hand, however, Paul does affirm that the wife is subordinate to her husband. In the New Testament too woman is considered subordinate to man in the created order (1 Cor 11:3). Here, however, there is no question of any diminution of her dignity any more than Christ's dignity is diminished in relation to God. What Paul shows, rather, is how the basic law of dependence permeates the whole of the divine order. There is nothing here, therefore, which women could have felt as particularly objectionable. The requirement that women shall wear veils in the communal assemblies (1 Cor 11:5ff) appears to have been an external expression determined by the customs actually prevailing at that time of woman's dependence on man for her very existence. 'Woman was taken from man and created for man: in the presence of the angels she must bear the sign of this dependence...' (F. Prat, *La théologie de Saint Paul*, Paris 1945, 573). In this a clear reference to Gen 2:18, 21 and 23 can be seen.

Whereas in 1 Cor 11 all that is forbidden is for women to take part in the communal assemblies unveiled, 1 Cor 14:34f requires that women shall be absolutely silent. Thus a certain development of ideas can be discerned, reaching its climax in 1 Tim. 1 Cor 11:5 permits charismatic utterances to women provided that they are veiled. 1 Cor 14:34 forbids women natural speech in the public assembly. Finally, 1 Tim 2:12 contains a prohibition of public teaching, and the reasons given for this are domestic in character, and based upon the natural position of women themselves. The pastoral practice of modern catholicism is to this day based upon the position adopted by the early christians. Woman's natural vocation is the bearing of children. It is through this that woman finds her rightful place in the divine order, provided she has faith and love (1 Tim 2:15). Thus with regard to the priesthood she is not simply thrust into the background even though this office is reserved to the male sex alone, but is rather called from the very outset to co-operate in its dissemination in her role as mother.

The pauline letters thus give a clear and consistent picture of women's position in the church and in celebrations of the liturgy. By comparison with those of men, the rights of women are clearly limited. It is fitting for a woman to show her piety in good works (1 Tim 2:10). A widow, if she genuinely remains a widow (1 Tim 5:3), may take up a specific position in the service of the church in connection with works of charity. In this case she is to be entered on a special list and must fulfil three requirements: she must be over sixty, have been only once married, and must lead an authentic christian life, expressed in actions prompted by love of her neighbour, bringing up children, hospitality, 'washing the feet of the saints' (ie, selfless and humble service), relieving the afflicted and 'doing good in every way' (1 Tim 5:9f). Younger widows, on the other hand, ought to marry, to avoid being tempted to break the promise they make to Christ and the church on their entry into the service of the community (1 Tim 5:11–14).

Women are, however, barred from preaching the word in liturgical celebrations, whether in a free and charismatic or an official form. They must conform to the order of the liturgy and leave the preaching of the word to men. This ruling is based on the order of creation; Adam was created first, and then Eve (1 Tim 2:13), and this order remains valid in the liturgy after the redemption as well. The differences between the sexes in the order of creation are not in contradiction to their equality in the order of redemption—as G. Fitzer claims in support of his case for striking out the *mulier taceat* verse as unpauline because of its incompatibility with 1 Cor 11. The differences between men and women arising from the creation and the unity and equality of the sexes as a result of the redemption are two different things, and on different levels. The equality of the sexes, being 'all one in Christ Jesus' (Gal 3:28), does not imply a theological equality, but refers to the status of being children of God, which men and women equally inherit through baptism. The priority established in the order of creation is a fact which remains unchanged. 1 Cor 14:34 cannot therefore be simply an example of a temporally conditioned judgement about the position of women in the liturgy, but must be a conscious decision of fundamental significance. The pauline rule of *mulier taceat* in the liturgy has lost none of its importance, but is still valid today.

The right relation between the order of creation and the order of redemption must be preserved, and the unanimous practice of the whole church, to which Paul refers in 1 Cor 14:33b, should under no circumstances be overlooked. Attempts to give men and women a basically equal position in the liturgy, such as have been undertaken in some protestant communities, should therefore give way before the contrary practice of nearly two thousand years.

Bibliography: H. Zschokke, *Die biblischen Frauen des AT*, Freiburg 1882; P. Tischleder, *Wesen und Stellung der Frau nach der Lehre des heiligen Paulus* (*NA* 10/3-4), Münster 1932; J. Sickenberger, *Die Briefe des heiligen Paulus an die Korinther und Römer*, Bonn 1932; J. Coppens, 'La soumission de la femme à l'homme d'après Gen 3:16b', *ETL* 14 (1937), 632ff; A. Oepke, *TDNT* 1, 776-89; P. Ketter, *Christus und die Frauen* 1 and 11, Stuttgart 1949/50; G. von le Fort, *Die ewige Frau*, Olten 1949[12]; K. Neulinger, *Frauengestalten des NT*, Vienna 1950 (dissertation); N. J. Hommes, 'Taceat mulier in ecclesia', *Arcana Revelata* (*Festschrift Grosheide*), 1951, 33-43; A. Adam, *Christus und die Frau*, Ettal 1951; Haag 494; G. Reidick, *Die hierarchische Struktur der Ehe*, Munich 1953; J. Leipold, *Die Frau in der antiken Welt und im Urchristentum*, Berlin 1962; C. Seltmann, *La Femme dans l'antiquité*, Paris 1956; L. Hick, *Die Stellung des heiligen Paulus zur Frau im Ramen unserer Zeit*, Cologne 1957; F. Horst, *RGG* 11[3], 1067f; H. Greeven, *RGG* 11[3], 1069f; H. Renckens, *Urgeschichte und Heilsgeschichte*, Mainz 1959; A. Rosenberg, *Die Erhebung des Weiblichen. Ordnung und Austand der Frau in unserer Zeit*, Olten 1959; J. Michl, *LTK* 1v[2], 294ff; E. Kähler, *Die Frau in den paulinischen Briefen*, Zurich 1960; H. Rusch, *Töchter des Glaubens*, Mainz 1960; de Vaux 39f; E. Gössmann, *Die Frau und ihr Auftrag*, Freiburg 1961; E. Gössmann, *Mann und Frau in Familie und Oeffent-*lichkeit, Munich 1964; F. Rienecker, *Lexikon zur Bibel*, 1503ff; P. Morant, *Die Anfänge der Menschheit*, Lucerne 1962[2]; Georg Richter, *Deutsches Wörterbuch zum NT*, Regensburg 1962, 254-65; G. Heinzelmann, *Frau und Konzil*, Zürich 1962; G. Fitzer, *Das Weib schweige in der Gemeinde*, 1963; G. G. Blum, 'Das Amt der Frau im NT', *NT* 7 (1964), 142-62; M. Rosseels, *Der Frau aber geziemt es zu schweigen*, Vienna 1964; *Die Frau im Aufbruch der Kirche*, Munich 1964.

Elisabeth Koffmahn

Word

A. *Old Testament*. To the Hebrew mind the word is more than the expression of an idea spoken aloud. Hebrew man sees in it something dynamic that presses on towards a further realisation. This applies to human words of blessing and cursing. Once these have been uttered they can no longer be revoked, and their effectiveness extends into the far future (Gen 20:7; Josh 6:26; 1 Kings 16:34). But it is Yahweh's word above all that is powerful in its effects: 'For as the rain and the snow come down from heaven and return not thither but water the earth, making it bring forth and sprout, giving seed to the sower and bread to the eater, so shall my word be that goes forth from my mouth. It shall not return to me empty, but it shall accomplish that which I purpose and prosper in the thing for which I sent it' (Is 55:10f).

The Old Testament knows of Yahweh's word in three forms: 1. as a prophetic utterance; 2. as a legal utterance; and 3. as a creative utterance.

1. Yahweh *puts his words in the mouth of the prophet* (Jer 1:9), and he is

commissioned to proclaim Yahweh's word to the people (Is 6:8). The prophet cannot resist Yahweh's call. Even if he is unwilling to speak in his name the word of God burns in him like burning fire shut up in his bones, so that he cannot endure it (Jer 20:9). The word of God proclaimed by the prophets is the decisive force in the history of Israel (1 Sam 9:27; 15:13–23; 2 Sam 7:4; etc). It is carried out irresistibly (1 Kings 2:27; 2 Kings 1:17; 9:36; 22:16). In contrast to the falsehoods of the lying prophets, it is full of power like a hammer which shatters rocks (Jer 23:29). In itself Yahweh's word signifies *salvation* (Is 2:2–5; Jer 30:1), but when it is despised it takes effect in the form of *punitive judgement* (Jer 26:4–6).

2. The prophetic word is conditioned by the situation in which it is uttered. It is addressed, that is to say, to specific hearers at a specific point in time. The word of the law, on the other hand, applies to the whole people and for all ages. Israel receives her law ('the words' Ex 34:28; see also Ps 147:19) from Yahweh (Ex 20:1, 22). Yahweh expects Israel scrupulously to observe every word with which he has charged her (Deut 12:32). His directing word is not unattainable to Israel. It is present revelation which, handed on by word of mouth, can be taken into the heart and so acted upon (Deut 30:11–14). If Israel follows the word of Yahweh she will remain alive and increase, and Yahweh will bless her in the land of promise (Deut 30:15f). But if Israel does not hearken she will perish (Deut 30:18).

3. 'Word', therefore, stands for the revealed will of Yahweh, who inter-venes again and again in the destiny of his people, but also lays upon them a firm and immutable order. But it is only a short step from this to ascribe to the word of Yahweh the creation considered as a still broader sphere of divine revelation. By his word Yahweh forms the world (Gen 1; Is 48:13; Ps 33:9; Wis 9:1). His word maintains the course of natural events (Ps 147: 15–18). The powers of nature hearken to the word of the Lord (Ps 148:8). They do not disobey it (Sir 39:31).

The Old Testament ascribes to the divine word all the works which God has performed, the fashioning and directing of the world, the promise and the demand which he makes to his own people. But in the speculations of later Jewish theologians (insofar as these are available to us in the canonical scriptures) this divine activity is summed up not under the concept of word but under the image of ↗ wisdom. Only in a few passages is a greater degree of subsistence (Is 9:8; 55:11; Ps 107:20) and an activity of its own (Is 55:11; Ps 148:8; Wis 16:12, 26; 18:14–16) ascribed to the divine word. God's word always attains its goal (Is 55:11). It commands the powers of nature (Ps 148:8). It heals all things (Wis 16:12). It preserves the life of the faithful (Wis 16:26). Like a fierce warrior God's almighty word brings death to the enemies of his people (Wis 18: 14–16).

B. *New Testament.* In the New Testament 'word' is found chiefly with the following meanings: 1. the word of God in the Old Testament; 2. the particular sayings and the preaching of Jesus as a whole; 3. the early christian preaching about Jesus; and finally,

4. Jesus himself is called the Word.

1. Paul draws a contrast between the word of man, the content of which is merely the foolishness of human wisdom (1 Cor 1:17–21), and the word of God, which is ever powerful to take effect (1 Thess 2:13). It is full of life and power, and sharper than a two-edged sword (Heb 4:12) because it is precisely God's word, and as such penetrates the inmost heart of man so as to compel him to take a decision at that level. Primitive christianity found this significance in the word of God ready to hand in the Old Testament. The word directed to the prophets (Acts 3:25; 7:3, 6, 31f; see also Lk 2:29; 3:2) and the word preached by the prophets (Mk 7:13; Mt 1:22; 2:15; 15:6) is the word of God. The Old Testament word retains its binding character for Christians (Rom 12:19f; 13:8–10; see also Jn 10:35). But the Old Testament word and the New Testament word are not on the same plane. The word of God in the Old Testament is a mysterious pointer to the word of God of the new covenant. The word of God in the New Testament is the fulfilment of the word of God in the old covenant (see Col. 1:25).

2. *Individual sayings of Jesus* are called 'the word (of the Lord)' (Mt 26:75; Lk 22:61; Jn 7:36 [Lit. 'What is this word?']), and are cited as such in the New Testament (Acts 11:16; 20:35; 1 Thess 4:15; see also 1 Cor 7:10, 12, 25). Only in a few instances (Mk 2:2; 4:33; Lk 5:1; Acts 10:36) is Jesus' preaching taken as a whole called 'the word'. It is striking how seldom the word of the Lord is explicitly referred to outside the gospels. Often, however, the word of Christ is used in a freer form without being explicitly characterised as a word of the Lord (see 1 Cor 13:2—Mt 17:20). It is true in general that those responsible for transmitting the sayings of Jesus do not cling over-anxiously to their exact historical wording (see the beatitudes: Mt 5:3–12; Lk 6:21–6) and the discourse at the last supper (Mt 26:26–9; Mk 14:22–5; Lk 22:15–20; 1 Cor 11:23–5). The first christians had not as yet acquired a book in which the exact wording of these sayings was precisely established. The word of the Lord was made known to them in the preaching of the apostles, who were commissioned by Christ and supported by his authority in order that they might bear witness to him (Mt 28:18–20). The fact that this word of the Lord possessed an unique authority for the first christians is apparent from the very manner in which Paul relies upon the commandments of Christ in deciding his own personal dispositions (1 Cor 7:10, 12, 25).

The synoptics record for us how the words of Jesus were received by those who heard them. The hearers sense the *claim* underlying these words. Some of them take scandal. They say that Jesus is possessed because of his words (Jn 10:20). Others, however, are astonished (Mk 1:27). They are profoundly impressed by the authority which is manifest in his words (Mt 7:28f; Lk 4:32). Jesus does not speak like the scribes, who invoke the support of scripture and tradition (Mt 7:29), but with the authority of the Son (Mt 11:27; Lk 10:22). The Son does not speak of himself; his word comes from the Father who has sent him (Jn 14:10, 24; 17:8). Since the Father is at work in the utterances of Jesus (Jn 14:10), his word is powerful to take effect. It heals the sick (Mt 8:8; Lk 7:7, 15), controls nature (Mk 4:39; Lk 5:5) and drives out devils (Mk 1:25f).

But for all this *the hearer is free to accept or to reject the word of Jesus*. He either receives it and keeps it or fails to keep it (Jn 8:51; 12:47f; 14:24; 15:20). To reject the word of Jesus implies the judgement of God (Jn 12:47f). But he who receives the word of Jesus with faith is 'clean' (Jn 15:3), 'he has eternal life; he does not come into judgement but has passed from death to life' (Jn 5:24). Assuredly only he to whom the Father has given it can receive the words of Jesus rightly (Mt 19:11; Mk 4:11; Lk 9:45; Jn 6:44, 65).

3. Together with prayer the apostles regard the 'ministry of the word' as their essential task (Acts 6:4). The word which the apostles proclaim (Acts 13:5; 15:36) is not the word of Old Testament revelation (see Acts 17:11), nor is it simply a repetition of the teaching of Jesus. Rather it is preaching about Jesus, about his words and deeds (Lk 1:2; Acts 1:1). It is the joyful message (Acts 15:7) of the salvation bestowed in Jesus Christ (Acts 13:26; Rom 5; Eph 1:13). The apostolic preaching is the word of God (Acts 4:31; 6:2, 7) because God himself has spoken the word (1 Thess 2:13). The apostle is anxious to guard against altering it or falsifying it (2 Cor 2:17; 4:2). He is a *minister of the word* (see Lk 1:2). He has to spread the word spoken by God, throughout the earth (Rom 15:9).

Since the apostolic preaching is derived from God, it is guaranteed by him who originates it to be effective. It is by his power that the word increases (Acts 19:20). It is itself the power of God (1 Cor 1:18). Hence it is active (Heb 4:12; 1 Thess 2:13) and sharper than a two-edged sword (Heb 4:12; see also Eph 6:17). Where it is received with faith it brings about redemption (Jas 1:21).

4. In his Son God has uttered his word finally and for all time. The revelation of the Old Testament was ordered to this word and finds its fulfilment in it (Col 1:25–7). The life of Jesus, his words and deeds, constitute a central revelation of God. The revelation in the Son, who says of himself: 'Before Abraham was I am' (Jn 8:58), does not, however, begin only at Jesus' birth. Led by the Spirit (Jn 14:26; 16:13) the first Christians scrutinise the Old Testament scriptures (Acts 8:35; 17:2f, 11), which bear witness to Jesus (Jn 5:39f). They realise that all revelation has been made through the Son. Where the Old Testament scriptures speak of the divine word or the divine wisdom as a medium of revelation, there is Christ already at work in his pre-existent state. Through the Son, the reflection of the glory of God (Heb 1:3; 2 Cor 4:4; Col 1:15—Wis 7:26), the world was formed (Heb 1:2—Wis 9:1). In him all things have their being (Col 1:17—Wis 8:1). In the form of wisdom (Wis 10:15–11:1) and word (Wis 16:12, 26; 18:22) the pre-existent Christ has accompanied Israel through the wilderness and bestowed spiritual food and spiritual drink upon her (1 Cor 10:1–4). In his vocation vision (Is 6:1–13) Isaiah saw the glory of

Christ (Jn 12:41). The revelation in the Son, therefore, is not *one revelation among many*, but *all revelation* has been made through the Son: the Old Testament revelation through the pre-existent Christ, the final revelation of the New Testament through Jesus, the Son of God become man. The pre-existing and the incarnate Christ is *the* revelation in the absolute, or, according to Jn 1:1, *the* word (see 1 Jn 1:1; Rev 19:13). As Jesus allows himself to be known as the bread of life in the distribution of bread (Jn 6), as the resurrection and the life in the raising of Lazarus (Jn 11), and as the light of the world (Jn 8:12; see also 9:39) in the healing of the blind (Jn 9), so too in his word (Jn 14:10, 24) he manifests the fact that he is *the* Word (the *Logos*) (Jn 1:1, 14).

Bibliography: P. Heinisch, *Das 'Wort' im AT und im Alten Orient* (*BZF* x 7–8), 1922; O. Grether, *Name und Wort Gottes im Alten Testament* (*BZAW* 64), 1934; Cullmann 255–75; Heinisch 122–7; Eichrodt II, 32–8; Procksch 468–75; Imschoot I, 188–95; von Rad II, 80–98; Jacob 103–9; Vriezen 74–93 and 214–17; Stauffer 38–42; O. Procksch and G. Kittel, *TDNT* IV, 89–140; Haag 1036–9 and 1718–23. See also: Bultmann (see Index); L. Dürr, *Die Wertung des göttlichen Wortes im AT und im Antiken Orient*, Leipzig 1938; C. Westermann, *Grundformen prophetischer Rede*, Munich 1960; G. Ebeling, *Wort und Glaube*, Tübingen 1962²; H. Schlier, *Wort Gottes*, Würzburg 1962².

Georg Ziener

Work

The conceptual range attached to the word *work* embraces so much material that it is difficult to fix upon any one clear definition. It includes the work of God in the creation as well as the wearisome toil of the slave. Again in the New Testament we encounter a third usage of the word, namely, as applied to the work of Christ and to work for the gospel. Every aspect of this threefold usage will be briefly reviewed in the pages which follow.

The work of God is creative work. No man can act like God, and furthermore none of the gods can act as God acts (Ps 85:8). All that exists is the work of God's hands (Ps 8; 18; 9:1). But these anthropomorphic ideas are to be found only in the more primitive descriptions. Already in the Priestly narrative of Gen 1:1, 2, 3 the sublime idea is inculcated that God has called all things into existence by his word and his will alone. Through the idea of the creative word of God—'He spoke and it took place'—the thought of the bible has given expression in the most effective possible way to its consciousness of the absolute power and transcendence of God in relation to his creation. In all this, however, work is by no means regarded as degrading. The bible does not hesitate constantly to apply anthropomorphic usages to God. Apart from the childlike simplicity of the Yahwist, a simplicity which lives on still in the words of Our Lord concerning God who feeds the sparrows and clothes the lilies of the field, we have only to think of the images of Deutero–Isaiah, such as that of the potter and the clay (Is 45:9). Thus in one way or another the biblical authors have found a way of expressing no less a truth than the absolute power of God as Creator.

The bible never describes the work of man as creative. Indeed it actually shows itself in a certain sense hostile to human creative work, as for instance in the decoration of the sanctuary, for in this the danger of idolatry may lie if images are set up. The second commandment of God is designed to avert this danger. Thus work was never regarded as a participation in the creative work of God. What the biblical authors had in mind was their own daily work in all its toilsomeness: God sets his blessing upon it. Day by day the amount of work done remains constant (Ps 104:19ff). The wisdom books praise industry and diligence (Prov 6:6). Even kings do not consider it beneath their dignity to work (1 Sam 11:5). Work is an element in the divinely ordained structure of the world and of human nature. So much is work an integral part of the divinely willed order of life that the decalogue contains no vestige of any commandment such as: 'Thou shalt not be idle'. On the contrary, a special prescription has to be included in it to make man rest from his work.

Already before the fall work is an integral element in human life (Gen 1:28; 2:15). And yet 'cursed is the ground because of you; in toil you shall eat of it all the days of your life . . .' (Gen 3:17ff). It is not until man rebels against God's wise law that the cosmic order is upset and the curse makes itself felt, particularly in the sphere of work.

The work of Christ. Christ himself is a worker (*tektōn*). This is normally translated as 'carpenter' (Mk 6:3), although the term may have been intended in a more general sense as signifying craftsman, skilled worker in general. The evangelists have no further interest in the fact that Jesus was a worker. John does not mention it at all. Paul does perhaps refer to it when he says that Christ assumed the form of a servant (Phil 2:7). Servant (*doulos* in Greek) was at that time used to designate slaves, the 'workers' of antiquity. But, as has been said, the evangelists take no further notice of this truth, which is assuredly of far-reaching significance for theology. For them the work of Jesus is not his work as a craftsman but his work as Redeemer of the world. John brings out this significance most clearly in his use of the word *work*. 'My food is to do the will of him that sent me, and to accomplish his work' (4:34; 5:17; 6:28f; 9:4). The works of Christ are the↗ miracles, the signs which manifest to the believers his unique work of↗ revelation and↗ redemption. The service which Jesus performs, culminating on the↗ Cross, is the accomplishment of the work entrusted to him by God (17:4). Hence the fourth gospel actually records the last words of the dying Messiah as the pregnant exclamation: 'It is consummated' (19:30; see also 5:28). The work of Christ, the deed of redemption once and for all consummated on behalf of mankind, has been accomplished.

It follows that *the work of the Christian* consists equally in↗ faith and in acting in conformity with faith. 'This is the work of God, that you believe in him whom he has sent' (Jn 6:29; Phil 2:13; 2 Thess 1:11). God works in us. Our work is wholly and entirely his work. Thus we are actually 'fellow workmen for God' (1 Cor 3:9; 2 Cor 6:1; Mk 16:20). Properly speaking the work of Christians consists in promoting the gospel and helping to further the

996

salvation willed by God. The Christian is one who works for the harvest, sows the word, plants (1 Cor 3:6ff; Jn 4:35ff), one who works as the ambassador of divine atonement (2 Cor 5:20ff). As a member of the body of Christ everyone has his own special task assigned to him (1 Cor 12). This is the work for which the christian is called; it is for this that he has been empowered with the Holy Spirit. This is his particular 'vocation'. The christian must remain faithful to his calling (1 Cor 7:20ff), for the worldly position in which he finds himself is not decisive. It is not the goal at which he aims, but only the means of attaining that goal. It makes no difference even if he is a slave. It is possible that even the bishops of the early church were slaves (Eucharistos) whose freedom was purchased with money raised by the communities. But by and large the axiom holds good: 'Remain in that state in which you were when you came to the faith'. When God calls a man into his service to do his 'work' it can entail a change in his worldly occupation (Mk 1:18: 'They left their nets and followed him'), but this by no means necessarily follows. All this is not to say that the worldly calling could be a matter of indifference to the christian, but it does mean that it is in some sense secondary (as Paul deliberately carried on the work of tent-making, Acts 18:3).

The *New Testament* attitude on the subject of work is expressed in the 'rules of life' (*Haustafeln*) inserted in the epistles (Col 3:22–4:1; Eph 4:5–9; 1 Tim 6:1ff; Tit 2:9ff; 1 Pet 2:18–25). What it is principally concerned with is the duties of workers, of 'slaves', and the space devoted to them is a clear indication of the social stratum from which the first christians derived (see 1 Cor 1:26: 'For consider your call, brethren; not many of you were wise according to worldly standards, not many were powerful, not many were of noble birth; but God chose what is foolish in the world ... what is weak in the world ...').

The authors of the epistles do not altogether omit to mention the responsibilities of slave owners: they must give their workers what is right because they know that they themselves have a Master in heaven (Col 4:1) who is also the Master of their servants, and who is not impressed by personal status (Eph 6:9). No criticism of the social system or of the institution of slavery is to be found in the New Testament. No-one who truly apprehends the nature of the gospel preached by the apostles will be surprised at this. Inevitably it required a long period of time before the Church realised the implications of its own preaching; that when it preached a message which had to do with the setting free of the world—a world, moreover, which was liable to judgement and was already passing away—this entailed certain general consequences with regard to the setting free of those in the world who were fettered by society. Nevertheless, consequences of this sort did take effect in the practical life of the church right from the outset. In the community of the church there was no distinction between poor and rich, slaves and freemen (Jas 2:1–13; Gal 3:28). Furthermore it should be noticed that the kind of slavery involved was not that of galley-slaves or forced labour in the mines, and that it was neither necessarily nor customarily harsh in character. Slaves could attain to high positions in their master's household, and were often held in affection and respect as members of the family (1 Pet 2:18). The 'rules of life' have as the basis of their exhortations the truth that the christian worker does his work, not in the first instance for those who are his masters 'in the flesh', but for Christ himself: 'Slaves, be obedient to those who are your earthly masters, with fear and trembling, in singleness of heart, as to Christ; not in the way of eye-service, as men-pleasers, but as servants of Christ, doing the will of God from the heart, rendering service with a good will as to the Lord and not to men' (Eph 6:5-7). The ultimate motive behind the christian ethic of work is not any natural law, not even a divine dispensation contained in the Old Testament. Rather it is that ↗obedience which the christian owes to his heavenly Master. The earthly master is the 'type' of Christ. He represents 'our Lord' himself. Such work keeps the name of God from being defamed (1 Tim 6:1).

On this interpretation the fulfilment of God's commandment to work becomes possible for man when he has been redeemed no longer from motives of obedience to the law or from a sense of duty but, like all acts inspired by christian morality, from the motive of thankfulness (↗thanksgiving) to the heavenly Lord: 'Whatever your task work heartily as serving the Lord and not men' (Col 3:23). The redemption took place 'that he might purify for himself a people of his own who are zealous for good deeds' (Tit 2:11-

14). The first vision of Christ is for those who see in it with the eyes of faith the sign of the coming eschatological Redemption which will be completed at his second coming, and which even now bears its fruit in the christian life and in the daily work of christians (Richardson, 32). A passage of Paul deserves special mention at this point because it affords us a deep insight into the connections between atonement and salvation: 'Yet woman will be saved through bearing children (if, of course, she continues in faith and love and holiness with modesty)' (1 Tim 2:15). From Gen 3:16 onwards the bearing and rearing of children, and a kind of motherhood that is painful, is imposed by God upon woman in expiation for the fault of the first mother. Paul now says that woman can actually achieve her salvation by fulfilling her duties of motherhood, because thereby she is submitting herself to the dispensation of God, always presupposing, of course, that she possesses the basic virtues and attitudes appropriate to the christian life. What applies to a woman surely applies to man also whose situation is in this respect wholly parallel. As the pains of motherhood are imposed on woman as an expiation, so too the hardships, toil and disappointments which man endures in the work of his calling are laid upon him. Now if woman achieves salvation by fulfilling this work of expiation laid upon her, why should the same not apply to man? He too, as he performs his allotted work, and still more if he accepts all the hardships and privations which it entails, will be performing the work of his own salvation.

Christ himself, the fulfiller of the

whole law of God, has also fulfilled the commandment to work. 1 Peter and Titus regard the service of the christian worker as an imitation of Christ. Even though Christ's work was primarily the work of redemption, still as man he has fulfilled the whole law of God, and perhaps the fulfilment of the command to work is integrally bound up with the act of redemption, as it seems legitimate to conclude from a consideration of the passage in 1 Tim 2:15 cited above. Until about his thirtieth year Jesus was a village craftsman. We have perfectly sound evidence for this fact, even though the hagiographers did not choose to dwell upon it. None of the facts concerning the Lord recorded in the gospels can be devoid of significance for the belief and moral conduct of christians. Christian piety has always loved to dwell upon the image of Jesus in the carpenter's workshop. The Master who spoke of his yoke as 'light' was the good workman who knew the difference between a well-made and a badly-made yoke which the poor ox would have to bear at the plough. It is certainly no less justifiable for the church to hold up the example of Christ in the workshop for the edification of christian workers than for Peter or Paul to make use of the example of his patience in suffering as the model for christian love, always provided that we do not treat sentimentally of what our redemption has cost, or entertain any such idea as that Christ redeems us from sin and redeems us in our working life merely by his example (Richardson, 20).

The New Testament teaching on work may already seem unpopular in the eyes of progressives by the very fact that it makes obedience one of the principal virtues of society. The 'rules of life' show that the master–servant relationship is one of the most fundamental relationships which has been established by God and has been sanctioned by God's natural law, in the same way as the relationship between ruler and ruled, husband and wife, parents and child. The structure of the human community is necessarily hierarchical and not egalitarian. The health of society consists in the fact that the individual takes his due responsibility for the duties entailed by his position within the organism as a whole. Even in the immense ramifications of modern industry there will always be a basic *kurios–doulos* (master–servant) relationship, to which these rules of life in the New Testament point. But what this relationship implies will have to be worked out by those whose lives are governed by it.

The bible knows nothing of a 'problem of leisure time'. Man works so long as it is day (Ps 104:22ff; Jn 9:4). A six or eight-hour day never entered into consideration. On the contrary it was counted as folly (sin) to be idle between daybreak and sunset! The free days in antiquity were the holy days: religious festivals brought freedom from the burden of daily work and relaxation. Moreover the sabbath law had its humanitarian aspect (Ex 20:10): to provide rest for man and beast. Its principle purpose, however, was religious in character, the sanctification of the sabbath, for in six days the Lord made heaven and earth and the sea and all that are therein, but on the seventh day he rested. Theological insights are to be found here which go far deeper than our discussion of free time. The meaning and purpose of human life as a whole are entered into here. The author of Hebrews (3:7–4:11) has developed these thoughts in a surprising manner. In the rhythmic alternation of work and rest is to be found a reflection of the image of God in which we were created. The work of man, like that of his Creator, culminates in rest, and his principle goal is not work but that eternal rest, that eternal joy which is to be found in God. The lukan pericope concerning Mary and Martha (10:42) is also explicit in making clear this order of priorities: Mary has chosen 'the better part', for the highest act which man is capable of on earth is the worship of God. In the last analysis the question is not whether our work results in great achievements and accomplishments on the human level; we must not put our trust in the work of our hands. Ultimately all our work will vanish from heaven and earth. The significance of our work is to be found not here but in the world to come, and the question is whether the Lord will be able to say: 'Well done, good and faithful servant; enter into the joy of your Master' (Mt 25:21; see also 25:34). Thus it is not its worldly value or the profit that accrues to us from our life of toil which gives our work its christian meaning, but its ultimate eschatological bearing on the heavenly goal. 'Therefore, my beloved brethren, be steadfast, immovable, always abounding in the work of the Lord, knowing that in the Lord your labour is not in vain!' (1 Cor 15:58). What is here being spoken of is not in some sense the dissemination of the gospel tidings, but all the work and toil of the christian (see Rev 14:13).

Work as sacrifice. As members of Christ we offer up ourselves, 'our bodies and souls' (see Rom 12:1ff). The eucharist, the church's sacrifice, is the offering of the body of Christ (see Augustine, *The City of God*, x, vi). Bread and wine are symbols of ourselves, our souls and our bodies, but also of our daily work, without which there would be neither bread nor wine. Moreover, the 'elements' with the help of which the miracle of our nourishment is accomplished are 'brought' or 'presented' to the Master himself. Without this 'bringing to' or 'offering' there would have been no sacrifice. It is striking that in John, who speaks with such emphasis of the bread 'which comes from heaven', we should find a unique presentation of the miracle of the loaves. Suddenly the disciples (in contrast to the synoptic accounts) recede into the background. It is Jesus who plays the central role. It is not the disciples who draw his attention to the people's hunger. Instead he acts on his own initiative. It is not, as in the synoptics, the apostles who bring the loaves to the Master, but a boy (*paidarion*). Thus in the version of the fourth gospel the loaves and fishes are the materials presented or offered by the people and not by the apostles. Could it be that even as early as the time of John it was the liturgical custom that the offertory was made, not by the bishop-presbyters (representing the apostles), but by the deacon in the name of the people, and that the evangelist is deliberately trying to underline the significance of the sacrifice of the community in the sacrament of the bread of heaven? But whatever the purpose of the author may have been, one point is clear, namely that the final impression left by his sixth chapter consists in the great emphasis he lays on the truth that there is no gift of the living Bread unless the sacramental elements have first been brought in faith by the liturgical community (Richardson, 51f).

The christian ethic of work, the meaning of work according to New Testament doctrine, applies only to christians. The christian understands the hardships of work as such in a world affected by the fall, and bears them joyfully for the Lord, to whom his service is really given. Every work which the christian performs has an eschatological bearing in that it belongs, so to say, to the dimension of time and space, in which, in the existing state of the divine dispensation, our testing and our redemption are worked out. It is in this dimension of time and space that the good works according to which each individual will be judged are performed in order that he may enter into God's rest. Rest from work comes to stand as an image to remind us of the final purpose and the final goal, which consist precisely in that rest with God. Still more the connection between our work and the liturgy shows that our work is taken up in the liturgy as that which the sacrament presupposes, just as our creaturehood in all its fallen state must be there in order to make its redemption possible (*quod 'mirabiliter condidisti, mirabilius reformasti'*).

Bibliography: A. Richardson, *The Biblical Doctrine of Work*, London 1952. We sometimes follow Richardson's work very closely, occasionally supplementing his presentation. This book meets with our agreement except for the negative judgement on Sirach (pp 14 and 39). See also: N. Peters, *Das Buch Jesus Sirach*, Münster 1913, 318; J. A. Kleist, 'Ergon', *CBQ* 6 (1944), 61–8; G. Bertram, *TDNT* II, 635–52; *BTHW* 35–7; Allmen 463f; A. Steinmann, *Jesus und die soziale Not der Gegenwart*, Paderborn 1929², 49–70 (p 49 for further bibliography); S. Kalischer, 'Die Wertschätzung der Arbeit in Bibel und Talmud', *Festschrift H. Cohens*, Berlin 1912, 579–608; E. Beijer, *Svensk Teologisk Kvartalskrift* 29 (1953), 25–41; H. Weinstock, *Arbeit und Bildung*, Heidelberg 1954; P. Termes Rós, *El trabajo según la Biblia*, Barcelona 1955; H. Rondet, *Die Theologie der Arbeit*, Würzburg 1956; W. Bienert, *Die Arbeit nach der Lehre der Bibel*, Stuttgart 1956²; P. Benoit, *LV* 20 (1955), 73–86; A. Vögtle, *LTK* I², 801–3; J. B. Bauer, *Der Seelsorger* 25 (1955), 344–51; J. B. Bauer, *BL* 24 (1957), 198–201; F. Gryglewicz, *Bbl* 37 (1956), 314–37; B. Prete, *Sacra Doctrina* 2 (1956), 280–309; P. de Haes, *Collectanea Mechlinensia* 43 (1958), 370–73 and 497–500; R. Falconer, *JBL* 60 (1941), 375–9 (on 1 Tim 2:14f); W. Bienert, 'Die Arbeit nach der Lehre der Bibel', *Studium Generale* (1961), 151–62; F. Storni, 'El trabajo en la Biblia', *Ciencia y Fe* 13 (1957), 321–32; E. Testa, *Il lavoro nella Bibbia*, Assisi 1959; F. Vattioni, 'Il lavoro nei primi tre capitoli della Genesi', *Studi Sociali* 1 (Rome 1961), 109–19.

Johannes B. Bauer

World

A. It is illuminating to notice how different the Greek conception of 'world' is from that of the Old Testament. In it God and world are not two entities at opposite poles from one another. Instead the *kosmos* is the 'all-embracing divine'. Both are included in a single order, which is opposed to chaos. Cosmogony is theogony. Thus there is no unbridgeable gulf between God and the world, any more than there is between God and man. The remote origins of cosmology are delineated by Homer, Hesiod, and the Orphics. From the chaos of the beginning emerged the domain of light, from which in turn the theogony develops. For Hesiod the divine element in the world still persists. It is God as the supreme power which has two distinct aspects, the cosmic and the ethical. Other authors point in the same direction. Anaximenes, for example, is responsible for the characterisation of the world as *kosmos*, that is, as 'world-as-order'. For Heraclitus the primordial power becomes *logos*, and so constitutes a unity of human and world intelligence and a world-order that informs all things—unity as a harmony of opposites. Faith in the divine *logos* has a spiritualising effect upon nature religion. The Pythagoreans discover that number is the principle of the cosmos of things, and according to the principle of correspondence this becomes the first law of man and society in ethics and politics. Anaxagoras understands the deity as the *nous* (=mind, intelligence) which governs the world throughout: since *pronoia* (=providence) is absent from it, the world remains a mechanism which can be understood in purely causal terms. On this theory the world is a *unio mystica* in virtue of the divine power which permeates it and controls it. This *unio mystica* is understood as *pneuma* (spirit), the outward manifestations of which are *aretai* (virtues) or *energeiai* (activities), which are understood ontologically, and which constitute the bond which holds all together: *sumpatheia* ('sympathy'). This in turn is the expression of the *hen zōon* ('the single living thing') in which the supreme god conceals himself. He acts through the *deuteros theos* (lit = 'second god') or demiurge. The basic law of the cosmos is 'the eternal return of the same' (compare Nietzsche). But man does not see himself as blessed in the cosmos because he finds himself in the 'prison of the Heimarmene'—otherworldly longings. The problem, the tension which exists between the transcendent god on the one hand and, on the other, the eternal timeless world permeated and controlled by divine power yet distinct from the deity, also defeated Plato and his school.

But for all this the problem of the *kosmos* has been analysed from so many different points of view that the concept is capable of becoming a vehicle of revelatory language. Here admittedly the question is transposed from the purely philosophical and cosmological plane to that in which the question of supernatural redemption arises. The problem is spiritualised in neoplatonism. Philo expands the concept into *kosmos noētos* (='the world of reason') and *kosmos aisthētos* (='the world of perception'), Plotinus into that of *kosmos houtos* ('this world') and *kosmos ekeinos* ('that world'). He thereby mitigates the dualism and establishes a bridge between the two opposing principles by means of the concept of the world as *eikōn* (image, likeness). It is this that Augustine takes over and makes the basis of his cosmology. The Gnosis of the Corpus Hermeticum takes cosmos as 'the body of God' (W. Nestle, *Vom Mythos zum Logos. Die Selbstentfaltung des griechischen Denkens*, 1942[2]).

B. The basic characteristics of the Greek concept of *kosmos* are: unity, immanent norm, duty, the interrelationship of cosmos, society, and human nature. These provide a point of contact with the judaism of the Old Testament which separates heaven, earth, and 'the all' in its manner of speaking. In hellenistic thought the cosmos is understood in spatial terms. It is only in the Wisdom books and Maccabees that we find the concept of the universe as consisting of earth and mankind (compare the later anti-Gnostic mysticism of the Merkaba).

C. The use of the concept of *kosmos* in the New Testament is based upon the development described above. In it we must distinguish the following distinct senses:

1. *kosmos* regarded more from the cosmological and speculative point of view, that is from the philosophical aspect, or *kosmos* as interpreted cosmogonically. In this sense it is true to say that scripture has in the first instance nothing to do with it. The ideas which are worked out scientifically, a mixture of neoplatonist and gnostic speculations with an element of stoicism, provide a foil to New Testament interpretation. It is not the function of revelation to develop a cosmology in the true sense, except for recognising that the *kosmos* is a created entity. The New Testament image of the world considered from the aspect of natural science and philosophy remains indefinite. The conception of the world as presented here is simply taken over from philosophy. That is, the world is conceived of as a space divided into three parts: heaven, earth, and the underworld. We have no intention here of examining the influence on the early christian conception of the world exercised by early cabbalistic or gnostic views entertained by Jewish christians. These combined typically Jewish ideas with mysticism. Here, however, we must confine ourselves to indicating the following expressions which seem to betray this influence: *stoikheia tou kosmou* (= 'the elemental principles of the world': Gal 4:3; Col 2:8, 20); *ek tou kosmou— en tō(i) kosmō(i)* (= 'out of the world— in the world': Jn 15:19; 17:11). (See Jonas, *Gnosis und spätantiker Geist*, 1934, 153 n 1). This world is *the sphere, the arena of human life,* and so from the point of view of intellectual interpretation neutral.

2. In particular cases it is impossible to establish precisely whether *kosmos* is intended to signify the arena in which human action takes place or the human race which enlivens it. In the following passages it is probably to be understood in the first of these senses: 'light of the world' (Jn 8:12); according to Jn 3:17, Christ has been sent into the world as the evangelist too has been sent; according to Jn 8:23, Christ is not of this world, and according to Jn 18:36 neither is his 'kingdom'. According to Jn 3:16 he has been sent by the Father and has come from motives of love for the world; he presides in judgement over the 'prince *(arkhōn)* of this world'. 2 Cor 5:19 provides a typical example in which *kosmos* is used in the sense of the arena in which the drama takes place. The opposition between God and the world becomes wholly apparent only in Christ, but at the same time so does God's atoning activity: *kosmos* = the world of humanity, mankind as a whole. But to the extent that the *kosmos* concept is taken in the sense of the

universe as the arena of salvific history it extends beyond the limits of merely human history. The entire universe is included in the development of this world history, which nevertheless does not cease to remain a truly human history. Christ is precisely 'the first-born of all creation' (Col 1:15). A further idea is that the state of having fallen into evil necessarily follows from man's involvement in the *kosmos*. This idea, which is mentioned by the apostle, has something of the ancient concept of *anağkē* (= necessity, inevitability) in it. We shall be returning to treat explicitly of it at a later stage. Imprisonment in the Heimarmene of the sublunar regions and of *anağkē* gives way to the redeemed state of the cosmos. But once it is redeemed it loses this sense and becomes instead the 'dominion of God', 'the aeon to come', the 'new heaven' and the 'new earth', so that these concepts of the New Testament must be regarded as the end of the development of the idea of *kosmos* in the history of ideas. Paul takes the concept quite broadly as signifying *the universe as such*, in which he also includes the world of angels, thereby making it analogous to the stoic explanation of cosmos as the system of gods and men taken as a whole, with the aim of contrasting this new cosmos with the world which is totally hostile to God. John takes a similar view when he regards world history as a dramatic struggle.

3. *Kosmos* can only be intended to signify *humanity* in these passages: 'The sin of the world' blotted out by the Lamb according to Jn 1:29; 'Saviour of the world' in Jn 4:42; 'the world knows him not' in Jn 1:10; and, in contrast with this, 'all the world has gone after him' in Jn 12:19. In these cases mankind is always understood *collectively*, and this is also the sense of Jn 14:27; 1 Jn 4:4; 1 Jn 5:19—believers are 'of God', and unbelievers 'in (the power of) the evil one'. By this John intends to give expression to the supreme point in his theology, namely, that salvation history is a duel, but nevertheless a duel the issue of which is in fact already decided: 'I have overcome the world' (Jn 16:33). But when 'the world' is taken in this sense, it is inevitable that it should cease to be regarded as *alien to God*. Apart from this opposition between that which belongs to God and that which is alien to him (compare the concepts of 'inclination' and 'alienation' in Plotinus I 1:12), 'world' cannot be explained, a fact which applies particularly to the 'supernatural cosmology' in the johannine prologue. This idea is not far removed from what the Mandeans mean when they speak of 'the worlds', the equivalent of the *aiōnes* in hellenistic thought (yet another relationship would be that between 'world' and 'heaven'). (On the effect of this upon early christian times, see J. Ritter, 'Mundus intelligibilis', *Philos. Abhanlungen* VI, 1957, 19.) It is precisely these interpretations of *kosmos* that are carried over as definitions into mysticism on the one hand, and which, on the other hand, in the non-christian sphere are 'demonised', with the result that from the idea 'world = darkness' and 'the whole world lies in the power of the evil one' (1 Jn 5:19), it is only a short step to the rejection of 'the wisdom of this world'—to which, again, is related

the idea of 'the rulers of the world' who are hostile to 'the kingdom (rule) of God'. *Kosmos* as an expression of that which is alien to God cannot, however, have anything to do with the unredeemed state in the New Testament sense, but is rather derived from a mixture of philosophical, Old Testament, and mystical ideas. The New Testament then takes it over and develops it further.

4. *Kosmos* as 'mankind' contains a special and pregnant shade of meaning in the New Testament when it signifies 'mankind as fallen' and is brought into connection with Christ and the redeeming activity of God. Since, therefore, according to 1 Tim 1:15 Christ has come to redeem sinners, it follows that those who are redeemed constitute his kingdom (Col 1:13), so that the *ekklēsia* (=christian church) does not belong to the world. The 'saints' live in the *kosmos* (1 Cor 5:10) but they honour the Creator (Acts 17:24) and are thankful for God's natural gifts (Acts 14:15). According to 1 Cor 7:31 the saints must 'deal with the world' while at the same time conducting themselves as though they did not 'deal with it' (1 Cor 7:30; 2 Cor 6:10). For *kosmos* connotes of its very nature unregeneracy, hostility to God, a hindrance to true christian living, and it is emphasised again and again that it is the duty of christians to keep themselves uncontaminated by it (Jas 1:27: 'to keep oneself unstained from the world'). See Rom 12:2; 1 Cor 7:31. In Jas 4:4 'friendship with the world is enmity with God'.

In the pauline and johannine theology of redemption the problem of the cosmos is thrust right into the foreground. In John, however, the idea seems to be taken in a still more unequivocal sense than in Paul. The latter understands the 'world' in a narrower sense, in that cosmos only becomes explicable from the fact that there is a 'Saviour of the world' (1 Jn 4:14). This is the sense implicit in *aiōn houtos* (='this age (world)') as contrasted with *aiōn ekeinos* (='that age', 'the other world') (see Eph 1:21). In 1 Cor 1:20 'the wisdom of the world' is equivalent to 'folly with God' (1 Cor 3:19). According to 1 Cor 1:26, other standards apply with God than those prevailing in the world: compare the contrast between 'worldly grief' and 'godly grief' in 2 Cor 7:10. Sin constitutes the basis for the opposition between God and the world: 'the whole world may be held accountable to God' (Rom 3:19) as sinful. This is also the reason why Jn 3:17 and 1 Cor 6:2 speak of 'condemning/judging the world'. The condemnation of the world in 1 Cor 11:32 is similarly motivated. Israel, inasmuch as she has rendered herself liable to judgement, is included in the 'whole world' (Rom 3:19), and thereby set in contrast to the just. Again, in 1 Cor 2:8 it is the world as having fallen under the curse that is meant when the accusation of having crucified the Lord is applied to 'the rulers of this age'.

It can be seen, then, that the idea of *kosmos* is divided up into several different shades of meaning. Nevertheless, while the concept cannot be taken as expressing definitively any one concrete sense, it can be taken to stand in the neoplatonist sense for the unifying concept that lies behind a whole system of ideas which are abstract in character.

This is particularly applicable when it is combined with terms such as 'kingdom' (*basileia*).

5. On the meaning of *kosmos* when Jesus Christ is taken to be its model, measure, and dominant idea, and when it is understood to be analogous on the supernatural plane to the *Logos* of antiquity, ⟋ creation, likeness, word.

Bibliography: W. Kranz, 'Kosmos', *Archiv für Begriffsgesch.* II 1 and 2, ed. E. Rothacker, 1955/7; A. Jenni, *ZAW* 23 (1952), 197–248; 24 (1953), 1–35; H. Sasse, *TDNT* III, 867–98; F. Mussner, *Christus das All und die Kirche*, Trier 1955; E. Walter, *Christus und der Kosmos*, Stuttgart 1948; R. Schnackenburg, *Die Johannesbriefe*, Freiburg 1953, 117–20; G. Kittel, *TDNT* III, 857–98; G. Liddell and R. Scott (ed.), *A Greek–English Lexicon* I, Oxford 1940, 985.

Albert Auer

Wrath

I. *Human anger.* 1. *Holy anger.* Anger is justified and holy when used to vindicate the rights of others and especially God's sovereignty and sanctity (David, 2 Sam 12:5; Nehemiah, Neh 5:6; Moses, Ex 16:20; 32:19, 22; Num 31:14; Lev 10:16; Elisha, 2 Kings 13:19; Jesus, Mk 3:5; see also Jn 11:33, 38; Paul Acts 17:16). 2. *Anger in the sapiential books of the Old Testament.* Anger will result in injustice (Prov 14:17; 29:22) and work disaster; it destroys health, it impedes God's mercy and provokes His divine judgement (Prov 27:4; Sir 28:3–5; 30:24). The wise man is patient, the quick-tempered a fool (Prov 14:29; 15:18; 16:32; 14:17, 29). The incompatibility of anger with ⟋ wisdom is one of the tenets of old Egyptian wisdom: the boisterous cannot be wise (see also

J. Fichner, *Die altorientalische Weisheit in ihrer israelitisch-jüdischen Ausprägung*, 1953, 20f). In particular, anger with God is condemned (Job 18:4; see also 40:6). God even punishes anger at the good fortune of the wicked, for they will be judged by God himself (Prov 24:17f; Ps 37:7–9). 3. *Anger in the New Testament.* The New Testament generally disapproves of anger, although it does not reject it completely. Anger is, above all, an attribute of the devil and his henchmen (Rev 12:17; see also 12:12; of Herod, Mt 2:16). Jesus warns against wilful and unjustified anger with our fellow men, 'for anger is equal to murder' (Mt 5:22), and leads to words and acts which cannot be right in God's eyes (Jas 1:19f). Anger in the opinion of Paul is a sin (Col 3:8; Eph 4:31): love is not angry (1 Cor 13:5). Those who are angry interfere with the rights of God (Rom 12:19): they give way to the devil as sin is impending over those who are angry (Eph 4:26f). Anger is followed by God's judgement (Col 3:8; Rev 11:18). The Christian should, therefore, never be angry or incense others (Eph 6:4). Those who stand close to God must control their passions (those who pray, 1 Tim 2:8; the bishop, Tit 1:7).

II. *The wrath of God.* 1. *In the Old Testament.* The numerous expressions of anger or wrath are much more frequently used for God than for man. They describe the emotion of anger as an inner fire, and its effect as the snorting, foaming, boiling, and bursting of pent-up energy (see Is 30:27f; 34:5–10). God's wrath is very realistically described as flame, fire and storm (Ps 2:11; Is 13:13; Jer 15:14;

30:23; Ps 83:15). This anthropomorphism—ascribing human passions to God—is less strong in later periods. The word 'anger' is then used without the name of God (Is 63:5), and God's anger (2 Sam 24:1) is replaced by 'Satan' (1 Chron 21:1).

Yahweh's wrath is sometimes described as incomprehensible, 'irrational': Gen 32:23–33 (Jacob's struggle); Ex 4:24 (attack on Moses); Ex 33:20; Judg 13:22; Is 6:5 (the fatal effect of seeing God); Ex 19:9–25; 20:18–21; Num 1:51; 1 Sam 6:19. Even in these passages, God's features are not described as 'demoniacal' (P. Volz, *Das Dämonische in Jahweh*, 1924, 7–17): the expression of his displeasure is not arbitrary, but only indicates his incomprehensibility and sanctity (Haag 1754f; Eichrenrodt I, 170f). God's anger is a reaction against man's offensive actions, and is caused by sin and violation of the covenant. God's wrath falls on Israel as it rebels against the divine dispensation (Num 11:1; 17:6–15; 13:25–14:38; Deut 1:34f), shows contempt for God, falls away from him and turns to strange gods (Ex 32; Num 25; Deut 11:16f; 12:29–13:19; 29:15–17; see also 9:18; Judg 2:14; 3:8; 10:7; 1 Kings 14:15; 16:33 and many other instances). The historical pattern of the period of the judges and kings is apostasy, God's wrath, conversion. The central motive for God's anger in the prophetical sermon is the offended love of God: God's love is despised by his own people (Hos 5:10; 8:5; Is 9:11; Jer 4:4; Ezek 5:13; 7:3 and many other instances; see also Amos 2:9–11; 3:2; Hos 11:1–6; Is 1:2f; 5:1–7; 17:10; Jer 2:1–3; 31:1–3; Ezek 16:4–14).

God has the absolute dominion over all nations. He is angry when in their pride they refuse to acknowledge it (Gen 11), or on their own authority go beyond their commission to chastise his people, the Jews (Is 10:5–15; see also 14:4–6; Ezek 25:15–17; Zech 1:15). The Old Testament makes man the subject of God's wrath because he is sinful. In ancient history (Gen 2–11), the path of mankind goes from the fall of our first parents (Gen 2–3), through fratricide (4) and growing perversion of the generation of the flood (6–8), to the hybris of the Tower of Babel and its punishment. Being guilty (Ps 90:8; Job 14:1–4; see Heinisch 219), man will fade away under God's anger (Ps 90:7).

Man in the Old Testament can perceive God's wrath whenever his existence is being threatened. The law (Deut 7:4; 9:8, 19 and other instances) and the prophets (Is 30:27f; 34:2, 5; 63:1–4; Jer 50:13; Ezek 22:31; 43:8) announce his 'destructive anger'. In historiography and in the preaching of the prophets historical disasters are imputed to God's wrath: drought, famine, epidemics and plagues, pestilence and extradition to the enemy (Num 11:1, 10; 12:9; 17:10; 2 Sam 24); but especially exile is given in prophetical preaching as the result of God's wrath. Here we also find the proclamation of a judgement of wrath at the end of time ('Day of Wrath' Amos 5:18f; Is 2:9–21; Zeph 1:15–18). The effects of God's wrath on the fate of the individual—with whom only later periods are concerned—are illness, affliction caused by personal enemies, premature death and absence of God (Job; Ps 88:16f; 90:7f; 102:9–12 and other instances).

God's wrath is frequently kindled against the sinners (Ex 19:12; Num 11:33; 12:9; 17:6–11; 25:9–11; 2 Sam 6:7), but God often shows patience (Ex 34:6f; Num 14:18; Neh 1:8f; Is 48:9; Ps 103:8). God warns through these blows before he destroys (Amos 4:6–11; Is 9:11; Jer 4:4): in his forbearance he gives time for repentance (Jon 4:2). About the duration of divine wrath Jer 3:12 says, 'I will not be angry for ever'. Yahweh has hidden his face from his people in exile, convulsed with anger, but only for a little while, and he shows mercy with them in his everlasting kindness (Is 54:8–10). The apocalyptists came to understand that the end of God's wrath must come before the time of grace (Dan 8:19; Is 26:20). Yahweh's enemies are struck by his anger for ever (Nahum 1:2; Mal 1:4).

Divine legislation (Deut 6:14), the preaching of the prophets and public worship (Num 1:53) have prevented his destroying wrath. The prayers of those affected by his wrath (Judg 3:8f; Is 64:8; Jer 10:24; Ps 6:2; 38:1) and the intercessory prayers for them (of Moses: Ex 32:11f; Num 11:1f; 14:11–19; Deut 9:18; Ps 106:23; Num 12:13; of Amos: Amos 7:2–6; of Jeremiah: Jer 14:7; 18:20; of Job: Job 42:7f) cry out for the mercy of the angry God. God's wrath is a reaction against sin and violation of his sanctity; therefore he demands expiation as a condition for giving up his anger (Num 25:1–5; 6–11; Jos 7:1, 25). Peace-offerings are also mentioned (Num 16:46; 2 Sam 24). The prophets therefore demand serious conversion and repentance (Jer 4:4, 8; 36:7). God puts an end to 'the judgement of wrath' of the exile after Israel has drunk 'the cup of "wrath"', paid her debt, and 'received from God's hand double for all her sins' (Is 51:17, 22; 40:2).

Although in the Old Testament God's wrath is frequently mentioned, anger is never (except in Nah 1:2 'the Lord is a revenger and has wrath') given as an essential attribute of God (like holiness in the expression 'the Holy One of Israel', Is 1:4 and other instances). Anger is kept in check by the ↗ righteousness of God (allegiance to the covenant) (Jer 10:24; Ps 6:1; 38:1). God's mercy prevails over his wrath (Is 54:8–10; Ps 30:6; Is 12).

2. *In the New Testament.* The proclamation of God's wrath is not only peculiar to the Old Testament; John the Baptist, Jesus, Paul, and John all mention it. Jesus never ascribes anger to God directly. Most passages give the impression that God's wrath represents something independent, existing outside of God but depending on him; the ↗ judgement, the reckoning. The thought of the effect is stronger than 'the psychic reaction'; theological thinking outweighs psychological appreciation. Nevertheless, God's anger is never dissociated from emotion (Rom 9:22; especially Heb 3:11; 4:3 quoting Ps 95:11).

Anger attributed to God is also part of the picture given of Jesus, most explicitly in Mark where theological reflection is most scarce. Luke tones down the passionate features in Christ (J. Schmid, 'Das Evangelium nach Lukas', *RNT* 3 (1955³), 19). Anger and wrath as such are hardly ever mentioned, but the expression of his anger is frequently related in the gospel.

Jesus is angry with the powers of wickedness and their activities. He inveighs against Satan, who tempts him (Mt 4:10); against Peter, who, failing to understand Christ's passion, 'did not think of the things that are of God, but only of the things that are of men' (Mt 16:23 and parallel passages); he scolds the devils (Mk 1:25; 9:25; Lk 4:41), and is angry at the sight of the lepers (Mk 1:41) as illness is an evil which was not in God's original plan but came into the world through the sin of man. He is indignant at the Pharisees and the devilish behaviour of man (Mt 23; Jn 8:44). Jesus' anger with the Pharisees is mixed with compassion; he is angry at the resistance against the message of God's mercy and is filled with sorrow since this proclamation of love was also meant for them (Mk 3:5; see also 15:28). Jesus' anger springs from despised love (see Lk 15:28; Mt 18:34). He is angry where the honour of his father is offended (when casting the traders out of the temple Mt 21:12 and parallel passages; Jn 2:14–17). For the impenitent he has only words of threatening anger (Mt 11:20–24 and parallel passages; Mk 11:14; see also Lk 13:7). Here already is manifest the anger of the judgement which Jesus will display at the end of time (Mt 25:41).

God's wrath in the preaching of John the Baptist is eschatological in character ('the wrath to come', Mt 3:7). The divine judgement which the Baptist threatens is the unquenchable hell-fire (Mt 3:12). Only 'the worthy fruit of penance' can save (Mt 3:8). This proclamation of God's wrath is the echo of the preaching of the prophets and is taken over by Jesus, even though this has not explicit-ly been reported and the words of Jesus handed down to us do not contain the actual expression 'God's wrath' in this particular sense or context. In the parable of the royal marriage feast and that of the merciless servant, the angry king (or lord) passes judgement (Mt 22:7; 18:34). The punishment is 'destruction' (Lk 19:27; 12:46 and parallel passages; see also Mt 22:7) and merciless imprisonment until the debts have been paid (Mt 18:34), being cast into the hell-fire (Mt 13:42; 25:41).

Pauline theology connects the idea of God's wrath (or in short: wrath) with its fundamental themes. In the eschatological present time, God reveals his justice (Rom 1:17) as well as his wrath (Rom 1:18) which is only known by faith (Rom 1:17). God's wrath is already present. Paul regards the immorality of the heathens, their idolatry, fornication, and heartlessness as the effects of his wrath ('God has given them up', Rom 1:24, 26, 28). Their sinfulness is not regarded as the cause but as the result of the judgement (anger), as such it only becomes manifest in the death and resurrection of Christ (see Rom 3:25f; O. Kuss, *Der Römerbrief*, 1, Regensburg 1957, 32–5). In order to punish those who resist his ordinance, God avails himself of the worldly powers which are thought of as the instruments of God's wrath active in the present (Rom 13:4f). According to the 'anti-semitic' passage 1 Thess 2:16, God's wrath falls upon the Jews for their resistance against salvation, for killing the prophets and the Messiah, and for persecuting the apostles (Acts 17:5–9:13); and from this moment 'until the end' God's wrath will manifest itself most severely to the people of Israel (not 'for ever'; see also Rom 11:25–32). God has given them up to their↗ hardness of heart, through which they not only persist in their unbelief, but even try to prevent the salvation of the gentiles.

God's wrath, already active in this sinful human generation, will only be fully effective in the future; also Paul regards God's wrath as essentially eschatological. God's sanctity and dominion will finally be established with the punishment of all those who oppose him (Rom 2:5; 3:5; 5:9; 9:22; 1 Thess 1:10; 5:9; Col 3:6; Eph 5:6; it is not clear whether reference is made to the present or the future, Rom 4:5; 12:19). For Paul, too, the day of judgement is the 'Day of Wrath' (Rom 2:5). The final judgement will bring 'anger and wrath', 'tribulation and anguish' Rom 2:8); wrath is 'punishment'.

All men are subjected to God's wrath since they are all sinners (Rom 1:18–3:20); they are all 'by nature' ('as far as we ourselves or our own contribution is concerned'; H. Schlier, *Der Brief an die Epheser*, Düsseldorf 1957, 107) 'children of wrath', subject to the divine judgement (Eph 2:3); what in point of fact is mentioned here is the effect of original sin (see H. Schlier, *loc. cit.*; J. Mehlmann, *Natura filii irae*, Rome 1959). Man is a 'vessel of wrath', since God has destined him to fall a victim to his wrath (not without man's own fault). The reasons for this divine wrath are the sin of man, his contempt for the revelation of God himself in the creation of the world (Rom 1:18, 21f), his contempt for God's works in the revelation of his law (Rom 2:17–24; 3:19f), contempt for his holy love

(Rom 2:4; 1 Thess 2:14f), and returning uncharitableness for God's love (Rom 2:5). Obduracy and impenitence 'treasure up wrath against the Day of Judgement' (Rom 2:5). Contention with God and inobedience to the revealed truth bring wrath and indignation (Rom 2:8).

God's wrath is thought to be connected with his mercy and patience (Rom 9:22f). God has shown great patience with the 'vessels of wrath', the guilty men 'fitted for destruction' (damnation) (see Rom 2:4; 3:25f) in order to manifest his wrath (see the demonstration of the power of God's wrath Rom 1:18–3:20) and to reveal his power to defeat sin. God wants to proclaim the abundance of his glory to 'the vessel of his mercy', man, to whom he wants to show his mercy and whom he had predestined to glory. Paul sees in God's tolerance of evil a means to secure good objects; it justifies God's attitude towards the impenitence and obduracy of Israel. God's benignity will lead to penance (Rom 2:4). Man should never impatiently try to anticipate God's wrath, which is waiting in patience (Rom 12:19).

Man seeks salvation from God's wrath, which he won't find through the Law, for the Law is not only powerless but even 'works wrath' (Rom 4:15; see also 3:20; 5:20; 7:7–13; Gal 3:19). The law, according to Pauline theology, is a cause of transgression and therefore of damnation (God's wrath); promise and faith are the only ways of escaping God's wrath. Salvation from this wrath is brought by Jesus Christ. God has not predestined the christian for wrath but for salvation through Jesus Christ our Lord. Jesus has snatched us from the wrath to come (1 Thess 1:10). Through the continued pneumatic activity of Christ's death (or through his intervention in the eschatological judgement) all christians who have been justified and reconciled will be able to stand this eschatological judgement for which also they have to appear (Rom 5:9).

The drama of the eschatological events revealed in the Book of Revelation is the drama of the battle between God's wrath and the anger of Satan (Rev 12:7) and his henchmen (anger of the nations 11:18). The day of judgement, when this battle will take place is 'the great day of their wrath', of the wrath of him who sits on the throne and the wrath of the Lamb (6:16f; 11:18). The battlefield is the church. Satan is thrown down to earth raging with fury (12:12) and persecutes the church in return (12:13). God condemns all the powers of wickedness to death and destruction. He warns against the adoration of the Beast and threatens with the wine of the wrath of God, which has been prepared undiluted in the cup of his wrath (14:9f), with damnation (see 4:11). The great Babylon who has made all nations drink of the wine of her fornication (14:8; 18:3) falls; she has led other nations into apostasy, and this apostasy itself is a punishment ('wine of the wrath of God'; see Rom 1:18–32). God's judgement is compared to a vintage, cast into the great press of God's wrath (Rev 14:19; see also Is 63:1–6). God's wrath finds its completion in the execution of his judgement; seven angels with the seven last plagues are shown (Rev 15:1). One of the four living creatures passes to the seven angels seven golden vials full of the wrath of God to be poured out upon the earth (16:1). The great city of Babylon is given 'the cup of the wine of the indignation of his wrath' (16:19). Christ, the conqueror in this final battle, appears as the one who stamps the wine-press; he treads 'the wine-press of the fierceness of the wrath of God the Almighty' (19:15). God's wrath is victorious after all has been subjected to Christ (1 Cor 15:28).

In the other writings of John, the expression 'wrath of God' appears only once (Jn 3:36). Mankind stands guilty under God's wrath, subject to his judgement. In contradistinction to 'wrath' or 'anger' stands 'life everlasting'. The choice for or against Christ is decisive of whether man will be lost for ever or be saved from divine judgement and attain eternal life (see Jn 3:17f). In the faith in Christ, which is obedience, the eschatological gift of freedom from God's wrath has become a reality already in this present time (johannine eschatology).

Bibliography: Haag, 1754–7; H. Kleinknecht, J. Fichtner, G. Stählin, and others, *TDNT* III, 167f and v, 382–447 (= *Wrath* [*BKW* XIII], London 1964); Eichrodt I, 258–69; Meinertz II, 33ff; Bultmann, 238ff; G. Schrenk, *Unser Glaube an den Zorn Gottes nach dem Röm*, 1944; A. von Jüchen, *Der Zorn Gottes*, 1948.

Alois Stöger

Supplementary Bibliography

Analytical Index
of Articles
and Cross-References

Index of
Biblical References

Index of
Hebrew and Greek Words

Supplementary Bibliography

This supplement contains the most important books and articles which have appeared since the publication of the third German edition of the *Encyclopedia* in 1967. It has been specially prepared for this edition by the editor of the original, Professor J. B. Bauer, in the hope of thereby increasing the value of the *Encyclopedia* to English-speaking users.

Abraham

H. Werner, 'Abraham. Der Erstling und Repräsentant Israels', *Exempla Biblica* 1, 1965; N. A. Dahl. 'The Story of Abraham in Luke-Acts', *Festschrift P. Schubert*, Nashville/New York 1966, 139–58; K. Berger. 'Abraham in den paulinischen Hauptbriefen (Gal 3; 4, 21–31; Röm 4; 9–11; 2 C 11, 22)', *MTZ* 17 (1966), 47–89; A. González, *Abraham, Father of Believers*, London/New York 1968; H. Gaubert, *Abraham, Loved by God*, New York 1969.

Adam

A. J. Campbell, 'Adam', *Theology* 69 (1966), 216–22; P. Lengsfeld, 'Adam und Christus. Die Adam-Christus-Typologie im NT und ihre dogmatische Verwendung bei M. J. Scheeben u. K. Barth', *Koinonia . . .* 9 (1965); H. Müller, 'Der rabbinische Qal-Waeḥomer-Schluss in paulin. Typologie. Zur Adam-Christustypologie in Röm 5', *ZNW* 58 (1967), 73–92.

Almsgiving

S. J. Assaf, *La notion de l'aumône chez les Mésopotamiens, les Phéniciens et dans l'AT*, Strasbourg 1967 (dissertation).

Amen

J. C. G. Greig, *Abba and Amen: Their relevance to Christology (Studia Evangelica)* V, 2, *TU* 103 (1968), 3–20.

Angel

M. Takahashi, 'An Oriental's Approach to the Problem of Angelology', *ZAW* 78 (1966), 343–350; J. Quinlan, 'Engelen en duivels', *Tijdschrift voor Theologie*, 7 (1967), 43–61, English summary 62; É. Pascal, *Les anges dans la littérature préexilienne de l'AT*, Rome 1965/6 (dissertation).

Apostle

S. Freyne, 'The Twelve Apostles—An Essay in Redaction Criticism', *ITQ* 34 (1967), 242–53; F. Agnew, 'Vocatio primorum discipulorum in traditione synoptica', *VD* 46 (1968), 129–47; F. Bovon, 'L'origine des récits concernant les apôtres', *RTP* 100 (1967) 345–50; R. P. Meye, *Jesus and the Twelve: Discipleship and Revelation in Mark's Gospel*, Grand Rapids, Michigan 1968.

Ascension

J. Heuschen, *The Bible on The Ascension*, 1965; J. M. Egan, 'Meaning of the Ascension', *CrossCrown* 18 (1966), 164–74.

Asceticism

J. Leipoldt, *Griechische Philosophie und frühchristliche Askese*, Berlin 1961; H. A. Wenning, 'Die Askese im Zeugnis der Bibel', *ZeugBib* 8, 1966; H. A. Wennink, *The Bible on Asceticism*, St Norbert Abbey Series 14, 1966.

Atonement

D. Hill, 'Greek Words and Hebrew Meanings. Studies in the Semantics of Soteriological Terms', London/New York 1967.

Ban

A. Dekkers, *Der Kriegsherem und das Naturrecht. Mit einem religionswissenschaftlichen Vergleich*, Vienna 1964 (dissertation); B. Löbmann, 'Die Exkommunikation im NT', *Theologisches Jahrbuch*, 8 (1965), 446–58; W. Doskocil, 'Exkommunikation', *RAC* 7, 49 (1966), 1–22.

Baptism

D. M. Stanley, 'The NT Doctrine of Baptism', D. M. Stanley, *The Apostolic Church in the NT*, Westminster, Md, 1965, 140–94, 421–28 = *TS*

18 (1957), 169–215; E. C. Whitaker, 'The History of the Baptismal Formula', *JEH* 16 (1965), 1–12; W. Bieder, *Die Verheissung der Taufe im NT*, Zürich 1966; J. Pryke, 'The Sacraments of Holy Baptism and Holy Communion in the Light of the Ritual Washings and Sacred Meals at Qumran', *RQ* 5 (1966), 543–52; D. W. B. Robinson, 'Born of Water and Spirit: Does Jn 3:5 Refer to Baptism?', *Reformed Theological Review*, 25 (1966), 15–23; O. Böcker, *Dämonenfurcht und Dämonenabwehr. Ein Beitrag zur Vorgeschichte der christlichen Taufe*, Stuttgart 1969.

Baptism of Jesus

E. Wehrli, 'Jesus' Baptism and Ours', *TheolLife* 8, 1 (1965), 24–34; S. L. Jr. Johnson, 'The Baptism of Christ', *Bibliotheca Sacra*, 123 (1966), 220–29; M. Sabbe, 'Le baptême de Jésus. Étude sur les origines littéraires du récit des Évangiles synoptiques', *Don. natal. J. Coppens* 2 (Gembloux/Paris 1967), 184–211; J. K. Howard, 'The Baptism of Jesus and its Present Significance', *Evangelical Quarterly*, London 39 (1967), 131–38.

Blessing

W. Bieder, *Segnen und Bekennen; eine biblische und eine historische Studie*, Basle 1965; W. Schenk, *Der Segen im NT (eine begriffsanalytische Studie)*, Jena 1965 (dissertation); F. Asensio, 'Trayectoria histórico-teológica de la "bendición" bíblica de Yahweh en labios del hombre', *Greg* 48 (1967), 253–83.

Blood

G. Kiefer, *Das Blut im Kult des Alten Bundes. Ein Beitrag zur Theologie des alttest. Kultes*, Trier 1966 (dissertation).

Blood of Christ

E. F. Siegman, 'The Blood of Christ in St. Paul's Soteriology', *Contemp. NT Studies* (Collegeville, Minn. 1965), 359–74.

Body

Bo Reicke, 'Body and Soul in the NT', *ST* 19 (1965), 200–12.

Brethren of Jesus

J. Blinzler, *Die Brüder und Schwestern Jesu*, Stuttgart 1967².

Building up

M. E. Thrall, 'The Meaning of oikodomeo in Relation to the Concept of syneidesis (1 Cor 8:10)', *Stud. Ev.* 4, 1 (1968), 468–72.

Charisma

O. Perels, 'Charisma in NT', *Fuldaer Hefte* 15 (1964).

Church

A. Cole, *The Body of Christ. A NT Image of the Church*, Philadelphia 1965; G. S. R. Cox, 'The Emerging Organization of the Church in the NT, and the Limitations Imposed Thereon', *Evangelical Quarterly*, 33 (1966), 22–39; B. F. Meyer, 'The Initial Self-Understanding of the Church', *CBQ* 27 (1965), 35–42; R. Schnackenburg, *The Church in the NT*, London/New York 1965; D. J. O'Connor, 'Is the Church the New Israel?', *ITQ* 33 (1966), 161–64; D. M. Stanley, *The Apostolic Church in the NT*, Westminster, Md, 1965; *Volk Gottes. Zum Kirchenverständnis der kath., evang. und anglikanischen Theologie. Festgabe für Josef Höfer*, ed. R. Bäumer and H. Dolch, Freiburg i. B, 1967; M. J. Le Guillou, *Christ and Church: A Theology of the Mystery*, New York 1966; F. Hahn and P. Rieger (ed.), *Anfänge der Kirche im NT (Ev Forum 8)*, 1957; O. Kuss, 'Hat Jesus die Kirche eigentlich gewollt? Rückblick auf das NT', *Kontexte* 4 (1962), 15–22; W. G. Kümmel, *Kirchenbegriff und Geschichtsbewußtsein in der Urgemeinde und bei Jesus*, Göttingen 1968; R. J. McKelvey, *The New Temple. The Church in the New Testament*, Oxford 1969.

Circumcision

E. Isaac, 'Circumcision as a Covenant Rite', *Anthropos* 59 (1964), 444–56; R. Schwarzenberger, *Bedeutung und Geschichte der Beschneidung im AT mit besonderer Berücksichtigung der Forschungsergebnisse aus Ethnologie und alter Geschichte*, Vienna 1964 (dissertation).

Clean and unclean

W. Kornfeld, 'Reine und unreine Tiere im AT', *Kairos* 7 (1965), 134–47; J. Raasch, 'The Monastic Concept of Purity of Heart and its Sources', *StMonast* 8 (1966), 7–33, 183–213.

Confession

W. Bieder, *Segnen und Bekennen; eine biblische und eine historische Studie*, Basle 1965; F. B. Craddock, 'The Meaning of Confession in the NT', *MidStream* 6, 2 (1967), 17–28.

Conscience

M. E. Thrall, 'The Pauline Use of syneidesis', *NTS* 14 (1967), 118–25.

Consolation

C. J. Bjerkelund, *Parakalô. Form, Funktion und Sinn der parakalô-Sätze in den paulinischen Briefen*,

Oslo 1967; A. Grabner-Haider, 'Paraklese und Eschatologie bei Paulus. Mensch und Welt im Anspruch der Zukunft Gottes', *NA* N.F. 4 (1968); F. W. Danker, '1 Peter 1, 24–2, 17—A Consolatory Pericope', *ZNW* 58 (1967), 93–102.

Contest

V. C. Pfitzner, 'Paul and the Agon Motif. Traditional Athletic Imagery in the Pauline Literature', *Suppl. to NT* 16 (1967).

Conversion

S. Smalley, 'Conversion in the NT', *Churchman* 78 (1964), 193–210; W. Trilling, 'Metanoia also Grundforderung der neutest. Lebenslehre', *Einübung des Glaubens, Festschrift K. Tilman*, Würzburg 1964, 178–90; A. Hulsbosch, *The Bible on Conversion*, St Norbert Abbey Series 18 (1966); B. Prete, 'La conversione nei Vangeli', *Sacra Doctrina* 11 (1966), 173–93; R. Schnackenburg, 'Umkehr-Predigt im NT', R. Schnackenburg, *Christliche Existenz nach dem NT* 1, Munich 1967, 35–60 = *MTZ* 1, 4 (1950), 1–13, considerably revised.

Covenant

D. J. McCarthy, 'Covenant in the OT: The Present State of Inquiry', *CBQ* 27 (1965), 217–41; F. Asensio, 'Teología e historia del pacto: en torno a una interrogación bíblica', *Greg* 47 (1966), 665–84; W. Eichrodt, 'Covenant and Law. Thoughts on Recent Discussion', *Interpretation* 20 (1966), 302–21; G. Fohrer, 'AT—"Amphiktyonie" und "Bund"?', *TLZ* 91 (1966), 801–16, 893–904; M. H. Woudstra, 'The Ark of the Covenant from Conquest to Kingship', *Bibl. & Theol. St.* 1965; A. Deissler, 'Die Bundespartnerschaft des Menschen mit Gott als Hinwendung zur Welt und Mitmenschen', J. B. Metz. (ed.), *Weltverständnis im Glauben*, Mainz 1965, 203–23; J. Swetnam, 'Diatheke in the Septuagint Account of Sinai', *Biblica* 47 (1966), 438–44; P. Altmann, *Erwählungstheologie und Universalismus im AT*, 1965; W. Eichrodt, 'Covenant and Law: Thoughts on Recent Discussion', *Interpretation* 20 (1966), 302–21; F. C. Fensham, 'Covenant, Promise and Expectation in the Bible', *TZ* 23 (1967), 305–22.

Creation

P. Haes, *Die Schöpfung als Heilsmysterium. Erforschung der Quellen*, Mainz 1964; G. Schneider, *Kainē Ktisis. Die Idee der Neuschöpfung beim Apostel Paulus und ihr religionsgeschichtlicher Hintergrund*, Trier 1959 (dissertation); H. F. Weiss, 'Untersuchungen zur Kosmologie des hellenist-

ischen und palästinischen Judentums', *TU* 97 (1966); 'Die Schöpfung im NT', *Ex auditu verbi, Festschrift G. C. Berkouwer*, Kampen 1965, 56–72.

Cross

G. Q. Reijners, 'The Terminology of the Holy Cross in Early Christian Literature as Based upon OT Typology', *Graecitas Christianorum Primaeva* 2, Nijmegen 1965; E. Dinkler, 'Comments on the History of the Symbol of the Cross', *Journal for Theology and the Church*, 1 (1965), 124–45; F. Dölger, 'Beiträge zur Geschichte des Kreuzzeichens VII', *Jahrbuch für Antike und Christentum* 7 (1964, ed. 1966), 5–38; E. Dinkler, *Signum Crucis*, Tübingen 1967.

Cult

A. S. Kapelrud, 'The Role of the Cult in Old Israel', J. P. Hyatt (ed.), *Bible in Mod. Scholarship*, New York 1965, 44–56; response by B. Vawter: 57–64; by H. G. May: 65–73; H. J. Kraus, *Worship in Israel. A Cultic History of the OT*, Oxford/Richmond, Va, 1966; H. H. Rowley, *Worship in Ancient Israel. Its Form and Meaning*, London 1957; S. Herrmann, 'Kultreligion und Buchreligion. Kultische Funktionen in Israel und in Ägypten', *BZAW* 105 (1967), 95–105; A. Z. Idelzohn, *Jewish Liturgy and its Development*, New York 1967; H. H. Rowley, *Worship in Ancient Israel*, Philadelphia 1967; J. G. Trapiello, 'Mito y culto en el AT', *Angelicum* 44 (1967), 449–77.

Cup

G. Braumann, 'Leidenskelch und Todestaufe', *ZNW* 56 (1965) 178–83.

Death

N. Tromp, *Primitive Conceptions of Death and After-Life in the OT with Special Regard to Ugaritic Literature*, Rome 1967 (dissertation); P. Grelot, 'La théologie de la mort dans l'Écriture Sainte', *VS* Suppl. 77 (1966), 143–93; B. van Iersel, 'Vragen naar dood en leven in het NT', *Verbum* 33 (1966), 185–96; P. H. Menoud, *Le sort des trépassés d'après le NT*, Neuchâtel 1966[2]; N. J. Tromp, 'De conceptionibus primitivis orci et mortis in V.T. occurrentibus, consideratis in luce litteraturae ugariticae', *VD* 45 (1967), 209–17.

Decalogue

K. Kinoshita, *A Study of the Decalogue*, New York 1963 (dissertation); H. Gese, 'Der Dekalog als Ganzheit betrachtet', *ZTK* 64 (1967), 121–38.

Demon

P. E. S. Thompson, 'Die Dämonen in der bibl. Theologie', G. Rosenkranz (ed.), Beiträge zur biblischen Theologie, Munich 1967, 148–63; J. E. Bruns, 'Toward a New Understanding of the Demonic', *Ecumenist* 4 (1965), 29–37; O. Böcker, *Dämonenfurcht und Dämonenabwehr. Ein Beitrag zur Vorgeschichte der christlichen Taufe*, Stuttgart 1969.

Demythologising

C. Duncan, 'The Bible and Objectifying Thinking—What Does Bultmann Mean by Demythologizing?', *Australian Biblical Review*, 14 (1966), 24–32; H. Fries, *Bultmann–Barth and Catholic Theology*, Duquesne Studies, Theol. Ser., 8, Pittsburgh, Pa, 1967; E. Hübner, 'Entmythologisierung als theologische Aufgabe', *Festschrift K. Barth*, Zürich 1966, 238–60; J. Knox, *Myth and Truth: An Essay on the Language of Faith*, London 1966; W. H. Schmidt, 'Mythos im AT', *ET*. N.S. 27 (1967), 237–54; K. Ward, 'Myth and Fact in Christianity', *SJT* 20 (1967), 385–96.

Discipline

J. A. Muirhead, *Education in the NT* (Monographs in Christian Education, No. 2), New York 1965; J. N. Sevenster, 'Education or Conversion: Epictetus or the Gospels', *NVT* 8 (1966), 247–62; V. C. Pritzner, *Paul and the Agon Motif. Traditional Athletic Imagery in the Pauline Literature*, Suppl. to *NT* 16, Leiden 1967; J. Gray, 'The Nature and Function of Adult Christian Education in the Church', *SJT* 19 (1966), 457–63.

Dream

F. Schmidtke, 'Träume, Orakel und Totengeister als Künder der Zukunft in Israel und Babylonien', *BZ* 11 (1967), 240–46.

Easter

P. Grelot and J. Pierron, *The Paschal Feast in the Bible*, Baltimore 1966; W. Huber, 'Passa und Ostern. Untersuchungen zur Osterfeier der Alten Kirche', *BZNW* 35 (1969).

Eucharist

N. Hook, *The Eucharist in the NT*, London 1964; E. J. Kilmartin, *The Eucharist in the Primitive Church*, Englewood Cliffs, NJ, 1965; Jr. S. McCormick, *The Lord's Supper. A Biblical Interpretation*, Philadelphia 1966; J. J. von Allmen, 'Essai sur le repas du Seigneur', *Cahiers théologiques* 55 (1966); W. Elert, *Eucharist and Church Fellowship in the First Four Centuries*, St Louis, Mo., 1966; J. Jeremias, *The Eucharistic Words of Jesus*, Rev. ed. London/New York 1966; W. Barclay, *The Lord's Supper*, London 1967; F. Hahn, 'Die alttest. Motive in der urchristlichen Abendmahlsüberlieferung', *ET* N.S. 27 (1967), 337–74; E. Schweizer, *The Lord's Supper acc. to the NT*, Philadelphia 1967; J. Wilkinson, *The Supper and the Eucharist*, London 1965; S. Accame, *L'istituzione dell'Eucaristia*, Naples 1968.

Faith

(S.) J. Heijke, *The Bible on Faith*, St Norbert Abbey Series 22, De Père, Wisc. 1966; A. L. Mulka, '"Fides quae per caritatem operatur" (Gal 5, 6)', *CBQ* 28 (1966), 174–88; H. Ljungman, 'Pistis, a Study of its Presuppositions and its Meaning in Pauline Use', *Acta Reg. Soc. Hum. Lit. Lundensis*, 64 (1964).

Fasting

F. G. Cremer, 'Die Fastenansage Jesu. Mk 2, 20 (u. Parr.) in der Sicht der patristischen und scholastischen Exegese', *BBB* 23 (1965); J. O'Hara, 'Christian Fasting (Mt 5, 15–18)', *Scripture* 19 (1967), 3–18; R. Arbesmann, 'Fasten', 'Fastenspeise', 'Fasttage', *RAC* 7, 447–93, 493–500, and 500–24.

Father

J. Jeremias, 'Die Botschaft Jesu vom Vater', *Calwer Hefte* 92 (1968); P. Gutiérrez, *La paternité spirituelle selon S. Paul, Études Bibliques*, Paris 1968

Fear

J. Becker, 'Gottesfurcht im AT', *AnBib* 25 (1965).

Flesh

A. Sand, 'Der Begriff "Fleisch" in den paulinischen Hauptbriefen', O. Kuss (ed.), *Biblische Untersuchungen* 2, Regensburg 1967.

Freedom

D. Doughty, '"Heiligkeit u. Freiheit"—eine exegetische Untersuchung der Anwendung des paulinischen Freiheitsgedankens in 1 Kor 7', Göttingen 1965 (dissertation); C. Johansson, *Concepts of Freedom in the OT*, New York 1965; G. Moran, 'Freedom in Christian Revelation', *Proc. Soc. Cath. College Teachers of Sacred Doctrine* 11 (1965), 59–77; J. Cambier, 'La liberté chrétienne dans le NT', *Bbl* 48 (1967), 116–27; G. de Ru, *Over Vrijheid*, Wageningen 1967; D. Nestle, *Eleutheria. Studien zum Wesen der Freiheit bei den Griechen und im NT. Teil I. Die*

Griechen (Hermeneut. Unters. z. Theologie 6), Tübingen 1967.

Fulfilment

K. Runia, 'The Interpretation of the OT by the NT', *Vox Reformata* 5 (1965); L. Goppelt, 'Erfüllen', *TWNT* VIII (1966), 246–60; W. Rothfuchs, *Die Erfüllungszitate des Matthäus-Evangeliums*, Stuttgart 1969.

God OT

B. van Iersel, *The Bible on the Living God*, London 1965; J. S. Chesnut, *The OT Understanding of God*, Philadelphia 1968; R. C. Dentan, *The Knowledge of God in Ancient Israel*, New York 1968; A. Jukas, *The Names of God in Holy Scripture*, Grand Rapids, Michigan 1967; H. D. Preuss, *Jahweglaube u. Zukunftserwartung* (*BWANT* 87), 1968.

God NT

A. W. Argyle, *God in the NT*, London 1965; T. Müller, *Gottesbild und Gottesbeziehung im NT*, Zürich/Frankfurt a.M. 1966; R. M. Grant, *The Early Christian Doctrine of God*, Charlottesville, Virginia 1966; J. Pfammatter, 'Eigenschaften und Verhaltensweisen Gottes im NT', Feiner-Löhrer (ed.), *Mysterium Salutis* 2 (Einsiedeln/Köln 1967), 272–90; K. H. Schelkle, 'Gott der Eine u. Dreieine', K. H. Schelkle, *Wort u. Schrift* (Düsseldorf 1966), 81–95; F. J. Schierse, 'Die neutestamentliche Trinitätsoffenbarung', Feiner-Löhrer (ed.), *Mysterium Salutis* 2 (Einsiedeln/Köln 1967), 85–131; R. Schulte, 'Die Vorbereitung der Trinitätsoffenbarung', Feiner-Löhrer (ed.), *Mysterium Salutis* 2 (Einsiedeln/Köln 1967), 55–73 (49–84).

Gospel

O. Michel, 'Evangelium', *RAC* 6, 47 (1965), 1107ff

Government

W. Schneemelcher, *Kirche und Staat im NT: Festschrift H. Kunst*, Berlin 1967; J. M. Paupert, *The Politics of the Gospel*, New York 1969.

Grace

O. J. Thomas, 'Irresistible Grace', *Vox Evangelica* 4 (1965), 55–64.

Holy

D. S. Shapiro, 'The Meaning of Holiness in Judaism', *Tradition* 7, 1 (1965), 46–80.

Hope

W. Zimmerli, *Der Mensch und seine Hoffnung seit den Aussagen des AT*, Göttingen 1968; J. Moltmann, *Theology of Hope*, London/New York 1967; H. Sasse, 'Some Thoughts on Christian Hope', *Reformed Theological Review* 26 (1967), 41–54.

Hour

H. van den Bussche, 'De Betekenis van het Uur in het vierde Evangelie', *Collationes Gandavienses* 2 (1952), 5–16; J. Leal, 'La hora de Jesús, la hora de sa Madre (Joh 2:4)', *Estudios Eccl.* 26 (1952), 147–68; J. Michl, 'Bemerkungen zu Joh 2:4', *Bbl* 36 (1955), 492–509; C. F. Ceroke, 'The Problem of Ambiguity in John 2:4', *CBQ* 21 (1959), 316–40; A. Feuillet, 'L'Heure de Jésus et le Signe de Cana', *ETL* 36 (1960), 5–22; R. Schnackenburg, *Das erste Wunder Jesu*, Leipzig 1960[3]; W. Thüsing, *Die Erhöhung und Verherrlichung Jesu im Johannesevangelium*, Münster 1960.

Inheritance

A. M. Brown, *The Concept of Inheritance in the OT*, New York 1965 (Columbia dissertation); J. D. Hester, 'The "Heir" and Heilsgeschichte: A Study of Gal 4:1ff', *Oikonomia, Festschrift O. Cullmann* (Hamburg 1967), 118–25.

Intercession

H. Zillikens, 'Segenssprüche und Fürbitten in der Frömmigkeit des Alten Bundes', *LitgJb* 17 (1967), 96–102.

Jerusalem

N. W. Porteous, 'Jerusalem–Zion: The Growth of a Symbol', N. W. Porteous, *Living the Mystery* (Oxford 1967), 93–111.

Jesus Christ

R. H. Fuller, *The Foundations of NT Christology*, London/New York 1965; F. Gogarten, *Jesus Christus. Wende der Welt. Grundfragen zur Christologie*, Tübingen 1966; A. T. Hanson, *Jesus Christ in the OT*, London 1965; A. J. B. Higgins, *Jesus and the Son of Man*, London/Philadelphia 1965; R. Marlow, 'The Son of Man in Recent Journal Literature, *CBQ* 28 (1966), 20–30; M. Kähler, *The So-Called Historical Jesus and the Historic Biblical Christ*, Philadelphia 1964; H. K. McArthur, *The Quest through the Centuries: The Search for the Historical Jesus*, Philadelphia 1966; H. Berkhof, *Christ the Meaning of History*, London/Richmond, Va 1966; L. Sabourin, *The Names and Titles of Jesus. Themes of Biblical Theology*, New York

1967; S. H. Hooke, *The Resurrection of Christ as History and Experience*, London 1967; N. Clark, *Interpreting the Resurrection*, London 1967; G. W. H. Lampe and D. M. MacKinnon, *The Resurrection*, London/Philadelphia 1966; T. Boman, *Die Jesus-Überlieferung im Lichte der neueren Volkskunde*, Göttingen 1967; C. K. Barrett, *Jesus and the Gospel Tradition*, London 1967; R. C. Foster, *Introduction and Early Ministry. Studies in the Life of Christ*, Grand Rapids, Michigan 1966; E. J. Goodspeed, *A Life of Jesus*, New York 1967; W. K. Kümmel, 'Jesusforschung seit 1950', *Theologische Rundschau*, Tübingen 31 (1966) 15–46, 289–315; E. W. Saunders, *Jesus in the Gospels*, Englewood Cliffs NJ, 1967; V. Taylor, *The Life and Mystery of Jesus*, New York 1967; W. Trilling, *Fragen zur Geschichtlichkeit Jesu*, Düsseldorf 1967²; H. R. Balz, 'Methodische Probleme der neutest. Christologie', *WissMonANT* 25 (1967); F. H. Borsch, *The Son of Man in Myth and History*, London/Philadelphia 1967; R. E. Brown, *Jesus God and Man. Modern Biblical Reflections*, Milwaukee 1967; J. Knox, *The Humanity and Divinity of Christ. A Study of Pattern in Christology*, London/New York 1967; W. E. Lynch, *Jesus in the Synoptic Gospels*, Milwaukee 1967; R. Slenczka, 'Geschichtlichkeit und Personsein Jesu Christi', *Forschungen zur systematischen und ökumenischen Theologie* 18 (1967); H. Flender, *Die Botschaft Jesu von der Herrschaft Gottes*, Munich 1968; K. Niederwimmer, *Jesus*, Göttingen 1968; R. Schippers, *Jezus Christus in het historisch Onderzoek*, Kampen 1969; H. Braun, *Jesus*, Stuttgart 1969; G. Strecker, 'Die historische und theologische Problematik der Jesusfrage', *ET* 29 (1969), 453–76.

Joy

A. B. du Toit, *Der Aspekt der Freude im urchristl. Abendmahl*, Winterthur 1965.

Justification

P. Crowley, 'Justification by Faith in St. Paul', *Scripture* 18 (1966), 91–111; K. Kertelge, '*Rechtfertigung*' *bei Paulus. Studien zur Struktur und zum Bedeutungsgehalt des paulinischen Rechtfertigungsbegriffs* (*NA* 3), 1967.

Lamb of God

J. Blenkinsopp, 'The Lamb of God', *Clergy Review* 50 (1965), 868–72; F. Gryglewicz, 'Das Lamm Gottes', *NTS* 13 (1966), 133–46; N. Hillyer, '"The Lamb" in the Apoc.' *Evangelical Quarterly* 39 (1967), 228–36; J. D'Souza, *The Lamb of God in the Johannine Writings*, Allahabad 1968.

Law

O. Kuss, 'Nomos bei Paulus', *MTZ* 17 (1966), 173–227.

Life

S. H. Hooke, 'Israel and the After-Life', *Expository Times*, 76 (1964), 236–39; 'The Extra-canonical Literature, ib. 273–76; G. Dautzenberg, *Sein Leben bewahren. Psyché in den Herrenworten der Evangelien*, (*Studien zum Alten und Neuen Testament* 14, 1966); A. J. Feldman. *The Concept of Immortality in Judaism Historically Considered*, New York 1964; M. Carbonara Naddei, 'L'immortalità dell'anima nel pensiero dei Greci', *Sophia* 33 (1966), 272–300; R. Taylor, 'The Eschatological Meaning of Life and Death in the Book of Wisdom I–V', *ETL* 42 (1966), 72–137 = *Analecta Lovaniensia Biblica et Orientalia* 4 (1966).

Lord's day

L. T. Geraty, 'The Pascha and the Origin of Sunday Observance', *Andrews University Seminary Studies* 3 (1965), 85–96; F. A. Regan, 'Dies dominica and dies solis. The Beginnings of the Lord's Day in Christian Antiquity. An Abstract of a Dissertation', *Cath. Univ. of America. St. in S. Theol* 125A (1961); P. Delhaye and J. L. Lecat, 'Dimanche et Sabbat', *Mélanges de Science Religieuse*, 23 (1966), 3–14, 73–93; J. W. Leitch, 'Lord Also of the Sabbath', *Scottish Journal of Theology* 19 (1966), 426–33; W. Rordorf, *Sunday. The History of the Day of Rest and Worship in the Earliest Centuries of the Christian Church*, London/Philadelphia 1968.

Love

T. Barrosse, *Christianity: Mystery of Love. An Essay in Biblical Theology*, Notre Dame, Ind., 1964; C. Spicq, *Agape in the NT*, 3 vols, London/St Louis 1963–1966; J. T. Sanders, 'First Cor. 13. Its Interpretation since the First World War', *Interpretation* 20 (1966), 159–87.

Man

Leo Adler, *Der Mensch in der Sicht der Bibel*, Munich/Basle 1965; W. Zimmerli, 'Der Mensch und seine Hoffnung nach den Aussagen des AT', *Festschrift T. C. Vriezen*, Wageningen 1966, 389–402; W. Mork, *The Biblical Meaning of Man*, Milwaukee 1967; D. Burkhard (ed.), *Man before God: Toward a Theology of Man*, New York 1966.

Marriage

K. H. Schelkle, 'Ehe und Ehelosigkeit im NT', *WW* 29 (1966), 1–15; G. N. Vollebregt, *The*

Bible on Marriage, London 1965; A. Isaksson, *Marriage and Ministry in the New Temple. A Study with Special Reference to Mt 19, 3–12* (!) *and 1 Cor 11, 3–16*, Lund 1965; J. Cambier, 'Le grand mystère concernant le Christ et son Église, Éph 5, 22–33', *Bibl* 47 (1966), 43–90; K. Kahana, *The Theory of Marriage in Jewish Law*, Leiden 1966; H. Crouzel, 'Séparation ou remariage selon les Pères anciens', *Greg* 47 (1966), 472–94; H. Doms, 'Zur biblischen Sicht der Ehe', Feiner-Löhrer (ed.), *Mysterium Salutis* 2, Einsiedeln/Köln 1967, 724–37; V. J. Pospishil, *Divorce and Remarriage*, New York/London 1967; E. Schillebeeckx, *Marriage: Secular Reality & Saving Mystery*: I. *Marriage in OT and NT*, II. *Marriage in the History of the Church*, London 1965; R. Patai, *L'amour et le couple aux temps bibliques*, Tours 1967; R. Yaron, 'The Restoration of Marriage', *Journal of Jewish Studies* 17 (1966), 1–11; H. Baltensweiler, 'Die Ehe im NT. Exegetische Untersuchungen über Ehe, Ehelosigkeit und Ehescheidung', *Abhandlungen zur Theologie des Alten und Neuen Testaments* 32 (1967); W. J. Harrington, *The Bible on Marriage*, Dublin 1963; M. Thurian, *Matrimonio y celibato*, Saragosa 1966; A. Mahoney, 'A New Look at the Divorce Clauses in Mt 5, 32 and 19, 9', *CBQ* 30 (1968), 29–38.

Mary

J. Çantinat, *Mary in the Bible*, Westminster, Md., 1965; J. Galot, *Mary in the Gospel*, Westminster, Md, 1965; J. F. Craghan, *Mary's Vow of Virginity*, Munich 1965 (dissertation); A. Vögtle, 'Mt 1, 25 und die Virginitas B.M. Virginis post partum', *Tübinger Theologische Quartalschrift* 147 (1967), 28–39; B. Rinaldi, *Mary of Nazareth: Myth or History?*, Westminster, Md, 1966; F. M. Braun, *Mother of God's People*, Staten Island 1967; J. F. Craghan, *Mary. The Virginal Wife and the Married Virgin, The Problematic of Mary's Vow of Virginity*, Rome 1967; P. de Rosa, 'The Significance of Mary's virginity', *Clergy Review* 51 (1966), 419–29; *Maria in S. Scriptura. Acta Congressus Mariologici-Mariani in Republica Dominicana anno 1965 celebrati*, Rome 1967; H. Räisänen, 'Die Mutter Jesu im NT', *Annales Acad. Scient. Fennicae* Ser. B 158 (1969).

Mediation

H. Langkammer, *Christus als Schöpfungsmittler. Die biblischen Texte und der Ursprung des Glaubens*, Diss. Pont. Inst. Biblici, Rome 1966 (Biblical Institute dissertation); R. Bring, 'Der Mittler und das Gesetz. Eine Studie zu Gal 3, 20', *KD* 12 (1966), 292–309.

Meditation

M. L. Danieli, *Il concetto di contemplazione nell'AT*, Bologna 1965.

Messianism

S. Zeitlin, *The Origin of the Idea of the Messiah: Festschrift A. H. Silver*, New York 1963; P. Zerafa, 'Priestly Messianism in the OT', *Angelicum* 42 (1965), 318–41; S. Herrmann, *Die prophetischen Heilserwartungen im Alten Testament. Ursprung und Gestaltwandel*, Stuttgart 1966; J. Coppens, 'Le prémessianisme vétérotestamentaire', *Recherches Bibliques* 8 (1967), 153–79; *Il Messianismo: Atti della XVIII Settimana Biblica*, Brescia 1966; J. Scharbert, 'Der Messias im AT und im Judentum', *Stud. und Berichte der Katholischen Akademie in Bayern* 33 (1965), 47–78; Martin Rehm, 'Der königliche Messias im Licht der Immanuel-Weissagungen des Buches Jesaja', *Eichstätter Studien* (NF Bd 1) (XII und 432), 1968.

Millenarianism

R. D. Culver, *Daniel and the Latter Days* (*A Study in Millennialism*),[2] Chicago 1965; H. Schumacher, *Das tausendjährige Königreich Christi auf Erden. Eine biblische Untersuchung im Lichte des Fortschreitens der göttlichen Heilsoffenbarung und Heilsgeschichte*, Stuttgart 1964.

Miracle

Miracles: Cambridge Studies in their Philosophy and History, ed. C. F. D. Moule, London 1965; J. Scharbert, 'Was versteht das AT unter Wunder?', *Bibel und Kirche* 22 (1967) 37–46; A. de Groot, *The Bible on Miracles*, St Norbert Abbey Series 19, 1966; B. B. Warfield, *Miracles: Yesterday and Today*, Grand Rapids, Mich., 1965; A. Heising, *Multiplicatio panum: Die Botschaft der Brotvermehrung*, Stuttgart 1966; L. Monden, *Signs and Wonders—A Study of the Miraculous Element in Religion*, New York 1966; R. D. Smith, *Comparative Miracles*, St Louis, Mo., 1965; R. H. Fuller, *Interpreting the Miracles*, London 1966; D. Connolly, 'Ad miracula sanationum apud Mt', *VD* 45 (1967), 306–25; K. Tagawa, 'Miracles et Évangile: La pensée personnelle de l'évangéliste Marc', *Ét. d'hist. et phil. rel.* 62 (1966); H. Baltensweiler, 'Wunder und Glaube im NT', *TZ* 23 (1967), 241–56; F. Mussner, *Die Wunder Jesu. Eine Hinführung*, München 1967; G. Schille, 'Die urchristliche Wundertradition. Ein Beitrag zur Frage nach dem irdischen Jesus', *Arb. z. Theol.* 1, 29 (1967).

Moses

I. H. Weisfeld, *This Man Moses*, New York 1966; K. Kastner, *Moses im NT*, Munich 1967

Supplementary Bibliography

(dissertation); W. A. Meeks, 'The Prophet-King: Moses' Traditions and the Johannine Christology', Suppl. to *NT* 14 (1967); H. Schmid, 'Mose', *BZAW* 110 (1968).

Mystery

F. Gavin, *The Jewish Antecedents of the Christian Sacraments*, New York 1969.

Name

H. H. Rowley, *Dictionary of Bible Personal Names*, London 1968.

Neighbour

F. Mussner, 'Der Begriff des "Nächsten" in der Verkündigung Jesu. Dargelegt am Gleichnis vom barmherzigen Samariter', F. Mussner, *Praesentia Salutis* (Düsseldorf 1967), 125–32 (= *TTZ* 64 (1955), 91–9).

Oath

S. Mayence, *La parole de Jésus sur le serment (Mt 5, 33–37; Jac 5, 12). Tradition et rédaction dans l'Év. de Mt*, Louvain 1965 (dissertation).

Obedience

B. Schwank, '"Gehorsam" im NT: Erbe und Auftrag', *Beuron* 42 (1966), 469–76.

Original Sin

A. M. Dubarle, *The Biblical Doctrine of Original Sin*, London/New York 1964/1965; Z. Alszeghy and M. Flick, 'Il peccato originale in prospettiva personalistica', *Greg* 46 (1965), 705–32; W. T. Bruner, *Children of the Devil: A Fresh Investigation of the Fall of Man and Original Sin*, New York 1966; K. Condon, 'The Biblical Doctrine of Original Sin', *ITQ* 34 (1967), 20–36; P. Grelot, 'Réflexions sur le problème du péché originel', *NRT* 99 (1967), 337–75, 449–84; J. P. Mackey, 'Original Sin and Polygenism: The State of the Question', *ITQ* 34 (1967), 99–114; P. Grelot, 'Réflexions sur le problème du péché originel', *Cah. de l'Act. rel.* 24 (1967); P. De Rosa, *Christ and Original Sin*, London/Milwaukee 1967; J. Scharbert, *Prolegomena eines Alttestamentlers zur Erbsündenlehre*, Freiburg i.B. 1968; K. H. Schelkle, *Schuld als Erbteil*, Einsiedeln/Köln 1968.

Parable

J. Dupont, 'Le chapitre des paraboles', *NRT* 89 (1967), 800–20; C. J. Galloway, 'The Point of Parable', *Bible Today* 28 (1967), 1952–60; D. O. Jr. Via, *The Parables: Their Literary and Existential Dimension*, Philadelphia 1967.

Paradise

B. Hemelsoet, 'Das Paradies im Zeugnis der Bibel', *Zeugnis der Bibel* 6 (1965).

Parousia

A. L. Moore, 'The Parousia in the NT', Suppl. to *NvT* 13 (1966); I. H. Marshall, 'Martyrdom and the Parousia in the Revelation of John', *Studia Evangelica* 4, 1 (1968), 333–9.

Passion of Jesus

E. Best, *The Temptation and the Passion: The Markan Soteriology*, Cambridge/New York 1965; Fr. Normann, *Christos Didaskalos. Die Vorstellung von Christus als Lehrer in der christlichen Literatur des ersten und zweiten Jahrhunderts* (Münsterische Beiträge zur Theologie 32), Münster 1967; H. Conzelmann, 'Historie und Theologie in den synoptischen Passionsberichten', F. Viering (ed.), *Die Bedeutung des Todes Jesu* (Gütersloh 1967), 35–54; A. Vanhoye, *Structure and Theology of the Accounts of the Passion in the Synoptic Gospels* (Bible Today, Suppl. 81. 1), Collegeville, Minn., 1967; C. D. Peddinghaus, *Die Entstehung der Leidensgeschichte. Eine traditionsgeschichtliche und historische Untersuchung des Werdens und Wachsens der erzählenden Passionstradition bis zum Entwurf des Markus*, Heidelberg 1966 (dissertation); *Zur Bedeutung des Todes Jesu. Exegetische Beiträge* (von) H. Conzelmann, E. Käsemann, E. Haenchen, E. Flesseman-van Leer, E. Lohse: Schriftenreihe des Theol. Ausschusses der Ev. Kirche der Union, Gütersloh 1967; J. Knox, *The Death of Christ. The Cross in NT History and Faith*, London 1967; F. W. Bantz (ed.), *Das Wort vorm Kreuz. Evangelische und kath. Theologen verkündigen Christus, den Gekreuzigten*, Cologne 1967; F. Schütz, *Der leidende Christus. Die angefochtene Gemeinde und das Christuskerygma der lukanischen Schriften*, Stuttgart 1969.

Perfection

V. Luck, *Die Vollkommenheitsforderung der Bergpredigt*, München 1968.

Persecution

A. Harr, *The Theme of Jewish Persecution of Christians in the Gospel acc to Mt*, New York 1963 (Union Theological Seminary dissertation).

Poverty

A. Gelin, *The Poor of Yahweh*, Collegeville, Minn., 1964; L. E. Keck, 'The Poor among the Saints in the NT', *ZNW* 56 (1965), 100–29; H. J. Degenhardt, *Besitz und Besitzverzicht nach den lukanischen Schriften*, Stuttgart 1965.

Power

R. Penna, 'La Dynamis Theou; riflessione in margine a 1 Cor 1, 18–25', *Rivista Biblica ... Italiana* 15 (1967), 281–94.

Praise

R. J. Ledogar, 'Verbs of Praise in the LXX Translation of the Hebrew Canon', *Bibl* 48 (1967), 29–56.

Prayer

J. de Fraine, *Praying with the Bible*, New York 1964; W. Ott, *Gebet und Heil. Die Bedeutung der Gebetsparänese in der lukanischen Theologie* (Studien zum Alten und Neuen Testament 12), München 1965; J. Gnilka, 'Jesus und das Gebet', *Bibel und Leben* 6 (1965), 79–91; G. Bernini, 'La Preghiera nell'AT', R. Boccassino, *La Preghiera*, ed. R. Boccassino, Milan/Rome 1967, 321–417, 417–46; A. González, *La oracion en la Biblia*, Madrid 1968.

Preaching

D. M. Stanley, 'The Primitive Preaching: The Traditional Schema', *Concilium* 20 (1966), 88–100; R. C. Worly, *Preaching and Teaching in the Earliest Church*, Philadelphia 1967.

Priest(hood)

A. H. J. Gunneweg, *Leviten und Priester. Hauptlinien der Traditionsbildung und Geschichte des israelitisch-jüdischen Kultpersonals* (FRLANT 89), Göttingen 1965; K. H. A. Schelkle, *A Priestly People*, London 1965; J. C. G. Greig, *The Eschatological Ministry* (Essays in Mem. of G. H. C. Macgregor), Oxford 1965, 99–131; J. Baker, 'The Priesthood of All Believers', *Theology* 69 (1966), 60–65; C. (= K.) Romaniuk, *Le Sacerdoce dans le NT*, Le Puy/Lyons 1966; R. A. Stewart, 'The Sinless High-Priest', *NTS* 14 (1967), 126–35; J. Blenkinsopp, 'Presbyter to Priest: Ministry in the Early Church', *Worship* 41 (1967), 428–38; Y. Congar, *Priest and Layman*, London 1967; J. Blank, O. Schreuder, K. Rahner, A. Görres, F. Klostermann, *Weltpriester nach dem Konzil.* (Münchener Akademie-Schriften, ed. F. Henrich, Bd. 46), Munich 1969; A. Cody, *A History of Old Testament Priesthood*, Rome 1969.

Primacy

Il primato di Pietro nel pensiero contemporaneo, Bologna 1965; Š. Porúbčan, 'The Consciousness of Peter's Primacy in the NT', *Archivum Historiae Pontificiae* 5 (1967), 9–39; W. J. Tobin, 'La primauté de Pierre selon les évangiles', *Lumen Vitae* 22 (1967), 629–73; B. Rigaux, 'S. Pierre et l'exégèse contemporaine (bulletin)',

Concilium 3, 27 (1967), 129–52; *San Pietro.* Scritti di A. Bea ecc: Atti della XIX Settimana Biblica (dell')Associazione Biblica Italiana, Brescia 1967.

Principalities and powers

W. Manson, 'Principalities and Powers: The Spiritual Background of the Work of Jesus in the Synoptic Gospels', W. Manson, *Jesus & The Christian* (London 1967), 77–88.

Rebirth

E. Stein, 'Der Begriff der Palingenesie im talmudischen Judentum', *MGWJ* 83 (1939, ed. 1964), 194–205.

Redemption

G. W. Grogan, 'The Experience of Salvation in the Old and NT', *Vox Evangelica* 5 (1967), 4–26; E. M. B. Green, *The Meaning of Salvation*, London 1965; W. G. Most, 'A Biblical Theology of Redemption in a Covenant Framework', *CBQ* 29 (1967), 1–19; M. E. McIver, 'The Cosmic Dimensions of Salvation in the Thought of St. Paul', *Worship* 40 (1966), 156–64; R. Zehnle, 'The Salvific Character of Jesus' Death in Lucan Soteriology', *TS* 30 (1969), 420–44.

Rest

J. Cadet, 'Repos dominical et loisir humain', *MD* 83 (1965), 71–97; M. D. Philippe, 'Le repos du Père et l'Alliance éternelle', *Verbum Caro* 20, 79 (1966), 9–25.

Restoration

S. Rayburn, 'Cosmic Transfiguration', *Church Quarterly Review* 168, London 1967, 162–67.

Resurrection

G. Wied, *Der Auferstehungsglaube im späten Israel in seiner Bedeutung für das Verhältnis von Apokalyptik und Weisheit*, Bonn 1964/65 (dissertation); L. Swain, 'The Resurrection in the OT. Eternal Life in the OT', *Clergy Review* 51 (1966), 949–54, 52 (1967), 104–09; S. K. Aboa, *Die Entstehung der Auferstehungshoffnung im AT*, Hamburg 1966/67 (dissertation); E. Brandenburger, 'Die Auferstehung der Glaubenden als historisches und theologisches Problem', *Wort und Dienst* 9 (1967), 16–33; J. Schmid, 'Auferstehung des Fleisches. I. Biblisch', *Sacramentum Mundi* 1 (Freiburg i.B. 1967), 385–97; J. Comblin, *The Resurrection in the Plan of Salvation*, Notre Dame, Ind., 1966.

Revelation

D. Lührmann, *Das Offenbarungsverständnis bei Paulus und in den paulinischen Gemeinden* (*WissMonANT* 16) 1965.

Reward

A. Marmorstein, *The doctrine of merits in old Rabbinical literature*, 2 vols, New York 1968.

Righteousness (justice)

O. Kaiser, 'Dike und Sedaqa. Zur Frage nach der sittlichen Weltordnung. Ein theologisches Präludium', *Neue Zeitschrift für systematische Theologie und Religionsphilosophie* 7 (1965), 251–73; P. Stuhlmacher, 'Gerechtigkeit Gottes bei Paulus', *FRLANT* 87 (1965).

Sabbath

S. T. Jr. Kimbrough, 'The Concept of Sabbath at Qumrân', *RQ* 5 (1966), 483–502; J. H. Meesters, *Op zoek naar de oorsprong van de Sabbat* (Studia Semitica Neerl. 8.), Assen 1966; N. A. Barack, *A History of the Sabbath*, New York 1965.

Satan

M. E. Boismard, 'Satan selon l'Ancien et le NT', *LV* 15, 78 (1966), 61–76; R. S. Kluger, *Satan in the OT*, Evanston, Ill., 1967; C. Duquoc, 'Satan—Symbol oder Person?', *Christus vor uns . . .*, Bergen-Enkheim 1966, 49–57; P. von der Osten-Sacken, *Gott und Belial*, Göttingen 1969.

Scandal

W. Molinski, 'Ärgernis', *Sacramentum Mundi* 1 (Freiburg i.B. 1967), 318–27.

Scripture

J. Bright, *The Authority of the OT*, New York/London 1967; J. C. Wenger, *God's Word Written; Essays on the Nature of Biblical Revelation and Authority*, Scottdale, Pa., 1966.

Shepherd

O. Kiefer, *Die Hirtenrede. Analyse und Deutung von Joh 10, 1–18*, Stuttgart 1967; A. J. Simonis, *Die Hirtenrede im Johannes-Evangelium. Versuch einer Analyse von Joh 10, 1–18 nach Entstehung, Hintergrund und Inhalt* (*Analecta Biblica* 29), Rome 1967; P. de Robert, *Le Berger d'Israël. Essai sur le thème pastoral dans l'AT* (*Cahiers Théologiques* 57), Neuchâtel/Paris 1968.

Sin

R. Knierim, *Die Hauptbegriffe für Sünde im AT*, Gütersloh 1965; A. Buechler, *Studies in Sin and Atonement in the Rabbinic Literature of the First Century*, New York 1967; B. F. Malina, 'Some observations on the Origin of Sin in Judaism and St. Paul', *CBQ* 31 (1969), 18–34; L. van den Wijngaert, 'Die Sünde in der Priesterschriftlichen Urgeschichte', *Theologie und Philosophie* 43 (1969), 35–50.

Sonship

P. Wülfing von Martitz, G. Fohrer, E. Schweizer, E. Lohse, W. Schneemelcher, *TWNT* VIII (1967), 334–84.

Spirit

H. Berkhof. *The Doctrine of the Holy Spirit*, Richmond, Va., 1964; K. McNamara, 'The Holy Spirit in the Church', *ITQ* 32 (1965), 281–94; G. H. Davies, 'The Holy Spirit (=HS) in the OT', ibid., 129–34; F. Stagg, 'The HS in the NT', ibid., 135–47; *De Spiritu Sancto. Bijdragen tot de leer van de Heilige Geest bij gelegenheid van het 2e eeuwfeest van het Stipendium Bernardinum*, Utrecht 1964; D. Moody, *Spirit of the Living God. The Biblical Concepts Interpreted in Context*, Philadelphia 1968.

Suffering

A. Bertrangs, *The Bible on Suffering*, St Norbert Abbey Series 11, 1966.

Temple

B. Gärtner, *The Temple and the Community in Qumran and the NT* (SocNTS Monograph Series), Cambridge/New York 1965; R. E. Clements, *God and Temple*, Oxford/Philadelphia 1965; K. Baltzer, 'The Meaning of the Temple in the Lukan Writings', *Harvard Theological Review* 58 (1965), 263–77; L. Gaston, 'The Theology of the Temple. The NT Fulfillment of OT Heilsgeschichte', *Oikonomia, Festschrift O. Cullmann*, Hamburg 1967, 32–41; H. Lignée, *The Temple of Yahweh*, Baltimore 1966; N. Poulssen, *König und Tempel im Glaubenszeugnis des AT*, Stuttgart 1967.

Temptation

B. van Iersel, *The Bible on the Temptations of Man* (St Norbert Abbey Series 12), 1966; C. B. Houk, Peirasmos, 'The Lord's Prayer, and the Massah Tradition', *Scottish Journal of Theology* 19 (1966), 216–25; H. Clavier, 'Tentation et anamartésie dans le NT', *RHPR* 47 (1967), 150–64; J. Dupont, *Les tentations de Jésus au désert* (Studia Neotest., 4), Bruges/Paris 1968; 'The Origin of the Narrative of Jesus' Temptations', *Theology Digest* 15 (1967), 230–35.

Three

G. Delling, 'Drei', *TWNT* VIII (1966), 215–325.

Time

P. Brunner, 'Die Zeit im christlichen Glauben', Brunner, *Pro Ecclesia* II, Berlin/Hamburg 1966, 50–59; J. V. L. Casserley, *Toward a Theology of History*, London 1965; A. E. Willingale, 'Time in the Bible', *Faith & Thought* 96, 1 (1967), 25–53; C. Mugler, 'Le retour éternel et le temps linéaire dans la pensée grecque', *Bulletin de l'Association G. Budé* 25, 4 (1966), 405–19.

Tradition

Y. M. J. Congar, *Tradition and Traditions: An Historical and a Theological Essay*, London/New York 1966/1967; H. T. Mayer, 'Scripture, Tradition, and Authority in the Life of the Early Church', *Concordia Theological Monthly* 38 (1967), 19–23; *Holy Book and Holy Tradition*, Intern. Coll., Manchester, 1968.

Transfiguration

A. M. Ramsey, *The Glory of God and the Transfiguration of Christ*, London 1967; L. F. Rivera, 'Interpretatio Transfigurationis Jesu in redactione evangelii Marci', *VD* 46 (1968), 99–104.

Truth

H. Blocher, 'La notion biblique de vérité', *Ét. Év.* 26, 4 (1966), 145–58; L. Goppelt, 'Wahrheit als Befreiung. Das neutest. Zeugnis von der Wahrheit nach dem Jo.-Ev.', H. R. Muller-Schwefe (ed.), *Was ist Wahrheit?*, Göttingen 1965; R. Schnackenburg, 'Zum Begriff der "Wahrheit" in den beiden kleinen Johannesbriefen', *BZ* 11 (1967), 253–58.

Virgin Birth

H. v. Campenhausen, *The Virgin Birth in the Theology of the Ancient Church*, London/Naperville, Ill., 1964; J. Bligh, 'The Virgin Birth', *Heythrop Journal* 6 (1965), 109–197; J. F. Craghan, *Mary's Vow of Virginity*, Munich 1965 (dissertation); J. Riedl, *Die Vorgeschichte Jesu*, Stuttgart 1968; R. Kilian, *Die Verheißung Immanuels*, Stuttgart 1969; J. Michl, 'Die Jungfrauengeburt im NT', *Mariologische Studien IV* (1969), 145–84.

Virginity

D. W. Trautman, *The Eunuch Logion of Mt 19, 12: Historical and exegetical Dimensions as Related to Celibacy*, Rome 1966 (Angelicum dissertation); L. Swain, 'St. Paul on Celibacy', *Clergy Review* 51 (1966), 785–91; K. H. Schelkle, 'Ehe und Ehelosigkeit im NT', K. H. Schelkle, *Wort und Schrift*, Düsseldorf 1966, 183–98 = *WW* 29 (1966), 1–15; J. Blenkinsopp, *Celibacy, Ministry, Church*, London and New York 1968.

Vocation

J. de Fraine, *The Bible on Vocation and Election*, St Norbert Abbey Series 21, 1966.

Water

L. Goppelt, 'Wasser', *TWNT* VIII (1966), 313–33.

Way

E. Repo, *Der "Weg" als Selbstbezeichnung des Urchristentums. Eine traditionsgeschichtliche und semasiologische Untersuchung* (Annales Academiae Scientiarum Fennicae B, 132, 2), Helsinki 1964; N. Brox, *Der Glaube als Weg*, München/Salzburg 1968.

Wine

R. Borig, *Der wahre Weinstock. Untersuchungen zu Jo 15, 1–10* (Studien zum Alten u. Neuen Testament 16), Munich 1967; A. Smitmans, *Das Weinwunder von Kana. Die Auslegung von Jo 2, 1–11 bei den Vätern und heute* (Beiträge zur Geschichte der bibl. Exegese 6), Tübingen 1966.

Wisdom

B. De Pinto, 'Word and Wisdom in St. John', *Script* 19 (1967), 19–27; M. Conti, 'La Sophia di 2 Petr 3, 15', *Rivista Biblica Italiana* 17 (1969), 121–38.

Witness

J. C. Hindley, 'Witness in the Fourth Gospel', *Scottish Journal of Theology* 18 (1965), 319–37.

Woman

J. Bottéro, 'La femme dans l'ancien Israël', *Hist. mondiale de la femme* 1, Paris 1965, 224–47; R. Loewe, *The Position of Women in Judaism*, London 1966; K. Stendahl, *The Bible and the Role of Women. A Case Study in Hermeneutics*, Philadelphia 1966; T. Maertens, *La promotion de la femme dans la Bible: Points de repère*, Tournai 1967; C. J. Vos, *Woman in Old Worship*, Delft 1968 (dissertation).

Work

J. L. Gómez de Morales, *El trabajo en la Biblia*, Madrid 1966.

World

G. Hierzenberger, *Weltbewertung bei Paulus nach 1 Kor 7, 29–31. Eine exegetisch-kerygmatische Studie* (KomBeitrANT), Düsseldorf 1967; R. Schnackenburg, 'Der Christ und die Zukunft der Welt', R. Schnackenburg, *Christl. Existenz nach dem NT* 2, Munich 1968, 149–85; idem, 'Das Verständnis der Welt nach dem NT', ib., vol. 1, Munich 1967, 157–85.

Analytical Index of Articles and Cross-References

This analytical index has been compiled to enable readers to derive maximum benefit from the encyclopedia, and to locate easily and quickly important passages dealing with a given biblical-theological theme.

Words in bold type are the main entries for the articles in the encyclopedia: the italicised words indented below each bold-type entry indicate cross-references to the article in question from other articles. All arrowed cross-references in the text itself are included, and many more besides.

Words in roman type are cognates, synonyms, antonyms, etc. for themes treated in the italicised articles indicated after the arrow.

Abraham 3–6
Covenant 142
Father 262
Justification 453
Mediation 567
Spirit 875
Temptation 903f
Three 911
Vision of God 948
Vocation 955

Absolution ↗ *Goodness, Mercy, Reconciliation*

Abstinence ↗ *Asceticism, Fasting, Self-denial*

Abundance ↗ *Riches*

Abyss ↗ *Creation, Sea*

Acceptance ↗ *Sacrifice*

Accuser ↗ *Satan*

Acknowledgement ↗ *Confession*

Adam 6–9
Body 81
Covenant 142
Light 505
Likeness 509–13
Man 542–5
Marriage 551f
Messianism 576
Original sin 620–24
Paradise 629–33
Sin 849, 861
Spirit 871f

Adoption ↗ *Father, Inheritance, Sonship*

Adoration 9–15
Antichrist 31
Conversion 138–40
Flesh 274f
Hypocrite 390–92
Prayer 679f, 682f
Spirit 877–88
Truth 932

Adultery ↗ *Marriage*

Advent ↗ *Parousia, Visitation*

Adversary ↗ *Enemy, Satan*

Affliction ↗ *Persecution, Sickness*

Agape 15–16
Church 111
Eucharist 232, 237
Goodness 327
Love 518–41

Ages ↗ *Time*

Allegory ↗ *Parable*

Alliance ↗ *Covenant*

Almsgiving 16–19
Death 184
Love 524–7, 529–31, 535–8
Mercy 574
Riches 775–80
Righteousness 784

Altar ↗ *Sacrifice*

Amen 19–20
Faith 244
Truth 927

Anathema ↗ *Ban*

Angel 20–28
Demon 192, 194f
Glory 298
Heaven 367f
Mediation 569, 571f
Mission 589
Paradise 629–32
Principalities 712–16
Revelation 771
Satan 808–12
Scripture 824
Sonship 863
Temptation 904

Anger ↗ *Wrath*

Anointing ↗ *Jesus Christ*

Antichrist 28–32
Adoration 14f
Hell 370
Parousia 635
Scandal 815

Apocalypse ↗ *Revelation*

Apokatastasis ↗ *Restoration*

INDEX OF BIBLICAL REFERENCES

The books of the Bible are listed in the order in which they appear in the Revised Standard Version of the Bible (Catholic Edition). The individual references to a given book of the Bible are listed in their natural order of chapter and verse, but where two or more passages of differing lengths begin with the same verse precedence is taken by the longer or more inclusive reference.

All references to individual verses and chapters and to groups of verses and chapters are included. References to whole books of the Bible are not included, however.

In the synoptic gospel listings certain entries appear in italic type. These represent the references to parallel passages directly implied, but not explicitly cited, by the text. All parallel passages directly implied by textual references to a particular synoptic gospel passage *and parallels* are included, but such parallel passages are only entered in this index if a textual reference calls for them. For example, under Mark the following roman-type entry appears:

9:7   37, 123, 225, 434, 528,
                    531, 924

This means that there is an explicit reference to Mk 9:7 on each of the seven text pages listed. On two of these pages, however—pp 528 and 531—the reference is in the form 'Mk 9:7 and parallels'. One of the parallels to Mk 9:7 is Lk 9:35, and it will be seen that there are two consecutive entries for this latter reference:

9:35   123, 695
9:35 (|| Mk 9:7)   *528, 531*

The roman-type entry signifies that explicit references to Lk 9:35 will be found on pp 123 and 695. The italic-type entry signifies that implicit references to Lk 9:35 will be found on pp. 528 and 531 in the form 'Mk 9:7 and parallels'.

This feature is designed to help readers derive full benefit from the encyclopedia, while using it alongside the Bible or a biblical commentary, or while preparing sermons, lectures, etc., based on particular passages of the synoptic gospels.

OLD TESTAMENT

Genesis	page	Genesis—cont.	page	Genesis—cont.	page
1-5	6	1:26	366, 509, 511	2:8-15	339
1	511, 809, 825, 992	1:26b	544	2:8-14	630
1:1-2	504	1:27	93, 509, 511, 545, 989	2:8ff	629
1:1ff	224, 301, 302, 366, 585, 586	1:28	69, 71, 366, 552, 724, 996	2:8	147, 319
1:1	147, 995	1:29	349	2:9-17	316, 317
1:2-9	825	1:30	366	2:10	357
1:2	826, 871, 878, 879, 887, 995	1:31	147, 519	2:15ff	630
		2-11	1007	2:15	319, 629, 897, 996
1:3-30	871	2-3	317, 319, 320, 1007	2:16	319, 629
1:3f	504	2	511, 629, 631	2:17	181, 182, 317, 319, 339, 500, 620
1:3	504, 533, 995	2:1	366	2:18ff	630
1:4	505, 519	2:2f	797, 798, 799	2:18	551, 985, 989
1:6-8	366	2:3	372	2:19-23	319, 366
1:6	533	2:4-3:24	629	2:19	147, 339, 879
1:7	147	2:4-7	630	2:20	319, 551
1:10	519	2:4	147	2:21-4	630
1:11	349	2:5	6, 339, 542	2:21ff	81, 545, 985
1:14-17	366	2:7ff	519	2:21	273, 989
1:14ff	149	2:7	6, 8, 81, 147, 181, 281, 283, 307, 319, 446, 500, 542, 547, 872, 887	2:22	90, 339, 552
1:22	69, 71, 724			2:23-4	261, 274, 319
1:26-7	549			2:23f	9
1:26ff	6, 7, 81, 519, 544, 985	2:8-3:24	620	2:23	551, 983, 989

NEW TESTAMENT

INDEX OF HEBREW AND GREEK WORDS

1. *Hebrew words and roots*

2. *Greek words and prepositional phrases*